Antitrust in the Decentralized Economy

Antitrust in the Decentralized Economy

DeFi, Central Bank Digital Currencies, and Blockchain

KONSTANTINOS STYLIANOU
Professor of Competition Law and Regulation, University of Glasgow, UK

OXFORD
UNIVERSITY PRESS

OXFORD
UNIVERSITY PRESS

Great Clarendon Street, Oxford, OX2 6DP,
United Kingdom

Oxford University Press is a department of the University of Oxford.
It furthers the University's objective of excellence in research, scholarship,
and education by publishing worldwide. Oxford is a registered trade mark of
Oxford University Press in the UK and in certain other countries

Published in the United States of America by Oxford University Press
198 Madison Avenue, New York, NY 10016, United States of America

British Library Cataloguing in Publication Data
Data available

Library of Congress Control Number: 2025931090

ISBN 9780192842893

DOI: 10.1093/9780191925504.001.0001

Printed and bound by
CPI Group (UK) Ltd., Croydon, CR0 4YY

The manufacturer's authorised representative in the EU for product safety is Oxford University Press España S.A. of El Parque Empresarial San Fernando de Henares, Avenida de Castilla, 2 – 28830 Madrid (www.oup.es/en or product.safety@oup.com). OUP España S.A. also acts as importer into Spain of products made by the manufacturer.

MIX
Paper | Supporting responsible forestry
FSC® C013604
FSC www.fsc.org

Acknowledgements

Writing is, in many ways, a solitary activity. But no book is ever a product of its author alone. This is no less true for this monograph, and I want to take this opportunity to thank the people that contributed to this writing endeavour. Above all, my family whose support for this monograph started long before the research for and writing of it. Then, in alphabetical order, I want to thank Nic Carter, Marc de Vries, Maurice Herlihy, Kathleen Moran, Vasilis Ramopoulos, Ilias Trispiotis, and the wonderful people at Oxford University Press, especially Charlotte Kershaw and Peter Daniell. If I am forgetting anyone, it is not for lack of gratitude, but out of tiredness at the end of this project; please accept my apologies.

Contents

Detailed Contents ix
List of Figures xiii
List of Tables xv
Table of Cases xvii
List of Abbreviations (Excludes cryptoassets, currencies, and case parties) xxvii

PART I. FUNDAMENTALS

1. ANTITRUST IN THE DECENTRALIZED ECONOMY 3
2. PERSONAL AND MATERIAL SCOPE: ECONOMIC ACTIVITY AND UNDERTAKINGS IN THE DECENTRALIZED ECONOMY 23

PART II. MARKET ANALYSIS

3. MARKET DEFINITION 47
4. MARKET SHARES 79
5. MARKET POWER 115
6. BARRIERS TO ENTRY AND EXPANSION 143

PART III. OFFENCES

7. ABUSE OF DOMINANCE AND MONOPOLIZATION 173
8. ANTICOMPETITIVE AGREEMENTS AND RESTRAINTS OF TRADE 219

ADDENDUM 259
Index 261

Detailed Contents

List of Figures xiii
List of Tables xv
Table of Cases xvii
List of Abbreviations (Excludes cryptoassets, currencies, and case parties) xxvii

PART I. FUNDAMENTALS

1. ANTITRUST IN THE DECENTRALIZED ECONOMY 3
   (A) General 3
   (B) A working definition of the decentralized economy 5
   (C) The applicability of antitrust law in the decentralized economy 8
   (D) The special features of the decentralized economy for antitrust 11
      i) The decentralized nature of DLT products, services, and markets 11
      ii) The prevalence of social production 13
      iii) Governance as a new arena of economic activity 17
      iv) Application of tokenomics 20
2. PERSONAL AND MATERIAL SCOPE: ECONOMIC ACTIVITY AND UNDERTAKINGS IN THE DECENTRALIZED ECONOMY 23
   (A) General 23
   (B) Economic activities and undertakings in the decentralized economy 24
      i) Definitions 24
      ii) Consensus-building, mining, staking, and pools as economic activities 28
      iii) Protocol and software development as economic activity 30
      iv) Central Bank Digital Currency (CBDC) issuance 32
   (C) Single economic unit, intra-enterprise conspiracy, and imputability: Pools, foundations, and developers as (in)dependent actors 35
      i) Single economic units, intra-enterprise conspiracy, employees, subsidiaries, and agents 37
      ii) Mining and staking pools, and development foundations 42

PART II. MARKET ANALYSIS

3. MARKET DEFINITION 47
(A) General 47
(B) How to think about 'markets' in the decentralized economy 50
(C) Marked definition based on substitutability: exchanges, mining and validation, assets and asset pools 52
i) Standard substitution analysis: application to exchanges, mining and validation 53
ii) Correlation analysis: application to assets 57
iii) Platform markets: application to crypto-exchanges and DeFi asset pools 59
(D) Ecosystem and proximity-based definitions of areas of effective competition 64
i) DLTs and metaverses as ecosystems 65
a) Cluster markets and clustering: application to cryptoassets 67
b) Factor analysis: application to metaverses 70
c) Snowball selection process: application to token ecosystems 73
ii) Proximity analysis and strategic groups 76

4. MARKET SHARES 79
(A) General 79
(B) The complications of calculating market shares in DLT markets 82
(C) Calculation of cryptoasset and DeFi protocol market shares 85
i) Market capitalization 86
a) Inert supply 87
b) Supply inheritance 90
c) Supply arbitrariness 92
ii) Transaction count and volume 93
iii) Total Value Locked 96
(D) Calculation of mining and staking pool market shares 98
i) Output and capacity: hashrate and block count 99
ii) Revenue and profits 102
iii) Validator/miner/staker count 104
(E) Calculation of crypto-exchange and trading platform market shares 106
i) Trading volume 107
ii) Trade count 109
iii) Trader count 111

5. MARKET POWER 115
(A) General 115
(B) Types of market power 117
i) Power over price: Mining/staking fees and cryptoasset price manipulation 117
a) Definition and use 117
b) Transaction fees and mining fees and rewards as price 118
c) Mining and staking fees charged by pools as price 119
d) Cryptoasset price manipulation 120

ii) Power to exclude: Exclusion through delisting, governance, oversupply 123
a) Definition and use 123
b) Conventional exclusion in crypto markets 124
c) Exclusion through governance 125
d) Exclusion through oversupply 126
iii) Architectural power: Controlling governance and monetization 126
a) Definition and distinction from power over price and exclusionary power 126
b) Expressions of architectural power: coercion, dependency, soft power 129
c) Architectural power in the metaverse 130
iv) Engagement power: exploitation and exclusion due to 'stickiness' 131
a) Definition and use 131
b) Engagement power vs power in aftermarkets 133
(C) Factors limiting market power 134
i) Forking 134
ii) DLT interoperability 135
iii) Design and governance choices 137
iv) Token effects and bootstrapping new DLT networks 140

6. BARRIERS TO ENTRY AND EXPANSION 143
(A) General 143
(B) Network effects 146
i) Network effects in cryptoassets and CBDCs 148
a) Existence and measurement of network effects in cryptoassets 148
b) Switching and competition between cryptoasset and CBDC incumbents and competitors 151
ii) Network effects in ICOs, dApps, and DLT platforms 152
iii) Network effects in mining and staking pools 155
(C) Economies of scale and scope 157
i) Economies in mining and validation 159
ii) Economies in DLT applications and services 162
iii) Assessing the impact of economies of scale and scope in DLT markets 164
(D) Branding and economies of trust 167

PART III. OFFENCES

7. ABUSE OF DOMINANCE AND MONOPOLIZATION 173
(A) General 173
(B) Defining and extending the concepts of abuse and monopolization in the decentralized economy 174
i) The standard merit-based definitions and tests of abuse and monopolization 175
ii) Abuse and monopolization in the decentralized economy: beyond merit 178

(C) Types of abuse and monopolization: Introducing governance abuse 183
i) The standard classifications of abuse and monopolization and their links to applicable legal tests 183
ii) Governance abuse 186
a) Description and function of governance abuse 186
b) Relevant markets in governance abuse 191
(D) Specific abuse and monopolization practices 194
i) Refusal to deal and the essential facilities doctrine: Access to DLT networks, products, services, and consortia 194
ii) Discrimination, self-preferencing, neutrality 204
a) Discrimination in Article 102(c) TFEU and Robinson Patman Act: Application to delisting, AMMs, and MEV 206
b) Self-preferencing: Filling the gaps of traditional discrimination 213
c) Blockchain neutrality 216

8. ANTICOMPETITIVE AGREEMENTS AND RESTRAINTS OF TRADE 219
(A) General 219
(B) Aggravating and mitigating collusion factors in DLT markets 221
(C) Meaning of collusion (agreements, restraints of trade, concerted activity) 224
(D) Impermissible contacts and information exchange on private and public DLT networks and DLT markets 228
i) Meaning and role of contact between undertakings 228
ii) Private contacts and information exchange on private (permissioned) DLT networks 231
iii) Public sharing of information in DLT markets 235
(E) Illicit coordination vs legitimate cooperation in DLT markets 239
i) Can DLT cooperative activities be exempt from competition law? 240
ii) Coordination and cooperation in DLT markets as ancillary restriction and objective necessity 242
iii) Cooperation in DLT markets as standard-setting or joint venture 245
iv) The by object/effect and per se/rule of reason treatment and its determinants in the decentralized economy 252

ADDENDUM 259
Index 261

Figures

2.1 Competition law and individual code developers, miners, and stakers 36
2.2 Imputability of activity based on control, risk, and interest alignment 42
3.1 Pearson correlation between Bitcoin and the S&P500 index 58
3.2 Clustering of cryptoassets by two dimensions 70
3.3 An application of factor analysis to the metaverse 72
3.4 A non-exhaustive definition of the Cardano ecosystem 75
4.1 Evolution of exchange market share by volume 2019–2024 81
4.2 Market shares of major mining pools 2020–2024 81
4.3 Comparison between transaction count and market capitalization across Bitcoin (BTC) and EOS 84
4.4 Bitcoin supply per year of last move 88
4.5 Total market capitalization vs trailing year active capitalization 89
4.6 Bitcoin realized capitalization vs total market capitalization 90
4.7 Total supply of Bitcoin, Bitcoin Cash, and Bitcoin SV 91
4.8 Bitcoin fork uptake 92
4.9 Ratio of Bitcoin payment-per-transaction 94
4.10 Total transaction volume vs adjusted transaction volume in Bitcoin 96
4.11 AAVE's total value locked and virtual market capitalization 97
4.12 Miner revenue from transaction fees and total miner revenue including fees and block rewards 103
4.13 A side-by-side comparison of Coinbase and Coinbene 110
6.1 Network effect observations and distribution in six cryptocurrencies 150
6.2 Market shares of major mining pools 155
6.3 Total cost of a one-hour attack of the Bitcoin network 163
6.4 Miner revenue (USD) per hash 167

Tables

1.1 Governance typology in the decentralized economy 19

3.1 Transaction volumes of Uniswap currency pair pools (June 2024) 64

4.1 An example of concentration rates measured by mining pool and by individual miners 106

4.2 Reported transaction volume vs adjusted transaction volume 108

6.1 Competition among fiat currencies, CBDCs, stablecoins, and cryptocurrencies 153

6.2 Factors cutting in favour and against concentration in the mining/staking market 158

Table of Cases

EU CASES

European Commission

A. Ahlström Osakeyhtiö and others v Commission, Joined cases C-89/85, C-104/85, C-114/85, C-116/85, C-117/85 and C-125/85 to C-129/85, ECLI:EU:C:1993:120 . . . . . 228n.50
ABG/Oil Companies operating in the Netherlands, IV/28.841, Commission Decision of 19 April 1977 . . . . . 202n.125
Amazon Buy Box, AT.40703, Commission Decision of 20 December 2022 . . . . . 213–14, 216
Amazon Marketplace, AT.40462, Commission Decision of 20 December 2022. . . . 65–66n.78, 214n.181, 216n.190
Anheuser-Busch Incorporated - Scottish & Newcastle, IV/34.237/F3, Commission Decision of 14 December 1999 . . . . . 225n.25
Apple – App Store Practices (music streaming), AT.40437, Commission Decision of 04 March 2024. . . . . 133n.96, 191
AstraZeneca, A. 37.507/F3, Commission Decision of 15 June 2005. . . . . 215n.186
Bayer/Monsanto, M.8084, Commission Decision of 29 May 2018. . . . . 158n.73
Container Shipping, AT.39850, Commission Decision of 7 July 2016 230
Credit Suisse First Boston/Barclays, M.1068, Commission Decision of 19 December 1997 . . . . . 83n.21
Deutsche Boerse/NYSE Euronext, M.6166, Commission Decision of 1 February 2012 . . . . . 83n.19, 107n.80
Deutsche Post AG - Interception of cross-border mail,C-1/36.915, Commission Decision of 25 July 2001 . . . . . 196n.94, 208
Deutsche Telekom AG, C-1/37.451, 37.578, 37.579, Commission Decision of 21 May 2003 . . . . . 67n.85
EFIM, Rejecting the complaint in Case C-3/39.391, Commission Decision of 20 May 2009 . . . . . 133n.95
Eurofix-Bauco v. Hilti, IV/30.787 and 31.488, Commission Decision of 22 December 1987 . . . . . 54n.29
FAG - Flughafen Frankfurt/Main AG, IV/34.801, Commission Decision of 14 January 1998. . . . . 202n.126
German Postal Legislation Relating to Mail Preparation Services, COMP/38.745, Commission Decision of 20 October 2004 208–9
Glaxo Wellcome and others, IV/36.957/F3, Commission Decision of 8 May 2011. . . . . 253n.176
Glencore/Xstrata, M.6541, Commission Decision of 21 November 2012 . . . . . 57n.44
Google/Fitbit, M.9660, Commission Decision of 17 December 2020. . . . . 65–66n.78
Google Android, AT.40099, Commission Decision of 18 July 2018 . . . . . 65–66n.78, 127n.64
Google Search (AdSense), AT.40411, Commission Decision of 20 March 2019 . . . . 132n.90
Google Search (Shopping), AT.39740, Commission Decision of 27 June 2017. . . . . . . 80n.5, 80n.11, 167n.101, 168, 182, 192n.78
GVG/FS, 37.685, Commission Decision of 27 August 2003 . . . . . 199n.114
GVL, IV/29.839, Commission Decision of 29 October 1981. 207
Hasselblad, IV/25.757, Commission Decision of 2 December 1981 238–39

Huntsman Corporation/Equity Interests, M.7061, Commission Decision of 10 September 2004. . . . 58n.45
Intel, COMP/37.990, Commission Decision of 13 May 2009 . . . 158n.73, 167n.101, 168n.103, 168, 177n.22
Marine Harvest/Morpol, M.6850, Commission Decision of 30 September 2013. . . . 59n.50
MasterCard, EuroCommerce, and Commercial Cards, Joined Cases 34.579, 36.518, and 38.580, Commission Decision of 19 December 2007 . . . 84
Microsoft, C-3/37.792, Commission Decision of 24 March 2004. . . . 192n.78
Microsoft/Skype, M.6281, Commission Decision of 7 October 2011 . . . 83n.17, 105n.76
Morgan Stanley/Visa International, D1/37860, Commission Decision of 3 October 2007 . . . 83n.20, 93n.40
NDC Health/IMS Health (Interim measures), D3/38.044, Commission Decision of 3 July 2001 . . . 199n.112
Nestlé/Perrier, IV/M.190, Commission Decision of 22 July 1992. . . . 57n.44
Nuovo CEGAM, 1984 IV/30.804, Commission Decision of 30 March . . . 225n.24
Polypropylene, IV/31.149, Commission Decision of 23 April 1986. . . . 224n.20, 226n.35, 237n.97
Pre-insulated Pipe cartel, IV/35.691/E-4, Commission Decision of 21 October 1998 . . . 197n.100
Qualcomm (Exclusivity Payments), AT.40220, Commission Decision of 24 January 2018. . . . 52n.21
Rewe/Delvita, M.4590, Commission Decision of 25 April 2007. . . . 67n.84
Rewe/Meinl, IV/M.1221, Commission Decision of 3 February 1999 . . . 67n.84
Ryanair-Aer-Lingus, M.4439, Commission Decision of 27 June 2007. . . . 57n.44
Scandlines Sverige AB v Port of Helsingborg, A.36.568/D3, Commission Decision of 23 July 2004 . . . 212n.170
Slovak Telekom, AT.39523, Commission Decision of 15 October 2014 . . . 214n.184, 215n.186
Telekomunikacja Polska, 39.525, Commission Decision of 22 June 2011. . . . 196n.96
Tetra Pak II, IV.31043, Commission Decision of 24 July 1991. . . . 121–22, 192
Visa International, 29.373, Commission Decision of 9 August 2001 . . . 83n.20, 83
Yen Interest Rate Derivatives, AT.39861, Commission Decision of 4 February 2015 . . . 231n.66, 234
Zinc Producer Group, IV/30.350, Commission Decision of 6 August 1984 . . . 237n.96

Court of Justice

Aéroports de Paris v Commission, Case C-82/01 P, ECLI:EU:C:2002:617 . . . 28n.29
Activision Blizzard Germany GmbH v Commission, Case C 260/09 P, ECLI:EU:C:2011:62 . . . 225n.26
AKZO Chemie BV v Commission, Case C-62/86, ECLI:EU:C:1991:286 . . . 79–80, 175–76, 177n.22, 177
Akzo Nobel and Others v Commission, Case C-97/08 P, ECLI:EU:C:2009:536 . . . 39
Alphabet and Others v Autorità Garante della Concorrenza e del Mercato, Case C-233/23, ECLI:EU:C:2025:110. . . . 195n.90, 199n.111, 201n.119, 201n.123
Albany International BV v Stichting Bedrijfspensioenfonds Textielindustrie, Case C-67/96, ECLI:EU:C:1999:430. . . . 26n.23
Allgemeine Elektrizitäts-Gesellschaft AEG-Telefunken AG v Commission, Case C-107/82, ECLI:EU:C:1983:293. . . . 39n.70
Allianz Hungária Biztosító Zrt. and Others v Gazdasági Versenyhivatal, Case C-32/11, ECLI:EU:C:2013:160. . . . 253–54
Beef Industry Development Society and Barry Brothers, Case C-209/07, ECLI:EU:C:2008:643 . . . 255n.193

Brasserie De Haecht v Wilkin Janssen, Case C-23/67, ECLI:EU:C:1967:54 254
British Airways plc v Commission, Case C-95/04 P, ECLI:EU:C:2007:166....... 205n.142
Bundeskartellamt v Volkswagen AG and VAG Leasing GmbH, Case C-266/93, ECLI:EU:C:1995:345 39
Bundesverband der Arzneimittel-Importeure eV and Commission v Bayer AG, Joined Cases C-2/01 P and C-3/01 P, ECLI:EU:C:2004:2.................. 225n.28
Centrafarm BV and Adriaan de Peijper v Sterling Drug Inc., Case 15/74, ECLI:EU:C:1974:114 ....40n.74
Cisal di Battistello Venanzio & C. Sas and Istituto Nazionale Per L'Assicurazione Contro Gli Infortuni Sul Lavoro (INAIL), Case C-218/00, ECLI:EU:C:2002:36 ....28n.29
Commission v Anic Partecipazioni SpA, Case C-49/92 P, ECLI:EU:C:1999:356 .... 225n.33, 226n.36
Commission v Italy, Case C-118/85, ECLI:EU:C:1987:283 ....25n.13
Commission v Siemens Österreich and Others, Case C-231/11, ECLI:EU:C:2014:256 ....39n.72
Commission and France v Ladbroke Racing, Joined Cases C-359/95 P and C-379/95 P, ECLI:EU:C:1997:531 ....9n.34
Coöperatieve Vereniging "SuikerUnie" UA and others v Commission, Joined Cases 40 to 48, 50, 54 to 56, 111, 113 and 114/73, ECLI:EU:C:1975:174 .... 38n.67, 219n.2
Corinne Bodson v SA Pompes funèbres des régions libérées, Case 30/87, ECLI:EU:C:1988:225 ....27n.25
Criminal Proceedings against Jean Claude Becu and others, Case C–22/98, ECLI:EU:C:1999:419 ....38n.64
Deutsche Post AG v Gesellschaft für Zahlungssysteme mbH GZS) (C-147/97) and Citicorp Kartenservice GmbH, Case C-147/97, ECLI:EU:C:2000:74 ..... 207n.148
Deutsche Telekom AG v Commission, Case C-280/08, ECLI:EU:C:2010:603 .... 9n.32, 9, 182n.49
Diego Calì & Figli Srl v Servizi ecologici porto di Genova SpA, Case C-343/95, ECLI:EU:C:1997:160 ....28n.27
Dole Food Company and Dole Fresh Fruit Europe v Commission, Case C-286/13 P, ECLI:EU:C:2015:184 .... 227n.47, 255n.192
'Eturas' UAB and others v Lietuvos Respublikos konkurencijos taryba, Case C-74/14, ECLI:EU:C:2016:42.............225n.33, 231n.70, 232n.73, 234n.83
European Superleague Company, Case C-333/21, ECLI:EU:C:2023:1011..........175n.8
Europemballage Corp and Continental Can Co Inc v Commission, Case C-6/72, ECLI:EU:C:1973:22 .... 48n.6, 175n.11
FENIN v Commission, Case C-205/03 P, ECLI:EU:C:2006:453.............7n.25, 25n.10
Firma Ambulanz Glöckner v Landkreis Südwestpfalz,Case C-475/99, ECLI:EU:C:2001:577 ....7n.25, 25n.10
Gerhard Züchner v Bayerische Vereinsbank AG, Case C-172/80, ECLI:EU:C:1981:178 .... 9n.32, 230n.62
Gesellschaft zur Verwertung von Leistungsschutzrechten bmH (GVL) v Commission, Case C-7/82, ECLI:EU:C:1983:52 .... 205n.144
Groupement des cartesbancaires (CB) v Commission, Case C-67/13 P, ECLI:EU:C:2014:2204 253–54
Hilti AG v Commission, Case C-53/92P, ECLI:EU:C:1994:77.....................80n.5
Hoffmann-La Roche & Co. AG v Commission, Case C-85/76, ECLI:EU:C:1979:36 ....77n.127, 79n.2, 79–80, 104n.72, 116n.3, 175n.12, 183n.51
Hüls v Commission, Case C-199/92 P, ECLI:EU:C:1999:358................... 227n.48
Hydrotherm Gerätebau GmbH v Compact del Dott. Ing. Mario Andreoli & C. Sas., Case 170/83, ECLI:EU:C:1984:271 .... 26n.16, 37n.62, 41n.86

Imperial Chemical Industries (ICI) v Commission, Case 48/69,
ECLI: EU:C:1972:70 . . . . 39n.69, 226n.37, 226n.42, 228, 229n.51, 231n.66
IMS Health GmbH & Co. OHG v NDC Health GmbH & Co. KG., Case C-418/01,
ECLI:EU:C:2004:257 . . . . 195–96, 199nn.113–114, 200n.116, 201, 201n.120
Istituto Chemioterapico Italiano SpA and Commercial Solvents Corporation v
Commission, Joined Cases 6-7/73, ECLI:EU:C:1974:18 . . . . 198–99n.108
Italian Republic v Commission, Case 13/63, ECLI:EU:C:1963:20 . . . . 211n.162
Jan and Kristian Jæger AS v. Opel Norge AS, Case E-3/97, (1998) OJ C 263. . . . . 225n.28
Kanal 5 Ltd and TV 4 AB v Föreningen Svenska Tonsättares Internationella
Musikbyrå (STIM) upa., Case C-52/07, ECLI:EU:C:2008:703 . . . . 211n.165
Kattner Stahlbau GmbH v Maschinenbau- und Metall- Berufsgenossenschaft,
Case C-350/07, ECLI:EU:C:2009:127. . . . . .28n.29
Klaus Höfner and Fritz Elser v Macrotron GmbH, Case C-41/90,
ECLI:EU:C:1991:161 . . . . .24n.3, 28n.31
LG Electronics Inc and Koninklijke Philips Electronics NV, Case C-588/15,
ECLI:EU:C:2017:679 . . . . 251n.168
MasterCard and Others v Commission, Case C-382/12 P,
ECLI:EU:C:2014:2201 . . . . 243n.130, 254n.184
MEO–Serviços de Comunicações e Multimédia SA v Autoridade da
Concorrência, Case C-525/16, ECLI:EU:C:2018:270 . . . . 205n.141
Město Žamberk v Finančníředitelství v Hradci Králové, Case C-18/12,
ECLI:EU:C:2013:95 . . . . 197n.99
MOTOE v Elliniko Dimosio, Case C-49/07, ECLI:EU:C:2008:376 . . . . .25n.8
Oscar Bronner GmbH & Co. KG v Mediaprint Zeitungs- und Zeitschriftenverlag
GmbH et al., Case C-7/97, ECLI:EU:C:1998:569. . . . 195–96, 198–99n.108, 199n.111,
199n.114, 201n.120, 216
Pavlov et al. v Stichting Pensioenfonds Medische Specialisten,
Cases C-180–184/98, ECLI: EU:C:2000:428. . . . . .7n.25, 25n.12
Post Danmark A/S v Konkurrencerådet, Case C-209/10, ECLI: EU:C:2012:172. 206
Post Danmark A/S v Konkurrencerådet, Case C-23/14, ECLI:EU:C:2015:651 184–85
Radio Telefis Eireann (RTE) and Independent Television Publications Ltd (ITP) v
Commission, Joined cases C-241/91 P and C-242/91 P, ECLI:EU:C:1995:98 . . . . 195n.91
SAT Fluggesellschaft v Eurocontrol, Case C-364/92, ECLI:EU:C:1994:7 . . . . .27n.25
SELEX Sistemi Integrati SpA v Commission, Case C-113/07 P,
ECLI:EU:C:2009:191 . . . . 25n.11, 28n.29
Servizio Elettrico Nazionale SpA and Others v Autorità Garante della Concorrenza e
del Mercato and Others, Case C-377/20, ECLI:EU:C:2022:379 . . . . . .175–76, 176n.15
Slovak Telekom, a.s. v Commission, Case C-165/19 P, ECLI:EU:C:2020:678. 203–4
Société Technique Minière (L.T.M.) v Maschinenbau Ulm GmbH (M.B.U.),
Case 56-65, ECLI:EU:C:1966:38 254
Sot. Lélos kai Sia EE and Others v GlaxoSmithKline AEVE Farmakeftikon Proïonton,
formerly Glaxowellcome AEVE, Joined cases C-468/06 to
C-478/06, ECLI:EU:C:2008:504 . . . . 199n.110
Tomra Systems and Others v Commission, Case C-549/10 P,
ECLI:EU:C:2012:221 184–85
T-Mobile Netherlands BV v Raad van Bestuur van de Nederlandse
Mededingingsautoriteit, Case C-8/08, ECLI:EU:C:2009:343 . . . . . . .226n.37, 227n.47,
230n.59, 230n.62, 231n.66, 233n.76
Tepea v Commission, Case 28/77, ECLI:EU:C:1978:133 . . . . 225n.23
Tetra Pak v Commission, Case C-333/94 P, ECLI:EU:C:1996:436 . . . . 121–22, 192–93
United Brands Company and United Brands Continentaal BV v Commission,
Case 27/76, ECLI:EU:C:1978:22 . . . . 104n.72, 116n.3, 123n.43, 205n.144, 232n.73

Viho Europe BV v Commission, Case C-73/95 P, ECLI:EU:C:1996:405 ....41n.86
Volkswagen AG v Commission, Case C-338/00 P, ECLI:EU:C:2003:473 .... 225n.30
Wouters v Algemene Raad van de Nederlandsche Orde van Advocaten,
Case C-309/99, ECLI: EU:C:2002:98 .... 16n.72, 26n.21

General Court

AC-Treuhand AG v Commission, Case T-99/04, ECLI:EU:T:2008:256....233n.74, 234–35
Bayer v Commission, Case T-41/96, ECLI:EU:T:2000:242...............224–25, 225n.31
BPB plc v Commission, Case T-53/03, ECLI:EU:T:2008:254.................... 225n.22
British Airways v Commission, Case T-219/99, ECLI:EU:T:2003:343...... 79–80, 81n.12, 176n.14, 182, 205n.142
Cimenteries CBR and others v Commission, Joined cases T-25/95 et al, ECLI:EU:T:2000:77...............................226–27, 230n.61, 233nn.75–76
Coats Holdings Ltd v Commission, Case T-36/05, ECLI:EU:T:2007:268 .... 234n.84
DaimlerChrysler AG v Commission, Case T-325/01, ECLI:EU:T:2005:322 40–41
Deutsche Telekom v Commission, Case T-271/03, ECLI:EU:T:2008:101................9
E.ON Ruhrgas and E.ON v Commission, Case T-360/09, ECLI:EU:T:2012:332.....26n.16
European Federation of Ink and Ink Cartridge Manufacturers (EFIM) v Commission, Case T-296/09, EU:T:2011:693 .... 133n.95
European Night Services Ltd (ENS) et al. v Commission, Joined Cases T-374/94, T-375/94, T-384/94 and T-388/94, ECLI:EU:T:1998:198 .... 123n.43
FNSEA v Commission, Cases T-217/03 and T-245/03, ECLI:EU:T:2006:391........25n.9
Fresh del Monte v Commission, Case T-587/08, ECLI:EU:T:2013:129........... 226n.41
Google and Alphabet v Commission (Google Shopping), Case T-612/17, ECLI:EU:T:2021:763 ....184–85, 197, 204, 209–10, 213–14, 214n.182
Heineken Nederland v Commission, Case T-240/07, ECLI:EU:T:2011:284....... 225n.27
H. Lundbeck A/S and Lundbeck Ltd v Commission, Case T-472/13, ECLI:EU:T:2016:449 .... 254n.181
Infineon Technologies AG v Commission, Case T-758/14, ECLI:EU:T:2016:737.... 230n.60
Irish Sugar plc v Commission, Case T-228/97, ECLI:EU:T:1999:246...... 175–76, 182–83
Limburgse Vinyl Maatschappij NV and others v Commission (PVC II), Joined Cases T-305/94 and others, ECLI:EU:T:1999:80.................... 225n.27
Mastercard Inc, Mastercard International Inc, and Mastercard Europe SPRL v Commission, Case T-111/08, ECLI:EU:T:2012:260 ....48n.5, 49n.9, 52n.20
Métropole television (M6) and Others v Commission, Case T-112/99, ECLI:EU:T:2001:215 .... 242nn.122–123, 243n.129
Microsoft Corp. v Commission, Case T-201/04, ECLI:EU:T:2007:289................ 201
RENV Intel Corporation v Commission, Case T-286/09, ECLI:EU:T:2022:19 .... 132n.90
SA Hercules Chemicals NV v Commission, Case T–7/89, ECLI:EU:T:1991:75.... 225n.31
SELEX Sistemi Integrati SpA v Commission, Case T-155/04, ECLI:EU:T:2006:387 .... 176n.14
Shell International Chemical Company Ltd v Commission, Case T-11/89, ECLI:EU:T:1992:33... 37–38
Spain v Commission, Case T-398/07, ECLI:EU:T:2012:173........................9n.35
Tate & Lyle v Commission, Case T-202/98, ECLI:EU:T:2001:185 .... 225n.29
Tetra Pak v Commission, Case T-83/91, ECLI:EU:T:1994:246 ....122n.38, 192–93
Tiercé Ladbroke SA v Commission, Case T-504/93, ECLI:EU:T:1997:84........ 199n.109

Advocate General (AG) opinions

Albany International BV v Stichting Bedrijfspensioenfonds Textielindustrie, Case C-67/96, ECLI:EU:C:1999:28, Opinion of AG Jacobs 37–38

AOK Bundesverband and Others, Joined Cases C-264/01, C-306/01, C-354/01 and C-355/01, ECLI:EU:C:2003:304, Opinion of AG Jacobs 25n.15
Beef Industry Development and Barry Brothers, Case C-209/07, ECLI:EU:C:2008:467, Opinion of AG Trstenjak 165n.97
'Eturas' UAB and others v Lietuvos Respublikos konkurencijos taryba, Case C-74/14, ECLI:EU:C:2015:493, Opinion of AG Szpunar 225, 232
Jean Reyners v Belgian State, Case C-2/74, ECLI:EU:C:1974:59, Opinion of AG Mayras 33n.54
T-Mobile Netherlands BV et al. v Raad van bestuur van de Nederlandse Mededingingsautoriteit, Case C-8/08, ECLI:EU:C:2009:110, Opinion of Advocate General Kokott 253n.175
MEO–Serviços de Comunicações e Multimédia SA, ECLI:EU:C:2017:1020, Opinion of AG Wahl in Case C-525/16 . . . . 205n.141
Oscar Bronner GmbH & Co KG v Mediaprint Zeitungs- und Zeitschriftenverlag GmbH & Co KG, Mediaprint Zeitungs vertriebsgesellschaft mbH& Co KG and Mediaprint Anzeigengesellschaft mbH& Co KG, Case C-7/97, ECLI:EU:C:1998:264, Opinion of AG Jacobs 201n.119, 201n.122
Pierre Fabre Dermo-Cosmétique SAS v Président de l'Autorité de la concurrence and Ministre de l'Économie, de l'Industrie et de l'Emploi, Case C-439/09, ECLI:EU:C:2011:113, Opinion of Advocate General Mazák 256n.194
Wouters v Algemene Raad van de Nederlandsche Orde van Advocaten, Case C-309/99, ECLI:EU:C:2001:390, Opinion of AG Léger 28n.30
Ziegler SA v Commission, C-439/11 P, ECLI:EU:C:2012:800, Opinion of AG Kokott 47n.2

US CASES

Supreme Court

Abbott Labs. v. Portland Retail Druggists Association, Inc., 425 U.S. 1 S.Ct. 1305 (1976) 205n.144
Allied Tube & Conduit Corp. v. Indian Head, Inc., 486 U.S. 492 (1988) 197n.101, 241n.118, 248n.155
American Needle, Inc. v. National Football League, 130 S. Ct. 2201 (2010) 40n.75, 40, 41, 43, 251n.169
American Tobacco Co. v. United States, 328 U.S. 781 (1946) 117n.7, 224n.20, 227n.43
Aspen Skiing Co. v. Aspen Highlands Skiing Corp., 472 U.S. 585 (1985) 176, 194n.85, 195–96, 198, 198–99n.108, 201–2
Bell Atlantic Corp. v. Twombly, 550 U.S. 544 (2007) 233n.79
Broadcast Music, Inc. v. Columbia Broadcasting System, Inc., 441 U.S. 1 (1979) 243, 245, 256n.194
Brooke Group Ltd. v. Brown & Williamson Tobacco Corp., 509 U.S. 209 (1993) 205n.142
Brown Shoe Co. v. United States, 370 U.S. 294 (1962) 48n.3, 49n.13
Business Electronics Corp. v. Sharp Electronics Corp., 485 U.S. 717 (1988) 255
California Dental Association v. FTC, 526 U.S. 756 (1999) 253n.176, 253n.178, 255, 255n.189
Chicago Board of Trade v. United States, 246 U.S. 231 (1918) 253n.174, 255, 255n.192
Continental T.V., Inc. v. GTE Sylvania Inc., 433 U.S. 36 (1977) 255n.188
Copperweld Corp. v. Independence Tube Corp., 467 U.S. 752 (1984) . . . 40, 41n.85, 220n.3
Fashion Originators' Guild of America v. FTC, 312 U.S. 457 (1941) 197n.101
FTC v. Fred Meyer, Inc., 390 U.S. 341 S.Ct. 904 (1968) 205n.144
FTC v. Indiana Federation of Dentists, 476 U.S. 447 (1986) 48n.7, 253n.177

Goldfarb et Ux. v. Virginia State Bar et al., 421 U.S. 773 (1975) 23n.1, 28n.28
Interstate Circuit v. United States, 306 U.S. 208 (1939) 227n.47
Kiefer-Stewart Co. v. Joseph E. Seagram & Sons, Inc., 340 U.S. 211 (1951) 40
Leegin Creative Leather Products, Inc. v. PSKS, Inc., 551 U.S. 877 (2007) 255
Lorain Journal Co. v. United States, 342 U.S. 143 (1951). 122n.41, 194n.85, 195–96
Matsushita Electric Industrial Co. v. Zenith Radio Corp.,
475 U.S. 574 (1986). 177
Monsanto Co. v. Spray-Rite Service Corp., 465 U.S. 752 (1984) 226, 227n.45, 229n.57
National Society of Professional Engineers v. United States, 435 U.S. 679 (1978) 176–77
Northwest Wholesale Stationers, Inc. v. Pacific Stationery & Printing Co.,
472 U.S. 284 (1985). 255n.188
Ohio v. American Express Co., 585 U.S. 529 (2018). 49n.11, 116n.2
Ohio et al. v. American Express, 138 S. Ct. 2274 (2018) 10n.42, 48n.7
Pacific Bell Telephone Company v. Linkline Communications Inc.,
129 S Ct 1109 (2009) 185n.62
Perma Life Mufflers, Inc. v. International Parts Corp., 392 U.S. 134 (1968) 40n.76
Spectrum Sports, Inc. v. McQuillan, 506 U.S. 447 (1993) 175n.9
Standard Oil Co. v. United States, 221 U.S. 1 (1911). 52n.20, 252n.173
Tampa Electric Co. v. Nashville Coal Co., 365 U.S. 320 (1961) 48n.3, 182
United States v. American Tobacco Co., 221 U.S. 106 (1911) 252n.173
United States v. Colgate & Co., 250 U.S. 300 (1919) 194n.86
United States v. E.I. du Pont de Nemours & Co., 351 U.S. 377
(1956) 53n.23, 54n.28, 116n.2
United States v. E.I. du Pont de Nemours & Co., 353 U.S. 586 (1957) 47n.1, 123
United States v. Grinnell Corp., 384 U.S. 563 (1966) 67n.86, 176
United States v. Paramount Pictures, Inc., 334 U.S. 131 (1948) 224n.20
United States v. Philadelphia National Bank, 374 U.S. 321 (1963) . . . 67n.86, 68n.92, 83n.18
United States v. Phillipsburg National Bank and Trust Co., 399 U.S. 350
(1970) 68n.91, 83n.18
United States v. Socony-Vacuum Oil Co., 310 U.S. 150 (1940). 241n.119
Verizon Communications Inc. v. Law Offices of Curtis v. Trinko, LLP,
540 U.S. 398 (2004). 9n.36, 194n.85, 194n.87, 195–96, 198, 201n.122
Walker Process Equipment, Inc. v. Food Machinery & Chemical Corp.,
382 U.S. 172 (1965). 48n.7

Circuit and District Courts (Decisions, Orders, and Filings)

Bit Global Digital Ltd. v. Coinbase Global, Inc., 3:24-cv-09019-AMO (2024). 125n.53, 196–97, 199–200
Bit Global Digital Ltd. v. Coinbase Global, Inc., Defendant's Opposition to
Ex Parte Emergency Motion for Temporary Restraining Order and
Preliminary Injunction in Case 3:24-cv-09019-AMO (2024). 199–200n.115
Berkey Photo, Inc. v. Eastman Kodak Co., 603 F.2d 263 (1979) 175n.10, 184n.53
City of Tuscaloosa v. Harcros Chemicals, Inc., 158 F.3d 548 (1998). 229n.55
Crown Zellerbach Corporation v. Federal Trade Commission,
296 F.2d 800 (1961) 67n.86
Dahl v. Bain Capital Partners, LLC, 589 F. Supp. 2d 112 (2008) 10n.38
David Leibowitz et al. v. iFinex, Inc et al., 1:19-cv-09236-KPF (2019) 32n.47, 121n.33
Electronic Trading Group, LLC v. Bank of America Securities, LLC,
588 F.3d 128 (2009) 10n.38
Exxon Corporation v. Berwick Bay Real Estates Partners, 748 F.2d 937 (1984). 80n.10
FTC v. Facebook, 1:20-cv-03590-JEB (2021) 128n.69

FTC v. Whole Foods Market, Inc., 548 F.3d 1028 (2008) 52n.21
Geneva Pharmaceuticals Technology Corp. v. Barr Labs., 386 F.3d 485 (2004) 82n.16
In re Crude Oil Commodity Futures Litigation, 913 F. Supp. 2d 41 (2012) 122n.38, 122–23
In re LIBOR-Based Financial Instruments Antitrust Litigation, Docket Nos. 13-3565-cv (L) et al. (2016).. 241n.116
In re Libor-Based Financial Instruments Antitrust Litigation, 11 MD 2262(NRB) (2011) 10n.43
In re Libor-Based Financial Instruments Antitrust Litigation, 935 F. Supp. 2d 666 (2013) (LIBOR I) 231, 240–41, 241n.120, 248
In re Libor-Based Financial Instruments Antitrust Litigation, 11 MDL 2262 (NRB) (2015) (LIBOR II) 231, 240, 241n.121
In re Rail Freight Fuel Surcharge Antitrust Litigation, 587 F.Supp.2d 27 (2008) ... 248n.155
In re Tether and Bitfinex Cryptoasset Litigation, 1:19-cv-09236-KPF (2021) 32n.47, 86n.27, 120n.27, 121n.33, 121n.35, 122n.42, 126n.60, 192n.79
In re Tether and Bitfinex Crypto Asset Litigation Defendants' Memorandum of Law in Opposition to Plaintiffs' Motion for Leave to Amend, 1:19-cv-09236-KPF (2023).. 121n.35
In re Text Messaging Antitrust Litigation, 782 F.3d 867 (2015)..................... 221n.8
Kreuzer v. American Academy of Periodontology, 735 F. 2d 1479 (1984)......... 203n.130
Lamartine Pierre et al. v. Apple, Inc., 5:23-cv-5981 (2023)................ 195n.88, 220n.6
Los Angeles Land Co. v. Brunswick Co., 6 F.3d 1422 (1993) 144n.5
Marjorie Webster v. Middle States Association, 432 F.2d 650 (1970)..... 7n.25, 26n.17, 26n.20
Mayor & City Council of Baltimore & City of New Britain Firefighters & Police Benefit Fund, Texas Competitive Electric Holdings Company LLC v. Credit Suisse Group AG et al., In re: LIBOR-Based Financial Instruments Antitrust Litigation, No. 1:11-md-2262 (S.D.N.Y. Sept. 10, 2013) (Doc. 406),"Second Consolidated Amended Complaint" 240n.110
MCI Communications Corp. v. AT&T, 708 F.2d 1081 (1983) 240n.110
Meyer v. Kalanick, 174 F.Supp.3d 817 (2016) 245n.138
New York v. Facebook, Inc., 549 F. Supp. 3d 6 (2021) 198n.107
Novell, Inc. v. Microsoft Corp., 731 F.3d 1064 (2013) 198
Nurse Midwifery Association v. Hibbertt, 918 F.2d 605 (1990)...................... 37n.62
Olympia Equipment Leasing Co. v. Western Union Telegraph Co., 797 F.2d 370 (1986) 176
Pan-Islamic Trade Corp. v. Exxon Corp., 632 F.2d 539 (1980) 229n.56
PLS.Com, LLC v. National Association of Realtors, 32 F.4th 824 (2022)............. 49n.11
Polk Bros., Inc. v. Forest City Enterprises, Inc., 776 F.2d 185 (1985) 244n.134
Pollock v. Citrus Associates of N.Y. Cotton Exchange, 512 F.Supp. 711 (1981)...... 120n.27
Rebel Oil Co., Inc. v. Atlantic Richfield Co., 51 F.3d 1421 (1995) 144n.5, 158n.73
Rio Grande Royalty Co. v. Energy Transfer Partners, L.P., 786 F.Supp. 2d 1190 (2009) 49n.8
Rothery Storage & Van Co. v. Atlas Van Lines, Inc., 792 F.2d 210 (1986).......... 242n.126
Swink v. Uber Technologies, Inc., 4:16-cv-01092 (2016) 245n.138
Symbiont.io Inc. v. Ipreo Holdings, LLC, 2021WL 3575709 (2021).............. 251n.163
Thompson's Gas & Electric Service, Inc. v. BP America Inc., 691 F.Supp.2d 860 (2010) 123n.45
Toys "R" Us, Inc. v. FTC, 221 F.3d 928 (2000) 49n.8
Transamerica Corp. v. Board of Governors, 206 F.2d 163 (1953) 123n.46
United American Corp. v. Bitmain, Inc. et al., 530 F. Supp. 3d 1241 (2021)..... 5n.13, 32n.47, 125, 187n.67, 197–98, 220n.6, 237n.100
United States v. Airline Tariff Publishing Co., 1994-2 Trade Case (CCH) 61, (1993).... 231

United States v. Aluminum Co. of America, 148 F.2d 416 (1945) 80n.8, 177n.21
United States v. Amax, Inc., 402 F.Supp. 956 (1975). 83
United States v. Dentsply International, Inc., 399 F.3d 181 (2005) .80n.9
United States v. Microsoft Corp., 253 F.3d 34 (2001). 49n.8, 146n.16, 174n.3
U.S. v. Brown University, 5 F.3d 658 (1993) 7n.25, 26n.18, 26n.22
U.S. v. Visa USA Inc., Visa International Corp., and Mastercard International Inc., 344 F.3d 229 (2003). 10n.41
US DoJ v. AT&T and Deutsche Telecom, 1:11-cv-01560 (2011). 111n.92
Van Loon v. Department of Treasury, 2023 WL 5313091 (2023) 250–51
Viamedia, Inc. v. Comcast Corp., 951 F.3d 429 (2020) 198n.106
Wallace v. International Business Machines Corp., 467 F.3d 1104 (2006). 30–31, 245
Weiss v. York Hospital, 745 F.2d 786 (1984). 79n.2
Williamson Oil Co. v. Philip Morris USA, 346 F.3d 1287 (2003) 229n.55

NATIONAL CASES

UK Cases

Notice of an Application to Commence Collective Proceedings Under Section 47b of the Competition Act 1998 Case No. 1523/7/7/22 (2022). . . .125n.53, 195n.89, 220n.6

CASES SPECIFIC TO THE DECENTRALIZED ECONOMY (DUPLICATE LIST)

Bit Global Digital Ltd. v. Coinbase Global, Inc., 3:24-cv-09019-AMO (2024). 125n.53, 196–97, 199–200
Bit Global Digital Ltd. v. Coinbase Global, Inc., Defendant's Opposition to Ex Parte Emergency Motion for Temporary Restraining Order and Preliminary Injunction in Case 3:24-cv-09019-AMO (2024). 199–200n.115
David Leibowitz et al. v. iFinex, Inc et al., 1:19-cv-09236-KPF (2019) 32n.47, 121n.33
In re Tether and Bitfinex Cryptoasset Litigation, 1:19-cv-09236-KPF (2021) 32n.47, 86n.27, 120n.27, 121n.33, 121n.35, 122n.42, 126n.60, 192n.79
In re Tether and Bitfinex Crypto Asset Litigation Defendants' Memorandum of Law in Opposition to Plaintiffs' Motion for Leave to Amend, 1:19-cv-09236-KPF (2023). 121n.35
Lamartine Pierre et al. v. Apple, Inc., 5:23-cv-5981 (2023). 195n.88, 220n.6
United American Corp. v. Bitmain, Inc. et al., 530 F. Supp. 3d 1241 (2021). 5n.13, 32n.47, 125, 187n.67, 197–98, 220n.6, 237n.100
Van Loon v. Department of Treasury, 2023 WL 5313091 (2023) 250–51
Notice of an Application to Commence Collective Proceedings Under Section 47b of the Competition Act 1998 Case No. 1523/7/7/22 (2022). 125n.53, 195n.89, 220n.6

Abbreviations (Excludes cryptoassets, currencies, and case parties)

AG	Advocate General
AICOA	American Innovation and Choice Online Act
ALD	Accumulation-Lift-Distribution
AMM	Automated Market Maker
ASIC	Application-specific Integrated Circuit
ATPCO	Airline Tariff Publishing Company
BoB	Blockchains-of-Blockchains
CBDC	Central Bank Digital Currency
CEX	Centralized Exchange
CoJ	Court of Justice
CRPA	National Cooperative Research and Production Act of 1993
DAO	Decentralized Autonomous Organization
dApp	Decentralized Application
DeFi	Decentralized Finance
DEX	Decentralized Exchange
DLT	Distributed Ledger Technology
ETF	Exchange-Traded Fund
GC	General Court
GPL	GNU General Public License
HHI	Herfindahl–Hirschman Index
ICO	Initial Coin Offering
IP	Intellectual Property
ISDA	International Swaps and Derivatives Association
KYC	Know Your Customer
LIBOR	London Inter-Bank Offered Rate
M&A	Mergers and Acquisitions
MEV	Maximal Extractable Value
MiCA(R)	Markets in Crypto-assets (Regulation)
MIF	Multilateral Interchange Fee
NFL	National Football League
NFT	Non-Fungible Token
OECD	Organisation for Economic Cooperation and Development
PoET	Proof of Elapsed Time
PoS	Proof of Stake
PoW	Proof of Work
R&D	Research and Development
RoR	Rule of Reason

R–P Act	Robinson–Patman Act of 1936
SEC	Securities and Exchange Commission
SSNIP	Small but Significant and Nontransitory Increase in Price
SSNRQ	Small but Significant and Nontransitory Reduction in Quality
SSO	Standard Setting Organization
SWIFT	Society for Worldwide Interbank Financial Telecommunication
TFEU	Treaty on the Functioning of the European Union
ToS	Terms of Service
TVL	Total Value Locked

PART I

FUNDAMENTALS

1

ANTITRUST IN THE DECENTRALIZED ECONOMY

(A) General 3
(B) A working definition of the decentralized economy 5
(C) The applicability of antitrust law in the decentralized economy 8
(D) The special features of the decentralized economy for antitrust 11
i) The decentralized nature of DLT products, services, and markets 11
ii) The prevalence of social production 13
iii) Governance as a new arena of economic activity 17
iv) Application of tokenomics 20

(A) General

Every time a new foundational technology emerges, the antitrust (competition law)[1] community goes into introspection mode trying to assess the relevance and role of antitrust law and policy in the new markets ushered in by the technology. During the first computer era, scholars posited that 'it is quite possible that the advantages to society of computer utilization will force a radical redefinition of antitrust law'.[2] The existential crisis came back with greater force in the internet era, when the new innovation economics cast into doubt antitrust's efficacy due to its slow pace and rigid framework.[3] Today once again, the rise of the decentralized economy, encompassing such technologies and domains as blockchain, central bank digital currencies (CBDC) and fintech, reignites the debate.

[1] Antitrust (law) and competition law are used interchangeably in this monograph. The choice of terminology depends on the context for ease of reading.
[2] Binder Denis, 'Computers and Market Dominance: An Emerging Antitrust Problem' (1975) 26 Mercer Law Review 427, 427.
[3] John Lopatka and William H Page, 'Antitrust on Internet Time: Microsoft and the Law and Economics of Exclusion' (1999) 7 Supreme Court Economic Review 157; Lawrence Sullivan, 'Is Competition Policy Possible in High Tech Market?: An Inquiry Into Antitrust, Intellectual Property, and Broadband Regulation as Applied to "The New Economy"' (2001) 52 Case Western Reserve Law Review 41; David J Teece and Mary Coleman, 'The Meaning of Monopoly: Antitrust Analysis in High-Technology Industries' (1998) 43 Antitrust Bulletin 801.

Antitrust in the Decentralized Economy. Konstantinos Stylianou, Oxford University Press.
 DOI: 10.1093/9780191925504.003.0001

Reassuringly, even a cursory look at the state of antitrust theory and practice today reveals that not only has antitrust not been rendered irrelevant by any technological development so far, but its application in high-technology markets has ballooned.[4] Antitrust law has proven extremely adaptable and relevant as it applies horizontally across all markets and all economic actors, and its laws and concepts are so abstract that they can be ported into any economic context and any economic activity.[5] Its resilience is grounded in its ability to maintain elastic concepts and an all-encompassing reach across the economy. As long as this evolutionary process continues, antitrust will have a place in regulating new economic activities. The decentralized economy does not nullify antitrust law, nor does it create the need for a new type of antitrust law. What is needed is an understanding of the decentralized economy—its processes, actors, business models, and practices—and the occasional development of new concepts or tools to fill the gaps.

A great deal has already been written about the decentralized economy and its main technological underpinning, the blockchain. Its supporters extol its potential for a new economic order where wealth and power is distributed and access to capital is democratized;[6] its critics deride the lack of real world uses, its increasing capture by incumbent interests, and the underwhelming deliverables.[7] The truth lies somewhere in the middle, and even though the decentralized economy may have failed to live up to its initial lofty aspirations, it has captured the attention and active involvement of every major stakeholder group, including governments,[8] central banks,[9] financial incumbents and financial startups,[10] international

[4] There is vast literature on digital markets and on the work competition authorities have undertaken; for high-level summaries see European Commission, 'Competition Policy for the Digital Era' (2019); OECD, 'Handbook on Competition Policy in the Digital Age' (2022); US House Committee on the Judiciary, 'Investigation of Competition in Digital Markets' (2021).

[5] Richard Posner, 'Antitrust in the New Economy' in Rosa Greaves, *Dominance and Monopolization* (Routledge 2016).

[6] Marion Labouré and Nicolas Deffrennes, *Democratizing Finance: The Radical Promise of Fintech* (Harvard UP 2022); Yan Chen, 'Blockchain Tokens and the Potential Democratization of Entrepreneurship and Innovation' (2018) 61 Business Horizons 567; Yan Chen, Jack I Richter, and Pankaj C Patel, 'Decentralized Governance of Digital Platforms' (2021) 47 Journal of Management 1305. See also Brett Scott, 'How Can Cryptocurrency and Blockchain Technology Play a Role in Building Social and Solidarity Finance?' (2016) United Nations Research Institute for Social Development Working Paper No. 2016-1.

[7] OECD, 'The Uncertain Promise of Blockchain for Government', OECD Working Papers on Public Governance No. 43 (2020); Eric White, 'What Does Finance Democracy Look Like?: Thinking Beyond Fintech and Regtech' (2023) Transnational Legal Theory 1; Belen Suarez Lopez, David Issó García, and Antonio Vargas Alcaide, 'Blockchain Technology Facing Socioeconomic Challenges. Promise versus Probability' (2019) 3 SocioEconomic Challenges 13; Barber Gregory, 'What's Blockchain Actually Good for, Anyway? For Now, Not Much' *Wired* (28 October 2019).

[8] See eg Svein Ølnes, Jolien Ubacht, and Marijn Janssen, 'Blockchain in Government: Benefits and Implications of Distributed Ledger Technology for Information Sharing' (2017) 34 Government Information Quarterly 355.

[9] See eg European Central Bank, 'Central Bank Digital Currency and Bank Intermediation' (2022) Occasional Paper Series No 293.

[10] See eg the special issue 'Fintech and Banking. Friends of Foes?' (2017) 2 European Economy Banks, Regulation, and the Real Sector.

organizations,[11] regulatory authorities,[12] and individual users, developers, and infrastructure providers.

As the decentralized economy gradually embeds itself in economic life, it is only to be expected that actors with market power, anticompetitive conduct, and the occasional distortion of competition will make their appearance. Already, the first cases[13] and investigations and policy responses[14] have begun outlining the challenges the decentralized economy poses for competition law and policy. On the one hand, these initial exploratory steps expose the limits of current antitrust thinking, but on the other, they serve as a reminder that the law seeks to ascertain its relevance and applicability in new domains of economic life, and the decentralized economy is no exception.

To perform this task correctly, one needs to appreciate the special features of the decentralized economy. Are products, services, markets, and actors in the decentralized economy any different from mainstream economy, and if so, how? Once the differentiating features have been distilled, one can start seeing the gaps in current antitrust theory and practice and filling them in.

This chapter first defines the concept of the decentralized economy to establish a 'working space' and discusses the applicability of antitrust law within that domain. Then, it identifies the high-level features of the decentralized economy to provide analytical clarity on how antitrust law applies in the markets within the decentralized economy. These high-level features permeate economic activity in the decentralized economy, and they represent concepts and characteristics that antitrust scholars and practitioners will have to keep coming back to.

(B) A working definition of the decentralized economy

There is no single authoritative definition of the decentralized economy. In terms of technology, at its core lies the blockchain technology, which provides the technological infrastructure for distributed processing, transmission, and storage of data,

[11] See eg OECD, 'Recommendation of the Council on OECD Legal Instruments Blockchain and Other Distributed Ledger Technologies' (2024) OECD/LEGAL/0470.

[12] See eg the comprehensive regulatory response of the European Union to crypto-assets: Regulation (EU) 2023/1114 of the European Parliament and of the Council on Markets in Crypto-assets, L 150/40 (MiCA).

[13] The first major antitrust case in the space was brought in 2018 but was eventually thrown out: *United American Corp. v. Bitmain, Inc. et al.*, 530 F. Supp. 3d 1241 (2021). See commentary in Konstantinos Stylianou, 'What Can the First Blockchain Antitrust Case Teach Us About the Crypto-Economy?' (2019) Harvard Journal of Law and Technology (online), https://jolt.law.harvard.edu/digest/what-can-the-first-blockchain-antitrust-case-teach-us-about-the-crypto-economy.

[14] Numerous investigations, policy responses, and reports by competition and regulatory authorities have been launched. Among the high-profile ones, see US Department of Commerce, 'Responsible Advancement of U.S. Competitiveness in Digital Assets' (2022); UK Digital Regulation Cooperation Forum, 'Insight Paper on Web3' (2023); European Commission, 'Commission Staff Working Paper: An EU Initiative on Web 4.0 and Virtual Worlds: A Head Start in the next Technological Transition' (2023) SWD(2023) 250 final.

which most commonly represents transactions between actors.[15] Transactions in the blockchain context encompass any type of data transfer, processing, and storage, whether they represent monetary value, identity information, health records, art, etc.[16] Blockchain brings together a multitude of actors to function, from protocol developers, to validators, to various intermediaries, none of whom needs to know, trust, or negotiate with each other outside of the blockchain transaction, which explains why the technology is decentralized; it does not per se necessitate central control points, even if de facto some may arise.[17] Because blockchain is not the only technology that enables this type of distributed transaction processing, a better way to describe the core technology of the decentralized economy is distributed ledger technology (DLT).[18] DLT describes technologies that enable secure distributed databases, which can be read and modified by anyone who follows the governance and consensus rules on the state of the database.[19] Blockchain is one such technology. DLT will be the preferred technology reference herein.

In terms of type of activity, most of the products, services and applications built on DLT (and predominantly blockchain) are in the field of financial services.[20] Cryptoassets, crypto-exchanges, innovations such as decentralized lending protocols, and associated supporting services such as mining and staking represent the lion's share of the activity taking place in the decentralized economy. The term 'decentralized finance' (DeFi) is sometimes used to describe such activities.[21] But the decentralized economy goes beyond DeFi in that other DLT-based products, services, and applications that do not primarily concern financial activities also exist;

[15] There is vast technical literature on blockchain, but for accessible introductions see Mohan Menon and Ashraf Mady, 'Blockchain: A Non-Technical Primer for Marketing Academics' (2022) 32 Marketing Education Review 186; Arvind Narayanan and others, *Bitcoin and Cryptocurrency Technologies: A Comprehensive Introduction* (Princeton UP 2016).

[16] Andrew J Ehrenberg and John Leslie King, 'Blockchain in Context' (2020) 22 Information Systems Frontiers 29.

[17] Ashish Rajendra Sai and others, 'Taxonomy of Centralization in Public Blockchain Systems: A Systematic Literature Review' (2021) 58 Information Processing & Management 102584; Carlo Campajola and others, 'The Evolution of Centralisation on Cryptocurrency Platforms' (2022) arXiv:2206.05081; Johannes Rude Jensen, Victor von Wachter, and Omri Ross, 'How Decentralized Is the Governance of Blockchain-Based Finance: Empirical Evidence from Four Governance Token Distributions' (2021) arXiv:2102.10096.

[18] Arvind Panwar and Vishal Bhatnagar, 'Distributed Ledger Technology (DLT): The Beginning of a Technological Revolution for Blockchain' (2020) 2nd International Conference on Data, Engineering and Applications (IDEA) 1.

[19] Ali Sunyaev, 'Distributed Ledger Technology' in Ali Sunyaev, *Internet Computing* (Springer International Publishing 2020). See also UK Government Office for Science, 'Distributed Ledger Technology: Beyond Block Chain' (2016).

[20] David Mills and others, 'Distributed Ledger Technology in Payments, Clearing, and Settlement' (Federal Reserve Board 2016) 2016–095; Yan Chen and Cristiano Bellavitis, 'Blockchain Disruption and Decentralized Finance: The Rise of Decentralized Business Models' (2020) 13 Journal of Business Venturing Insights e00151.

[21] Chen and Bellavitis, ibid. See also Mariana de la Roche and Mirko Zichichi, 'Bringing Clarity to the DeFi Sector: A Cross-Sector Proposal for a Unified DeFi Definition' (2023) IOTA Foundation.

these can include identity verification, e-government, logistics, etc.[22] Relevant also here is fintech, which is used to describe financial products, services, and applications that rely on technology to compete with or extend traditional financial services.[23] Fintech has both a broader and a narrower scope than the decentralized economy, since it encompasses also products and services that are commonly not decentralized (such as robo-advisers and wealth management apps), while at the same existing exclusively within the financial sector.[24] As a result, there is only partial overlap between the decentralized economy and fintech.

Moreover, the decentralized economy is closely associated with financial activities that may not be purely economic, at least as understood by competition law. Competition law applies to economic or commercial activities, which are usually defined as the offering of goods or services in a given market on a competitive basis.[25] The most prominent use case that challenges this boundary is central bank digital currencies (CBDC). CBDCs are digital currencies issued by central banks and are commonly—but not always—implemented on a DLT.[26] Because CBDCs can be functionally equivalent to cash and cash-like instruments, and as such they are an expression of governments' sovereign monetary policy, their existence and role transcends the predominantly commercial competitive activity that competition law regulates. That said, not only may CBDCs encompass commercial activities (eg hybrid CBDCs), which would bring them within the scope of competition law,[27] but they provide similar functionality to offerings of the decentralized economy, chiefly stablecoins,[28] and therefore compete with them. Consequently, governments' initiatives in this space can also be included in the scope of the decentralized economy.

In sum, the decentralized economy's identity is defined by the technology that underpins it—decentralized ledgers and predominantly blockchain; by the nature and subject matter of the activities—predominantly, but not exclusively, of

[22] Mahdi H Miraz and Maaruf Ali, 'Applications of Blockchain Technology beyond Cryptocurrency' (2018) 2 Annals of Emerging Technologies in Computing 1; Shiho Kim and Ganesh Chandra Deka (eds), *Advanced Applications of Blockchain Technology*, vol 60 (Springer 2020).

[23] Patrick Schueffel, 'Taming the Beast: A Scientific Definition of Fintech' (2017) 4 Journal of Innovation Management 32.

[24] Claire Ingram Bogusz and Jonas Valbjørn Andersen, 'The Boundaries of Fintech: Data-Driven Classification and Domain Delimitation' in Konstantinos Stylianou, Marios Iacovides, and Björn Lundqvist (eds), *Fintech Competition: Law, Policy, and Market Organisation* (Hart Publishing 2023).

[25] See Case C-475/99 Firma Ambulanz Glöckner v Landkreis Südwestpfalz ECLI:EU:C:2001:577; Case C-205/03 P FENIN v Commission ECLI:EU:C:2006:453; Cases C-180–184/98 Pavlov et al v Stichting Pensioenfonds Medische Specialisten ECLI:EU:C:2000:428; *Marjorie Webster v. Middle States Association*, 432 F.2d 650 (1970); *U.S. v. Brown University*, 5 F.3d 658 (1993). For more details, see Chapter 2 section B.i.

[26] Shobit Seth, 'What Is a Central Bank Digital Currency (CBDC)?' *Investopedia* (14 June 2024).

[27] Daniel Schwarz, 'Central Bank Digital Currencies and Competition Laws: Recognising the Importance of Competition Laws in the CBDC Ecosystem' (2023) 02/23 Butterworths Journal of International Banking and Financial Law 107, 109.

[28] Stablecoins are cryptoassets that maintain a fixed value pegged to a fiat currency, most commonly the US Dollar. Examples include USDT, USDC, Dai, etc.

financial nature; and by the intricate links with government financial policies that affect the competitive conditions in the relevant markets.

Markets within those boundaries have distinguishing features that inform how antitrust law applies (see section C below): they are decentralized, they rely on social production, they are defined by endogenous governance processes, and their economics are influenced by the existence and function of tokens (tokenomics). These features create challenges around the application of antitrust law in these markets, without that meaning that the standard analytical framework of antitrust law is inapplicable. As becomes apparent from the analysis undertaken in the following chapters, most of competition law's analytical tools remain relevant, despite some necessary adaptations and new concepts.

(C) The applicability of antitrust law in the decentralized economy

Antitrust law applies horizontally across markets and is considered a backstop mechanism for bad business conduct.[29] Since it applies horizontally, it can also apply in markets comprising the decentralized economy. It is a backstop mechanism because the implicit assumption is that businesses are free to conduct themselves as they wish in the market, and it is only when they harm the competitive process that their conduct is constrained (by antitrust law). By extension, if businesses' freedom is curtailed by regulation, then there is less need for a backstop mechanism, because the implicit assumption in that case is that competition considerations are embedded in regulation, and regulatory compliance entails servicing said competition considerations as well. The more detailed and prescriptive the regulation, the less the residual freedom of companies in the market, and the smaller the margin for engaging in anticompetitive conduct.

Perhaps the most paradigmatic highly regulated industry is the financial industry, and since financial products, services, and applications account for the majority of the activity in the decentralized economy, the question arises of whether and to what degree antitrust law applies in the decentralized economy.[30] Financial services are traditionally known for features that are usually red flags for antitrust law, such as obscure pricing, high levels of profit (and possibilities for rent extraction), high levels of concentration, and horizontal inter-connections and information exchange between competing firms.[31] If these features are carried over to the

[29] Howard Shelanski, 'The Case for Rebalancing Antitrust and Regulation' (2011) 109 Michigan Law Review 683, 727 et seq.

[30] See Iris HY Chiu and Despoina Mantzari, 'Regulating Fintech and BigTech: Reconciling the Objectives of Financial Regulation and Promoting Competition' in Stylianou, Iacovides, and Lundqvist (n 24).

[31] David Harrison, *Competition Law and Financial Services* (Routledge 2014) 2; Andrea Lista, *EU Competition Law and the Financial Services Sector* (Informa Law 2013) 19–20.

decentralized economy too, then the application of antitrust law in the finance-oriented decentralized economy becomes particularly imperative.

The European Union and the United States are taking somewhat contrasting views on the applicability of antitrust law in highly regulated industries, with the European Union seeing more scope for application, whereas the United States remains more reticent. In fact, EU competition law is only minimally forborne from applying in heavily regulated markets such as financial services and utilities.[32] The early case of *Züchner* set the tone by having the Court of Justice (CoJ) declare that banking services are not automatically exempted from EU competition law by virtue of their 'special nature'.[33] In *Ladbroke* the CoJ stated that EU competition law is only inapplicable if 'anticompetitive conduct is *required* of undertakings by national legislation, or if the latter creates a legal framework which itself *eliminates any possibility of competitive activity* on their part' (emphasis added).[34] In *Deutsche Telekom*, the company argued that, because the range of wholesale rates it could charge was set by the German telecom regulator, any rate within that range could not possibly violate EU competition law, but the General Court (GC) disagreed, stating that 'the fact that the [Deutsche Telekom's] charges had to be approved by RegTP does not absolve it from responsibility under Article 82 EC [now Article 102 TFEU]'.[35]

The United States, on the other hand, is quicker to preclude the application of antitrust law when detailed regulatory regimes are in place. Famously in *Trinko*, which concerned a monopolization claim in the face of the 1996 Telecommunications Act, the Supreme Court stated that 'the enforcement scheme set up by the 1996 Act is a good candidate for implication of antitrust immunity, to avoid the real possibility of judgments conflicting with the agency's regulatory scheme'.[36] More specifically in the financial sector, the *Billing* case made clear that securities law can well be incompatible with the application of antitrust law, in which case antitrust law would be forborne, under the conditions that: (a) the activity in question is in 'an area of conduct squarely within the heartland of securities regulation'; (b) there is 'clear and adequate Securities and Exchange (SEC) authority to regulate' the conduct; (c) the conduct has been subject to 'active and ongoing agency regulation', and; (d) a 'serious conflict' exists or can arise between the antitrust and regulatory regimes.[37] These criteria have sometimes been

[32] For the financial services industry see principally European Commission, 'Commission Report on Competition' Policy (Vol 2)' (1972) nos 51–57. Case C-172/80 Gerhard Züchner v Bayerische Vereinsbank AG ECLI:EU:C:1981:178; for the utilities sector see principally Case T-271/03 Deutsche Telekom v Commission ECLI:EU:T:2008:101; upheld on appeal in Case C-280/08 Deutsche Telekom AG v Commission ECLI:EU:C:2010:603. At the national level, national laws have often created obstacles to the application of competition law in the financial services sector; see eg Lista (n 31) 129–33.

[33] Züchner (n 32) paras 6 et seq.

[34] Joined Cases C-359/95 P and C-379/95 P Commission and France v Ladbroke Racing ECLI:EU:C:1997:531, para 33.

[35] Deutsche Telekom (n 32) para 107. See also Case T-398/07 Spain v Commission ECLI:EU:T:2012:173.

[36] *Verizon Communications Inc. v. Law Offices of Curtis v. Trinko, LLP*, 540 U.S. 398, 406 (2004).

[37] *Credit Suisse Securities LLC v. Billing*, 551 U.S. 264, 285 (2007).

interpreted against the applicability of antitrust law,[38] and are reminiscent of other antitrust exemptions in US financial laws, such as insurance, which was recently repealed.[39]

Despite a certain measure of scepticism towards antitrust laws in the United States when heavy regulation is in place, they still retain their relevance. For one thing, recent financial laws include antitrust savings clauses; for example, section 6 of the Dodd–Frank Act states that 'nothing in this Act, or any amendment made by this Act, shall be construed to modify, impair or supersede the operation of any of the antitrust laws, unless otherwise specified'.[40] Additionally, the Department of Justice has actively pursued anticompetitive conduct in financial services, albeit in areas that were less regulated, for instance, exclusivity arrangements in card issuance,[41] anti-steering provisions,[42] or the notorious LIBOR rate fixing.[43]

It follows that that even if the decentralized economy is heavily skewed toward financial activities, it will not be exempt from the application of antitrust laws neither in the United States nor in the European Union. To the extent that the logic of antitrust enforcement is the same across industries (ie maintaining competitive markets that safeguard welfare) it will continue to be appropriate for application in decentralized economy markets as well.[44] This is even more true considering that much of the activity taking place within the scope of the decentralized economy remains unregulated, despite the often remarkable similarity with activities in more traditional financial markets, which are regulated. This is a regulatory gap that will eventually close (already the European Union has passed the first comprehensive regulation on cryptoassets, the Markets in Cryptoassets Regulation—MiCA),[45] but until then, the case for antitrust forbearance on the grounds of heavy regulation does not seem to apply with the same force in the decentralized economy as in traditional financial markets.

[38] See eg *Electronic Trading Group, LLC v. Bank of America Securities, LLC*, 588 F.3d 128 (2009). But see *Dahl v. Bain Capital Partners, LLC*, 589 F. Supp. 2d 112 (2008).

[39] McCarran-Ferguson Act, 15 U.S.C. §§ 1012(b); 1013(b), repealed by H.R.1418 - Competitive Health Insurance Reform Act of 2020.

[40] Dodd–Frank Wall Street Reform and Consumer Protection Act, Pub. L. 111-203, 124 Stat. 1376 (2010), sec 6 and sec 541.

[41] *U.S. v. Visa USA Inc., Visa International Corp., and Mastercard International Inc.*, 344 F.3d 229 (2003).

[42] The Department of Justice sued Visa, Mastercard, and American Express, but Visa and Mastercard settled, while American Express litigated the case, culminating in a favourable decision by the Supreme Court; see *Ohio et al. v. American Express*, 138 S. Ct. 2274 (2018).

[43] *In Re Libor-Based Financial Instruments Antitrust Litigation*, 11 MD 2262(NRB) (2011).

[44] Lawrence White, 'Antitrust and the Financial Sector – with Special Attention to "Too Big to Fail"' (2014) NYU Working Paper No. 2451/33582 21.

[45] MiCA (n 12).

(D) The special features of the decentralized economy for antitrust

It is impossible to talk about the decentralized economy without mentioning such features as immutable, secure, cryptographic, disintermediated, etc. While all of them are valid, they do not necessarily weigh heavily on how antitrust law applies to the decentralized economy. It is worth, instead, zeroing in on those features that differentiate the decentralized economy from traditional economies in ways that may challenge and stretch existing antitrust frameworks, call for a modified application of antitrust laws, or even require the creation of new antitrust concepts or doctrines.

Doing so requires abstracting away from any specific product, service, implementation, or business model. What remains is characteristics that should apply to all offerings of the decentralized economy, although they may not be equally determinative in all cases. The list presented below introduces those characteristics and shows how they relate to competition law and policy. It is not meant to engage in any analysis of the relevant issues—this is reserved for the chapters that follow.

i) The decentralized nature of DLT products, services, and markets

Perhaps the most notable feature of the decentralized economy is, as the name suggests, that it is decentralized. The epithet has been widely used without always referring to the same property, and its factual accuracy is contested,[46] but it does remain key to the decentralized economy. In the context of antitrust law, decentralization means that the performance of economic activity ordinarily involves the contribution and input of a multitude of actors that are otherwise unknown to and uncoordinated with one another. Decentralization characterizes at least three facets of the decentralized economy: network, consensus, and governance.[47] So, simply saying that an economic activity is (de)centralized does not convey much information about which of its operations are (de)centralized or to what degree. This can often result in confusion as different observers may focus on different facets and will form a different picture about the decentralized nature of said economic activity. To the extent that antitrust policy is often concerned with concentration resulting from centralization, this confusion may become misleading.

Network decentralization refers to the degree to which the underlying network infrastructure of DLT systems is distributed across different actors.[48] Network

[46] Sirio Aramonte, Wenqian Huang, and Andreas Schrimpf, 'DeFi Risks and the Decentralisation Illusion' (2021) BIS Quarterly Review.

[47] Luyao Zhang, Xinshi Ma, and Yulin Liu, 'SoK: Blockchain Decentralization' (2022) arXiv:2205.04256.

[48] Adem Efe Gencer and others, 'Decentralization in Bitcoin and Ethereum Networks' in Sarah Meiklejohn and Kazue Sako (eds), *Financial Cryptography and Data Security*, vol 10957 (Springer 2018).

infrastructure comprises any physical and logical components that make up a DLT system. This can include the equipment used to validate transactions (eg mining equipment) and the communication networks used by DLT participants to communicate with each other.

Consensus decentralization refers to the degree to which the consensus layer of DLT systems is distributed across different actors.[49] Consensus is the process by which nodes agree on the state of the network such that they all see and accept the same distributed ledger. No transaction and therefore no economic activity can take place on a DLT system without nodes reaching consensus about it. In permissionless DLT systems, any actor who abides by the system's consensus rules can become part of the consensus process, and as a result permissionless DLT consensus processes tend to be spread across hundreds or thousands of nodes. In permissioned DLT systems, additional authorization criteria apply, which create some centripetal forces, but do not necessarily detract from the decentralized model.

Governance decentralization refers to the degree to which a DLT system's governance power and authority are distributed among different actors.[50] Governance is the set of written and unwritten rules and norms that determine the operation of a DLT system, that is, how proposals are submitted and voted on, who can vote and how power is distributed among voters, how the system's finances are structured, etc.[51]

In all three cases, it is important to note that decentralization is not a binary state but rather it exists on a spectrum. DLT systems are virtually never fully centralized or decentralized, and in fact, the level of decentralization is not static; changes in industry conditions and governance dynamics can affect the degree of decentralization in DLT systems.[52] Also, the three facets mentioned previously are interconnected but distinct from each other, and so they can reflect different degrees of (de)centralization within the same DLT system. For example, all mining equipment may be manufactured by a single firm, but operated/controlled by a multitude of actors, which would indicate some centralization in the network layer, but less so in the consensus layer. An accurate description of an economic activity as decentralized will reflect the facets and degrees of decentralization, rather than simply affix the epithet.

For antitrust law, which is concerned with the undue exercise of (concentrated) power but also collusion between market actors, decentralization becomes an

[49] Zhang, Ma, and Liu (n 47).

[50] Wessel Reijers, Fiachra O'Brolcháin, and Paul Haynes, 'Governance in Blockchain Technologies & Social Contract Theories' (2016) 1 Ledger 134.

[51] Andrej Zwitter and Jilles Hazenberg, 'Decentralized Network Governance: Blockchain Technology and the Future of Regulation' (2020) 3 Frontiers in Blockchain 12.

[52] Angela Walch, 'Deconstructing "Decentralization": Exploring the Core Claim of Crypto Systems' in Chris Brummer (ed), *Cryptoassets: Legal, Regulatory, and Monetary Perspectives* (OUP 2019) 50.

influential feature of the economy. On the one hand, the fact that a multitude of actors need to come together to make the decentralized economy work diffuses power across them and therefore eases the build-up of power in the hands of one single actor, which can then be abused.[53] Where in the mainstream economy, products and services could be developed and offered largely under the control of a single firm,[54] in the decentralized economy the same operations require the input of multiple separate stakeholders. While market power can still be accumulated in the hands of dominant undertakings, the fragmentation of economic activity in the decentralized economy means that they will grow dominant in a market that, like highly disintegrated markets, represents a smaller segment of the economic activity taking place in the decentralized economy.[55] Naturally, nothing stops firms from integrating into adjacent markets and eventually controlling a larger part of economic activity, thereby mimicking the role and function of actors in the mainstream economy, but the decentralized economy is far from integrating back to the level of mainstream centralized economy.

On the other hand, the multiplication of actors that need to cooperate for the provision of products and services in the decentralized economy elevates the risk of collusion. Economic activity that in the mainstream economy took place internally to the firm, requires the input of different actors in the decentralized economy, and where there is need for cooperation there is opportunity for collusion.[56] This is not to say that decentralization changes economic incentives—it simply means that it creates more decision making centres and therefore more scope for collusive activity among them.

ii) The prevalence of social production

At the heart of the decentralized economy is a commons-based production system.[57] The distributed nature of DLT and the various stakeholders involved in shaping the products and services of the decentralized economy make it a social production system, which is unlike the typical firm-driven systems that antitrust law usually applies to. From an antitrust perspective, the prevalence of social

[53] Giovanna Massarotto, 'Can Antitrust Trust Blockchain?' in Aurelien Portuese (ed), *Algorithmic Antitrust*, vol 12 (Springer 2022).
[54] Control does not necessarily entail production. Platforms and their ecosystems support and engender production of products and services but they are not necessarily the producers themselves.
[55] Christian Catalini and Katherine Tucker, 'Antitrust and Costless Verification: An Optimistic and a Pessimistic View of Blockchain Technology' (2018) 82 Antitrust Law Journal 861, 865–68.
[56] See Chapter 6 section B.
[57] Sarah Manski and Michel Bauwens, 'Reimagining New Socio-Technical Economics Through the Application of Distributed Ledger Technologies' (2020) 2 Frontiers in Blockchain 29; Vangelis Papadimitropoulos, *Blockchain and the Commons* (Routledge 2023); David Bollier, 'Reinventing Law for the Commons' in Melissa K Scanlan (ed), *Law and Policy for a New Economy* (Edward Elgar Publishing 2017) 153–54.

production in the decentralized economy informs fundamental concepts and principles of antitrust law: it can affect what is considered 'normal' competition (against which unlawful conduct is assessed); it can raise challenges for the scope of conduct that falls within the ambit of antitrust law as well as for the question of who conduct can be imputed to; and it can give rise to new forms of power that antitrust law will have to contend with.

Social production means that the design and offering of products and services takes the contribution of multiple stakeholder groups, which can be (and often de facto are) composed of a large number of people-peers working cooperatively.[58] Features associated with this 'commonist' organizational model include the self-organization of production and self-management by communities, as well as 'decentralism, autonomy, bottom-up power, collective decision-making, equality, reciprocity, solidarity, and cooperation'.[59] This is in contrast to the firm-based model where the productive capacity either lies exclusively within the firm, or the firm coordinates the production process across other firms (platforms and ecosystems would fall under this too). In the firm-based model, control is vested with the firm, whereas in the commons-based model, control is dispersed across all stakeholder groups and their members.[60]

Such commons-based social production systems are not new; open source software is perhaps the best known example.[61] But unlike previous forms of commons-based production systems, such as open source, where peers largely represented a single stakeholder group, the commons-based production model of the decentralized economy is one that brings together numerous stakeholder groups. Where in open source software the controlling stakeholder group was the programmers,[62] in the decentralized economy control is diffused across protocol developers, miners, validators, and even secondary actors such as equipment manufacturers and crypto-exchanges, to name the key players.[63] Moreover, while in some traditional peer production systems the peer activity is concentrated in only level of the value chain (usually as input on top of an existing infrastructure), in the decentralized economy, stakeholders feed into multiple layers, including the actual

[58] Yochai Benkler, *The Wealth of Networks: How Social Production Transforms Markets and Freedom* (Yale UP 2006).

[59] Hangwoo Lee, *Affective Capitalism: For a Critique of the Political Economy of Affect* (Springer Nature 2023) 184. See also Steve Huckle and Martin White, 'Socialism and the Blockchain' (2016) 8 Future Internet 49.

[60] Sinclair Davidson, Primavera De Filippi and Jason Potts, 'Disrupting Governance: The New Institutional Economics of Distributed Ledger Technology' (2016) SSRN 11–18.

[61] Charles Schweik and Robert English, *Internet Success: A Study of Open-Source Software Commons* (MIT Press 2012).

[62] Dany Di Tullio and D Sandy Staples, 'The Governance and Control of Open Source Software Projects' (2013) 30 Journal of Management Information Systems 49.

[63] Jakob Svennevik Notland, Mariusz Nowostawski, and Jingyue Li, 'An Empirical Study on Governance in Bitcoin's Consensus Evolution' (2023) arXiv:2305.04079; Richard Red, *Peer Production in the Crypto Commons* (2019) 27–33.

infrastructure.[64] Online content sharing platforms or peer-to-peer networks are often brought up as examples of commons-based social production systems, but the social production there is limited to the content created and shared on top of the platforms, not the platforms themselves. To the contrary, infrastructural components of the decentralized economy, such as protocols, distributed ledgers, security and integrity functions, etc, are themselves collectively generated by the stakeholders.

These complex dynamics of the decentralized economy's social production nature challenge antitrust law and competition policy in various ways. For one thing, the very concept of what is normal competition in social production systems can differ from firm-based systems, with which antitrust law has almost exclusively been concerned.[65] Antitrust law has needed to develop a concept of normal competition, because it is only by knowing what normal competition is that the law can then detect deviations which it seeks to prosecute as abusive or monopolistic conduct. With the firm being at the core of the competitive process, it was only natural that the concept of normal competition would be moulded around the nature and activity of the firm. Abuse of dominance and monopolization have developed around a concept of competition on the merits, with merit being understood in different ways reflecting performance, efficiency, progress, or welfare metrics.[66] Yet, in markets where the productive process shifts from the firm model to the social production model, the nature of competition itself needs to expand to account for how the multi-stakeholder community operates not just how the firm operates. In social production markets where the firm is not necessarily the entity that reigns supreme, normal competition should reflect how things are customarily and commonly done in such communities, which may not always be geared towards merit considerations such as progress and improvement, but instead, they may reflect ideological, sociological, or cultural considerations that have to do with the ethos and purpose of the decentralized economy,[67] with the promotion of social good (however defined) and wealth redistribution,[68] with the role of technology in society,[69] with inclusion and representation,[70] and with social power dynamics.[71] In

[64] Papadimitropoulos (n 57) ch 4.
[65] See Chapter 7 section B.
[66] Konstantinos Stylianou, 'Can Common Business Practices Ever Be Anticompetitive? Redefining Monopolization' (2020) 57 American Business Law Journal 169, 174–82.
[67] Nigel Dodd, 'The Social Life of Bitcoin' (2018) 35 Theory, Culture & Society 35.
[68] David Golumbia, *The Politics of Bitcoin Software as Right-Wing Extremism* (University of Minnesota Press 2016) chs 2 and 4.
[69] Toni Caradonna, 'Blockchain and Society' (2020) 43 Informatik Spektrum 40.
[70] Qiqi Gao and Jiteng Zhang, *Artificial Intelligence Governance and the Blockchain Revolution* (Springer 2024) ch 4.
[71] Malcolm Campbell-Verduyn, 'The Distributions of Distributed Governance: Power, Instability and Complexity in Polycentric Data Ordering' in Carolina Aguerre, Malcolm Campbell-Verduyn, and Jan Aart Scholte, *Global Digital Data Governance* (Routledge 2024).

turn, an expanded concept of normal competition will inform what conduct can be deemed as abusive or monopolistic in markets of the decentralized economy.

The social production nature of the decentralized economy does not simply affect the concept of normal competition but also the broader framework in which it operates. Antitrust law applies only to commercial activities, and it is only within the scope of such activities that the legality of competition is assessed. In the firm-centric mainstream economy, antitrust law has cast its web widely, and only a narrow tranche of activity escapes its reach: government activity and activity that belongs in the private sphere.[72] But in the decentralized economy, where peer production is prevalent, and the productive capacity lies partly in the hands of lay individuals, the boundaries of antitrust's scope may need to be further clarified or redrawn. Are the myriad actors in the decentralized economy, including protocol developers, miners, validators, lenders on decentralized exchanges, etc, subjects of the antitrust laws, even if or even when they only occasionally participate without even realizing that the law may regard their actions as economic activity? Even government activities need to be rethought, as in the case of issuance of CBDCs, which may express the exercise of sovereign functions normally excluded from antitrust laws, but can rely partly on commercial activities and can compete with other commercial offerings such as stablecoins.

Moreover, even assuming that some or all of the activities of stakeholders in the decentralized activity are subjects of antitrust laws, an imputability question is raised: when outcomes are the combined effect of the confluence of the numerous stakeholder groups and their members, who is the conduct attributable to?[73] For traditional antitrust law, which is firm-based, the internal mechanics of how firm conduct comes about, and which firm executives weighted in are irrelevant; the conduct will be attributed to the legal entity of the firm. But in the peer production model of the decentralized economy, the issue of attributability is thornier.[74]

The social production model further informs the typology of power in markets of the decentralized economy. Typically, power for antitrust purposes is understood as the ability to raise prices or exclude rivals, but it is increasingly accepted that in new models of economic organization, power can be expressed in different ways that are not well captured by traditional definitions. For instance, for economic activities that are organized as ecosystems, architectural power, which consists in the ability to dictate the terms of how participating actors conduct

[72] See Chapter 2 section B; Ioannis Lianos, Valentine Korah, and Paolo Siciliani, *Competition Law*, vol 1 (OUP 2019) 287. See also Case C-309/99 Wouters v Algemene Raad van de Nederlandsche Orde van Advocaten ECLI:EU:C:2002:98, para 57.

[73] Even if actions could easily be imputed to the obvious actors behind them, various layers of influence are at play in social production systems, which further complicates correct imputability. See Rewat Thapa and others, 'Identifying Influence Mechanisms in Permissionless Blockchain Communities: The Bitcoin Case', *ICIS 2021 Proceedings*, vol 8 (Association for Information Systems 2021).

[74] See eg Peder Østbye, 'Who Is Liable for Collusion in Cryptocurrency Protocol Development?' (2019) SSRN.

themselves in the ecosystem, becomes an important modality of power.[75] Not only is architectural power of elevated importance in the decentralized economy, since much of the economic activity within is organized around ecosystems, but a new form of power emerges too—engagement power—which expresses the ability to attract and lock in the market's productive resources by exploiting stickiness, stickiness being the property that expresses persistent behaviour even though the actor has choice.[76]

Social production systems do not only create new opportunities for the exercise of power, they also create ways to limit power. Since the productive capacity and associated decision-making is shared among different stakeholder groups and their members, design choices on the decentralized economy infrastructure or the products and services built on top of it can result in power shifts—sometimes sudden. To take a notable example, when Ethereum's developers decided to change the cryptocurrency's consensus model from proof of work to proof of stake, an entire class of key stakeholders—miners—became obsolete.[77] Miners and mining pools that commanded a sizeable share of the mining market saw their power and influence over the Ethereum ecosystem disappear unless they could port it to the staking market (by converting their assets to Ethereum). Such power shifts are characteristic of multi-stakeholder systems because stakeholders' positions in the market are affected not just by their own actions, but by the decisions of other stakeholder groups and their members.

iii) Governance as a new arena of economic activity

The social production model of the decentralized economy is underpinned by a system of governance. Governance is the collective decision-making process that determines a DLT product's or service's features, allocates roles in their development (eg who can validate transactions), and defines the processes of their development (eg voting for a protocol upgrade).[78] It sets the rules that regulate the working-together of stakeholder groups and their members, as well as codify the operation of products, services, and application of the decentralized economy.

Governance in the decentralized economy represents a new arena of economic activity that antitrust law must make sense of, particularly as regards its potential to open up new domains for monopolization/abuse of dominance and collusion.

[75] See Chapter 5 section B.iii; Ron Adner, 'Ecosystem as Structure: An Actionable Construct for Strategy' (2017) 43 Journal of Management 39.

[76] See Chapter 5 section B.iv.

[77] See Chapter 5 section C.iii.

[78] Roman Beck, Christoph Müller-Bloch, and John Leslie King, 'Governance in the Blockchain Economy: A Framework and Research Agenda' (2018) 19 Journal of the Association for Information Systems 1020; Primavera De Filippi and Greg McMullen, 'Governance of Blockchain Systems' (Coalition of Automated Legal Applications 2018).

Normally, competition law is oblivious to the internal managerial processes that culminate into the economic activity of undertakings; instead, it is the externalized economic activity of the undertaking—the outcome of the internal processes—that competition law has traditionally been concerned with. This is not to say that the internal processes that define business conduct are necessarily exempt from competition law scrutiny, but that in traditional (even digital) markets, they are mostly hidden behind the corporate veil, and competition law enforcement engages once these processes translate into externalized business conduct that affects the competitive process. The complication that DLT products and services present is that they often come into existence through open market activity *between* rather than *within* undertakings, and the decision-making process that defines their features and market positioning is no longer hidden behind the corporate veil of an undertaking-producer, but rather spread across undertakings in the open market each acting as a separate independent actor. This involves protocol developers, miners, validators, and sponsoring institutions. Such governance activities can well be economic of the kind that competition law applies to, they can be the subject of abuse or monopolization, and since they occur in the open market, they fall within the ambit of competition law.

Governance in the decentralized economy can be thought of as existing in a matrix of *what* is being governed and *how* it is being governed (see Table 1.1).[79] The 'what' that is being governed is (a) the (technical) infrastructure and (b) the overlaid economic activities. *Governance of the infrastructure* comprises those rules that control how the DLT and related infrastructure operates. Any products, services, and applications that are built on top of the infrastructure (overlaid economic activities) are also subject to rules, which may come from various sources. When these rules are imposed by the infrastructure, meaning rules encoded in the infrastructure that enable and constrain what those products, services, and applications are and how they operate, this reflects *governance by the infrastructure.*

In terms of how governance is codified, the infrastructure and the overlaid activities are governed either by rules and norms that are codified on-chain or off-chain.[80] *On-chain* refers to rules that have been encoded directly into the underlying infrastructure; they are embedded into the technical fabric of the infrastructure in a *code-is-law* fashion.[81] *Off-chain* rules are all other rules that control the operation of a decentralized economy system, such as those described in whitepapers, decisions that have been voted on by stakeholders, etc. On-chain rules are more formal and rigid, but limited in scope, and they are also self-executing since they are encoded in the infrastructure, whereas off-chain rules are

[79] De Filippi and McMullen (n 78).

[80] Primavera De Filippi, Morshed Mannan, and Wessel Reijers, 'Blockchain Technology and the Rule of Code: Regulation via Governance' (2022) hal-03883249 22–28.

[81] Taner Dursun and Burak Berk Üstündağ, 'A Novel Framework for Policy Based On-Chain Governance of Blockchain Networks' (2021) 58 Information Processing & Management 102556, 3.

Table 1.1 Governance typology in the decentralized economy.

<table>
<tr><th></th><th>How activity is governed (source of rules/norms)</th><th>What activity is governed (subject of rules/norms)</th></tr>
<tr><td>On-chain governance</td><td>Governance by the infrastructure</td><td rowspan="3">Infrastructure and overlaid economic activities</td></tr>
<tr><td rowspan="2">Off-chain governance</td><td>Governance by external-to-infrastructure rules/norms (eg markets)</td></tr>
<tr><td>Governance by internal-to-infrastructure rules/norms (eg whitepapers)</td></tr>
</table>

less formal, more flexible, may cover a wide range of activity, and require their own enforcement mechanism.

This body of governance rules and norms invariably influences the design, operation, and market positioning of products and services in the decentralized economy. Consensus models, product/service features, decision-making processes, interfaces, and interoperability rules, etc, are all regulated by the rules and norms that are collectively called governance—as well as by the usual exogenous forces of the law and the market, which are omnipresent whether in the decentralized economy or mainstream economy.[82] Such rules are, of course, in place in products and services of the mainstream economy too, but they are internal to the firm; the particular features and design of a product or service and their interoperation with other products and services are decisions that rest with the firm and exist within the firm that produces them. Antitrust law will engage only if the *outcome* of such decisions results in anticompetitive activity, but the *process* through which the decisions are taken is not per se caught by antitrust law.[83] At best, the process can provide informative indicia that add colour to the externalized conduct.

Contrariwise, due to the social production nature of the decentralized economy, the governance process more often than not takes place, wholly or partly, in the open market—it is no longer an internal-to-the firm process but a market process. This is true even in so-called permissioned networks, where participation is reserved for authorized entities only, since each entity is still a separate undertaking.

[82] See the classic model of modalities of regulation popularized by Lessig in Lawrence Lessig, *Code: And Other Laws of Cyberspace* (Perseus Books 2002). For use of that framework in the decentralized economy see De Filippi, Mannan, and Reijers (n 80).

[83] There are, of course, exceptions, whereby antitrust law is also involved in the internal decision-making process of the firm, notably with criminal liability of cartel executives, director disqualification, and horizontal shareholding. But these areas represent a minority of antitrust practice. See Florence Thépot, *The Interaction Between Competition Law and Corporate Governance: Opening the 'Black Box'* (CUP 2019).

Once we move from the intra-firm domain to the inter-firm domain (ie the market), antitrust law applies. Consequently, processes that in the mainstream economy were concealed from antitrust law now break new ground for application.

This affects both monopolizing/abusive and collusive conduct. Monopolization and abuse of dominance are no longer limited to the outcome of decision-making processes as reflected in firms' externalized conduct, but also to the decision-making process itself when this reflects the governance that shapes and controls a product or service of the decentralized economy.[84] In that sense, such governance activities as protocol development and voting procedures can themselves be the subject of monopolization or abuse of dominance. They can also be the subject of anticompetitive agreements since more than one undertaking is involved in the governance process. In either case, both monopolizing/abusive and collusive conduct can occur anywhere in the governance matrix: it can be on-chain (eg monopolization through protocol design) or off-chain (eg collusion among miners).

Additionally, since the governance process is a new domain of economic activity that competition law can apply to, antitrust law will have to contend with new forms of anticompetitive conduct or at least improve its understanding of how existing tools can apply in such new economic domains. At least two areas stand out, which are considered in more detail in the following chapters: one concerns the concept of governance abuse, deemed necessary to capture practices that compromise or manipulate the decision-making (governance) process of DLT-based products and services, as these may escape traditional understandings of abuse.[85] The second concerns how the multilateral governance of the kind encountered in the decentralized economy can be reconciled with antitrust law's traditional vision whereby the norm is independent activity among undertakings whereas in DLT markets, this vision breaks down because governance requires by nature cooperation and therefore contact between (competing) undertakings.[86]

iv) Application of tokenomics

Many products, services, and applications of the decentralized economy issue tokens as part of their business model and operation. Tokens can have a variety of functions, but most commonly they represent value and are used in transactions, they allow token holders to participate in the product, service, or application governance, and they enable programmability allowing the creation of further

[84] Even in decentralized governance systems, individual entities can still amass and wield significant power. See Jack Parkin, 'The Senatorial Governance of Bitcoin: Making (De)Centralized Money' (2019) 48 Economy and Society 463.
[85] See Chapter 7 section C.
[86] See Chapter 8 section E.

applications.[87] Whatever their use, tokens are central to the operation of decentralized economy products, services, and applications, and they are determinative of their economic structure and, by extension, success. The rules and principles of economics as applied on the economic structure of projects that rely on tokens are commonly called *tokenomics*. Similar to the importance of economics in general antitrust, tokenomics are influential in the antitrust treatment of the decentralized economy.

Perhaps the most fundamental insight of tokenomics relates to the use of tokens as a means to bootstrap new products or services.[88] A common problem of network products and services is coordination problems that result in users failing to reach a socially beneficial equilibrium of adoption, that is, users taking individualized decisions to not adopt the product or the service, even though if they all adopted it, it would be beneficial for all.[89] Tokens solve that early problem by promising appreciation of value once the product or service is more widely adopted, commitment of future access to the product or service, and often governance rights.[90] In fact, because these conditions and commitments are often baked into the technical infrastructure or governance procedures and are therefore hard to modify, they are more credible than those of traditional platforms, which have both the incentive and the ability to depreciate or refuse to honour early promises once the platform becomes successful.[91] By offering a solution to overcoming coordination problems and successfully launching new products or services, token issuance facilitates entry, lowers entry barriers, and reduces the cost of innovation. These factors are determinative for assessing market power.[92]

Moreover, tokenomics help explain the lifetime of tokenized systems' finances, which in turn illuminate economic incentives, constraints, and market structure. If one takes Bitcoin's tokenomics as an example, two prominent features are its capped supply and its issuance schedule.[93] Bitcoin's protocol caps Bitcoin issuance at 21 million Bitcoins and it also halves every four years the Bitcoins that are issued, as reward for mining. The implication is that Bitcoin is deflationary, and that

[87] Jonathan Rohr and Aaron Wright, 'Blockchain-Based Token Sales, Initial Coin Offerings, and the Democratization of Public Capital Markets' (2019) 70 Hastings Law Journal 463, 469–80.

[88] Christian Catalini and Joshua Gans, 'Initial Coin Offerings and the Value of Crypto Tokens' (2018) National Bureau of Economic Research w24418; Rowena Gan, Gerry Tsoukalas, and Serguei Netessine, 'Decentralized Platforms: Governance, Tokenomics, and ICO Design' (2023) 69 Management Science 6667.

[89] See Michael L Katz and Carl Shapiro, 'Product Introduction with Network Externalities' (1992) 40 Journal of Industrial Economics 55.

[90] See Ali Sunyaev and others, 'Token Economy' (2021) 63 Business & Information Systems Engineering 457.

[91] Yannis Bakos and Hanna Halaburda, 'Overcoming the Coordination Problem in New Marketplaces via Cryptographic Tokens' (2022) 33 Information Systems Research 1368; Michael Sockin and Wei Xiong, 'Decentralization through Tokenization' (2023) 78 The Journal of Finance 247.

[92] See Chapter 5.

[93] See Bitcoin Wiki, 'Controlled Supply' at <https://en.bitcoin.it/wiki/Controlled_supply> (all links were last accessed on 1 September 2024).

miner revenue gradually shifts from block rewards to transaction fees.[94] Among other things, these parameters affect the supply of Bitcoin, and in turn the size of the market in which Bitcoin exists, as well as the financing model of the Bitcoin mining market and, in turn, its profitability and competitiveness. All of these are essential characteristics for the assessment of market power and competitive conditions.

Thirdly, tokenomics are intricately intertwined with governance, since governance is often exercised through tokens.[95] Therefore, the rules that determine the supply, distribution, and value of tokens also determine governance rights and constraints, and through them the competitive positioning of the relevant products and services. For example, the MakerDAO financial system, which develops the stablecoin Dai, issues and burns native MKR tokens as necessary to maintain the stable value of Dai pegged to the US Dollar.[96] In that process, MKR token holders use their tokens to vote on governance parameters such approved assets that can be accepted as collateral, debt ceilings for issuance of new Dai, etc. As a result, token holders' governance decisions and the concomitant token issuance and burning rules determine risk management and whether Dai retains its 1:1 value to the US Dollar, and accordingly whether Dai meets its purpose. Since stablecoins compete largely on their stability, the economic rules that define their operation are closely tied to how competitive they remain.

94 See David Easley, Maureen O'Hara, and Soumya Basu, 'From Mining to Markets: The Evolution of Bitcoin Transaction Fees' (2019) 134 Journal of Financial Economics 91.

95 Jensen, von Wachter, and Ross (n 17) 2–3.

96 See the MakerDAO whitepaper at <https://makerdao.com/en/whitepaper/>.

2
PERSONAL AND MATERIAL SCOPE: ECONOMIC ACTIVITY AND UNDERTAKINGS IN THE DECENTRALIZED ECONOMY

(A) **General** 23

(B) **Economic activities and undertakings in the decentralized economy** 24

i) Definitions 24

ii) Consensus-building, mining, staking, and pools as economic activities 28

iii) Protocol and software development as economic activity 30

iv) Central Bank Digital Currency (CBDC) issuance 32

(C) **Single economic unit, intra-enterprise conspiracy, and imputability: Pools, foundations, and developers as (in)dependent actors** 35

i) Single economic units, intra-enterprise conspiracy, employees, subsidiaries, and agents 37

ii) Mining and staking pools, and development foundations 42

(A) General

As a form of market regulation, competition law is concerned only with entities that form part of economic life, trade, or commerce. Non-economic activities and actors, as understood in competition law, do not have to comply with competition law's rules and restrictions. Both in EU competition law and US antitrust law, the concepts of economic activity and economic actor (undertaking) are to be interpreted broadly so that there is little margin for activities that may, even remotely, affect the economy to escape the prescriptive power of the law.[1]

[1] For the breadth of the EU definition of economic activity see Vassilis Hatzopoulos, 'The Economic Constitution of the EU Treaty and the Limits between Economic and Non-Economic Activities' (2012) 23 European Business Law Review 973. For the US definition of commercial activity see *Goldfarb et Ux. v. Virginia State Bar et al.*, 421 U.S. 773, 787 (1975).

Antitrust in the Decentralized Economy. Konstantinos Stylianou, Oxford University Press.

DOI: 10.1093/9780191925504.003.0002

Decentralized Ledger Technology (DLT) markets present a particular challenge for the scope of competition law because the origin of the blockchain technology and its first mainstream application in the form of Bitcoin was grounded precisely on a desire to bypass traditional markets and existing economic systems.[2] As the technology matured and expanded, it entered mainstream economic life, but the original identity of blockchain as a grassroots decentralized and often subversive value proposition never went away. Importantly, the technological foundations of DLT products and services (and therefore markets) have remained the same, and as a result, many of the essential actors and activities that comprise DLT systems and markets still function in ways that were never modelled after economic forms or functions that standard competition law is traditionally concerned with.

This raises the question of which of the activities that take place in the frame of the decentralized economy as well as which of the associated actors can fall under the scope of competition law. The answer depends not only on the nature of the activity but also on the degree to which it is performed by the associated actors, since the social production model of the decentralized economy may encompass individuals that engage in activities in a non-habitual and ostensibly non-professional fashion.

(B) Economic activities and undertakings in the decentralized economy

i) Definitions

Undertakings and persons. The scope of competition law is delimited by who is acting and what kind of activity they engage in. EU competition law applies to *undertakings*, which are defined as 'entit[ies] engaged in an *economic activity*, regardless of the legal status of the entity and the way in which it is financed' (emphasis added).[3] US antitrust law applies to any '*person*'[4] who engages in '*trade or commerce*'.[5] Undertakings/persons can include private corporations and individuals but also government instrumentalities, with very limited exceptions, as long as they engage in economic activity (or commercial activity in US antitrust

[2] Jon Baldwin, 'In Digital We Trust: Bitcoin Discourse, Digital Currencies, and Decentralized Network Fetishism' (2018) 4 Palgrave Communications 14; Finn Brunton, *Digital Cash: The Unknown History of the Anarchists, Utopians, and Technologists Who Built Cryptocurrency* (Princeton UP 2020).

[3] Case C-41/90 Klaus Höfner and Fritz Elser v Macrotron GmbH ECLI:EU:C:1991:161, para 21.

[4] The Sherman and Clayton Acts define persons to include individuals, corporations, partnerships, and any other private judicial entity. See 15 U.S.C. §§ 7 and 12.

[5] See 15 U.S.C. §§ 1–2, 7, and 15; Federal Trade Commission, 15 U.S.C. § 45.

law terminology).[6] Economic/commercial activity therefore becomes the critical element around which the definition of undertaking/person revolves.[7] Case law is not always coherent in this area but it has distilled a number of factors that are relevant as well as factors that are not relevant for the determination of whether an activity is of the nature that is captured by competition law.

The factors are assessed on the basis of each activity in question separately, such that an entity may be found to be an undertaking for some activities but not for others.[8] Moreover, for the characterization of an entity as undertaking performing an economic activity it is also not necessary that all its members or all its activities could be characterized as such, as long as some can.[9] As a result, heterogeneous DLT systems such as mining pools, protocol developers, crypto-exchanges, and others, wherein some actors or activities may be non-economic, cannot, as a whole, be exempt from competition law, but rather each type of constituent actor has to be examined separately.

Economic and commercial activity. In its most basic sense, economic activity has been defined as the 'offering of goods and services on a given market'.[10] The economic nature of the activity is to be judged 'intrinsically and objectively'.[11] The definition does not necessitate a showing of an existing market for goods or services of the kind offered by the challenged undertaking; it is enough to show that the activity 'could, at least in principle, be carried on by a private undertaking in order to make profits'[12] as long as this activity takes place within the boundaries of 'a given market'.[13]

This is clearly a permissive definition, but it is not boundless. While, in theory, anything can be offered by a private undertaking in order to make profits,[14] these activities need to be able to arise in a marketplace context. There is no definition in competition law of what constitutes a marketplace activity, but the minimum requirement seems to be that a 'degree of competition' should at least be possible between the activity in question and other similar activities;[15] that, in other words,

[6] Commission Recommendation of 6 May 2003 concerning the definition of micro, small and medium-sized enterprises C(2003) 1422 IJ L124/36.

[7] The term 'economic activity and undertaking' will be used for simplicity to capture also commercial activity and person respectively, unless the context requires otherwise.

[8] Case C-49/07 MOTOE v Elliniko Dimosio ECLI:EU:C:2008:376, para 25.

[9] Cases T-217/03 and T-245/03 FNSEA v Commission ECLI:EU:T:2006:391, para 55.

[10] Case C-475/99 Firma Ambulanz Glöckner v Landkreis Südwestpfalz ECLI:EU:C:2001:577, para 19; Case C-205/03 P FENIN v Commission ECLI:EU:C:2006:453, para 25.

[11] Case C-113/07 P SELEX Sistemi Integrati SpA v Commission ECLI:EU:C:2009:191, para 94.

[12] Cases C-180–184/98 Pavlov et al v Stichting Pensioenfonds Medische Specialisten EU:C:2000:428, para 201.

[13] Case C-118/85 Commission v Italy ECLI:EU:C:1987:283, para 7.

[14] It is confusing that in some cases the language is such that it suggests that the existence of a market must be proven, rather than simply the possibility of one. See eg Case T-155/04 SELEX Sistemi Integrati SpA v Commission ECLI:EU:T:2006:387, para 61 ('In this case the applicant *has not shown* that there is a market for ...') (emphasis added, implying that the existence of a market must be proven).

[15] Opinion of AG Jacobs in Joined Cases C-264, 306, 354, and 355/01 AOK Bundesverband and Others ECLI:EU:C:2003:304, paras 38–40.

competition between different entities offering substitutable products or services is possible.[16]

US courts share the same broad understanding of what constitutes commercial activity; they have ruled that antitrust laws are 'tailored for the business world',[17] that they apply to 'transactions that are commercial in nature',[18] and that the commercial nature of the conduct is to be assessed 'based on the totality of circumstances'.[19] Any suspected anticompetitive activity must have 'an intent or purpose to affect the commercial aspects of the profession', since antitrust laws are aimed primarily at activities 'having commercial objectives'.[20]

Private vs economic activity: the contours of lay users. Given competition law's scope, there are only two types of activities that are excluded, even though they may otherwise appear to be of economic nature: activities that take place predominantly in the private sphere and activities that are reserved for the state.[21] Competition law therefore applies to economic activities that lie between the private sphere and the government sphere.

The separation between the private and the market spheres has not been an issue of great study traditionally, perhaps because activities at the borderline of the two spheres were not impactful enough for competition enforcement to engage. This might need to change in the decentralized economy as, by nature, the underlying DLT technology relies on social production and participation, which can look like it lies in the private sphere but that might be performed at a scale that crosses over to economic activity caught by competition law. It is not uncommon for lay people to engage in activities without realizing that they constitute part of the production process of DLT products or services; for instance, staking one's cryptoassets or lending computing power for cloud mining. Whether they do it for profit or not is immaterial; profit-seeking and profit-making are not defining characteristics of marketplace activities, although they are a helpful indication when they exist.[22] Activities that do not generate profit or do not seek to make profit or do not even have an economic purpose, for example amateurism activities, can still be found to be within the ambit of competition law.[23]

[16] Case 170/83 Hydrotherm Gerätebau GmbH v Compact del Dott. Ing. Mario Andreoli & C. Sas. ECLI:EU:C:1984:271, para 11; Case T-360/09 E.ON Ruhrgas and E.ON v Commission ECLI:EU:T:2012:332, para 84.

[17] *Marjorie Webster v. Middle States Ass'n*, 432 F.2d 650, 654 (1970).

[18] *U.S. v. Brown University*, 5 F.3d 658, 665 (1993).

[19] ibid.

[20] *Marjorie Webster* (n 17).

[21] See Case C-309/99 Wouters v Algemene Raad van de Nederlandsche Orde van Advocaten EU:C:2002:98, para 57, where the CJ ruled that competition laws 'do not apply to activity which . . . does not belong to the sphere of economic activity . . . or which is connected with the exercise of the powers of a public authority'. See also Ioannis Lianos, Valentine Korah, and Paolo Siciliani, *Competition Law*, vol 1 (OUP 2019) 287.

[22] *Brown University* (n 18) at 666 ('the exchange of money is a quintessential commercial transaction').

[23] Case C-67/96 Albany International BV v Stichting Bedrijfspensioenfonds Textielindustrie ECLI:EU:C:1999:430; Ambulanz Glöckner (n 10).

Clearly, however, it cannot be said that a one-off participation in the productive processes of the decentralized economy is the same as the activity performed professionally at scale. Guidance on the taxation of cryptoassets offers useful criteria on how to distinguish between private activity and economic activity that can be captured by competition law: degree of activity, organization, risk, and commerciality.[24] Degree of activity means the amount and frequency of the activity carried out; organization relates to the structure that has been set up (material or immaterial) to support the activity; risk relates to the degree to which the actor risks losing any investments (material or immaterial) going into the activity; and commerciality relates to whether the actor performs the activity with the intention of doing it on a commercial basis and with a view to the realization of profit. These elements are not cumulative, but are rather taken together as a whole, and there is no cut-off point beyond which an activity is clearly considered to be able to fall in the market sphere. To clarify, the fact that an activity can fall into the market sphere as a matter of principle does not automatically render it economic; it simply means that it *can* be economic, which will be further assessed, as per above, based on whether it consists in the provision of goods and services and it could, at least in principle, be carried on by a private undertaking in order to make profits.

Government activity vs economic activity. Apart from falling within the private sphere, the other reason why an activity may be exempt from the application of competition law, even though it can be of economic nature, is if it is deemed government activity, that is, linked to the exercise of public powers or fulfilling a social function. While the latter might be less likely to arise in the context of DLT markets, the classification as government activity is highly relevant in view of the rising significance of Central Bank Digital Currencies (CBDCs).

As a general matter, the exemption for government activities covers the exercise of sovereign powers of the state, tasks performed in the public interest, and administrative functions.[25] These situations must be distinguished from the doctrine of antitrust immunity (more developed in the United States than in the European Union), which concerns situations where the activity *is* economic in terms of nature, but is deemed to be protected ('immune') from competition law as a matter of policy decision—whether express or implied.[26] Government activities as understood herein are not economic in nature. To earn this characterization, they must *directly*

[24] See HM Revenue & Customs, 'Cryptoassets' (2018) at <https://www.gov.uk/government/collections/cryptoassets> (all links were last accessed on 1 September 2024). See also IRS, 'Internal Revenue Bulletin: 2014-16' (2014) at <https://www.irs.gov/irb/2014-16_IRB#NOT-2014-21>.

[25] Case C-364/92 SAT Fluggesellschaft v Eurocontrol ECLI:EU:C:1994:7; Case 30/87 Corinne Bodson v SA Pompes funèbres des régions libérées ECLI:EU:C:1988:225, para 118.

[26] For a detailed discussion on the scope of immunity see Herbert J Hovenkamp and Phillip E Areeda, *Antitrust Law: An Analysis of Antitrust Principles and Their Application* (Wolters Kluwer 2013) 240–43. Yet different again is the US antitrust concept of state action, which immunizes actions of state authorities from federal antitrust law: see ibid 221. For a comparison between federal antitrust immunity and state action see ibid 242d.

concern the exercise of powers akin to public authority or powers that form part of the essential functions of the state.[27] Similarly in the United States, activities that are simply 'prompted' by the state are not necessarily exempt: for the exemption to apply, the activities 'must be compelled by direction of the State acting as a sovereign'.[28]

The fact that the activity is required by law, or is carried out on publicly owned property, or simply has a social aim or function, is not sufficient to exclude it from competition law.[29] As Advocate General Léger has noted, 'once an entity carries on an activity which can, at least in principle, be carried on by a private operator in order to make a profit, it must be regarded as an undertaking. In that case, it is of small importance that its tasks are in the public interest or the public service'.[30] All the more so, if an activity is already being offered by private actors commercially (rather than it being a theoretical possibility), it is all but certain that it is not related to the exercise of public powers.[31] It seems, therefore, that the historical evolution of the activity in question can become relevant in assessing its state-monopoly status and therefore whether it is exempt from competition laws.

ii) Consensus-building, mining, staking, and pools as economic activities

The decentralized economy has been defined as economic activity that is underpinned by DLT.[32] At the heart of DLT systems is a consensus-building process, which enables involved parties to agree on the state of the network and therefore on the state of the product or service that is provided by the network. No transaction and no economic activity more generally can be performed on DLT systems without it being verified and agreed on by the system's consensus process. Most commonly, consensus is reached through mining or staking, although other technologies exist (eg proof of elapsed time (PoET)).[33] Mining is performed through proof of work (PoW), whereby processing power is contributed towards the solution of computational problems, whereas staking is usually performed through

[27] Case C-343/95 Diego Calì & Figli Srl v Servizi ecologici porto di Genova SpA ECLI:EU:C:1997:160, para 22.
[28] *Goldfarb* (n 1) at 791.
[29] See eg Case C-82/01 P Aéroports de Paris v Commission ECLI:EU:C:2002:617, para 70; SELEX (n 11) para 59; Case C-218/00 Cisal di Battistello Venanzio & C. Sas and Istituto Nazionale Per L'Assicurazione Contro Gli Infortuni Sul Lavoro (INAIL) ECLI:EU:C:2002:36, para 37; Case C-350/07 Kattner Stahlbau GmbH v Maschinenbau- und Metall- Berufsgenossenschaft ECLI:EU:C:2009:127.
[30] Opinion of AG Léger in Case C-309/99 Wouters v Algemene Raad van de Nederlandsche Orde van Advocaten ECLI:EU:C:2001:390, para 80.
[31] Höfner (n 3) paras 20–24.
[32] See Chapter 1 section B.
[33] International Monetary Fund, 'Blockchain Consensus Mechanisms: A Primer for Supervisors' (2022) Note 2022/003.

proof of stake (PoS), whereby assets native to the DLT system are escrowed and used as voting rights.[34]

Consensus-building has all the hallmarks of economic activity. Firstly, it constitutes a service provided to the network/users by the nodes consisting in validating the activity taking place on the network, and by doing so it ensures the operation, security, and integrity of the system. Therefore, users who contribute to consensus-building provide a service. Secondly, the provision of this service is done on a competitive basis. Miners and stakers compete with each other on who will succeed in processing the next transaction. The conditions of competition are predetermined and set by the respective consensus protocol. In principle, and within the conditions set by the consensus protocol, miners and stakers can increase their chances of being successful by investing more on computing power or assets. Thirdly, mining and staking are remunerated services: when miners and stakers successfully update the ledger, they receive compensation for their input in return—usually in the form of a token (or denomination thereof) native to the network and/or in the form of transaction fees.

Despite these features, consensus activities may fall outside of the scope of competition law if they are not offered in the market context but are instead limited in the private sphere. After all, the early vision and motivation behind the decentralized economy was precisely to bypass mainstream economy, and therefore to lie outside the scope of traditional institutional structures, including competition law.[35] While the maturation of the industry, the rise of fintech and enterprise DLTs, and the increasing involvement of governments mainly in the form of CBDCs have brought the decentralized economy more firmly into the scope of competition law, there is still a certain residual measure of private activity. To this day, numerous miners and stakers are lay users (regardless of whether they come together under the umbrella of a mining or staking pool). In the case of staking in particular, users engage in the consensus-building activity and receive staking rewards by simply putting up their assets for staking once, after which point they do not need to take any additional action (similar to gaining interest on deposits). But whether this level of activity is sufficient depends on the criteria identified previously: degree of activity, organization, risk, and commerciality.[36] For this reason, it becomes relevant to ask whether consensus activities can be economic activities in theory (they can), and also, under which circumstances.

One last point should be made with regard to consensus-building. Because consensus is costly to achieve as it requires the commitment of resources, it is common

[34] ibid.

[35] The original Bitcoin whitepaper states that 'proof-of-work is essentially one-CPU-one-vote'. See Satoshi Nakamoto, 'Bitcoin: A Peer-to-Peer Electronic Cash System' (2008) at 3 at <https://www.ussc.gov/sites/default/files/pdf/training/annual-national-training-seminar/2018/Emerging_Tech_Bitcoin_Crypto.pdf>.

[36] See Chapter 2 section B.i.

that actors participating in consensus-building combine their resources and form *pools*, that is, mining pools and staking pools. The activity of contributing mining or staking resources to a pool should be distinguished from the activity of setting up and managing a pool. Setting up and offering the organizational structure of a pool can be a service in and of itself distinct from the mining and staking activities taking place within it. The pool service consists in the *coordination* of the mining or staking activity among the participating miners or stakers, whereas the actual mining and staking service consists in running the consensus mechanism. In that sense, pools seem to be offering services to miners and stakers, not to the network/users. This explains why some pools explicitly characterize miners as consumers of their services.[37] Not only do pools provide a service, they do so on a competitive basis, since they compete with other actors in the consensus-building process, and they receive remuneration for their services (in the form of fees). As such, the provision of pooling services can also amount to economic activity.

iii) Protocol and software development as economic activity

Protocols as software. It should be fairly uncontroversial that, to the extent that products, services, and applications of the decentralized economy are essentially software (code), their production can constitute, in principle, economic activity. There is a long list of antitrust cases revolving around software development and the conditions of its placement on the market.[38] While the majority of those cases involved software developed in-house, the famous *Wallace* case concerned a claim against open source software, and while the District Court did not specifically talk about the formation of open source software, it implicitly confirmed the applicability of antitrust law in open source software.[39] Typical decentralized economy offerings, such as DeFi protocols, cryptoassets, and services, more often than not resemble the development process of open source software than in-house software, but others, such as enterprise DLT solutions, are more like traditional in-house software development. In any case, the internal organization—technical and managerial—of the product or service should not matter for the characterization of economic activity, and so decentralized economy products, services, and applications can well constitute economic activity for the purpose of competition

[37] See eg Braiins Pool, 'Terms and Conditions' at <https://braiins.com/pool/terms-and-conditions-braiins-mining-limited>.

[38] For useful summaries see Michael L Katz and Carl Shapiro, 'Antitrust in Software Markets', in Jeffrey A Eisenach and Thomas M Lenard (eds), *Competition, Innovation and the Microsoft Monopoly: Antitrust in the Digital Marketplace* (Springer 1999); Lawrence Sullivan, 'Is Competition Policy Possible in High Tech Market?: An Inquiry Into Antitrust, Intellectual Property, and Broadband Regulation as Applied to "The New Economy"' (2001) 52 Case Western Reserve Law Review 41.

[39] See eg *Wallace v. International Business Machines Corp.*, 467 F.3d 1104 (2006).

law enforcement. A decentralized exchange, such as Uniswap, is as much of an economic activity as a centralized exchange, like Coinbase.

Private vs marketplace protocol and software development. The difficulty, similarly to consensus-building activities, is to determine which of the decentralized economy software activities fall in the private sphere and which in the marketplace sphere. Only the latter can be brought under competition law's ambit.

While all developers may be performing tasks of similar nature, the degree to which they contribute and the roles they hold (formal or informal) can make a difference. The grassroots beginnings of the decentralized economy inspired masses of developers who believed the liberalist vision, but while some saw professional opportunities, many others got involved as amateurs practicing a hobby. The similarities with open source software are apparent, particularly given that many products and services in the decentralized economy are open source themselves. Popular belief may regard open source software as an amorphous horizontal community of developers, but in reality, it often has formal governance mechanisms in place that regulate how contributions are made, approved, and implemented.[40] In this organizational structure, some developers have authority, make binding decisions, and contribute critical components of the software, while others make incremental contributions or their input may even be completely ignored.[41] Linus Torvalds, the creator of Linux, is a notoriously controlling figure in the Linux community,[42] and similar examples of decisive exercise of authority exist in numerous decentralized economy projects as well.[43]

The governance structure of products and services in the decentralized economy reveals divisions of labour, voting rights, and responsibilities,[44] that make clear that not all developers are the same. Relevant criteria to assess whether a developer is acting in the private sphere or in the marketplace sphere can be sourced from different lines of research, including fiduciary duties, taxation, and research specific to identifying core versus peripheral developers.[45] Such criteria can be the

[40] Dany Di Tullio and D Sandy Staples, 'The Governance and Control of Open Source Software Projects' (2013) 30 Journal of Management Information Systems 49; Siobhán O'Mahony and Fabrizio Ferraro, 'The Emergence of Governance in an Open Source Community' (2007) 50 The Academy of Management Journal 1079.

[41] Maha Shaikh and Ola Henfridsson, 'Governing Open Source Software Through Coordination Processes' (2017) 27 Information and Organization 116.

[42] Steven Weber, *The Success of Open Source* (Harvard UP 2005) 157 et seq.

[43] Jack Parkin, 'The Senatorial Governance of Bitcoin: Making (De)Centralized Money' (2019) 48 Economy and Society 463.

[44] Paul Van Vulpen, Jozef Siu, and Slinger Jansen, 'Governance of Decentralized Autonomous Organizations That Produce Open Source Software' (2024) 5 Blockchain: Research and Applications 100166.

[45] See respectively Raina Haque and others, 'Blockchain Development and Fiduciary Duty' (2019) 2 Stanford Journal of Blockchain Law and Policy 139; Angela Walch, 'In Code(Rs) We Trust: Software Developers as Fiduciaries in Public Blockchains' in Philipp Hacker and others (eds), *Regulating Blockchain* (OUP 2019); Mitchell Joblin and others, 'Classifying Developers into Core and Peripheral: An Empirical Study on Count and Network Metrics', *2017 IEEE/ACM 39th International Conference on Software Engineering (ICSE)* (IEEE 2017); Ju Long, 'Understanding the Role of Core

degree of contribution to a product or service, the centrality of contribution, the level of responsibility, and the degrees of organization, risk, and commerciality of the activity.[46] Based on the above, developers who have an outsized influence over the direction of a product or service, who are remunerated and for whom this activity is a source of income, who contribute on a stable basis, and who have made investments (in time, resources, etc) in order to contribute are more likely to be performing an economic activity for the purposes of competition law. Also, if developers have set up an organizational structure to support their activities, for example a corporation or even a not-for-profit entity, this likely indicates economic activity.[47] For example, the Ethereum Foundation and the Ripple Foundation were set up to support the development of the respective namesake projects, among others, through financial means. Such economic structures show a level of organization which can contribute to the activity outgrowing the private sphere and entering the marketplace sphere. The fact that the legal entity may not itself pursue profit is immaterial.

iv) Central Bank Digital Currency (CBDC) issuance

Pure CBDCs. CBDC is a digital form of sovereign money.[48] They are usually divided into wholesale CBDCs and retail CBDCs, with wholesale CBDC being a payment system available only between central banks and commercial financial institutions, and retail CBDC being a payment system accessible to the public at large while maintaining direct central bank liability.[49] Wholesale CBDCs are generally seen as less of an innovation, because claims by financial institutions to central banks are already settled in digital money.[50] The main novelty of wholesale CBDCs lies in the DLT technology and what it enables (among others, programmability, interoperability with other DLT solutions, distributed consensus). Retail CBDCs, on the other hand, present more of a novelty because they enable retail

Developers in Open Source Software Development' (2006) 1 Journal of Information, Information Technology, and Organizations 75; HMRC (n 24).

[46] ibid.

[47] See eg the list of defendants in *United American Corp. v Bitmain, Inc. et al.*, 530 F. Supp. 3d 1241 (2021); *David Leibowitz et al. v. iFinex, Inc et al.*, 1:19-cv-09236-KPF (2019) (the decision issued in this case is *In re Tether and Bitfinex Cryptoasset Litigation*, 1:19-cv-09236-KPF (2021)).

[48] Tommaso Mancini-Griffoli and others, 'Casting Light on Central Bank Digital Currency' (2018) IMF Staff Discussion Notes 7.

[49] Morten Linnemann Bech and Rodney Garratt, 'Central Bank Cryptocurrencies' (2017) BIS Quarterly Review 55.

[50] Fabio Panetta, 'Demystifying Wholesale Central Bank Digital Currency', Speech by Fabio Panetta, Member of the Executive Board of the ECB, at the Symposium on Payments and Securities Settlement in Europe-today and Tomorrow, Deutsche Bundesbank (26 September 2022) at <https://www.ecb.europa.eu/press/key/date/2022/html/ecb.sp220926~5f9b85685a.en.html>.

users to maintain direct claim to the central bank as opposed to a financial intermediary. As such, CBDCs can compete with other forms of 'retail' money, such as cash, commercial bank deposits, narrow finance, and even cryptocurrencies.[51]

The fact that different forms of money exist and CBDCs can compete with some of them should not automatically lead to the conclusion that CBDCs exist in the marketplace sphere. Since CBDCs serve as the digital version of sovereign currency, they have the same role and functions as sovereign money. In modern monetary systems, the sovereign government has the exclusive prerogative to issue the sovereign national currency, which is inextricably tied to government policy.[52] The sovereign currency is designated by the government as the official unit of account through which debt and tax liabilities are settled and the vehicle through which monetary policy is executed.[53] Pure CBDCs are, therefore, an expression of sovereign function of the state and a manifestation of the exercise of public authority,[54] even if in the eyes of consumers CBDCs may be interchangeable with other forms of money, which in their own right may exist in the marketplace sphere and constitute economic activity.

Hybrid CBDC. Mixed forms of CBDCs may, however, be treated differently, because they involve private actors in varying degrees, which can change the character of the economic activity. As early as 1976 the idea of private money was popularized by Friedrich Hayek in his classic treatise *The Denationalisation of Money*, which advocated for the creation of private currencies by financial institutions competing for acceptance.[55] While not fully private, and still under the effective control of governments, hybrid CBDCs are a step in that direction as they rely on private actors to develop their full functionality. In 2019, the International Monetary Fund introduced the concept of a synthetic CBDC, whereby unlike pure CBDCs, where the central banks perform all of the functions of digital sovereign money such as 'customer due diligence, offering or vetting wallets, developing or selecting the underlying technology, offering a settlement platform, managing

[51] Mancini-Griffoli and others (n 48) 12–13.

[52] Joseph Huber, *Sovereign Money: Beyond Reserve Banking* (Palgrave Macmillan 2017) 39 et seq; Randall Wray, 'Understanding Modern Money' in Heiner Ganßmann (ed), *New Approaches to Monetary Theory* (Routledge 2011).

[53] William Mitchell, L Randall Wray, and Martin J Watts, *Macroeconomics* (Macmillan 2019) 135–36. See also Milton Friedman and Anna J Schwartz, 'Has Government Any Role in Money?' (1986) 17 Journal of Monetary Economics 37.

[54] In the words of AG Mayras in *Reyners*, '[o]fficial authority is that which arises from the sovereignty and majesty of the State; for him who exercises it, it implies the power of enjoying the prerogatives outside the general law, privileges of official power and powers of coercion over citizens'. Opinion of AG Mayras in Case C-2/74 *Jean Reyners v Belgian State* ECLI:EU:C:1974:59, at 664. The issuance of a digital form of sovereign money can match those features.

[55] Friedrich A von Hayek, *Denationalisation of Money: The Argument Refined* (3rd edn, Institute of Economic Affairs 1990).

customer data, monitoring transactions, and interacting with customer requests, complaints, and questions', in the case of the synthetic CBDC, 'the central bank would merely offer settlement services to e-money providers, including access to central bank reserves. All other functions would be the responsibility of private e-money providers'.[56] China's e-CNY (digital renminbi) is perhaps the most notable implementation of this type; e-CNY is built on a two-tier architecture whereby the People's Bank of China (China's central bank) is responsible for the issuance and disposal, inter-institution connections, and wallet ecosystem management, whereas commercial banks and institutions provide circulation and exchange services.[57]

Depending on how mixed forms of CBDCs are structured, layers of private competition activity can emerge. One layer of competition is among financial institutions to become a central bank's CBDC partner or partners to connect retail users with the central bank and to provide associated services (eg account management, points of payment, etc). In this layer, the conditions of competition can either be structured as a bidding process or,[58] if any actor who meets minimum requirements can be a CBDC partner, the competitive conditions are set within the parameters decided by the central bank.[59] The second layer of competitive activity emerges among financial service providers that accept the CBDC. In this layer, the acceptance of CBDCs as payment and any associated services, promotional offers, etc becomes the basis on which providers compete. For instance, service providers can offer interest on CBDC deposits, preferential exchange rates, integration with other financial products, etc. Both of these layers represent economic activity, as they consist in services offered in the market, most likely for profit, and under conditions of competition.[60]

[56] Tobias Adrian and Tommaso Mancini Griffoli, *The Rise of Digital Money* (International Monetary Fund 2019) 14; Alexander Kriwoluzky and Chi Hyun Kim, 'Public or Private? The Future of Money' (European Parliament 2019) PE 642.356 17–21.

[57] The People's Bank of China, 'E-CNY: Main Objectives, Guiding Principles and Inclusion Considerations' in Bank of International Settlements, *CBDCs in Emerging Market Economies*, vol 123 (Bank of International Settlements 2022) 45–48; Franklin Allen, Xian Gu, and Julapa Jagtiani, 'Fintech, Cryptocurrencies, and CBDC: Financial Structural Transformation in China' (2022) 124 Journal of International Money and Finance 102625, 6–8.

[58] See Erik Kloosterhuis, 'Defining Non-Economic Activities in Competition Law' (2017) 13 European Competition Journal 117, 140.

[59] This can take the form of the state delegating powers to private actors. See Amir Ibrahim, 'A Re-Evaluation of the Concept of Economic Activity for the Purpose of EU Competition Rules: The Need for Modernisation' (2015) 11 European Competition Journal 265, 276.

[60] Youming Liu and others, 'The Potential Competitive Effects of CBDC on Deposits, Payments and Bank Business Models' in Konstantinos Stylianou, Marios Iacovides, and Björn Lundqvist (eds), *Fintech Competition: Law, Policy, and Market Organisation* (Bloomsbury-Hart 2023).

(C) Single economic unit, intra-enterprise conspiracy, and imputability: Pools, foundations, and developers as (in) dependent actors

As mentioned earlier, competition law applies to undertakings/persons as long as they engage in economic/commercial activity. An implicit extension of this rule is that economic actors that are subsumed under another undertaking are not themselves subjects of competition law; rather, their actions are imputed to the main undertaking, and it is this main undertaking that becomes the subject of competition law. Common economic structures and arrangements that form expressions of this rule are corporations/enterprises and their *employees*, corporations and their *subsidiaries*, and principals and their *agents*. In all these situations, there is a main undertaking—the (parent) corporation or the principal—and the subsumed economic actors—the employees, subsidiaries, or agents. When one of the subsumed actors implements a decision in the course of their duty that results in a violation of competition law, competition law will apply to the main actor, not to the subsumed one.[61]

In the decentralized economy, it may not be immediately obvious where and when such relationships of dependency exist between economic actors. DLT, similar to other technological inflection points, has created new economic organizational forms and activities that do not map squarely onto existing conceptions of undertakings. Many common economic activities, such as mining, staking, protocol development, and decentralized lending, can be performed both on an individual basis and in the frame of organized activity. Whether competition law will apply to the individual actors or to the economic structures of which they form part will depend on the type and degree of dependency and integration they exhibit.

This is a fact-specific exercise, illustrated in Figure 2.1. There are two steps to it: firstly, establish the relevant criteria that define the boundaries between main and dependent actors; secondly, apply the criteria to the specific actor and action to determine whether an actor is a subject of competition law in their own right or, alternatively, their actions are ascribed to a main undertaking (in which case they are a dependent actor).

[61] There are exceptions for personal liability of the actor that perpetrates the illegal action, such as criminal liability and director disqualifications.

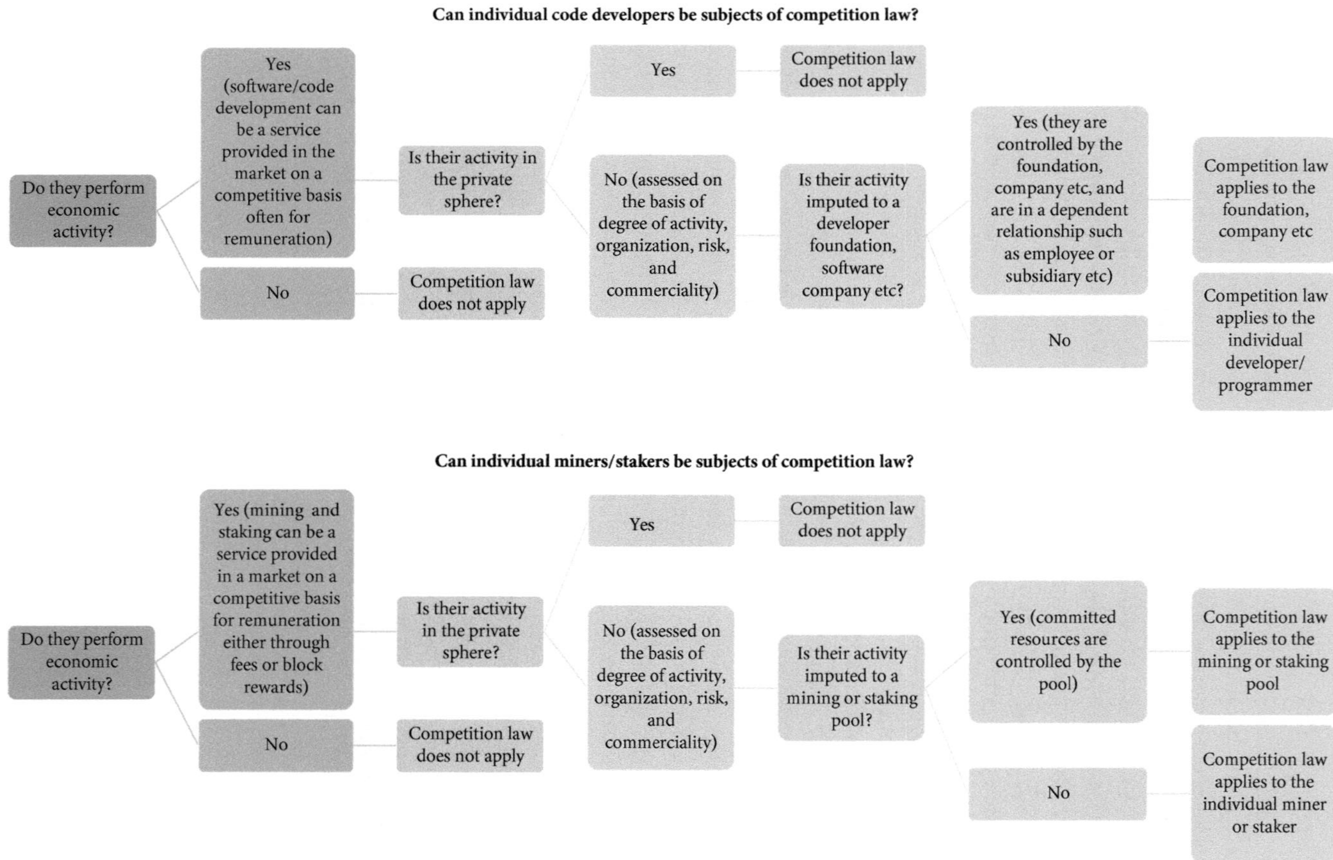

Figure 2.1 When does competition law apply to individual code developers, miners, and stakers, and when to pools and developer institutions?

i) Single economic units, intra-enterprise conspiracy, employees, subsidiaries, and agents

The criteria to determine the boundaries between undertakings, so as to know whether actors are separate or form a single economic unit, come from different strands of competition law and associated case law: one is the company–employee distinction, a second one is the parent company–subsidiary distinction, and a third one is the principal–agent distinction. In US antitrust law, these questions are dealt under the concept of the intra-enterprise conspiracy doctrine. While these strands are distinct, the criteria they employ can be synthesized in the following three: (a) the degree of control exercised from one actor to another; (b) the degree of risk assumed by actors when they engage in economic activity; (c) and the alignment of interest between actors. More control of one actor over another, greater risk assumption of one actor for the activity of another actor, and closer alignment of interests between actors indicate that the actors form a single economic unit; in other words a single undertaking. As the degree of control, risk assumption, and interest alignment erodes, so does the link between actors making it more likely that they will be treated as separate undertakings.

Even though the above criteria stem from different strands of competition law theory and case law, it is useful to consider them together when seeking to determine boundaries of undertakings in the economic contexts of the decentralized economy. After all, not only do these separate strands express similar considerations, but both EU and US courts have ruled that the labelling of actors (whether as employees, subsidiaries, etc) is not determinative, but it is rather their function that matters in whether they will be deemed to form a single economic unit with other actors, a judgement that is made dynamically on a case-by-case basis, so that an actor who is considered an employee or agent can form an economic unit with their employer or principal in one case, but be a separate actor (undertaking) in another.[62]

Control and risk. The elements of control and risk as determinative factors on whether two or more related actors are independent or form part of a single economic unit appear in different forms of economic dependency, including employees, subsidiaries, and agents, but all three express similar principles. The Court of Justice (CoJ) in *Shell* defined undertakings as 'economic units which consist of a

[62] See Hydrotherm (n 16) para 11 (stating that 'the term "undertaking" must be understood as designating an economic unit *for the purpose of the subject-matter of the agreement in question*') (emphasis added). See also Christopher Townley, 'The Concept of an "Undertaking": The Boundaries of the Corporation-A Discussion of Agency, Employees and Subsidiaries' in Giuliano Amato and Claus-Dieter Ehlermann (eds), *EC Competition Law: A Critical Assessment* (Hart Publishing 2007) 10, 15. See also *Nurse Midwifery Ass'n v. Hibbertt*, 918 F.2d 605 (1990) (where medical staff could be considered as employees of the hospital when they were performing functions that were not competing with it, but as separate entities when their activities were in competition with those of the hospital).

unitary organisation of personal, tangible and intangible elements which pursue a specific economic aim on a long-term basis and can contribute to the commission of a [competition law] infringement'.[63] Employees, on the other hand, according to the CoJ in *Becu*, are characterized by the fact that they 'perform the work in question for and under the direction of . . . undertakings' and that they are 'for the duration of that relationship, incorporated into the undertakings concerned and thus form an economic unit with each of them'.[64] Advocate General (AG) Jacobs in *Albany* elaborated on the distinguishing features of employees commenting that employees offer 'dependent labour[, which] is by its very nature the opposite of independent exercise of an economic or commercial activity. Employees normally do not bear the direct commercial risk of a given transaction. They are subject to the orders of their employer. They do not offer services to different clients, but work for a single employer'.[65]

By contrasting the concept of undertaking to that of employee, the prima facie differences seem to lie in the degree of *control* enjoyed by each actor and the share of commercial *risk* they assume. The more control an actor has over their activities and the greater the share of the commercial risk of the activity they assume, the more likely it is that they will be considered freestanding economic actors and therefore separate undertakings. As the degree of control and share of risk erode, economic actors start to lose their individual standing and begin to be integrated into the actor that exercises control over them and assumes the commercial risk of the activity they perform.

This is confirmed by the parallel line of cases that discuss the concept of agents. Agents are economic actors who are 'entrusted with the power to negotiate and/or conclude contracts on behalf of another person ("the principal")'.[66] Similar to employees, agents are in a form of dependency from their principals, and at first sight the function of an agent seems to be an extension of the principal that hires them, and therefore, together, they form a single economic unit. As the CoJ said in *Suiker Unie*, an agent 'can in principle be regarded as an auxiliary organ forming an integral part of the [principal's] undertaking *bound to carry out the principal's instructions* and thus, like a commercial employee, forms an economic unit with this undertaking' (emphasis added).[67]

[63] Case T-11/89 Shell International Chemical Company Ltd v Commission ECLI:EU:T:1992:33, para 311.

[64] Case C-22/98 Criminal Proceedings against Jean Claude Becu and Others ECLI:EU:C:1999:419, para 26.

[65] Opinion of AG Jacobs in Case C-67/96 Albany International BV v Stichting Bedrijfspensioenfonds Textielindustrie ECLI:EU:C:1999:28, para 215.

[66] Commission Guidelines on Vertical Restraints (2022/C 248/01) OJ C 248, para 29.

[67] Joined cases 40–48, 50, 54 to 56, 111, 113, and 114/73, Coöperatieve Vereniging 'Suiker Unie' UA and others v Commission ECLI:EU:C:1975:174, para 539.

But if the agent assumes a non-trivial share of the commercial risk of the economic activity or exercises considerable control and discretion over it, they may be regarded as separate undertakings. Regarding risk the CoJ concluded in *Volkswagen AG*, where the issue was whether car dealers that purchased cars from the manufacturer and leased them to customers were dependent agents of the manufacturer or undertakings in their own rights, that 'representatives can lose their character as independent traders only if they do not bear any of the risks resulting from the contracts negotiated on behalf of the principal'.[68] Since in this case the dealers undertook part of the commercial risk, particularly because they owned the cars they leased, they were considered independent traders.

The element of control is also key in the relationship between parent companies and subsidiaries. Parent companies can be held liable for the acts committed by their subsidiaries when the two can be considered to constitute a single economic unit, particularly if the subsidiary is wholly owned by the parent. In early case law, this was the case when subsidiaries were considered just an instrument of the parent company meaning that 'the subsidiary does not decide independently upon its own conduct on the market, but carries out, in all material respects, the instructions given to it by the parent company'.[69] In this line of case law, the control exercised in by the parent company needed to be proven.[70] In later case law, however, the fact that a parent and a subsidiary constituted a single economic unit could be deduced based on their relationship and not on the actual control the parent did or could have exercised in the challenged case at hand. Famously, in *AKZO*, the CoJ stated that '[i]n the specific case of a parent company holding 100% of the capital of a subsidiary . . . there is a simple presumption that the parent company exercises decisive influence over the conduct of its subsidiary'.[71] In fact, the CoJ clarified that 'it is not . . . because of a relationship between the parent company and its subsidiary in instigating the infringement, or a fortiori, because the parent company is involved in the infringement, but because they constitute a single undertaking . . . that the Commission is able to address the decision imposing fines to the parent company of a group of companies'.[72]

As controversial as this new presumption is,[73] it does not change the underlying reason why the presumption exists, which is that the 'decisive influence' that parent

[68] Case C-266/93 Bundeskartellamt v Volkswagen AG and VAG Leasing GmbH ECLI:EU:C:1995:345, para 19.

[69] Case C-48/69 Imperial Chemical Industries (ICI) v Commission ECLI:EU:C:1972:70, paras 33–35.

[70] See eg Case C-107/82 Allgemeine Elektrizitäts-Gesellschaft AEG-Telefunken AG v Commission ECLI:EU:C:1983:293, para 53.

[71] Case C-97/08 P Akzo Nobel and Others v Commission ECLI:EU:C:2009:536, para 60.

[72] ibid para 58. See also Case C-231/11 Commission v Siemens Österreich and Others ECLI:EU:C:2014:256.

[73] Andriani Kalintiri, 'Revisiting Parental Liability in EU Competition Law' (2018) 43 European Law Review 145.

companies (can) exercise on subsidiaries robbing them of any 'real autonomy in determining [their] line of conduct'[74] is what binds them together in a single economic unit allowing the acts of the subsidiary to be imputed to the parent.

In the United States, the above situations are dealt under the intra-enterprise conspiracy doctrine.[75] US case law is also concerned with control, but it is less presumptuous than EU competition law. In fact, in the early case of *Kiefer-Stewart* the Supreme Court stated that even in the case of wholly owned subsidiaries 'common ownership and control does not liberate corporations from the impact of the antitrust laws. The rule is especially applicable where, as here, respondents hold themselves out as competitors'.[76] While the Supreme Court in that instance did not provide further details, it did helpfully point out that when actors compete against each other they are more likely to be considered as separate actors each capable of being the subject of antitrust law, even if they, as a matter of form, belong in the same corporate structure.

This was a somewhat too permissive approach and later, in *Copperweld*, the Supreme Court overruled *Kiefer-Stewart* and declared that fully owned subsidiaries, much like unincorporated internal divisions of a company, are not separate economic actors and therefore cannot conspire among themselves.[77] This thinking was later confirmed in *American Needle* too, where the Supreme Court reiterated that the test to determine whether two entities are in a unitary organization revolves around whether their relationship is such that it 'deprives the marketplace of independent centers of decision-making',[78] adopting a functional rather than formalistic analysis of whether decisionmakers are genuinely independent and not simply a part of a unitary organization.[79]

Alignment of interests. In *DaimlerChrysler*, the General Court (GC) reasoned from *Suiker Unie*, which had stated that 'if ... an agent works for the benefit of his principal he may in principle be treated as an auxiliary organ forming an integral part of the latter's undertaking'[80] to clarify that '[t]he test is whether or not there is

[74] Case 15/74 Centrafarm BV and Adriaan de Peijper v Sterling Drug Inc. ECLI:EU:C:1974:114.

[75] Technically, the doctrine is now 'defunct' in that intra-enterprise conspiracy is no longer possible (ie section 1 Sherman Act does not apply), but the principle and reasoning why this is the case is still referred to under this name. See *American Needle, Inc. v. National Football League*, 130 S. Ct. 2201, IV (2010).

[76] *Kiefer-Stewart Co. v. Joseph E. Seagram & Sons, Inc.*, 340 U.S. 211, 215 (1951). See also *Perma Life Mufflers, Inc. v. International Parts Corp.*, 392 U.S. 134 (1968).

[77] *Copperweld Corp. v. Independence Tube Corp.*, 467 U.S. 752 (1984). See also John T O'Connor, 'Copperweld Corporation v. Independence Tube Corporation: The Death of a Doctrine' (1984) 5 Pace Law Review 879.

[78] *American Needle* (n 75) 2212.

[79] Warren S Grimes, 'American Needle and Justice Stevens' Supreme Court Antitrust Legacy' (2010) 4 Journal of Competition Law 430.

[80] Suiker Unie (n 67) para 480.

unity in their conduct on the market'[81] and that 'where an agent, although having separate legal personality, does not independently determine his own conduct on the market, but carries out the instructions of his principal' no two separate undertakings exist.[82] Rather, the agent and the principle form a single economic unit. Interestingly, the GC, by referencing working *for the benefit* of the principal and *unity in the conduct* in the market, hinted to the alignment of the commercial interests of the principal and the agent as part of the control that the principal exercises over the agent. In other words, in a true principal–agent relationship, the interests of both parties are aligned and accordingly, their conduct in the market is one of unity and this is why they are treated as a single economic unit.[83]

US antitrust law extends this thinking beyond agents. In *American Needle*, and referencing a long list of prior case law, the Supreme Court ruled that '[a] division within a corporate structure pursues the common interests of the whole rather than interests separate from those of the corporation itself . . . A parent and its wholly owned subsidiary have a complete unity of interest. Their objectives are common, not disparate . . . They share a common purpose whether or not the parent keeps a tight rein over the subsidiary; the parent may assert full control at any moment if the subsidiary fails to act in the parent's best interests'.[84]

Synthesis. If one were to synthesize the insights from these interwoven strands of case law on employees, agents, and subsidiaries, and combine control, risk, and alignment of interests, the full picture of the boundaries of the undertaking emerges: what competition law ultimately cares about is whether actors are *independent centres of decision-making*[85] 'capable of affecting the competitive position of third parties'.[86] The more they are capable of charting their own course of action, which implies being in control of their business actions, assuming the risk of it, and serving their own interests, which can conflict with those of other competitors, the more such actors are separate subjects of competition law, regardless of their legal structure and corporate organization, and accordingly their actions are not imputable to a parent undertaking/employer/principal: see Figure 2.2.

81 Case T-325/01, DaimlerChrysler AG v Commission ECLI:EU:T:2005:322, para 85.

82 ibid para 88.

83 Pinar Akman, 'Online Platforms, Agency, and Competition Law: Mind the Gap' (2019) 43 Fordham International Law Journal 209.

84 *American Needle* (n 75) IV.

85 *Copperweld* (n 77) at 769.

86 Case C-73/95 P Viho Europe BV v Commission ECLI:EU:C:1996:405, para 17. See also Hydrotherm (n 16) para 11.

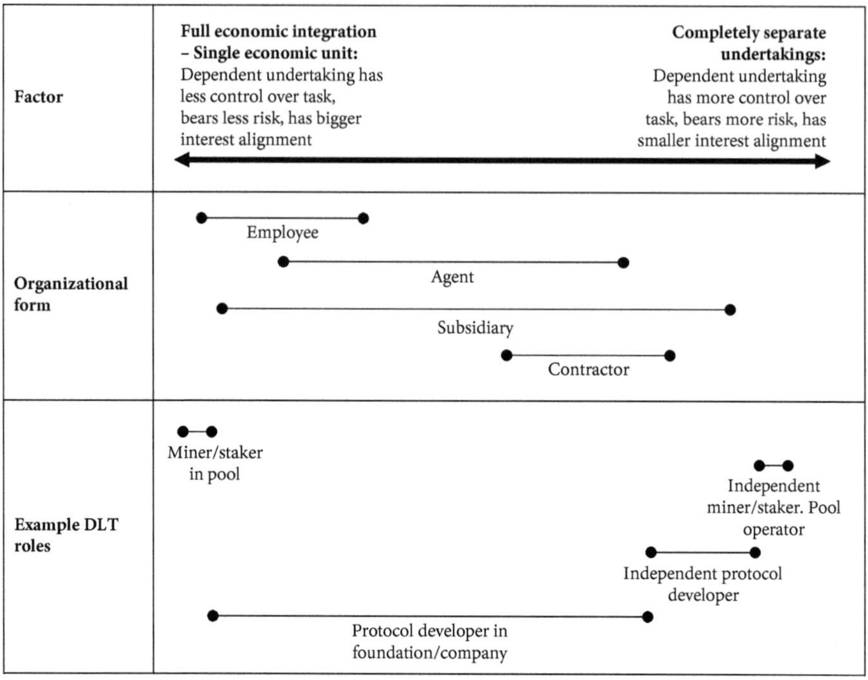

Figure 2.2 Imputability of activity based on control, risk, and interest alignment.

ii) Mining and staking pools, and development foundations

Paradigmatically, the decentralized economy differentiates itself from the traditional economy by replacing the defined economic structure of the firm with a distributed consensus mechanism that connects, coordinates, secures, records, and executes economic activities among otherwise separate and independent actors. And while this model can and does work, it soon became apparent that some form of organization and collaboration was still beneficial. Instead of mining alone, miners joined forces to create mining pools; instead of programming independently, protocol developers created foundations to coordinate the development of products and services; other organizational structures such as consortia, joint ventures, etc, emerged too.

When such economic structures are in place, the question arises whether the individual actors are part of a single economic unit, in which case competition law will apply to that larger entity, or whether they retain their own identity as separate undertakings, in which case they can constitute themselves subjects of competition law.

Miners, stakers, pools, and liquid staking. Mining and staking are the processes through which consensus is built, transactions are added to the DLT network, and the network is secured.[87] Because successful and efficient mining and staking require immense resources today, miners and stakers more often than not pool their resources together and share in the rewards.[88] Mining pools, staking pools, and liquid staking enable just that. Users commit their resources (processing power in mining, assets in staking) to a pool or a liquid staking smart contract or platform, where they join the resources of other users, and receive a share of the amassed rewards collected by the pool or liquid staking operation.

Other than commissioning and decommissioning resources, users have little to no control over the actual mining and staking operation. Where their resources are channelled and, therefore, how the mining/staking affects the market, is decided by the pool or smart contract operator. Individual miners and stakers do not retain control over how their resources are used, other than entering and exiting the pool. Also, their risk profile is assimilated into that of the pool or smart contract operation, since other than committing their resources to the pool they do not take any other economic decisions with regard to those resources for which they assume risk that is not already born by the pool (including the committed resources). Lastly, there is complete alignment of interests as both the pool as an organization and the actors committing resources to the pool aim at maximizing mining/staking rewards and rewards are shared equitably and in by predetermined rules across all participating actors.

In a way, individual miners and stakers cease to exist as independent decisionmakers once they commit their resources to the shared operation. In *American Needle*, where the teams of the National Football League (NFL) created an entity, NFLP, to exclusively license merchandise, the Supreme Court ruled that the teams cannot be shielded behind NFLP's actions; rather NFLP was a conspiracy among independent teams, which would otherwise compete for licensing their merchandise. In the words of the Supreme Court, '[t]he NFL teams do not possess either the unitary decisionmaking quality or the single aggregation of economic power characteristic of independent action . . . the teams compete in the market for intellectual property'.[89] This is not the case with pools and pooling smart contracts. Miners and stakers do not retain an independent identity once they give up their resources; their situation is closer to a 'temporary' merger (I acknowledge the misnomer) where the previously independent parties cease to exist and operate as separate entities. For this reason, the action of joining and leaving a pool is attributed to the owner of the committed resources, but the economic activity developed within the pool with the owner's resources should be attributed to the pool, not to the owner.

[87] Bahareh Lashkari and Petr Musilek, 'A Comprehensive Review of Blockchain Consensus Mechanisms' (2021) 9 IEEE Access 43620.

[88] Arvind Narayanan and others, *Bitcoin and Cryptocurrency Technologies: A Comprehensive Introduction* (Princeton UP 2016) 124–30.

[89] *American Needle* (n 75) V.

Developers, programmers, and foundations. The development of products, services, and applications in the decentralized economy ranges from projects built by independent individuals, to projects bringing together numerous developers often under the coordination of one or more entities, to projects that are developed within the boundaries of corporations. The two extremes of this spectrum do not present particular difficulties: independent individual developers, to the extent that they engage in economic/commercial activity, are undertakings themselves and competition law applies to them. For products, services, and applications developed by corporations, competition law applies to the corporation rather than to the developers employed by it. In between those extremes there is an indefinite number of organizational forms that economic activity can assume, and for each specific case, the degree of control, risk, and interest alignment will need to be assessed to determine whether the involved actors are undertakings in their own right, or if they form part of a larger single economic unit to which their actions are imputed.

Of particular interest here are the various forms of foundations and organizations that steer decentralized economy products or services without being the exclusive developers, rather other third-party developers also feed in the developments on a steady or occasional basis. The Hyperledger Foundation, HBAR Foundation, and Ethereum Foundation are examples of that. The Ethereum Foundation describes itself as 'hard to categorize. We are not a tech company, or a "normal" non-profit',[90] whereas the Hyperledger Foundation forms part of the Linux Foundation, which is also non-profit.

The functions of such organizations can span a wide spectrum but commonly include developer coordination, project financing, leadership, and project marketing around the product, service, or application that they sponsor. Because the degree to which these functions are exercised by such foundations and companies varies widely even within the same entity, it is difficult to even formulate presumptions of imputability. The fact that they assume the legal form of a foundation or a limited liability company does not automatically mean that the actions of all developers they bring together are attributed to foundation/company, because, as mentioned earlier the legal form is not a determinative factor,[91] and contributors may have different legal relationships with the foundation/company. In these cases, a functional approach, based on control, risk, and interest alignment, is necessary, and some developers may be considered to be in a dependent relationship with them, whereas others are not.

[90] Ethereum Foundation, 'Ethereum Foundation Report' (April 2022) at 5. Despite the marketing phrasing, the Foundation specifies in the report that it is legally a non-profit.
[91] See section B.i.

PART II
MARKET ANALYSIS

3
MARKET DEFINITION

(A) General 47
(B) How to think about 'markets' in the decentralized economy 50
(C) Marked definition based on substitutability: exchanges, mining and validation, assets and asset pools 52
i) Standard substitution analysis: application to exchanges, mining and validation 53
ii) Correlation analysis: application to assets 57
iii) Platform markets: application to crypto-exchanges and DeFi asset pools 59
(D) Ecosystem and proximity-based definitions of areas of effective competition 64
i) DLTs and metaverses as ecosystems 65
a) Cluster markets and clustering: application to cryptoassets 67
b) Factor analysis: application to metaverses 70
c) Snowball selection process: application to token ecosystems 73
ii) Proximity analysis and strategic groups 76

(A) General

Market definition is a ubiquitous tool in competition law analysis. While it has lost some of its authoritativeness due to the complexities of modern markets (and particularly digital markets),[1] it remains relevant and widely used in the analysis of unilateral conduct, agreements, and mergers.

Market definition performs several functions. At a very basic level, it sets the scope of each particular competition law investigation.[2] This scope—different

[1] It is telling that the 2010 U.S. Department of Justice Horizontal Merger Guidelines start with direct evidence of adverse competitive effects, and not with market definition, as it has been common in practice, and the Guidelines also note that '[t]he Agencies' analysis need not start with market definition. Some of the analytical tools used by the Agencies to assess competitive effects do not rely on market definition, although evaluation of competitive alternatives available to customers is always necessary at some point in the analysis'. See U.S. Department of Justice and the Federal Trade Commission, Horizontal Merger Guidelines, 19 August, 2010, § 4. See contra *United States v. E. I. du Pont de Nemours & Co.*, 353 U.S. 586, 593 (1957) (calling market definition a 'necessary predicate to a finding of a violation of the Clayton Act').

[2] Market definition is not a general abstract exercise, but it is tied to each particular case. See Opinion of AG Kokott in C-439/11 P Ziegler SA v Commission ECLI:EU:C:2012:800, paras 53–58. See also Simon Bishop and Mike Walker, *The Economics of Competition Law: Concepts, Application, and Measurement* (3rd edn, Sweet & Maxwell 2010) 104.

Antitrust in the Decentralized Economy. Konstantinos Stylianou, Oxford University Press.
 DOI: 10.1093/9780191925504.003.0003

in every case—is 'the area of effective competition',[3] it is the boundaries wherein competition authorities look for the 'active competitive forces central to the case'.[4] While in complex economies everything is ultimately interrelated and, in that sense, relevant, for enforcement to take place, the exercise must have a beginning and an end in the economy, and this is what market definition delineates. As a necessary corollary, a defined market is the area in which the alleged harm has occurred or is likely to occur; without it, there would be no meaningful end to where enforcers or courts should look for signs that the competitive process has been distorted and consumers have been harmed. By extension, the defined market is the area in which competition authorities and courts focus their discovery efforts.

More specifically, in unilateral conduct cases in the European Union (Article 102 Treaty on the Functioning of the European Union—TFEU), market definition is a prerequisite to assessing market power, since as the General Court (GC) explained in *MasterCard* '[f]or the purposes of Article [102 TFEU] the proper definition of the relevant market is a necessary precondition for any judgment as to allegedly anti-competitive behaviour, since, before an abuse of a dominant position is ascertained, it is necessary to establish the existence of a dominant position on a given market, which presupposes that such a market has already been defined'.[5] This follows from settled case law dating back to *Continental Can*, which explained that 'the possibilities of competition can only be judged in relation to those characteristics of the products in question by virtue of which those products are particularly apt to satisfy an inelastic need and are only to a limited extent interchangeable with other products'.[6] In US monopolization cases (section 2 of the Sherman Act), establishing market definition (and accordingly market power) can be skipped in case direct harm can be demonstrated, but to assess the magnitude of the harm one still needs to define a market.[7] In *Microsoft*, the Circuit Court

[3] *Brown Shoe Co. v. United States*, 370 U.S. 294, 324 (1962); *Tampa Elec. Co. v. Nashville Coal Co.*, 365 U.S. 320, 328 (1961).

[4] Gregory J Werden, 'Why (Ever) Define Markets: An Answer to Professor Kaplow' (2012) 78 Antitrust Law Journal 729, 729.

[5] Case T-111/08 MasterCard Inc, MasterCard International Inc, and MasterCard Europe SPRL v Commission ECLI:EU:T:2012:260, para 171.

[6] Case C-6/72 Europemballage Corp and Continental Can Co Inc v Commission ECLI:EU:C:1973:22, para 32.

[7] Compare *FTC v. Indiana Federation of Dentists*, 476 US 447, 460–61 (1986) ('Since the purpose of the inquiries into market definition and market power is to determine whether an arrangement has the potential for genuine adverse effects on competition, "proof of actual detrimental effect, such as a reduction of output" can obviate the need for an inquiry into market power, which is but a 'surrogate for detrimental effect') and *Ohio v. American Express Co.*, 138 S. Ct. 2274, 2285 (2018) ('Here, the plaintiffs rely exclusively on direct evidence to prove that Amex's antisteering provisions have caused anticompetitive effects in the credit-card market. To assess this evidence, we must first define the relevant market'); *Walker Process Equipment, Inc. v. Food Machinery & Chemical Corp.*, 382 U.S. 172, 177 (1965) ('To establish [monopolization], it would then be necessary to appraise the exclusionary power of the illegal patent claim in terms of the relevant market for the product involved. Without a definition of that market there is no way to measure [the defendant's] ability to lessen or destroy competition').

ruled that direct proof of monopoly can be sufficient for the purposes of a section 2 Sherman Act monopolization claim.[8]

In anticompetitive agreements cases (Article 101 TFEU, section 1 of the Sherman Act), 'the reason for defining the relevant market is to determine whether the agreement, the decision by an association of undertakings or the concerted practice at issue is liable to affect trade between Member States and has as its object or effect the prevention, restriction or distortion of competition within the common market'.[9] Since in agreements cases there is no need to measure dominance, market definition tends to be more flexible both in the European Union[10] and the United States.[11] Emphatically, in *American Express*, the Supreme Court reiterated precedent whereby '[g]iven that horizontal restraints involve agreements between competitors not to compete in some way, this Court [has] concluded [in such cases] that it did not need to precisely define the relevant market to conclude that these agreements were anticompetitive'.[12]

In merger cases, market definition aims at identifying product or service lines where the structural changes that will be effected through the merger may result in the creation or reinforcement of a dominant position, as a result of which effective competition[13] may be significantly impeded in a substantial part of the market. Market definition in mergers is helpful but not always required.[14]

Based on the above, market definition emerges as a *focusing* and a *measuring* tool. It helps focus investigations on the relevant market forces and actors, and within that scope it helps measure market power and anticompetitive effects.

The difficulty is that the main framework underpinning market definition has been developed for markets that, due to their characteristics, are representative of only part of today's economy, and as the economy has evolved to encompass newer and more diverse types of markets, it is no longer sufficient. The inadequacies of traditional market definition follow directly from its original focus: non-digital markets where businesses primarily compete on price on a product-per-product basis with horizontal competitors that offer substitute products. Digital markets

[8] *United States v. Microsoft Corp.*, 253 F.3d 34, 51–52 (2001). See *also Toys "R" Us, Inc. v. FTC*, 221 F.3d 928, 937 (2000); *Rio Grande Royalty Co. v. Energy Transfer Partners, L.P.*, 786 F.Supp. 2d 1190, 1197 (2009) ('A plaintiff, therefore, does not need to define a market if it can support its claim with direct evidence that the defendant controlled prices or excluded the competition').

[9] MasterCard (n 5).

[10] Commission Notice on the definition of the relevant market for the purposes of Union competition law (C/2023/6789) OJ C 372, para 9.

[11] *Ohio v. American Express Co.*, 585 U.S. 529, 543 n 7 (2018); *PLS.Com, LLC v. Nat'l Ass'n of Realtors*, 32 F.4th 824, 838 (2022).

[12] *American Express* (n 11).

[13] *Brown Shoe* (n 3) at 324 (1962) ('The "area of effective competition" must be determined by reference to a product market (the "line of commerce") and a geographic market (the "section of the country")'). Commission Notice on market definition (n 10) para 18.

[14] See n 1.

have challenged all of these conditions, and the decentralized economy presents yet more complexities.

Products and services in the decentralized economy exist almost entirely in the digital realm (with minor exceptions, such as physical wallets). As such, and in the long tradition of digital markets, many products and services are free, which makes price—a common parameter of market definition tests—impracticable. Moreover, while products and services in the decentralized economy can well exist in their own separate market, they often form part of a bundle or a system. In the eyes of consumers, while such products and services may technically have one-to-one substitutes, the decision to adopt or reject them is taken in conjunction with the rest of the bundle or system, and market definition should be adapted to account for such interdependencies. Thirdly, while existing horizontal competitors of substitute products or services continue to be the strongest force of competition, they are certainly not the only ones. To the extent that decentralized economy markets are often structured as non-hierarchical multi-lateral coöpetitive systems,[15] market definition should be able to capture any entity within that construct that can exert competitive pressure over the focal company. This is where ecosystem analysis comes in. Fourthly, because products and services in the decentralized economy are often underpinned by a governance structure, a separate governance market may need to be defined on top of the focal product or service market under investigation.

These challenges do not mean that market definition is futile. Market definition has received renewed approval from competition authorities, and it will continue to serve as a key step in competition law analysis.[16] The challenges mean that the market definition exercise needs to be tweaked, adapted, and complemented to account for the special features of decentralized economy markets. Moreover, as markets become more complex, there is no one single way to define any and all markets. Depending on the purpose of the investigation and the type of the market, different tools may be applicable, and indeed more than one way to define markets can be used in the same investigation.

(B) How to think about 'markets' in the decentralized economy

The decentralized economy introduces many new concepts and technologies: consensus, permissionless and permissioned networks, validators, miners, stakers, blocks, and myriad others. It is tempting to regard the existence of those functions, actors, or technologies as determinative for how market definition is performed in decentralized economy markets. Some discussion has indeed emerged

[15] These terms are analysed below in section D.
[16] See the new Commission Notice on market definition (n 10); *American Express* (n 11).

on whether market definition should be done on the basis of Distributed Ledger Technology (DLT) layers (eg settlement layer, consensus layer), whether open (permissionless) or closed (permissioned) networks should be brought together in the same market, or whether different consensus mechanisms should result in the definition of different markets.[17] While these distinctions may be valid and informative, one should not be too quick to stray from the basic principles of market definition.

Market definition is a tool to delineate the area of effective competition with the view to detect sources of competitive pressure, to determine where competitive effects should be investigated, and where remedies should be focused.[18] None of these functions of market definition is a priori contingent on specific technologies unless the technology engenders new and distinct economic activity. One example of this can be the emergence of a *governance market*, which encompasses the economic activity around the governance that gives shape to and supports the DLT product or service, and includes the consensus-building process (eg mining), protocol development, and any other process that feeds into a DLT network's governance structure.[19] While the individual economic activities that make up governance can be approached as separate markets, the governance market as a collection of such activities can be thought of as a unified market worth defining if, for example, the economic and legal facts of a case show that it is a market worth monopolizing or where anticompetitive agreements are concluded with their object or effect of distorting the governance process.

The broader point here is that the market definition tools we have, including modern ones that are only beginning to be used even in conventional competition law (such as ecosystems), can well be sufficient, and any deviation should have a well-specified raison d'être. Two families of market definition methodologies are discussed in this chapter: (a) market definition based on substitutability (see section C); and (b) ecosystem and proximity-based methodologies (see section D). If markets are to be defined based on substitutability, one proceeds by testing for substitutes of the focal product or service around which the market definition is performed; the particular technology employed by products or services does not make substitutability tests inapplicable and may only require adaptations. For example, while proof of work (PoW) consensus technology is markedly different from proof of stake (PoS) consensus technology, they can both be included in the same 'consensus-building' market if it can be shown that, for instance, undertakings can shift their operations from one to another; this would indicate supply-side substitutability. Similarly, if the area of effective competition is to be defined

[17] See Okan Yildiz and Rolf Weber, 'Market Definition and Market Power in the Era of Blockchain' (2023) 02/23 EuZ Zeitschrift für Europarecht C1; Florian Deuflhard and Philipp Heller, 'Defining Relevant Markets in the Crypto Economy' (2022) 02/22 Competition Policy International 1.

[18] See nn 2–14 and accompanying text.

[19] See Chapter 7 section C.ii.b.

as an ecosystem, then any product or service that matches the criteria of one of the appropriate methodologies presented below should be included in the defined ecosystem. For example, in a token ecosystem, the different layers of the DLT technology would not need to be disentangled from each other.

(C) Marked definition based on substitutability: exchanges, mining and validation, assets and asset pools

At the core of traditional market definition is substitutability. At its most basic form, the relevant market consists of the focal product or service under investigation and substitutes provided by competitors. The relevant market is the market within which market power is assessed.[20] It is the smallest grouping of sales wherein a hypothetical monopolist can profitably raise prices. This is usually defined as the threshold where demand and supply elasticities are low enough to enable the hypothetical monopolist to make a small but significant and nontransitory increase in price (SSNIP).[21] This conception of relevant market can be applicable in decentralized economy markets too to the extent that demand and supply elasticities based on price can be computed.

Three methods of market definition based on substitutability are discussed below. One, standard market definition performed on the basis of price (SSNIP) or other parameters of competition, such as output, and product or service quality. This type directly looks for substitutes to include in the relevant market by observing consumer and supplier switching in response to price increases or changes in other parameters of competition, and can find application in crypto-exchanges, mining and validation, and assets among others. Two, an indirect way to determine whether products or services should be in the same market is by observing the covariance of associated parameters attached to them, and if they covariate then this can be interpreted to mean that they respond to the same demand and supply conditions. This is called correlation analysis, and can find application in asset classes. Three, when two or more markets are intermediated by an actor who controls the interaction between the different markets, then such markets should be defined as platform markets, which accounts for the interaction between them. Trading platforms or Non-Fungible Token (NFT) platforms can avail

[20] MasterCard (n 5); *Standard Oil Co. v. United States*, 221 U.S. 1, 61 (1911) ('A showing of market power is a substantive element of plaintiff's monopolization claim . . . and plaintiff cannot escape proving her claims with reference to a particular market even if she intends to proffer direct evidence of controlling prices or excluding competition').

[21] See MB Coate and JH Fischer, 'A Practical Guide to the Hypothetical Monopolist Test for Market Definition' (2008) 4 Journal of Competition Law and Economics 1031; *FTC v. Whole Foods Market, Inc.*, 548 F.3d 1028 (2008); Commission Notice on market definition (n 10) paras 29–30. The European Commission has often found the SSNIP test unnecessary; see eg Commission decision of 24 January 2018 AT.40220 Qualcomm (Exclusivity Payments), sec 9.2.10.

of such definitions, and a variation whereby pairs of assets are treated as asset pools rather than intermediated trading platforms is also discussed.

i) Standard substitution analysis: application to exchanges, mining and validation

Substitutability based on price: application to exchanges. Consider the example of Coinbase, a platform that allows users to buy, sell, and exchange cryptoassets. In order of less to more generality, Coinbase is a 'cryptoasset exchange', an 'exchange', and a 'financial services provider'. Which of those is the relevant market? If the market is defined to be 'cryptoasset exchanges' and Coinbase raised its fees by a small but significant and nontransitory amount, say 10 per cent, would enough customers switch to other cryptoasset exchanges (demand elasticity), and would enough related companies switch to providing cryptoasset exchange services (supply elasticity) to make the increase unprofitable? If the answer is yes, then this is the market. If the answer is no, then the broader market of 'exchanges' must be tested. Perhaps if Coinbase raised its fees by 10 per cent, customers would not only switch to other cryptoasset exchanges, but they would switch some of their cryptoassets to other non-cryptoassets they can trade on 'exchanges'. If that is the case, then the relevant market in which Coinbase exists is 'exchanges' and not simply 'cryptoasset exchanges'. The exercise is repeated until the correct market boundaries are found.

This example reflects the importance of substitutes in defining the market and how the process works. The relevant market is built around a focal product and its substitutes which are defined in the European Union as those which are regarded as interchangeable or substitutable by the consumer, by reason of the products' characteristics, their prices, and their intended use.[22] Similarly, in the United States, the relevant product market consists in 'commodities reasonably interchangeable by consumers for the same purposes'.[23] In the above example, the relevant market includes any service that can be swapped for Coinbase.

To define a market based on substitutability, first a focal product or service (or groups thereof) is chosen as the starting point.[24] Focal product or service is the core product or service around which the effects of conduct are studied (in the example above, the Coinbase exchange service). Then demand and supply substitutions are calculated according to the SSNIP test. Demand substitution entails a determination of the range of products which are viewed as substitutes of the focal product

[22] Commission Notice on market definition (n 10) paras 22–24. See also Continental Can (n 6) para 32.

[23] *United States v. E. I. du Pont de Nemours & Co.*, 351 U.S. 377, 395 (1956).

[24] Office of Fair Trading, 'Market Definition' (2003), sec 3.17.

by the consumer.[25] If the increase is unprofitable, it means that consumers switched to substitutes and the market should be expanded to include those as well.[26] The step is repeated until the increase is profitable, which means that there are no more substitutes to turn to and this is where the boundaries of the market end.[27] A known risk with this method is that if an undertaking was already pricing at monopolistic levels, a further increase would simply cause consumers to exit the market, and it would therefore erroneously appear that there are no other substitute products.[28]

Supply substitution assesses the degree to which suppliers are able to switch production to the relevant products in response to the small but significant and non-transitory increase in the price of the focal product.[29] When this is the case, such suppliers should also be included in the relevant market. Supply substitution is distinct from completely new entry (potential competition), which expresses the possibility that firms that were not previously present in the market will decide to enter in response to the small but significant and non-transitory increase in price.[30]

SSNIP, demand substitution, and supply substitution can be used in decentralized economy markets, as long as there is a price element. In the above example, if a SSNIP in fees results in users switching to competing crypto-exchanges, then these should be included in the market definition as a matter of demand substitutability. The same with supply substitutability. Assume, for instance, that the focal service in question is margin trading (which allows users to trade asset values beyond their available balance) and a crypto-exchange effects a SSNIP in its margin trading fees. If crypto-exchanges that only offer spot trading service (which allows users to trade assets at current prices up to the amount of the available balance in their account), can easily expand into margin trading, then spot trading crypto-exchanges should be included in the supply substitution analysis of a SSNIP test on the relevant market of the focal service of margin trading.

Substitutability based on output: application to mining and validation. Validation is the process by which transactions are verified and confirmed for inclusion in a DLT network; it is the outcome of the consensus-building process in DLT networks (validation in this context includes mining and staking too). In PoW blockchains, validation is performed by miners and is often called mining, whereas in PoS networks it is performed by validators or stakers. Validation as a service presents an interesting case for the application of substitutability and this is

[25] Commission Notice on market definition (n 10) paras 25 et seq.

[26] Robert O'Donoghue and A Jorge Padilla, *The Law and Economics of Article 102 TFEU* (3rd edn, Hart Publishing 2020) 100.

[27] ibid 110.

[28] This is sometimes called the Cellophane fallacy. See *du Pont* (n 23). Commission Notice on market definition (n 10) n 55.

[29] Commission Notice on market definition (n 10) para 32 et seq; US Merger Guidelines (n 1) at 7. See also Continental Can (n 6) para 32; Commission Decision of 22 December 1987 IV/30.787 and 31.488 Eurofix-Bauco v. Hilti, para 55.

[30] Commission Notice on market definition (n 10) para 21.

because the relevant price is not set by the service provider but by the customer.[31] When a transaction is proposed in blockchain networks, it includes a transaction fee which is set by the party proposing the transaction. The transaction is held along with other transactions in a pool until it is allocated to or selected by a validator for verification and inclusion in a block, thereby confirming the transaction.[32] When that happens, the validator collects the transaction fee. Those proposing transactions have an incentive to include higher fees so that their transaction will be processed faster. When the network is uncongested, the incentive is small, because transactions are processed in a timely fashion.[33] But when the network is congested, higher transaction fees become essential. While validators are unable to set the transaction fee, a hypothetical monopolist could reduce network capacity, thereby increasing congestion, and accordingly, fees.[34] The substitution test, then, would, in theory, ask whether a hypothetical monopolist validator could profitably reduce output (network capacity) by a small but significant non-transitory amount in a given validation market.[35] If they can, then those boundaries define the market.

Applying the substitution test in this case shows both the importance of trusting the traditional tools of market definition and the limitations that technological characteristics place around it. Starting with why traditional substitution analysis is still relevant, one should note that, at first glance, one might expect that each validation market is separate since it is tied to the specific network it serves. For example, ETH (Ethereum) staking operations support the ETH network, whereas ADA (Cardano) staking operations support the ADA network, and therefore they do not appear as substitutes to each other. Yet, the substitution test asks on the demand side whether ETH users would switch to ADA if ETH transaction fees increased, and on the supply side, whether ADA validators would switch to ETH staking in response to the opportunities for collecting increased fees. If the answer is positive to the extent that it would make the reduction in output unprofitable, then then ETH and ADA staking operations should be included in the same market.[36] It is likely therefore that the staking market from a market definition perspective may not be as fragmented as it may seem from a technological perspective.

The test however is less straightforward for PoW networks, which rely on mining, and on the question of substitutability between PoW and PoS networks.

[31] See Arvind Narayanan and others, *Bitcoin and Cryptocurrency Technologies: A Comprehensive Introduction* (Princeton UP 2016) 62–63.

[32] ibid 52–53.

[33] Gur Huberman, Jacob D Leshno, and Ciamac Moallemi, 'Monopoly without a Monopolist: An Economic Analysis of the Bitcoin Payment System' (2021) 88 The Review of Economic Studies 3011.

[34] ibid.

[35] Florian Deuflhard and Philipp Heller, 'Antitrust Economics of Cryptocurrency Mining' (2023) 19 Journal of Competition Law & Economics 333.

[36] For an equivalent analysis see Deuflhard and Heller (n 17) at 5. Note however the additional technological considerations on mining explained in the main text in this section.

In PoW networks where validation is performed on the basis of mining, the PoW algorithm dynamically adjusts the hashing difficulty level, thereby bringing the network's available capacity in line with demand. As such, if the hypothetical monopolist miner reduced capacity and demand remained stable, the network would adapt to the reduced capacity in order to manage congestion and therefore mitigate the need for increased transaction fees. This process is not instantaneous, but it is questionable whether PoW algorithms' embedded adaptability would allow a profitable *non-transitory* reduction in output (capacity) as required by the hypothetical monopolist test to be safely modelled. Moreover, many mining operations are performed using application-specific integrated circuits (ASICs), customized chipsets that are specialized in one mining algorithm, and therefore do not perform as well in other mining contexts. As a result, switching capacity from one network to another can be impractical. The technological switch is even harder between mining to staking, because the relevant resource in staking is the incumbent asset, as opposed to mining, where the relevant resource is computing power. This means that investments and expertise in one type of validation are probably irrelevant for the other type. But in theory, if it can be shown that miners and staking validators can switch from one network to another, market definition should reflect that through substitutability analysis.

Substitutability based on quality metrics: application to exchanges. One obvious problem with traditional substitution analysis is that it relies on price. Numerous products and services in decentralized economy markets are commonly offered for free (eg wallets, custody services). If there is no price reference, it is impossible to calculate the increase that could cause consumers to switch to substitutes. This obstacle is usually circumvented by relying on other characteristics besides price, most notably the product or service quality. Then, instead of a small but significant and non-transitory increase in price, the test looks at a reduction in quality (SSNRQ).[37] If such a reduction in quality of the focal product or service causes consumers to turn to other substitutes, these should be included in the market definition.

In data-driven markets, quality can sometimes be measured on the basis of data—for example, an unwarranted increase in the amount of user data collected can be regarded as the equivalent of an increase in price as both are essential characteristics of the product or service and both can cause users to look for substitutes.[38] Other quality aspects can become relevant too. In exchanges, for instance, the spread between bid and ask prices and the depth of the orderbook are important and quantifiable parameters.[39] Using historical data of orderbook depth

[37] OECD Competition Committee, 'The Role and Measurement of Quality in Competition Analysis' (2013).

[38] See Magali Eben, 'Market Definition and Free Online Services: The Prospect of Personal Data as Price' (2017) 14 I/S: A Journal of Law and Policy for the Information Society 227.

[39] Conor Ryder, 'A Cheatsheet for Bid Ask Spreads' (2023) Kaiko Research.

and liquidity, authorities can simulate price slippage scenarios upon which user response to changes can be calculated.

Security features, know your customer (KYC) controls, track record, and regulatory compliance can also be considered as quality aspects,[40] although they are less amenable to quantification. They remain important, though, especially given the reputation of the crypto industry attracting criminality.[41] They may not be the most determinative, but they can be factored in as support.

ii) Correlation analysis: application to assets

In traditional market definition, competitors are grouped together in the same market because they respond to each other in a way that creates competitive pressure towards each other: when a competitor's price increases or decreases, other competitors' prices increase or decrease too; and when a competitor's output increases, it leaves less demand for others, and so their output decreases.[42] For instance, if two remittance services, A and B, are thought to be in the same market and fees are calculated based on capacity, a capacity reduction in A will result in increased fees for A, but also for B, because some of A's customers will turn to B, straining B's capacity as well, resulting in B increasing its fees accordingly.

A different way to think about market boundaries is to consider whether products or services belong in the same market because (some of) the variables that characterize them move in concert, presumably as a response to the same market forces. Since they are subject to the same forces and they are affected in a similar way, an argument can be made that they can be grouped together in the same market.

Correlation analysis does just that: it identifies variables that may explain similar market responses across products, services, or actors.[43] It is a measure of covariance between variables that characterize products or services. Correlation analysis has been used in a number of cases to define the relevant market.[44] The

[40] See Sascha Hägele, 'Centralized Exchanges vs. Decentralized Exchanges in Cryptocurrency Markets: A Systematic Literature Review' (2024) 34 Electronic Markets 33.

[41] See Ilias Kapsis, 'Crypto-Assets and Criminality' in Dan Jasinski, Amber Phillips, and Ed Johnston (eds), *Organised Crime, Financial Crime, and Criminal Justice* (Routledge 2023); Andy Greenberg, *Tracers in the Dark: The Global Hunt for the Crime Lords of Cryptocurrency* (Doubleday 2022).

[42] Herbert J Hovenkamp and Phillip E Areeda, *Antitrust Law: An Analysis of Antitrust Principles and Their Application* (Wolters Kluwer 2013) s 530a.

[43] Phillip A Cartwright, David R Kamerschen, and Mei-Ying Huang, 'Price Correlation and Granger Causality Tests for Market Definition' (1989) 4 Review of Industrial Organization 79; Sheldon Kimmel, 'Price Correlation and Market Definition' (Department of Justice, Antitrust Division 1987) Discussion Paper EAG 87-8.

[44] Commission Decision of 22 July 1992 IV/M.190 Nestlé/Perrier; Commission decision of 27 June 2007 M.4439 Ryanair-Aer-Lingus; Commission decision of 21 November 2012 M.6541 Glencore/Xstrata.

Commission has explained that 'the basic idea behind this approach is that prices [the discussed variable for two different products that belong to the same relevant market] should typically move in the same direction (co-movement in time) because of demand and/or supply-side substitution'.[45]

In finance, correlation analysis is often applied to determine whether different assets can be classed together.[46] For example, prices of two assets moving together may indicate that the same forces that affect the price of one asset also affect the other, and they may therefore belong in the same market. Conversely, if the prices move in opposite directions, it may indicate that consumers do not see the same use for them and therefore regard them as not belonging in the same market. Correlation analysis has been used to distinguish between asset classes based on variables such as risk, hedging ability, and volatility. Such analyses have been used to reject the proposition that gold and cryptoassets can be grouped together as safe heaven assets,[47] or to show that alternative cryptoassets (altcoins) and Bitcoin belong in the same market. See Figure 3.1 for the correlation between Bitcoin and the S&P500 index.[48]

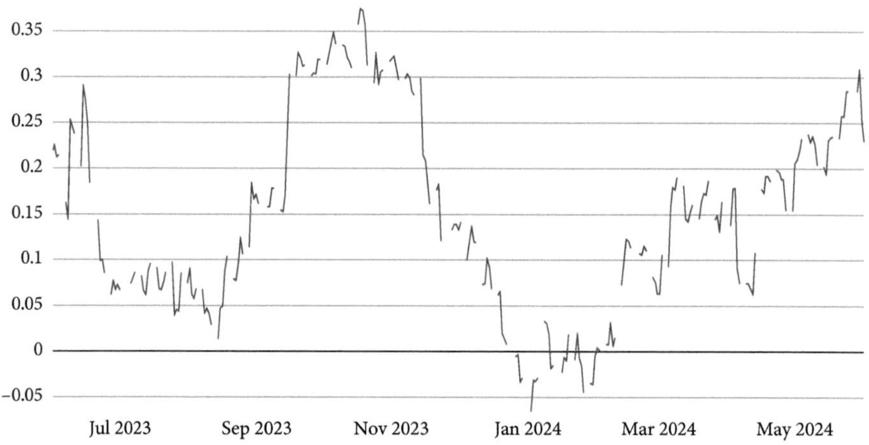

Figure 3.1 Pearson correlation between Bitcoin and the S&P500 index. Higher correlation means prices move in tandem. Gaps in graph represent weekends, where no S&P500 data are available.

Source: Coin Metrics

[45] Commission decision of 10 September 2004 M.7061 Huntsman Corporation/Equity Interests, para 143.

[46] Andrea Buraschi, Paolo Porchia, and Fabio Trojani, 'Correlation Risk and Optimal Portfolio Choice' (2010) 65 The Journal of Finance 393; Olha Holovatiuk, 'Cryptocurrencies as an Asset Class in Portfolio Optimisation' (2020) 54 Central European Economic Journal 33.

[47] Tony Klein, Hien Pham Thu, and Thomas Walther, 'Bitcoin Is Not the New Gold – A Comparison of Volatility, Correlation, and Portfolio Performance' (2018) 59 International Review of Financial Analysis 105.

[48] Artur Meynkhard, 'Effect of Bitcoin Volatility on Altcoins Pricing' in Radek Silhavy, Petr Silhavy, and Zdenka Prokopova (eds), *Software Engineering Perspectives in Intelligent Systems*, vol 1294 (Springer 2020).

Albeit helpful, correlation analysis is prone to errors. Firstly, correlation does not imply causation, and the fact that two variables are moving in the same direction may be coincidental.[49] This is why sometimes correlation analysis is best used as a separation test rather than an inclusion test, that is, it is used to determine that that products do *not* belong in the same relevant product market, rather than determine that they do.[50] Secondly, covariance may imply complementary rather than competitive relationships. For instance, when an asset's transaction volume or price increases, the number of user accounts associated with it may also increase; but it would be wrong to conclude that accounts (as a service) and the asset they are linked to are in the same market for purposes of antitrust analysis. As a result, correlation analysis is best used as an auxiliary rather than primary market definition method.

iii) Platform markets: application to crypto-exchanges and DeFi asset pools

In some market contexts, buyers and sellers may meet and transact directly, whereas in others they may rely on intermediaries to bring them together. The term 'two-sided markets' (or 'multi-sided markets') or 'platform markets' has often been used to describe such intermediated economic contexts, and a rich literature, and ample disagreement, exists on how to define intermediated and platform markets.[51] Numerous products and services in the decentralized economy have been described as platforms,[52] but not all uses of the term influence how the market around them should be defined. For the purposes of market definition, platforms merit special consideration when there are indirect effects between the two sides and the platform can control transaction parameters—usually the price—in order

[49] This would be a case of false positive. See n 45 paras 144–145.

[50] See eg Commission decision of 30 September 2013 M.6850 Marine Harvest/Morpol.

[51] Jean-Charles Rochet and Jean Tirole, 'Two-Sided Markets: A Progress Report' (2006) 37 The RAND Journal of Economics 645; Jens-Uwe Franck and Martin Peitz, 'Market Definition in the Platform Economy' (2021) 23 Cambridge Yearbook of European Legal Studies 91.

[52] For DLT as a platform for applications see Mohammad Jabed Morshed Chowdhury and others, 'A Comparative Analysis of Distributed Ledger Technology Platforms' (2019) 7 IEEE Access 167930. For blockchain as an institution that serves as a platform see Florian Glaser, Florian Hawlitschek, and Benedikt Notheisen, 'Blockchain as a Platform' in Horst Treiblmaier and Roman Beck (eds), *Business Transformation through Blockchain* (Springer 2019). For blockchain-enabled metaverses as platforms see Thien Huynh-The and others, 'Blockchain for the Metaverse: A Review' (2023) 143 Future Generation Computer Systems 401. For Decentralized Autonomous Organizations (DAO) as Platforms see Youssef Faqir-Rhazoui, Javier Arroyo and Samer Hassan, 'A Comparative Analysis of the Platforms for Decentralized Autonomous Organizations in the Ethereum Blockchain' (2021) 12 Journal of Internet Services and Applications 9.

to maximize participation on both sides.[53] If there are no indirect network effects between the two sides and the intermediary accordingly does not need to set the transaction conditions to reflect this externality, then it is sufficient to define the two sides of the platform separately and independently as per traditional market definition.[54] This is because no economically important interdependence exists between the two sides and so they can be analysed independently.

Decentralized vs centralized platforms. Before we look into market definition of platforms and asset pools, a point of clarification will be useful: whether a platform employs DLT or not to perform its function should not matter for market definition. Compare a centralized exchange like Coinbase, with a decentralized exchange like Uniswap; Coinbase allows users to swap assets by matching sellers and buyers through its centralized orderbook and then settles trades on the blockchain, whereas Uniswap works by creating liquidity pools through smart contracts which are themselves deployed on the Ethereum blockchain.[55] As regards their platform nature, both perform the same function, namely enabling users to swap assets, both are subject to indirect network effects, and both employ a pricing mechanism to encourage transactions between users. Therefore, both should be defined as platform markets regardless of whether Coinbase's technology is more akin to traditional exchanges, whereas Uniswap is a true Decentralized Finance (DeFi) service.

Two-sided platforms with indirect network effects: application to exchanges. In two-sided platforms that exhibit indirect network effects between the two sides, there are two methods to define markets. The method most faithful to what market definition traditionally reflects, namely the grouping of substitutable competitors that constrain one another, asks that each side of the platform be defined separately, but the externality of indirect network effects be accounted for.[56] Because platforms need to bring both sides to the table, they compete with rivals on both sides of the platform. For example, an exchange that facilitates trades between asset A and asset B must attract willing traders of both assets, and therefore competes in both the market for traders of asset A and the market for traders for asset B. At the same time, even though the markets for traders of A and traders of B will be defined separately, the platform recognizes that the number of traders of A affects the number of traders of B, that is, the more traders it has on one side, the more traders it can attract on the other side. This is the indirect effect externality, which will need to be taken into account in the substitutability analysis of the two

[53] Erik Hovenkamp, 'Platform Antitrust' (2019) 44 Journal of Corporate Law 713, 720–24; Hovenkamp and Areeda (n 42) ss 565d and 565d2.

[54] David Evans and Michael Noel, 'Defining Antitrust Markets When Firms Operate Two-Sided Platforms' (2005) 2005 Columbia Business Law Review 667, 696.

[55] Lucius Fang and others, *How to DeFi: Advanced* (CoinGecko 2021) 27 et seq.

[56] Jens-Uwe Franck and Martin Peitz, 'Market Definition and Market Power in the Platform Economy' (CERRE 2019) 22–46.

interrelated markets. Knowing that, and depending on the elasticities of both sides, the platform will set appropriate fees (:price) to traders of A and to traders of B in order to maximize transactions and therefore profits.

An alternative to this method would be to define only one market that includes both sides. This has been suggested as appropriate for transaction platforms, which are platforms where transactions are 'present between so-called end-users—that is, between customers on the two sides of the market'.[57] Non-transaction platforms, on the other hand, are those that connect different sides but the sides do not transact directly with each other. In transaction platforms, 'the product that is offered is the possibility to transact through the platform'. In the previous example of an exchange that facilitates asset, the exchange is a transaction platform, where, if it is defined as one market, the product of that single market would be the matchmaking that enables holders of assets A and B to exchange their assets.

The single-market methodology has been heavily criticized mainly on the grounds that, if only one market is defined, this would bring under the same market both competitors and complements, which defeats the main purpose of defining markets, namely to scope out the area of firms that can constrain the challenged firm by competing with it.[58] Competitors and complements behave in the opposite way in the market, and therefore it makes no economic sense to include them in the same market.[59] In the above example, traders of asset A compete with other traders of asset A but are complements relative to traders of B, because together they enable the exchange of assets. Therefore, traders of A and traders of B do not belong in the same market and they do not exert competitive pressure towards each other; quite the opposite. Proponents of the single-market methodology acknowledge this point and counter that 'defining a single market implies defining the market for *services to a transaction*. The product that is offered is the possibility to transact through the platform'[60] (emphasis added). In the words of the Supreme Court, which adopted this understanding in its notorious *American Express* decision, '[t]ransaction platforms are thus better understood as "suppl[ying] only one product"—transactions'.[61] The problem with this formulation is that logic mandates that if the product is the possibility to transact through the platform, then the only substitute products are also platforms (which equally offer the possibility to transact). Indeed, the Supreme Court continued to explain

[57] Lapo Filistrucchi, Damien Geradin, and van Damme, 'Market Definition in Two-Sided Markets: Theory and Practice' (2014) 10 Journal of Competition Law and Economics 293, 301.

[58] Hovenkamp and Areeda (n 42); Gunnar Niels, 'Transaction versus Non-Transaction Platforms: A False Dichotomy in Tow-Sided Market Definition' (2019) 15 Journal of Competition Law & Economics 327.

[59] Between competitors, prices move in the same direction and output in the opposite direction, whereas between complements prices moves in the opposite direction and output moves in the same direction.

[60] Filistrucchi, Geradin, and van Damme (n 57) 303.

[61] *American Express* (n 7) 2286.

that '[o]nly other two-sided platforms can compete with a two-sided platform for transactions'.[62] And yet, the very proponents of the single-market method that the Supreme Court relied on in its decision argue that 'candidate substitute products are not only other platforms that offer, to both sides, the possibility to transact, but also non-intermediated transactions'.[63] This is conceptually inconsistent.[64] To take Uber as an example, a single-market approach would put it in the market of connecting riders to drivers (ie 'the possibility to transact through the platform'), and not in the market of, for example, means of paid-for ground transportation, which would include taxis, buses, trams, city bike schemes, etc. Uber would then compete with the likes of Lyft, but not with other paid-for ground transportation alternatives, an approach that most people would find too restrictive.[65] If, instead, two separate markets were defined, one for riders and one for drivers, and Uber was thought to be present in both markets, then substitutability analysis on the drivers market would include not only other platforms similar to Uber, but also any other paid-for ground transportation options, a cleaner approach.

Asset pools instead of platforms—the case of DeFi. The usual view of the platform intermediary is that they connect an indefinite but large number of products, services, or actors on one side with an indefinite but large number of products, services, or actors on the other side.[66] For instance, NFT platforms that connect NFT creators with NFT buyers are commonly thought to list a large number of NFTs for sale to a large number of buyers (OpenSea, one of the largest NFT marketplaces, lists more than 80 million NFTs and has facilitated sales upwards of $20 billion).[67] When this is the case, then the methodologies presented previously are most appropriate. On other platforms, though, the intermediated interactions may take place predominantly between a select few products, services, or actors. If, despite the fact that the platform may be open to an indefinite and large number of products, services, or actors in total, certain pairs exhibit disproportionately higher volume, it may be helpful to define a market around the specific pair(s) rather than around the sides of the platform or the platform itself (depending on whether one subscribes to the separate market or single-market methodology).

DeFi market makers are the paradigmatic manifestation of such platforms. At a high level, DeFi market makers function similarly to exchanges, in that they link traders who wish to swap their assets for a different asset, and they implement a commission/interest mechanism to maximize participation.[68] But DeFi market

62 ibid 2287.
63 Filistrucchi, Geradin, and van Damme (n 57) 303.
64 Niels (n 58).
65 Hovenkamp and Areeda (n 42).
66 The utility of the platform function is maximized when they connect populous sides, see Melissa Schilling, 'Protecting or Diffusing a Technology Platform: Tradeoffs in Appropriability, Network Externalities, and Architectural Control' in Annabelle Gawer (ed), *Platforms, Markets and Innovation* (Edward Elgar Publishing 2011).
67 See OpenSea at <https://opensea.io/about> (all links were last accessed on 1 September 2024).
68 See Fang and others (n 55).

makers neither link traders directly nor do they serve as custodians of assets.[69] Instead, they create liquidity pools of asset pairs; each pair represents two groups of asset holders that wish to give up one asset in exchange for another.[70] For example, if a trader owns ETH and wants to receive BTC, they deposit their ETH in the BTC–ETH pool, and take out BTC. The protocol dynamically adjusts interest rates/commissions to ensure sufficient collateralization of assets and incentivization of traders. A different pool exists for every pair of assets that traders want to exchange.

The protocol managing the liquidity pools could well be defined as a platform that brings together asset traders, and a market can be defined around it as per above. But if certain pairs become more popular than others resulting in the respective liquidity pools dominating transactional activity, then it may make sense to define a market around the asset pools, not around the platform, if that would benefit the investigation. Assume, for instance, two DeFi protocols, A and B, which facilitate trading of the same assets, and whose total transaction volumes are similar. On protocol A, the BTC–ETH pool represents the bulk of the transactional activity, whereas on protocol B, the USDT–XRP pool represents the bulk of the transactional activity (Table 3.1). Because both protocols support all of the above assets and offer pools for all asset combinations, one can be inclined to define an asset trading market wherein protocols A and B are competing platforms. Yet, in reality, they exert very little competitive pressure towards each other considering that the bulk of the transactional activity on their platforms takes place between different asset combinations. If one instead defined markets around asset pools, it would be clear that the transactional activity on A does not compete with that on B, and it may emerge that A is competitively unconstrained despite B's existence as a service of equivalent functionality. At the same time, each pool would compete with services that offer exchange between the constituent pool assets, even if the competing service is not a platform itself. This would be in line with the Supreme Court's argument in *American Express* that transaction platforms only compete with other platforms:[71] not treating DeFi market makers as platforms allows us to acknowledge any relevant service as competitor regardless of whether it is structured as platform or not (eg exchange bureaus).

Moreover, while the assets contained in each pool may be combined with other assets, the particular pool combination is not fungible. Each pool has its own supply and demand curves separate from the rest of the protocol activity. This is different from traditional platforms whose supply and demand curves are generally calculated on the entire platform or at most per a small number of segments (eg

[69] Mohsen Pourpouneh, Kurt Nielsen, and Omri Ross, 'Automated Market Makers' (University of Copenhagen, Department of Food and Resource Economics 2020) IFRO Working Paper No. 2020/08 2. For examples, see Jiahua Xu and others, 'SoK: Decentralized Exchanges (DEX) with Automated Market Maker (AMM) Protocols' (2023) 55 ACM Computing Surveys 1M.

[70] ibid.

[71] See n 62 and accompanying text.

on credit cards, one might differentiate between business and personal users).[72] Any money transaction on a traditional platform changes the demand curve of the platform as a whole, but transactions in a given pool do not change the demand curves of the other pools handled by the protocol.

Table 3.1 Transaction volumes of Uniswap currency pair pools (June 2024). It is evident that the USDC/ETH pool accounts for the majority of transaction volume on the Uniswap market maker protocol.

Pool	Transactions	TVL	1 day volume	↓ 7 day volume	1 day APR
USDC/ETH 0.05%	7.0M	$470.3M	$58.0M	$2.4B	0.617%
ETH/USDT 0.05%	4.0M	$104.0M	$31.6M	$627.4M	1.519%
USDC/USDT 0.01%	813.3K	$29.6M	$16.2M	$295.1M	0.546%

Source: Uniswap

This refocusing of the market definition around asset pools rather than the platform could in theory be done for any platform. But the economic conditions to define the market around pools rather that platforms rarely arise on other platform contexts, because most platforms commonly intermediate transactions that are spread more evenly across the platform. Traditional platforms such as credit cards do not see their transaction volume dominated by one or a few merchants, and even if that were the case, the concentration would not be mirrored on the consumer side. It makes sense to define pools when transaction volume is disproportionately concentrated in one or a few pairs and each pair has its own demand and supply curve.

(D) Ecosystem and proximity-based definitions of areas of effective competition

Defining markets around substitutes expresses a specific economics-driven perception of competition: firms are disciplined by competition because they offer substitutable products or services to which consumers can switch. In that sense, a market of substitutes includes products or services that have *effective* and *immediate* impact on the focal product or service.[73] While straightforward, an exclusive focus on substitutes as a source of competitive pressure conceals other important constraints that act to discipline firms in the market.[74] To the extent that the main purpose of market

[72] Even traditional foreign currency exchanges, which are functionally closer to decentralized market makers as they operate on the basis of currency pairs, can benefit as a whole from the influx of a certain currency, because the influx will affect all the currency's pairs, and it can potentially be used to subsidize even other currency combinations through indirect exchanges.

[73] Commission notice on market definition (n 10) para 17.

[74] Ioannis Lianos, Valentine Korah, and Paolo Siciliani, *Competition Law*, vol 1 (OUP 2019) 229.

definition is to delineate the area of effective competition, alternative methods that do not rely on substitutability but still reveal sources of competitive pressure can be explored. Two such methods are discussed below: ecosystems and proximity analysis. The concept of ecosystem features prominently in the decentralized economy to describe agglomerations of economic activity around tokens or metaverse segments. Proximity analysis draws from management science to identify groups of actors that, due to their characteristics, compete closer with one another even if they may not necessarily produce substitutes.

i) DLTs and metaverses as ecosystems

The term 'ecosystem' has been used extensively in the decentralized economy to describe any number of vague agglomerations of economic activity. The International Telecommunications Union understands a DLT ecosystem as 'a collection of stakeholders such as organizations and users in conjunction with other entities, performing separate roles' comprising the hardware aspect, business aspect, software development aspect, and the protocol development aspect.[75] The World Economic Forum suggests that ecosystem thinking is essential in conceptualizing and implementing business applications based on blockchain: 'As blockchain projects almost always involve cross-enterprise workflows, collaboration is a critical success factor . . . Ecosystems enable integration across enterprise boundaries, allowing organisations to deliver products or services that they would otherwise not have the technological capabilities to deliver on their own, nor the end customer understanding to imagine'.[76] The International Association for Trusted Blockchain Applications, a leading industry body, describes metaverse ecosystems as comprising virtual reality, DLT features, DAO applications, and human–computer interfaces.[77] The heavy reliance on the concept of ecosystems to describe economic activity in the decentralized economy mirrors the proliferation of ecosystems in digital markets in general, with an increasing number of investigations and cases making use of the term.[78]

[75] International Telecommunications Union, 'Distributed Ledger Technology Overview, Concepts, Ecosystem' (2019) FG DLT D1.2 2.
[76] World Economic Forum, 'Blockchain Toolkit: Ecosystem' at <https://widgets.weforum.org/blockchain-toolkit/ecosystem/index.html>. See also Commission de Surveillance du Secteur Financier, 'Distributed Ledger Technologies & Blockchain: Technological Risks and Recommendations for the Financial Sector' (2022).
[77] International Association for Trusted Blockchain Applications, 'A Holistic Introduction to Virtual Worlds for Policy Makers' (2024) 10–13; Bank for International Settlements, 'The Crypto Ecosystem: Key Elements and Risks' (2023) Report submitted to the G20 Finance Ministers and Central Bank Governors; Commission de Surveillance du Secteur Financier (n 76); Michel Rauchs, 'Distributed Ledger Technology Systems: A Conceptual Framework' (Cambridge Centre for Alternative Finance 2018).
[78] See eg Commission decision of 18 July 2018 AT.40099 Google Android; Commission decision of 20 December 2022 AT.40462 Amazon Marketplace; Commission decision of 17 December 2020

Despite the common use of the term 'ecosystem', there is still not an accepted methodology on how to define boundaries of ecosystems similarly to how boundaries of markets are delineated in market definition, and fuzziness remains as to how one would delineate ecosystems in DLT markets.[79] Ecosystems are not based on substitutability; rather, they represent actors and activities that coordinate non-hierarchically and multilaterally with the view to jointly create value for end customers.[80] Often, such actors and activities are coordinated and even largely controlled by a central ecosystem orchestrator. For example, if one were to define an ecosystem around Meta's metaverse, Meta would be the orchestrator firm at the centre. Within and across ecosystems, competitive pressure does not stem only from substitutes, but also from complements, diagonal relationships, and neighbouring markets, and so the constituent parts of ecosystems are best considered together rather than in isolation each in their own market.[81] Even when focusing on a specific and well-delimited component of a system, upon which traditional substitution analysis could be performed, an ecosystem approach would still require that the individual component be seen in conjunction to the rest of the system.[82] This is because in the environment of a system, the decision to switch to a component competitor (substitution) is not taken in isolation, but rather by considering the rest of the system as well. While an insular one-to-one comparison between two competing components could reveal that they are substitutes in the sense that they have similar characteristics, price, and fulfil similar needs, users might still not be willing to switch if they needed to make other, perhaps far-reaching adaptations to the rest of the system the component functions in. As a result, methodologies for defining ecosystem boundaries should be able to capture these diverse relationships and interdependencies.

A number of methodologies have been proposed.[83] Defining ecosystems is not superior to defining markets. The question of whether it makes more sense to define markets or ecosystems depends on whether the economic activities under study are better seen as markets where products and services compete on a

M.9660 Google/Fitbit. See also US Department of Commerce, 'Competition in the Mobile Application Ecosystem' (2023); Competition and Markets Authority, 'Mobile Ecosystems Market Study' (2022).

[79] Efstathios Papanikolaou, Jannis Angelis, and Vassilis Moustakis, 'Which Type of Ecosystem for Distributed Ledger Technology?' (2023) 72 Technology in Society 102143.

[80] Ron Adner, 'Ecosystem as Structure: An Actionable Construct for Strategy' (2017) 43 Journal of Management 39; Daniel A Crane, 'Ecosystem Competition and the Antitrust Laws' (2019) 98 Nebraska Law Review 412.

[81] Frederic Jenny, 'Changing the Way We Think: Competition, Platforms and Ecosystems' (2021) 9 Journal of Antitrust Enforcement 1; Ioannis Lianos, 'Competition Law for the Digital Era: A Complex Systems' Perspective' (2019) SSRN; Thomas Eisenmann, Geoffrey Parker and Marshall Van Alstyne, 'Platform Envelopment' (2011) 32 Strategic Management Journal 1270.

[82] Michael G Jacobides and Ioannis Lianos, 'Ecosystems and Competition Law in Theory and Practice' (2021) 30 Industrial and Corporate Change 1199.

[83] The ensuing analysis draws on Konstantinos Stylianou and Bruno Carballa-Smichowski, '"Market" Definition in Ecosystems' (2024) Journal of Antitrust Enforcement jnae046.

substitutability basis, or as ecosystems, where products and services are in a non-hierarchical multilateral coöpetitive relationship. Defining ecosystems instead of or on top of markets can result in a richer picture of how economic segments are delineated and structured. Therefore, market definition and ecosystem definition should not be seen as mutually exclusive, but complementary. The applications and examples presented below are indicative and should not be read to mean that each discussed methodology only applies to the industry segment used as an example.

a) Cluster markets and clustering: application to cryptoassets

Cluster markets and the related one-stop markets[84] and aggregator markets[85] are familiar organizational forms in competition law, and can be a starting point on how ecosystem definition can work. They express groups of products or services that trade realities call to be analysed together,[86] but they only partially capture ecosystem dynamics. More developed clustering analysis can assist further.

Hovenkamp argues that cluster markets make sense if '1) "many customers" need or at least "prefer the convenience of receiving the defendant's grouping of products" rather than any single product, or (2) "economies of joint provision (economies of scope)" make it cheaper to distribute the cluster rather than each good separately, and (3) entering into competition with the cluster is difficult'.[87] This definition includes both demand (first and second conditions) and supply (third condition).[88] Ayres, in a more streamlined approach, draws the limits of cluster markets around the transactional costs of purchasing or using multiple products or services from a single provider.[89] Transactional costs here should be interpreted broadly to include search, purchase, use, and other costs involved in

[84] Commission decision of 3 February 1999 IV/M.1221 Rewe/Meinl, para 13 ('the broader experience of shopping at a supermarket or other type of food-retailing outlet where [the consumer] can find all the goods he needs on the spot (one-stop shopping) [is not comparable to] shopping at specialised outlets'); Commission decision of 25 April 2007 M.4590 Rewe/Delvita, para 12.

[85] Ben Thompson, 'Aggregation Theory' (*Stratechery*, 15 July 2015). See also Herbert Hovenkamp and Erik Hovenkamp, 'Complex Bundled Discounts and Antitrust Policy' (2009) 57 Buffalo Law Review 1227. Commission decision of 21 May 2003 COMP/C-1/37.451, 37.578, 37.579 Deutsche Telekom AG, para 117.

[86] *Crown Zellerbach Corporation v. Federal Trade Commission*, 296 F.2d 800 (1961), where the court defined a 'line of commerce' by looking for a product line which was 'sufficiently inclusive to be meaningful in terms of trade realities', a concept which was further elaborated on in *United States v. Philadelphia National Bank*, 374 U.S. 321 (1963), where the court defined a 'cluster of products (various kinds of credit) and services (such as checking accounts and trust administration) denoted by the term "commercial banking"' (at 374), and in *United States v. Grinnell Corp.*, 384 U.S. 563 (1966) where the court noted that 'it would be unrealistic . . . to break down the market into the various kinds of central station protective services that are available. Central station companies recognize that, to compete effectively, they must offer all or nearly all types of service. The different forms of accredited central station service are provided from a single office and customers utilize different services in combination' (at 572–73).

[87] Herbert Hovenkamp, 'Digital Cluster Markets' (2022) 1 Columbia Business Law Review 246, 253.

[88] ibid 254.

[89] Ian Ayres, 'Rationalizing Antitrust Cluster Markets' (1985) 95 Yale Law Journal 109, 109–10.

finding, using, or purchasing products and services. This can even include attention or cognitive aspects. To identify whether and which products and services can be grouped together in a cluster, bundle, aggregation package, or one-stop shopping experience, one should look at consumer purchasing or use behaviour and, secondarily, whether sellers offer or market them jointly (but not tie them).[90] When this is the case, the cluster has an economic significance beyond the individual products or services which it contains and it can therefore be seen as constituting a separate market of its own.[91]

Similar to the origins of cluster markets in banking,[92] where multiple products and services were offered by the same institution, one application of clustering in the decentralized economy can be in crypto-exchanges. Crypto-exchanges commonly offer multiple tightly integrated services, such as asset trading, derivative trading, wallets, and custody. Users can find these services from separate providers, but the integration, economic incentives in the form of lower fees for cross-service use, unified account verification, and financial regulation controls, etc, make getting them from a single provider appealing and cost-effective. Users do not always use all available services that exchanges offer, and each individual service offered by exchanges still competes with substitute services separately, but the exchange as a cluster of integrated services competes with other similarly structured exchanges on that aggregate level as well.[93]

An even more pertinent application of clustering is in cryptoassets.[94] There are currently over 10,000 cryptoassets in circulation with diverse features, uses, adoption dynamics, etc. While arbitrary groupings exist,[95] a proper methodological clustering would more accurately show which cryptoassets compete more closely together, revealing competitive affinity across the dimensions chosen by investigators.

Cluster markets have not found widespread adoption, although recent scholarship has provided new impetus.[96] Part of the problem has been that there is no cohesive methodology on clustering in competition law analysis, but porting insights from how cluster analysis is used in statistics can help fix that problem. Cluster

[90] ibid 120.

[91] *United States v. Phillipsburg National Bank and Trust Co.*, 399 U.S. 350 (1970) 360–62.

[92] See *Philadelphia National Bank* (n 86).

[93] For a similar argument about Amazon see Hovenkamp (n 87) 252–55.

[94] Below, two clustering methods are mentioned, hierarchical and K-means. For an application of K-means clustering in cryptoassets see Luis Lorenzo and Javier Arroyo, 'Analysis of the Cryptocurrency Market Using Different Prototype-Based Clustering Techniques' (2022) 8 Financial Innovation 7. For an application of hierarchical clustering see Jung Yoon Song, Woojin Chang, and Jae Wook Song, 'Cluster Analysis on the Structure of the Cryptocurrency Market via Bitcoin–Ethereum Filtering' (2019) 527 Physica A: Statistical Mechanics and its Applications 121339.

[95] For example, CoinMarketCap, a premier data analytics company, lists over 200 groupings of the cryptoasset population, some of them by type, others by use, others by industry sector, etc. See <https://coinmarketcap.com/cryptocurrency-category/>.

[96] See nn 83, 87.

analysis attempts to group together data observations/cases based on one or more variables across a given population.[97] The population is initially preselected, but observations that lie beyond a set score are excluded—this determines the outer boundaries of the ecosystem population. The threshold can be computed based on statistical analysis of the initial population so that observations beyond a degree of standard deviation are excluded. Two types of clustering are common: hierarchical clustering and K-means clustering.

In hierarchical clustering, one starts from a population of products/services and a criterion for determining similarity is selected, upon which the distance between them is measured.[98] Unlike traditional market definition based on substitutability, it is similarity (as expressed through the chosen variables) among products and services that serves as the grouping element.[99] Products/services that are closer to each other are clustered together resulting in a first order clustering of the population. Products/services whose distance is beyond a chosen threshold can be excluded as irrelevant to the studied ecosystem, which serves as the outer boundary of the ecosystem. Then, the exercise continues either with the same criterion or with a different criterion of similarity and the initially resulting clusters are merged together in bigger clusters. The exercise is repeated either until one big super-cluster is formed or until the investigator has applied all relevant criteria.

More useful is K-means clustering, which is used to group together observations/cases in a pre-selected number of distinct non-overlapping clusters.[100] Such division of observations/cases into clusters can result in two types of definitions for ecosystem analysis: (a) each cluster can represent a sub-ecosystem and the boundaries of each cluster delimit the boundaries of sub-ecosystems; or (b) the resulting clusters together can make up the ecosystem, in which case K-means clustering reveals the internal structure of the ecosystem. In both cases, score thresholds are established beyond which observations are excluded, as per above, and this serves as the outer boundary of the investigation. In K-means clustering, the number of clusters is predefined based on an initial determination (this can later be adjusted).[101] Then, a centroid for each cluster is selected and observations/cases are assigned to the clusters (randomly or based on a reasonable assumption). Then their fit in their assigned cluster is assessed, the goal being to minimize the sum of the squared distance between the cases/observations and the cluster's centroid. The cluster's

[97] Trevor Hastie, Robert Tibshirani, and Jerome Friedman, *The Elements of Statistical Learning: Data Mining, Inference, and Prediction* (2nd edn, Springer 2008) 501–02.

[98] Hans-Friedrich Köhn and Lawrence J Hubert, 'Hierarchical Cluster Analysis' in N Balakrishnan and others (eds), *Wiley StatsRef: Statistics Reference Online* (1st edn, Wiley 2015); Stephen C Johnson, 'Hierarchical Clustering Schemes' (1967) 32 Psychometrika 241.

[99] Sami Äyrämö and Tommi Kärkkäinen, 'Introduction to Partitioning-Based Clustering Methods with a Robust Example' (2006) Reports of the Department of Mathematical Information Technology Series C. Software and Computational Engineering 1–7.

[100] Margaret Dunham, *Data Mining Introductory and Advanced Topics* (Pearson 2020) 138, 140.

[101] For a description of the process see Hastie, Tibshirani, and Friedman (n 97) 460–61.

centroid is the arithmetic mean of all the cases/observations that belong to that cluster. The exercise is run repeatedly until every case/observation finds its best fit in one of the clusters. Additional criteria can then be applied to re-cluster cases/observations to reflect the multiple criteria. Essentially, K-means clustering attempts to find which cases/observations belong better together in each of the predefined clusters, thereby giving us the boundaries of each cluster.[102] Cases/observations within each cluster compete more closely together, and neighbouring clusters also compete more closely together.

To circle back to the example of cryptoassets, one could start from the total population of 10,000+ cryptoassets, select the parameters/features across which they would be measured for likeness, measure the parameters/features for all cryptoassets, determine the number of clusters (which can be adjusted), and then distribute the cryptoassets across the clusters (see Figure 3.2). Each cluster would reveal which cryptoassets are closer together in terms of competitive affinity across the selected parameters, and could be an area of effective competition for market definition purposes.

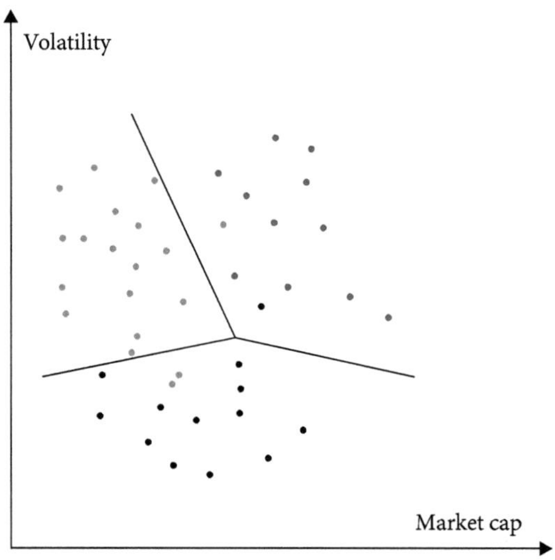

Figure 3.2 Clustering of cryptoassets by two dimensions. Each cluster can be an area of effective competition for market definition purposes.

b) Factor analysis: application to metaverses

Factor analysis helps not only answer the question of whether data observations should be included in a given ecosystem, but also which the relevant variables

[102] Gareth James and others (eds), *An Introduction to Statistical Learning: With Applications in R* (Springer 2013) 517–18.

are that indicate belonging of observations to the ecosystem. Factor analysis has found application in asset valuation, but not yet as a method to define ecosystems, without that meaning that it cannot be used for that purpose. Studies have used factor analysis to identify the factors that affect cryptoasset returns,[103] but increasingly also to identify joint behaviour of cryptoassets under the influence of a common set of factors.[104] This latter line of research is closer to using factor analysis to define ecosystems, as it results in the lumping together of individuals (in this case, cryptoassets) whose metrics respond to the same factors, and therefore can be seen to form a part of the same group. Those applications notwithstanding, factor analysis in ecosystem definition can be more helpful in constructing ecosystems around a core entity, for example a metaverse built around an orchestrator firm.

Factor analysis works by testing whether multiple observable variables covariate in response to an unobservable latent variable (the factor) across a set of individual cases (Figure 3.3).[105] The variables that are found to covariate are the relevant ones that explain and can be attributed to the latent factor. For use in ecosystem definition, the multiple *observable variables* would be the measurable parameters; the *individuals* would be the products and services that one wants to test whether they form part of the same ecosystem; the *unobservable latent variable* would be whether the individuals form part of the hypothesized ecosystem (versus not belonging in it).

How closely an observable variable is correlated with the latent variable is indicated by a *factor loading* score.[106] A factor loading with higher value indicates a stronger correlation with the latent variable. In essence, factor analysis obtains data on multiple variables across individual products and services and determines whether they are influenced (covariate) by a more limited set of factors, which in ecosystem analysis is whether they belong in the same ecosystem. In more complex versions, the factors can be expanded to include two or even more ecosystems, in which case factor analysis would show which variables are influenced by which factors (ie belonging in a given ecosystem). This would be useful in cases where the enforcer wants to test different ecosystem versions or different ecosystems.

[103] See eg Siddharth M Bhambhwani, Stefanos Delikouras, and George M Korniotis, 'Blockchain Characteristics and Cryptocurrency Returns' (2023) 86 Journal of International Financial Markets, Institutions and Money 101788.

[104] See eg Yukun Liu, Aleh Tsyvinski, and Xi Wu, 'Common Risk Factors in Cryptocurrency' (2022) 77 The Journal of Finance 1133.

[105] See generally Timothy A Brown, *Confirmatory Factor Analysis for Applied Research* (2nd edn, The Guilford Press 2015) 12–21; RO Mueller and GR Hancock, 'Factor Analysis and Latent Structure, Confirmatory', *International Encyclopedia of the Social & Behavioral Sciences* (Elsevier 2001); Rick H Hoyle, 'Confirmatory Factor Analysis', *Handbook of Applied Multivariate Statistics and Mathematical Modeling* (Elsevier 2000).

[106] On the methodology steps see Donna Harrington, *Confirmatory Factor Analysis* (OUP 2009) 21–24.

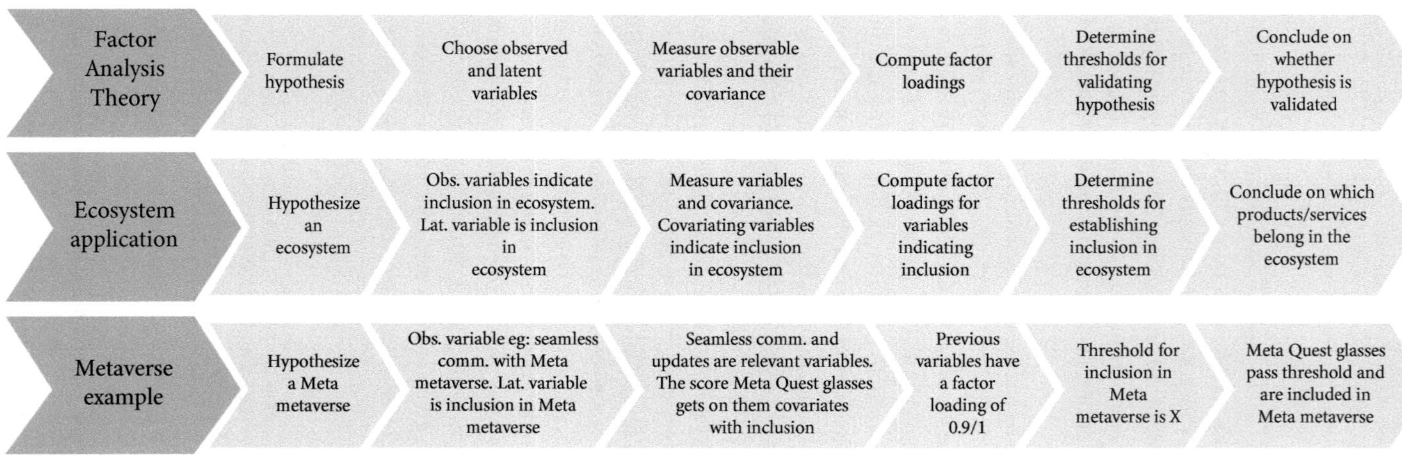

Figure 3.3 An application of factor analysis to the metaverse.

Consider the example of a metaverse built around Meta or Apple. Although there is no authoritative definition, the metaverse is considered a 'digital simulation of a multidimensional space'.[107] While it can consist of multi-actor sub-ecosystems, metaverses can also develop around individual firms.[108] Factor analysis can be used to determine which products and services are associated with a metaverse orchestrated by Meta or by Apple after helping determine which variables are relevant. Factor analysis starts from a hypothesized ecosystem, in this case a Meta or Apple metaverse. Different variables that are thought to indicate inclusion in the metaverse are selected and any candidate products or services are tested against those variables. The relevant variables can include joint purchasing/membership, integration, update cycles, pricing variations, compatibility, and interoperability among devices and services, etc. Examples of products and services that can be considered are Virtual Reality equipment, wearable interface control devices, digital identity services, payment and liquidity services, applications and games, etc. Then candidate products and services for inclusion in the hypothesized Meta or Apple metaverse would be checked against these variables, meaning that the variables would be measured for each candidate product or service. If the measured values covariate it means that the variables are linked back to the latent factor (belonging in the hypothesized metaverse); if not, then those variables are less indicative of belonging in the ecosystem and can be ignored. The value measurements of each of the products or services across the relevant variables indicate how closely each of the product or service is linked to the metaverse (eg product A gets a score of 4 out of 5 in the variable 'update cycle'). Then factor loadings are calculated (eg seamless communication gets a factor loading of 0.9 out of 1, indicating that seamless communication with the Meta or Apple metaverse is a crucial characteristic of belonging in that metaverse). Once this process is repeated for all candidate products and services, and all variables, the investigator can decide thresholds for inclusion to the metaverse and observe which products and services make the cut based on their scores in the relevant variables.

c) Snowball selection process: application to token ecosystems

In snowball selection the investigator starts from a convenience sample of subjects (seeds) which fit the investigation criteria, and which in turn refer other subjects matching the criteria and so on until either a target sample size or a saturation point has been reached.[109] The challenge with snowball selection process is to

[107] Mariusz Maciejewski, 'Metaverse' (European Parliament 2023) PE 751.222 145.

[108] Sofia Marlena Schöbel and Jan Marco Leimeister, 'Metaverse Platform Ecosystems' (2023) 33(12) Electronic Markets 1, 1–2.

[109] Charlie Parker, Sam Scott, and Alistair Geddes, 'Snowball Sampling', SAGE Research Methods Foundations (2019) at <https://eprints.glos.ac.uk/id/eprint/6781>. Patrick Doreian and Katherine L Woodard, 'Defining and Locating Cores and Boundaries of Social Networks' (1994) 16 Social Networks 267.

devise appropriate rules of reference from one subject to the next so as to avoid both stalling and infinite expansion.[110] Stalling occurs when the reference criteria are so strict that the waves of reference from one subject to the next are exhausted quickly, in effect resulting in very narrow ecosystems. On the other hand, infinite expansion occurs when the criteria are so loose that the ecosystem is virtually never saturated and becomes all-encompassing. Too narrow ecosystems will not accurately reflect competitive forces and constraints, whereas all-encompassing ecosystems are devoid of analytical value.

A proposed snowball selection process for ecosystems sees products/services as subjects, and starts with a single product/service (or a set thereof) or undertaking based on a strong specific inclusion rule.[111] Strong inclusion rules are those that define strict criteria of which products/services will be included in the initial selection, such that the initial selection comprises only products/services that the investigator thinks form the core of the ecosystem. This may sound like an arbitrary judgement, but it is no more arbitrary than the judgements that need to be made in regular market definition, among other things on the comparator products and services, the threshold of interchangeability, etc.[112] To some extent, it is impossible to kickstart the market or ecosystem definition process without making some initial arbitrary choices (which, incidentally, is one of the reasons why market definition has been criticized as pointless).[113]

The next step is to establish reference criteria. These are the criteria that will move the investigation outward from one product/service group to the one at the next degree of separation. Reference criteria can be different each time, but they must result in correct inclusion/exclusion to avoid stalling and infinite expansion. The criterion suggested here is non-generic complementarities, which is an authoritative way of defining ecosystems.[114] Non-generic complementarities between constituent parts (ie products and services) of an ecosystem are those that exhibit some degree of production or operation specificity towards one another.[115] This is contrasted to generic complementarities, which describes components that work together the same way that they work with any other component.

[110] Parker, Scott, and Geddes (n 109).

[111] See Mahin Naderifar, Hamideh Goli, and Fereshteh Ghaljaie, 'Snowball Sampling: A Purposeful Method of Sampling in Qualitative Research' (2017) 14 Strides in Development of Medical Education; Ilker Etikan, Rukayya Alkassim, and Sulaiman Abubakar, 'Comparison of Snowball Sampling and Sequential Sampling Technique' (2015) 3 Biometrics & Biostatistics International Journal 55.

[112] Richard S Markovits, 'The Inevitable Arbitrariness of Market Definitions and the Unjustifiability of Market-Oriented Antitrust Analyses' in Richard S Markovits, *Economics and the Interpretation and Application of U.S. and E.U. Antitrust Law* (Springer 2014).

[113] ibid; Louis Kaplow, 'Why (Ever) Define Markets?' (2010) 124 Harvard Law Review 437.

[114] Michael G Jacobides, Carmelo Cennamo, and Annabelle Gawer, 'Towards a Theory of Ecosystems' (2018) 39 Strategic Management Journal 2255.

[115] ibid 2261–63.

The reference criterion can therefore be formulated to be that subjects refer other subjects that serve as inputs or complements to them as long as they also exhibit non-generic complementarity to the seed subject(s). Note that components do not have to exhibit *exclusive* non-generic complementarities with components of only one ecosystem.

Consider the example of the Cardano ecosystem (Figure 3.4). The seed subject would be the Cardano protocol set (settlement layer, consensus layer, ADA token specifications, etc), which forms the core of the Cardano platform. First wave non-generic inputs and complements to the core platform include governance services (proposal tabling and voting), staking services, DeFi apps built on Cardano, ADA wallets, etc. These are non-generic because they require a specific investment in production or operation to make them suitable for Cardano. Examples of components that exhibit generic complementarities and are not to be included are general purpose developer tools, such as the programming language Java, which is used in Cardano but in the same way as in myriad other contexts and applications. Then, for every component identified in the first wave, one can apply the same criterion to graduate to the second wave. For instance, for the component of staking, staking pools exhibit complementarities to staking, because to enable staking for ADA they need to be specifically set up for it. Interestingly, staking pools that support ADA may support other tokens as well; in this case the non-generic complementarity is not exclusive, but it still fulfils the reference criterion.

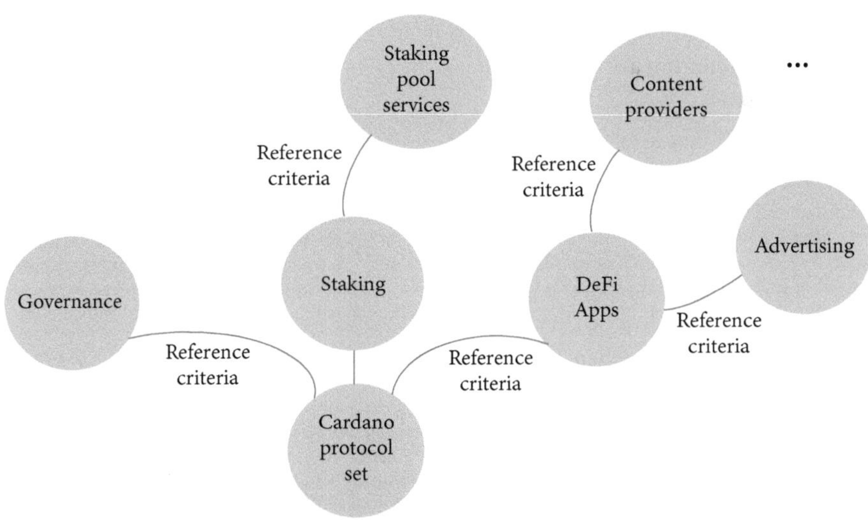

Figure 3.4 A non-exhaustive definition of the Cardano ecosystem using snowball selection process. Each steps proceeds based on selected reference criteria; here the criterion is that each outward step feeds into the previous step as a non-generic complement.

ii) Proximity analysis and strategic groups

Proximity-based market definition seeks to define an area wherein firms exert competitive pressure towards each other even if they may not necessarily produce substitutes. It looks at similarities among firms across different dimensions to identify those firms that belong closer together.[116] Closeness in the market was initially thought to reveal the potential for collaboration but it also reveals competitive affinity.[117] This conceptualization of markets has found application in mapping DeFi structures, which encompass a wide variety of systems and applications. For instance, a strategic group analysis of the DeFi structure on Ethereum, shows that the main constituent groups are token management applications, protocol platforms, aggregation platforms, and decentralized financial services.[118] Entities that fall within each of those groups exhibit greater affinity to each other across the selected parameters.

There are numerous dimensions across which proximity can be measured, each expressing a different aspect of affinity. A common classification recognizes three types of proximity: organizational, technological, and geographical proximity.[119] Organizational proximity refers to the level of similarity of the norms and routines between organizations.[120] Technological proximity is based on similar technological knowledge, which goes beyond knowledge of the technology itself and encompasses knowledge about the processes around developing and using technical know-how.[121] *Dynamic capabilities* are also related here, as they express a set of capabilities that allow firms to innovate and adapt to the changing environment (hence, dynamic), and therefore firms with similar dynamic capabilities may be able to exert greater competitive pressure towards each other.[122] Geographical proximity denotes territorial, spatial, local, or physical proximity.[123]

[116] Note that market definition revolves around substitute products, not firms. Proximity analysis revolves around firms under the assumption that proximate firms either produce or can produce substitute products, and therefore present either actual or potential competition, or can increase new entry or expansion opportunities, thereby still adding to competitive pressure.

[117] Michael Porter, 'Clusters and the New Economics of Competition' (1998) 76 Harvard Business Review 77; Catalin Boja, 'Clusters, Models, Factors and Characteristics' (2011) 1 International Journal of Economic Practices and Theories 34; Cheng Nie and others, 'A Strategic Group Analysis of Competitor Behavior in Search Advertising' (2021) 22 Journal of the Association for Information Systems 1659.

[118] Benedikt Christian Eikmanns and others, 'Is Ethereum the New iOS? Exploring the Platform Economy of Decentralized Finance' (2021) SSRN.

[119] Joris Knoben and Leo AG Oerlemans, 'Proximity and Inter-Organizational Collaboration: A Literature Review' (2006) 8 International Journal of Management Reviews 71.

[120] Andre Torre and Alain Rallet, 'Proximity and Localization' (2005) 39 Regional Studies 47; Douglass C North, 'Institutions' (1991) 5 Journal of Economic Perspectives 97.

[121] Michael L Tushman and Philip Anderson, 'Technological Discontinuities and Organizational Environments' (1986) 31 Administrative Science Quarterly 439.

[122] Sidney G Winter, 'Understanding Dynamic Capabilities' (2003) 24 Strategic Management Journal 991; David J Teece, 'Dynamic Capabilities and Strategic Management' (1997) 18 Strategic Management Journal 509; Vijaya Sunder M and LS Ganesh, 'Identification of the Dynamic Capabilities Ecosystem—A Systems Thinking Perspective' (2020) Group & Organization Management (online).

[123] Andre Torre Shaw and Jean-Pierre Gilly, 'On the Analytical Dimension of Proximity Dynamics' (2000) 34 Regional Studies 169.

Another way to look into proximity is through the lens of *strategic groups*, which describe similarly positioned companies in the market making them competitively relevant to each other.[124] Again, products by firms in the same group may not necessarily be substitutes, but they represent potential competition towards one another.[125] As Reger and Huff explain, 'managerial perception of similarities and differences among competitors influence strategic decision making . . . [and] strategists' grouping schemes may prove to be more significant . . . for understanding competition and performance because, through enactment processes, the way firms see themselves and their competitors is expected to have tangible effects on strategy reformulation and subsequent industry structure'.[126] Afterall, one manifestation of market power is the ability of firms to 'behave to an appreciable extent independently of their competitors',[127] and a tool that helps capture firms that can constraint such independent behaviour through potential competition or entry, can result in a meaningful market definition.

Unlike market definition based on substitutability, whereby products are or are not substitutes, proximity analysis and strategic groups do not operate on a strict binary inclusion/exclusion basis—rather they exhibit *membership gradience*,[128] where some products or firms form the core, some are more peripheral, and some are transient, meaning they are not always stable members of the same group but their strategic position is along dimensions common to other firms in the industry.[129] Clustering, which was described as a method for defining ecosystems, is also commonly used to identify strategic groups.[130] While firms/products are eventually allocated in one cluster, clustering reveals their relative position to each other making gradience observable.

124 Michael Porter, *The Competitive Strategy: Techniques for Analyzing Industries and Competitors* (Free Press 2004) 129; Kenneth J Hatten and Mary Louise Hatten, 'Strategic Groups, Asymmetrical Mobility Barriers and Contestability' (1987) 8 Strategic Management Journal 329.

125 Ken G Smith and others, 'Strategic Groups and Rivalrous Firm Behavior: Towards a Reconciliation' (1997) 18 Strategic Management Journal 149; Jay B Barney and Robert E Hoskisson, 'Strategic Groups: Untested Assertions and Research Proposals' (1990) 11 Managerial and Decision Economics 187.

126 Rhonda K Reger and Anne Sigismund Huff, 'Strategic Groups: A Cognitive Perspective' (1993) 14 Strategic Management Journal 103, 104.

127 Case C-85/76 Hoffmann-La Roche & Co AG v Commission ECLI:EU:C:1979:36, para 38.

128 Reger and Huff (n 126) 116.

129 ibid 117.

130 Deepika Nath and Thomas Gruca, 'Convergence Across Alternative Methods for Forming Strategic Groups' (1997) 18 Strategic Management Journal; Kathryn Rudie Harrigan, 'An Application of Clustering for Strategic Group Analysis' (1985) 6 Strategic Management Journal 55; H Hruschka, 'Market Definition and Segmentation Using Fuzzy Clustering Methods' (1986) 3 International Journal of Research in Marketing 117; Dean F Amel and Stephen A Rhoades, 'Strategic Groups in Banking' (1988) 70 The Review of Economics and Statistics 685.

4
MARKET SHARES

(A) General 79
(B) The complications of calculating market shares in DLT markets 82
(C) Calculation of cryptoasset and DeFi protocol market shares 85
i) Market capitalization 86
a) Inert supply 87
b) Supply inheritance 90
c) Supply arbitrariness 92
ii) Transaction count and volume 93
iii) Total Value Locked 96
(D) Calculation of mining and staking pool market shares 98
i) Output and capacity: hashrate and block count 99
ii) Revenue and profits 102
iii) Validator/miner/staker count 104
(E) Calculation of crypto-exchange and trading platform market shares 106
i) Trading volume 107
ii) Trade count 109
iii) Trader count 111

(A) General

Market share is an indication of firms' relative size; it reflects the portion of economic activity for which a firm accounts in the relevant market.[1] As a representation of firms' relative economic footprint, market shares are usually the first proxy competition law considers to deduce market power.[2] The calculation of market shares relies on an antecedent definition of the relevant market (see Chapter 3 section A), within which the share firms command is calculated.

The calculation of market shares is not an end in itself. Market shares serve as a proxy for market power, such that the higher the market share, the more power a firm likely has in the market (everything else equal).[3] Neither statutory law nor case law definitively specifies the thresholds above and below which firms can be considered to have or not have market power respectively. In the European Union, *Hoffmann-La Roche* initially spoke of 'very high market share' as indicative of

[1] Jonathan Jacobson, *Antitrust Law Developments* (6th edn, American Bar Association 2007) 341.

[2] See Case C-85/76 Hoffmann-La Roche & Co AG v Commission ECLI:EU:C:1979:36; *Weiss v. York Hospital*, 745 F.2d 786, 827 (1984).

[3] William Landes and Richard Posner, 'Market Power in Antitrust Cases' (1981) 94 Harvard Law Review 937, 944 et seq. See also Hoffman-La Roche (n 2) paras 39–41.

Antitrust in the Decentralized Economy. Konstantinos Stylianou, Oxford University Press.
 DOI: 10.1093/9780191925504.003.0004

dominance, an expression that was later quantified in *AKZO* to mean 50 per cent.[4] The *AKZO* threshold created a rebuttable presumption of dominance; it neither concluded that market shares over 50 per cent always point to dominance,[5] nor that shares below 50 per cent can never indicate dominance. Indeed, in *British Airways* the Court of Justice (CoJ) found British Airways to be dominant, with a market share of 40 per cent—the lowest ever recorded.[6] Sensing the paradox of finding dominance with a market share below 50 per cent, the CoJ engaged in a lengthy discussion on all other factors contributing to the finding and emphasized that market shares is just one of them.[7]

In the United States, a higher threshold applies. The classic formulation in *Alcoa* summarizes thresholds as follows: 'ninety percent is enough to constitute a monopoly; it is doubtful whether sixty or sixty-four percent would be enough; and certainly thirty-three per cent is not'.[8] There seems to be a widespread agreement among US courts that 'a share significantly larger than 55% has been required to establish prima facie market power'[9] and usually 70 per cent is required.[10]

Static market shares alone are not very instructive, as they reflect only a snapshot in time. Usually, only sustained market power is capable of resulting in the kind of market distortions competition law concerns itself with.[11] Therefore, a showing of sustained rather than transient market share is almost always necessary. As the decentralized economy is still in a nascent stage, characterized by elevated entry and experimentation, market shares are expected to show fluctuations.

To take two examples that demonstrate the historical volatility of market shares in Distributed Ledger Technology (DLT) markets, Figure 4.1 shows market shares of major crypto-exchanges (hereinafter, exchanges unless context requires clarification) from 2019 to 2024, while Figure 4.2 shows market shares of major mining pools between 2020 and 2024. The figures show not only major changes from year to year but also frequent entry and exit from the market.

4 Case C-62/86 AKZO Chemie BV v Commission ECLI:EU:C:1991:286, para 60.

5 Future cases confirmed that shares over 50% are most likely to be indicative of dominance. See Case C-53/92P, Hilti AG v Commission ECLI:EU:C:1994:77 (70–80% in PAF nails and cartridges); Commission decision of 27 June 2017 AT.39740 Google Search (85% in general search); Commission decision of 24 March 2004 C-3/37.792 Microsoft (90% in desktop operating systems).

6 Case T-219/99 British Airways v Commission ECLI:EU:T:2003:343, paras 211–112.

7 ibid paras 211–124.

8 *United States v. Aluminum Co. of America*, 148 F.2d 416, 424 (1945).

9 *United States v. Dentsply International, Inc.*, 399 F.3d 181, 187 (2005).

10 *Exxon Corporation v. Berwick Bay Real Estates Partners*, 748 F.2d 937, 940 (1984).

11 Lawrence Sullivan, Warren Grimes, and Christopher Sagers, *The Law of Antitrust: An Integrated Handbook* (3rd edn, West Academic Publishing 2016) 30–31. See also Google Search (n 5) para 266 ('An undertaking which holds a very large market share for some time . . . is by virtue of that share in a position of strength').

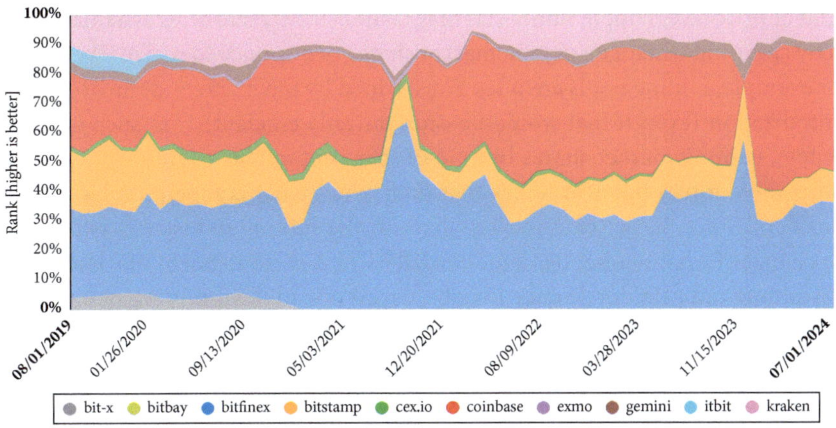

Figure 4.1 Evolution of exchange market share by volume 2019–2024.
Source: Bitcoinity

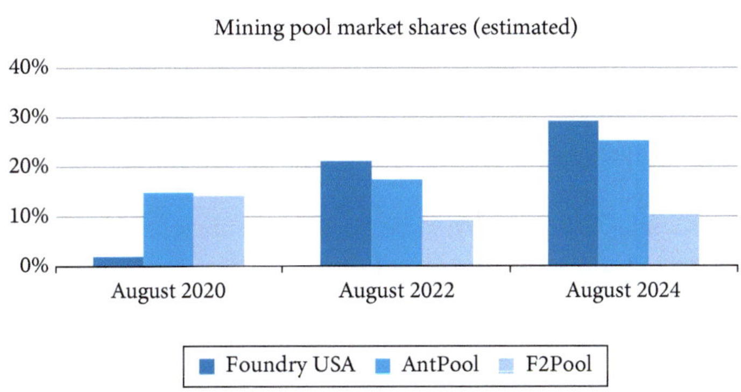

Figure 4.2 Market shares of major mining pools 2020–2024.
Source: Data from BTC.com, Hashrate Index, Cryproslate

Moreover, the figures reveal another important methodological point on the use of market shares, namely that market shares are most useful when looked at relative to each other, rather than in isolation.[12] A market with numerous players each having a comparable market share presents different competitive dynamics from a market with a small number of large players and a long tail of fringe players. Relatedly, one should recognize that technology and market features may place soft upper limits to the market share a firm may command. This is important because market shares are often used as proxy for market power, and so keeping in

[12] Alison Jones and Brenda Sufrin, *EU Competition Law* (6th edn, OUP 2016) 323–324. This point was crucial in *British Airways*, where the CoJ defended the finding of dominance at a low 40% market share, among others, because British Airways' market share 'invariably constitute[d] a multiple of the market shares of each of its five main competitors'. See British Airways (n 6) para 211.

mind any (de facto) upper limits that may characterize a market is essential in correctly assessing whether a certain market share corresponds to real market power. For example, mining pools are often constrained by the market's desire to prevent centralization (even if that would be economically efficient);[13] in such a market context, gaining market shares beyond 50 per cent entails overcoming not only competitive forces but also forces that go beyond what competition law usually considers. Since 50 per cent market share in the mining industry is realistically the ceiling of what market dynamics usually allow, an adjustment of what market shares may indicate dominance may be necessary. Indeed, mining pools with a share of around 40 per cent—a normally exceptionally low share to find dominance in most other markets—are considered dominant in the mining industry (everything else equal) and are regarded with suspicion.[14]

In the following sections we first look at factors that complicate the calculation of market shares in DLT markets. Then, detailed expositions of how to calculate market shares in different economics segments of the decentralized economy are presented.

(B) The complications of calculating market shares in DLT markets

Putting aside any general challenges of calculating market shares, which are addressed as needed below, DLT markets pose additional unique problems. While mitigation strategies may not always be possible or obvious, acknowledging the problems is still useful as, at least, it informs investigators about how confident they should be regarding their findings.

Appropriate metrics. The first challenge concerns the identification of appropriate metrics to calculate shares. In mainstream competition law, market shares are usually calculated on the basis of sales. This is reflected both in the Commission's Market Definition Notice[15] and in US antitrust case-law, which deems sales as 'the primary index of market power'.[16] Sales can be measured in terms of revenue or units, with revenue being a better indicator where products are not full substitutes.

[13] 'Bitmain's Mining Pools Now Control Nearly 51% of the Bitcoin Hashrate' *CCN Markets* (25 June 2018). For more detail see Chapter 5 sections B.i.b and B.i.c.

[14] Irni Eliana Khairuddin and Corina Sas, 'An Exploration of Bitcoin Mining Practices: Miners' Trust Challenges and Motivations' (2019) Proceedings of the 2019 ACM CHI Conference on Human Factors in Computing Systems 1.

[15] Commission Notice on the definition of the relevant market for the purposes of Union competition law (C/2023/6789) OJ C 372, para 111. See also Guidance on the Commission's enforcement priorities in applying Article 82 of the EC Treaty to abusive exclusionary conduct by dominant undertakings (2009/C 45/02), para 13.

[16] *Brown Show Co. v. United States*, 370 U.S. 294, 322 (1962). See also *Geneva Pharmaceuticals Technology Corp. v. Barr Labs.*, 386 F.3d 485, 500 (2004) ('Although market share is not functionally equivalent to monopoly power, it is nevertheless highly relevant to the determination of monopoly power').

However, under special conditions that characterize certain industries, sales may not always be the most reliable indicator of market shares, and instead other industry-specific indicators may be used.[17] This particularly concerns markets where DLT technologies often find application, such as fintech. Indeed, in fintech and financial markets in general a number of other relevant metrics have been used, among which total assets, deposits, and loans in the retail banking market;[18] transaction value and transaction volume in the stock exchange market;[19] number of cards and volume of card transactions in the credit/debit card market;[20] and 'league table' rankings in the investment banking market.[21] The sections below discuss numerous metrics that are appropriate in blockchain markets.

Conflicting metrics. Secondly, when multiple metrics become relevant, the question of which one should be primary arises. The choice can become decisive in cases where metrics point to different results. For instance, in *United States v. Amax* where the court could choose between sales and capacity as the appropriate measure of market positioning, the difference was significant since '[i]f sales were used it would reduce by almost half the market share which the Government, using . . . capacity as the measure, alleges Amax would control'[22] (the court chose capacity in the end).

In many cases, even if metrics deviate, they may still lead to the same conclusion, although failure to acknowledge the deviation and its potential effects confounds the analysis. For example, in *Visa International* the Commission cumulatively used various metrics without separately discussing each one's merits. It noted that '[o]n the national markets for cards . . . Visa holds, in terms of number of cards in circulation, a market share varying between 4% and 69%, [and in] terms of volume and value of Visa card transactions Visa's market share varies respectively from 2% to 95% and 2% to 93%'.[23] The conclusion was that, based on Visa's position in the market, its network indeed had an appreciable effect on competition, but we do not know whether the conclusion would have been the same if any one of the metrics considered suggested a markedly different market position.

[17] For examples of industry-specific metrics see Jones and Sufrin (n 12) 321–322. Also, in some markets multiple metrics become relevant all at the same time in varying degrees. For instance, in the market for online voice communication software (eg Skype, Messenger, etc), relevant metrics can include total users, active users, call volume, call duration, traffic volume, total revenue, or revenue from user subscriptions, all of which reflect a tranche of the full picture. See Commission decision of 7 October 2011 M.6281 Microsoft/Skype.

[18] See eg *United States v. Phillipsburg National Bank & Trust*, 399 U.S. 350 (1970); *United States v. Philadelphia National Bank*, 374 U.S. 321 (1963).

[19] See eg Commission decision of 1 February 2012 M.6166 Deutsche Boerse/NYSE Euronext.

[20] See eg Commission Decision of 9 August 2001 29.373 Visa International, para 51. See also Commission Decision of 3 October 2007 D1/37860 Morgan Stanley/Visa International, paras 80–93.

[21] See eg Commission Decision of 19 December 1997 M.1068 Credit Suisse First Boston/Barclays, para 9.

[22] *United States v. Amax, Inc.*, 402 F.Supp. 956, 961 (1975).

[23] *Visa International* (n 20) para 51.

In *Mastercard* the Commission considered the number of cards and transaction volumes as relevant metrics, but even though the two metrics diverged significantly, the Commission opined that the available data on transaction volumes were unreliable and did not end up using it, passing up an opportunity to discuss their relative value.[24]

In cryptoassets, metrics can diverge significantly, and the choice of preferred metric for market share calculation should be influenced by the nature and purpose of the investigation. For instance, Figure 4.3 shows that across two cryptoassets, Bitcoin and EOS, transaction count and market capitalization diverge widely, even if one could expect a positive correlation between them. Among other reasons, in this example, the correlation breaks down because EOS is a smart contract platform which incurs numerous transactions as part of the operation and governance of the services built on top of it, unlike Bitcoin, whose transactions are predominantly for value transfer.

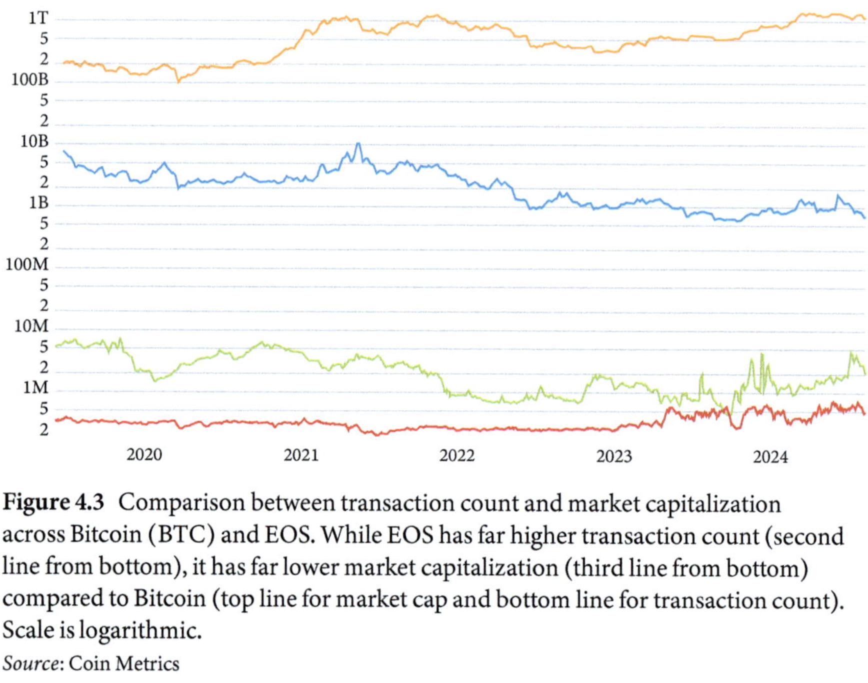

Figure 4.3 Comparison between transaction count and market capitalization across Bitcoin (BTC) and EOS. While EOS has far higher transaction count (second line from bottom), it has far lower market capitalization (third line from bottom) compared to Bitcoin (top line for market cap and bottom line for transaction count). Scale is logarithmic.
Source: Coin Metrics

Unreliable data. Thirdly, regardless of which indicator(s) one chooses to calculate market shares, they all necessitate clean data to be of any use. In most traditional markets it is assumed that the data required to perform market share calculation is available and reliable. This is often not the case in DLT markets. At the heart of

[24] Commission Decision of 19 December 2007 Joined Cases COMP/34.579 MasterCard, COMP/36.518 EuroCommerce and COMP/38.580 Commercial Cards, paras 105–117.

the decentralized economy, at least initially, were collaborative grassroots movements that lacked a single authority which could provide relevant and accurate data and disclosures—as compared with, for instance, public corporations, which issue quarterly reports or must regularly file forms to comply with regulatory oversight (eg 10-K).

And even when the data is available (since many products and services in the decentralized economy are permissionless so that anyone can tap into the data generated by such products and services) it is often unreliable owing to a variety of reasons, including manipulation, lack of well-developed standards and scientific methodologies, and ultimately lack of regulatory oversight that would ensure a level of transparency, quality, and trustworthiness. As the industry matures, it is expected that data will gain in integrity and accessibility, but as of now, caution is advised. Below, where appropriate, the reader will be alerted to potential issues with data availability or integrity.

Overall, the inquiry into market shares in DLT markets is partly familiar and partly unique: it is familiar in that it relies on multiple different indicators whose value is to be assessed on a case-by-case basis, much like in any other market investigation. It is unique in that the novelty of the industry and the underlying technology introduce new indicators alongside conventional ones, whose value however should be approached with caution in terms of reliability.

(C) Calculation of cryptoasset and DeFi protocol market shares

Cryptoassets are digital instruments of economic value that are developed and traded on DLT networks and most commonly on blockchain.[25] The function of cryptoassets resembles that of common financial instruments, like currencies, stocks, and derivatives. DLT equivalents include cryptocurrencies, tokenized equity, and crypto-derivates.

Cryptoasset market shares can primarily be measured on the basis of three metrics: market capitalization, transaction count, and transaction volume. Market capitalization is by far the most common method, likely because it was already widely employed in conventional markets, which contributed to its early adoption in blockchain markets as well. It is, however, beset with methodological difficulties, and does not fully capture the economic footprint of cryptoassets. For

[25] The vast majority of cryptoassets is developed and traded on blockchain networks, although there exist cryptoassets that rely on DLT but not on blockchain. A notable example is IOTA, whose distributed ledger does not consist of transactions grouped into a chain of sequential blocks as in a blockchain, but as a stream of individual transactions entangled together.

Decentralized Finance (DeFi) and fintech markets in particular, a preferred metric called Total Value Locked (TVL) is in use too.

i) Market capitalization

Market capitalization expresses the economic size of a cryptoasset as a function of the market price and count of its tokens. In its simplest form, market capitalization is calculated by multiplying the token market price by the circulating supply. For instance, if a cryptocurrency has issued one million tokens and at a given time the price of each token is £10, the market capitalization at that time is £10 million. This figure expresses an asset's market share vis-à-vis its value. While not commonly considered in market share calculation in traditional financial markets, market capitalization has been used in DLT markets to represent the economic size of cryptoassets. This may be both because the commonly used metrics of transaction count and volume in traditional financial markets are prone to extensive manipulation,[26] which has caused a turn to the more easily verifiable market capitalization, and because the market power of cryptoassets stems to a greater degree from their valuation compared to traditional companies, whose market power is better reflected in market adoption as expressed by output (ie transaction count, volume, etc). For example, in *Bitfinex*, the District Court took into account Tether's large market capitalization in the stablecoin market as a facilitating factor in its ability to monopolize the cryptocommodities market.[27]

To calculate market capitalization, we need the number of tokens and their price. Both can and do fluctuate, and therefore, for market capitalization to be an informative measure, accurate market price and circulating supply figures are necessary. These would ideally be considered over longer time horizons to smoothen out short-term fluctuations. Market price is easier to obtain accurately, whereas supply figures require more careful investigation.

In conventional financial markets the price of financial instruments is taken from the exchange on which they are traded. Because conventional financial instruments are commonly traded only on one exchange, obtaining their market price is uncomplicated. However, cryptoassets are commonly traded on multiple exchanges at the same time, each listing them at a different price. For the purposes of calculating market capitalization, the price discrepancies are usually negligible and can be ignored, although some notable discrepancies have been recorded at a scale that could matter.[28] To mitigate the effect of discrepancies an average price can be calculated across the various exchanges that list the cryptoasset in question.

[26] See below C.ii.
[27] *In re Tether and Bitfinex Cryptoasset Litigation*, 1:19-cv-09236-KPF (2021), at 57–58.
[28] See eg Kyungji Cho, 'Bitcoin's "Kimchi Premium" Has Vanished' *BusinessWeek* (2 February 2018).

It is good practice to rely only on trustworthy or regulated exchanges to calculate average prices. Otherwise, the calculation is prone to include outlier prices that may taint the analysis.

While obtaining accurate prices presents some difficulties, by far the trickiest part of calculating market capitalization is measuring supply. This is because there can be disagreement as to which tokens should be counted in a cryptoasset's supply. The relevant choices pertain to inert supply, inheritance of supply from a parent cryptoasset, and variable issuance rates among cryptoassets. Collectively, these issues can account for considerable differences in supply estimation, and, in turn, market capitalization.

a) Inert supply

The starting point of supply measurement is to look at the number of the cryptoasset tokens in question that have been issued. This information is usually publicly available; for example, we know that, as of mid-2024, around 19.5 million Bitcoins have been issued.[29] However, even though all of these tokens are nominally in circulation, not all of them are economically active, raising the question of whether they should be counted in. Inert supply refers to those tokens that may be economically irrelevant for market share calculation either because they are lost or because they are highly illiquid.

Lost tokens are those that can no longer be used because access to them has been lost. Unlike equities, where there is recourse if, for example, a physical share certificate is lost, in a distributed public key infrastructure like that which underpins cryptoassets, lost cryptographic keys result in a permanent loss of access to the asset. It is an open issue when one declares that access to tokens is permanently lost. For instance, in a major 2017 incident where a bug in a multi-signature contract led to the loss of over 500,000 Ether tokens (worth around $150 million at the time), the wallet provider that was responsible for the error pledged to try to restore access.[30] The effort was abandoned six months later.[31] If someone wanted to measure Ethereum's market capitalization in the meantime between the incident and the abandonment of the restoration attempt, it is questionable whether those tokens should be counted in. Similar to lost tokens are burnt tokens that are still visible on-chain, as these will eventually be removed from circulation.

An even higher degree of subjectivity characterizes choices on inactive tokens. Inactive tokens are those that have not been involved in a transaction for a period of time—to be defined arbitrarily. Tokens that move with extreme rarity or not at all are essentially out of circulation since they are economically dormant.

[29] See <https://www.blockchain.com/explorer/charts/total-bitcoins> (all links were last accessed on 1 September 2024).

[30] Camila Russo, 'Security or Not, Ethereum's Soul Searching Isn't Over' *Bloomberg* (27 June 2018).

[31] Molly Jane Zuckerman, 'Ethereum Proposal to "Resurrect" Disabled $360 Mln Parity Contract Shut Down' *CoinTelegraph* (24 April 2018).

The same can be said (again with a certain degree of arbitrariness) for tokens that are withheld by their issuing companies or foundations, or even tokens withheld by investors that have been formally restricted (through legal or smart contracts). Investigators are free to choose the temporal point beyond which they wish to consider tokens lost or inactive. In public blockchains, they can inspect the blockchain directly to ascertain the liveness of supply.

Bitcoin is a good case study because it has sufficient historical depth and liquidity to demonstrate the issue of inactive tokens. For instance, Figure 4.4 shows that in the first ten years (2009–2019), Bitcoins which have not moved and can safely be understood to be lost, amount to approximately 10.6 per cent of total supply. By another estimation, as of 2019, 3.6 million Bitcoins are either lost and out of circulation or held in wallets controlled by Bitcoin creator Satoshi Nakamoto, who is presumed to have abandoned the project and his/her coins.[32]

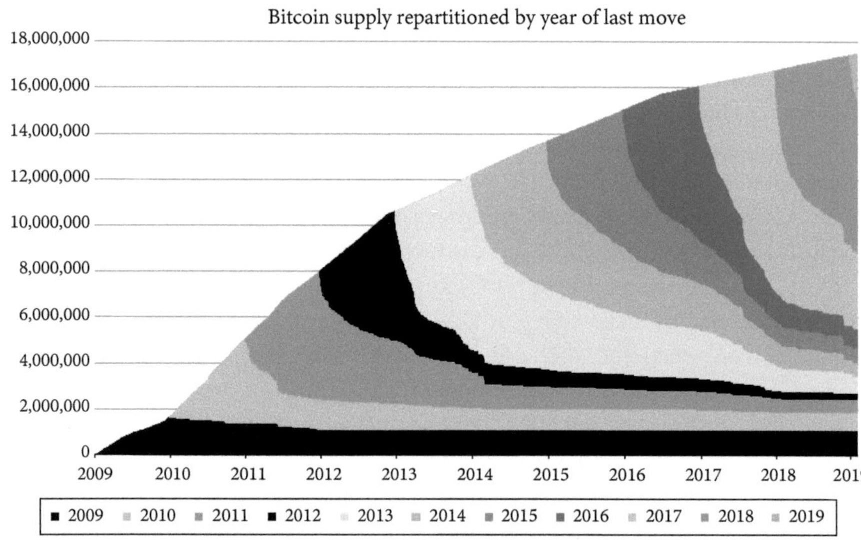

Figure 4.4 Bitcoin supply per year of last move. The graph shows that a large quantity of circulating supply has remained dormant over the years, whether out of choice or because owners lost access to it.
Source: Coin Metrics

In fact, total market capitalization and market capitalization based on the tokens moved in the past one trailing year can differ by as much as three times (Figure 4.5).

[32] Jeff John Roberts and Nicolas Rapp, 'Nearly 4 Million Bitcoins Lost Forever, New Study Says' *Fortune* (25 November 2017).

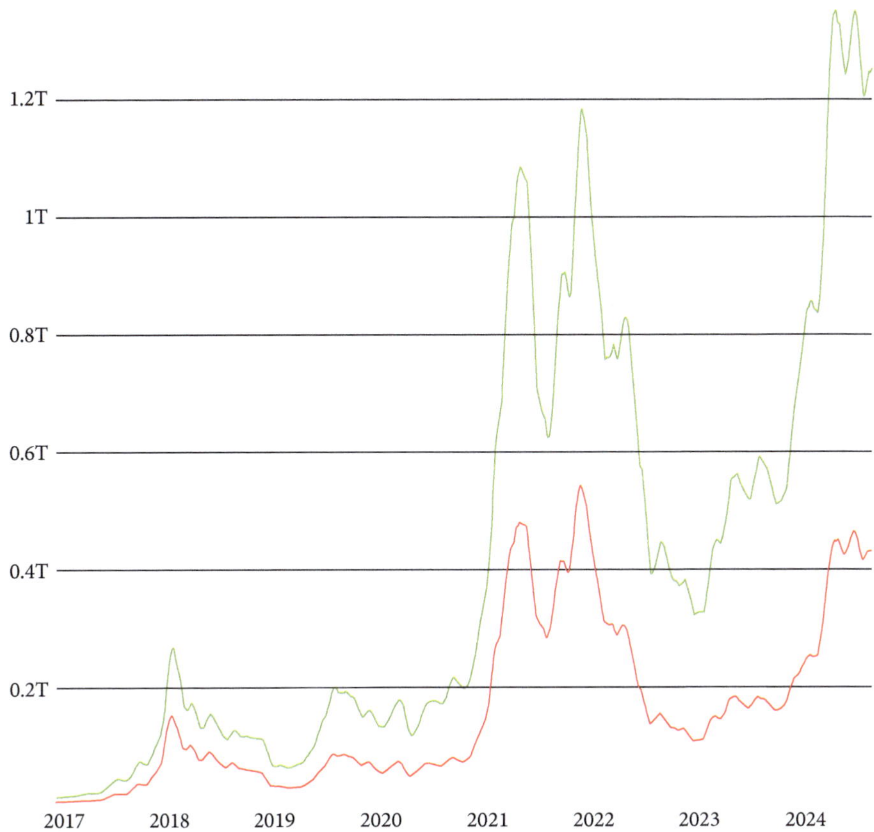

Figure 4.5 Total market capitalization (top line) vs trailing year active capitalization can differ by as much as 3x.
Source: Coin Metrics

Because of the inherent subjectivity of estimating supply by setting a cut-off point below which tokens are considered inactive, an alternative solution is to weigh each token according to the price when it last moved on the ledger. This method, referred to as *realized capitalization*, indexes the price of each token to their market value when they last settled on the ledger, instead of treating them all as homogeneous, thereby devaluing inactive tokens.[33] The last movement and corresponding price of tokens are observable on public blockchains, since settlement of transactions must occur on the ledger. The difference can be significant, particularly when the current token price is higher than historical levels or network activity is slower than historical levels, as shown in (Figure 4.6).

[33] Coin Metrics Data Encyclopedia, 'Realized Market Cap' at <https://gitbook-docs.coinmetrics.io/network-data/network-data-overview/market/market-capitalization#h>.

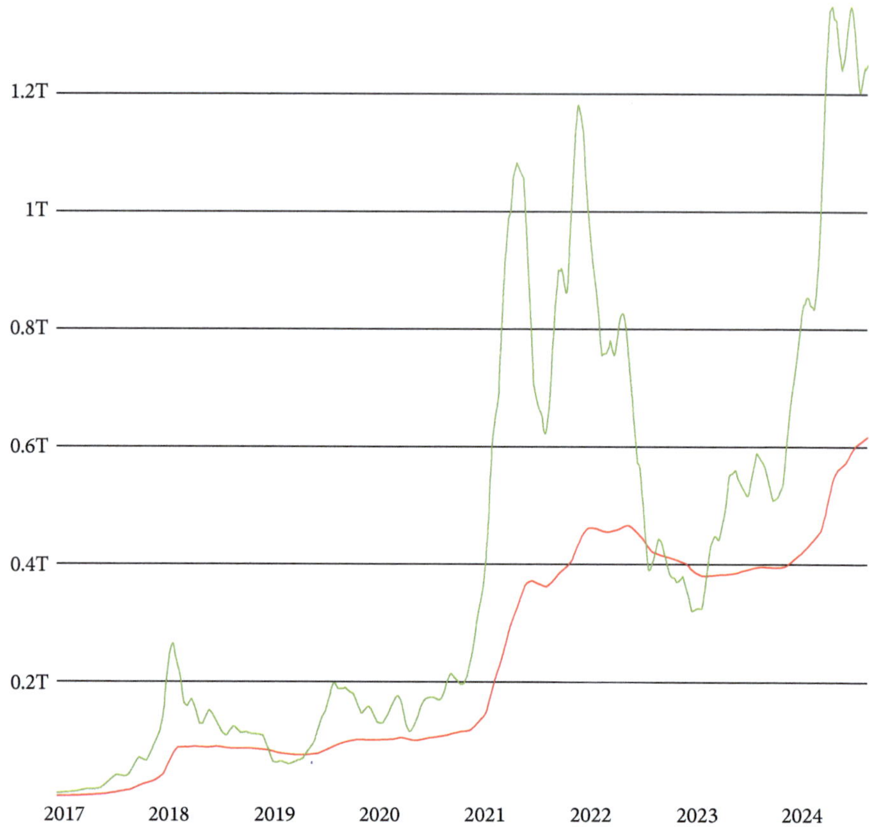

Figure 4.6 Bitcoin realized capitalization (bottom line) vs total market capitalization. In realized capitalization coins are weighted by historical movement and the corresponding prices at the time.
Source: Coin Metrics

b) Supply inheritance

Supply inheritance is an issue unique to cryptoassets and can greatly affect the supply figures that are considered for market share calculation. It refers to the erroneous counting of tokens of a parent ledger in the supply of a fork ledger. Forks are spin-off blockchain ledgers that derive from a parent when the cryptoasset's development team is split over the future direction of the cryptoasset, in which case two different versions of the cryptoasset will emerge—an original (parent) and a fork.[34] When this happens, the dissenting developers take a snapshot of the existing (unified) ledger of account balances while irredeemably altering some parameters such that the two ledgers cannot be reconciled after a split. The two

[34] Andreas M Antonopoulos, *Mastering Bitcoin: Programming the Open Blockchain* (2nd edn, O'Reilly Media 2017) 274–84.

resulting ledgers—original and fork—cannot each account for the full original supply at the same time. Doing so would inflate supply by double-counting the tokens as belonging both to the parent and the child fork.

Supply inheritance is a common problem, since forks are common, but reliable data analytics can ensure accurate counting. The case of Bitcoin Cash is illustrative.[35] In August 2017, a breakaway faction created an alternative version of Bitcoin (BTC) called Bitcoin Cash (BCH). Prior to the fork, owners of Bitcoin were issued prorated tokens of Bitcoin Cash. Since Bitcoin Cash came to obtain a meaningful economic value, many Bitcoin holders redeemed their Bitcoin Cash coins, either becoming active on the second chain or liquidating their new coins for Bitcoin. Subsequently, Bitcoin Cash itself bifurcated into Bitcoin ABC (this fork retained the original ticker BCH) and Bitcoin SV (BSV). It is important to note that BSV was a fork of the original Bitcoin Cash and thus two degrees of forks removed from Bitcoin. Erroneously, both BCH and BSV were assumed to possess the supply of the parent asset: for Bitcoin Cash, Bitcoin; for BSV, Bitcoin Cash, and a result all three assets are now showing an almost identical supply (Figure 4.7).[36] However, since units on newly forked chains must be initially moved to become active, simply porting over the supply of the parent chain overestimates the supply of the child chain, since many users choose to ignore their forked coins, leaving them

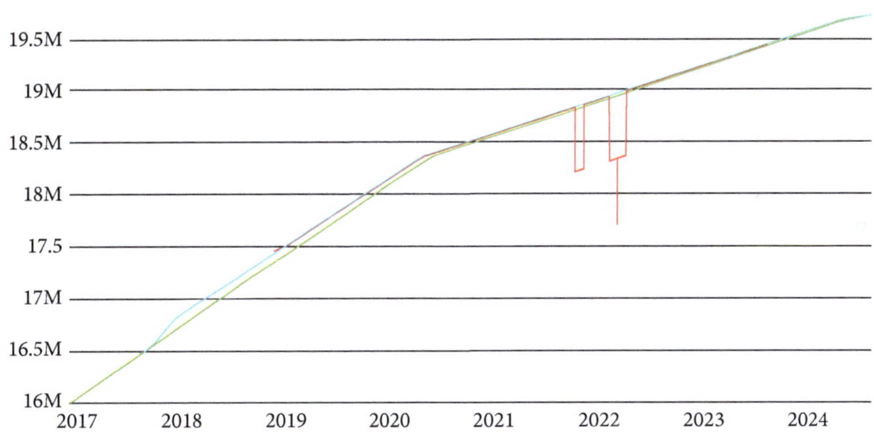

Figure 4.7 Total supply of Bitcoin, Bitcoin Cash, and Bitcoin SV showing as almost identical. Bitcoin Cash derives from Bitcoin and Bitcoin SV derives from Bitcoin Cash. It would be wrong to count the same tokens for all three cryptoassets because they are no longer sharing the same ledger, nor are they interchangeable.
Source: Coin Metrics

[35] For a history and analysis of Bitcoin Cash, see Marco Alberto Javarone and Craig Steven Wright, 'From Bitcoin to Bitcoin Cash: A Network Analysis' (2018) Proceedings of the 1st Workshop on Cryptocurrencies and Blockchains for Distributed Systems (CryBlock'18) 77.

[36] See eg CoinMarketCap's data on BSV and BCH showing identical supply for both currencies, at <https://coinmarketcap.com/currencies/bitcoin-sv> and <https://coinmarketcap.com/currencies/bitcoin-cash>.

inert. Using exclusively activated units to compute supply presents instead a more accurate picture (Figure 4.8).

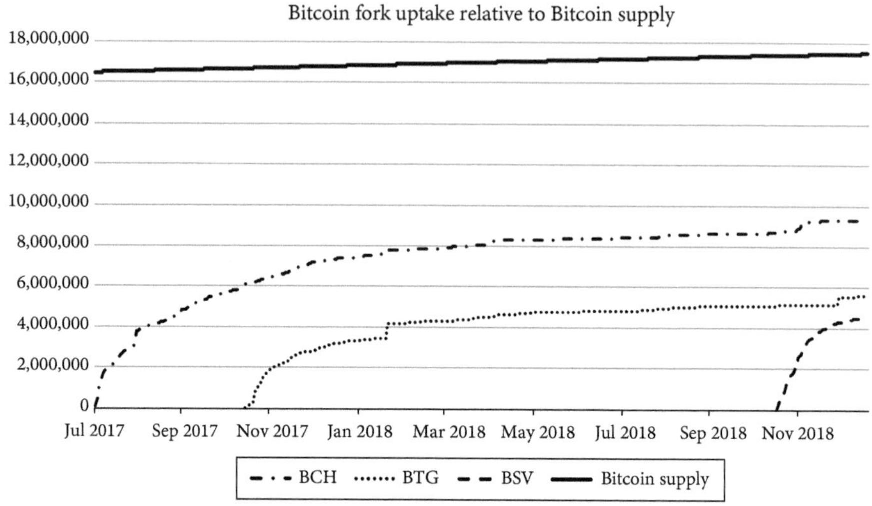

Figure 4.8 Bitcoin fork uptake. It is evident that forks do not account for the full original supply of the parent chain.
Source: Coin Metrics

c) Supply arbitrariness

Supply arbitrariness refers to situations where the total supply of a cryptoasset may be known in advance, but the time of release remains unknown and often at the discretion of a single entity. This creates uncertainty as to how supply is expected to change in the future, which casts in doubt the future-proof quality of any market share calculation. The question, then, arises of whether future increases—planned or predicted—should be taken into account even if they have not occurred yet.

The most accurate way would be to consider only actual circulating supply (free float) and eliminate from supply tokens held by the issuing entity, if one exists.[37] This method, however, presents the risk that supply held in the ostensibly out-of-circulation issuer wallets is liable to enter active supply unexpectedly, especially when issuance is not credibly set according to a rigid schedule. As a middle way and inspired by investor valuations, one could use a projection five years into the future and then the resulting expected supply figures are used for comparisons instead of the outstanding supply.[38] This method is safer when the supply

[37] See eg Bitwise's methodology for Bitwise Crypto Index Methodology (Bitwise Investments) <https://www.bitwiseinvestments.com/indexes/methodology>.

[38] See Nick French and Laura Gabrielli, 'Discounted Cash Flow: Accounting for Uncertainty' (2005) 23 Journal of Property Investment & Finance 75.

schedules are programmatic, and it may be useful for merger assessments since it is forward-looking.

A notable example of entities maintaining discretion over the supply of cryptoassets is XRP. XRP is created and sold by Ripple Labs. Around 100 billion XRP were created at inception in January 2013, but since then and as of the end of 2024 only 57 billion have entered circulation (through distribution events called 'airdrops' and through direct sales by Ripple Labs). Ripple Labs controls the remaining XRP and can issue them at their discretion. Ripple claims to have escrowed XRP on their ledger,[39] with that supply being progressively released, but since Ripple Labs maintains de facto control over the ledger and consensus system, that commitment is not as credible as a proof of work (PoW) system where issuance is codified for perpetuity at inception. XLM is issued by the Stellar Development Foundation with a degree of arbitrariness.

ii) Transaction count and volume

Unlike market capitalization, which sees cryptoassets as investment or store of value vehicles and measures their economic footprint as a function of their value, transaction count and volume treat cryptoasset networks as service providers that enable transactions, and measure their size as a function of the number of transactions that take place on their platforms and the volume they generate.

Transaction count. Transaction count has become a popular yardstick in the cryptoasset industry. It refers to the sum of all economically relevant actions occurring directly on a cryptoasset blockchain in a given time frame, usually per day. It is a familiar metric, as it has been in use in traditional payment systems, like credit cards, and it is a reasonable approximation of the share of the market a cryptoasset commands, based on the assumption that transactions reflect adoption of the cryptoasset and engagement with the service.[40]

There are two main caveats when relying on transaction count. The first relates to the technical specifications of cryptoasset networks. Cryptoasset networks differ widely in terms of how they structure and process transactions. For instance, Bitcoin is, by design, limited to a maximum capacity of seven transactions per second in its original iteration, and Ethereum initially could process fifteen, whereas newer networks, such as EOS, can process millions. By comparison, the Visa network can process 45,000 transactions per second. The large differences in transaction capacity across cryptoassets are explained by the function transactions are called to perform on the cryptoasset networks. For instance, on the EOS

[39] Ripple, 'Ripple Escrows 55 Billion XRP for Supply Predictability' (*Ripple Insights Blog*, 8 December 2017) at <https://ripple.com/insights/ripple-escrows-55-billion-xrp-for-supply-predictability>.

[40] See eg *Morgan Stanley/Visa International* (n 20) para 91.

network transactions perform numerous functions, from moving value, to enabling distributed apps, to setting up voting processes, to distributing and claiming voting rewards, and others.[41] Therefore, to compare cryptoassets purely based on the number of transactions they process per given time frame without first sorting them by function would not be instructive.

Moreover, what on the blockchain appears as one transaction can in fact constitute a collection of numerous independent transactions, a technique known as batching.[42] Batching originated as a means of lowering the cost of transactions on cryptoasset networks by allowing multiple payments to share overhead costs and fees. The average ratio of payment-per-transaction on the Bitcoin network ranges between 1.8 and 2.3, which means that almost double the number of payments take place as transactions shown (Figure 4.9). Additionally, while batched payments represent only a little over 10 per cent of all transactions on the Bitcoin network, they can account for over 40 per cent of volume.[43] Therefore, on cryptoasset networks where batching is observed to be common, it is more accurate to consider payments rather than transactions.

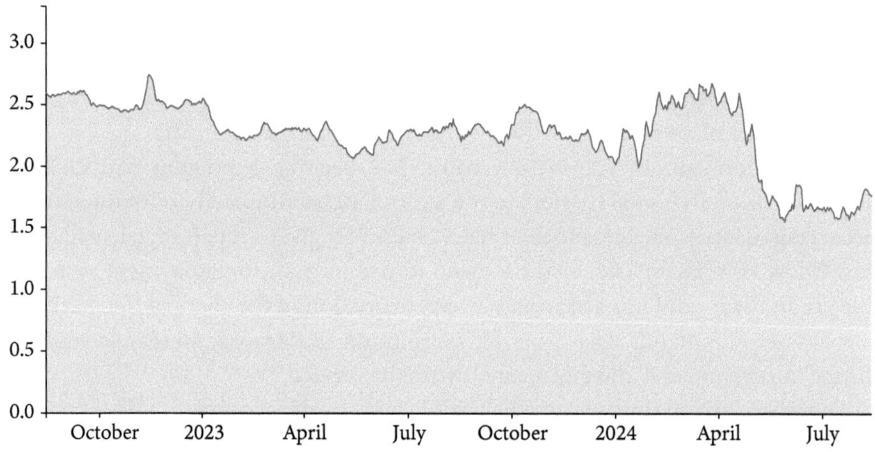

Figure 4.9 Ratio of Bitcoin payment-per-transaction. The economically relevant metric is payments; measuring just transactions may conceal the economic activity actually taking place on a cryptoasset network.
Source: Transactionfee

41 EOS Authority, 'Types of Transactions' (*EOS Authority Blog*, 26 June 2018) at <https://eosauthority.com/blog/types_of_transactions_on_eos_accounts>.

42 The more technical explanation of batching is that it is a technique whereby a single transaction has multiple inputs and outputs, such that one transaction can result in the transfer of value from multiple senders to multiple recipient addresses. See Coin Metrics, 'An Analysis of Batching in Bitcoin' (*Coin Metrics Blog*, 20 May 2018) at <https://coinmetrics.io/batching>.

43 ibid.

The second caveat on the use of transaction count concerns the manipulation or artificial inflation of transaction count, which affects the reliability of measurements. While the vast majority of transactions on traditional transfer of value services are performed to move value from one economic actor to another, many transactions on cryptoasset networks do not have meaningful economic utility. Rather, they are generated to serve other purposes—not all legitimate—and it is therefore doubtful that they should be counted in when comparing cryptoassets by transaction count.

An example of legitimate transactions, which however do not represent meaningful transfer of value, is change transactions. Change transactions, as the name suggests, are transactions whereby change is returned to a user when the amount transferred to another user exceeds the value of the transacted good or service.[44] Intuitively, if A pays with a £20 note for something that costs £15, the economically relevant amount is £15, not £25—£20 from paying and £5 from giving back change. Change transactions, while validly recorded on the blockchain, do not contribute to the meaningful amount that was moved from actor to actor, and therefore should be filtered out.

More difficult is the issue of transactions that appear as valid but have questionable purposes and similarly do not meaningfully transfer value between economic actors. For instance, mixers are services that repeatedly combine and mix transactions into new transactions to obscure the origin and ownership of cryptoassets.[45] Such practices may have legitimate goals, such as preservation of privacy, or they may be used to cover up tracks of criminal transactions. Either way, the transactions generated by mixers simply recycle economic value, rather than add new value. Other examples of transactions that simply recycle, rather than add economic value, are 'wash trading' and 'painting the tape' transactions, whereby users transfer tokens among themselves to artificially inflate transaction count.[46] This practice is popular on exchanges and is discussed in more detail in section E.i. An accurate measurement of transaction count should exclude all such transaction types that do not have meaningful economic utility.[47]

Transaction volume. Together with transaction count, transaction volume can also be considered as a relevant metric of cryptoassets' share of the market. Transaction volume is the aggregate value of transactions performed in a given time frame, usually per day. Since it is a function of transaction count, it is susceptible to the same caveats documented previously, and the volume that corresponds

[44] Antonopoulos (n 34) 20.

[45] Qi Feng and others, 'A Survey on Privacy Protection in Blockchain System' (2019) 126 Journal of Network and Computer Applications 45.

[46] Hacken, 'Investigation on Fake Trade Volume of Top Crypto Exchanges: BigONE' *Medium* (10 August 2018); Will Kenton, 'Painting the Tape' *Investopedia* (14 January 2018).

[47] See Coin Metrics, 'Introducing Our Adjusted Transaction Volume Estimates' (*Coin Metrics Blog*, 27 June 2018) at <https://coinmetrics.io/introducing-adjusted-estimates>.

to non-economically relevant transactions should accordingly be excluded. This can be a significant portion of total volume. Figure 4.10 indeed shows that the adjusted corrected volume can be significantly lower than the recorded volume of all transactions—almost by 60 per cent in some cases. Transaction volume can, however, be more difficult to spoof than transaction count, because to count the same value multiple times by recycling it in multiple transactions, one would first have to possess the assets of value. While it is easy to inflate transaction count by generating large numbers of empty transactions, significant manipulation of volume is mostly an option for owners/managers of high-value assets and incurs greater risk.

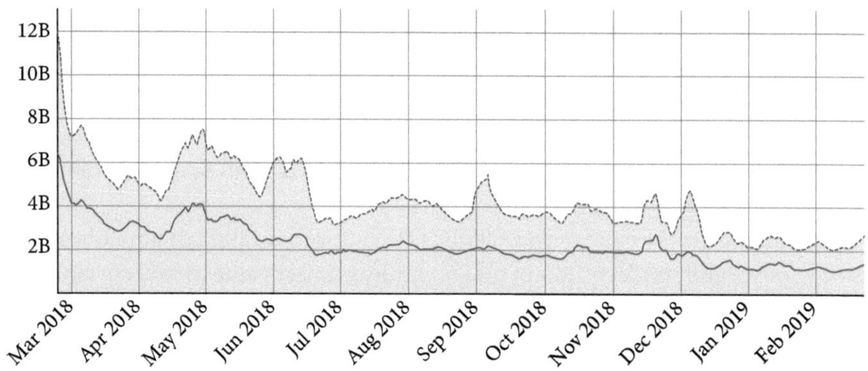

Figure 4.10 Total transaction volume (fill area) vs adjusted transaction volume (line) in Bitcoin. Adjusted transaction volume considers only economically relevant transactions.
Source: Coin Metrics

iii) Total Value Locked

Total Value Locked (TVL) is a metric used in DeFi and fintech markets because it better captures the economic significance of the underlying activities. TVL expresses the total value of virtual assets committed ('locked') on a particular DLT network, usually in the DeFi, decentralized apps (dApps), or more broadly, fintech space.[48] In this space, the most common type of services relates to loans, staking, and decentralized exchanges (DEX), all of which pool together different types of virtual assets. For example, the Aave liquidity protocol allows users to supply their assets for others to borrow thereby earning interest, or they can stake them

[48] Dominik Metelski and Janusz Sobieraj, 'Decentralized Finance (DeFi) Projects: A Study of Key Performance Indicators in Terms of DeFi Protocols' Valuations' (2022) 10(108) International Journal of Financial Studies, at 7–8.

as part of the protocol's consensus mechanism, thereby earning staking returns.[49] DeFi products like AAVE bring together numerous virtual assets, and so their economic footprint is the sum of those assets that are committed to the network for the various uses and services the network enables.

TVL is a useful metric for products or services that combine different assets, since it reflects the economic value across all assets that are committed to it, and it is these committed assets that enable the relevant services. Products and services with higher TVL are more likely to be liquid, secure, and by extension, popular among users. Additionally, such products and services most often issue their own virtual asset to enable and facilitate the provision of DeFi services, and that asset has its own supply and market price, and therefore it has its own market capitalization. But the native asset's market capitalization is distinct from the total assets locked in the network which the native asset supports. The native asset's market capitalization can be calculated according to the methodology presented previously. Figure 4.11 shows a comparison between AAVE's TVL and the market capitalization of its native asset (also called AAVE), which are two distinct metrics.

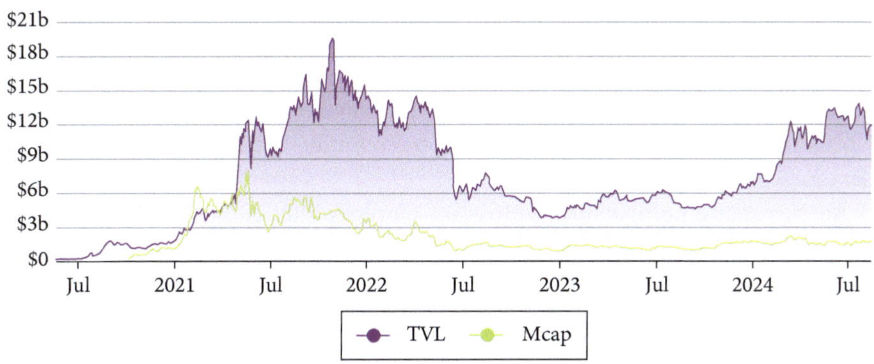

Figure 4.11 AAVE's (the protocol's) total value locked (top line) and AAVE's (the virtual asset's) market capitalization. The AAVE protocol serves a different purpose and is in a different market (DeFi lending) than the AAVE virtual asset (cryptocurrencies), and so their market shares are calculated using different methodologies.
Source: DefiLlama

The TVL is not immune to pitfalls like the ones identified in the calculation of market capitalization. One pitfall relates to the different versions of DeFi protocols wherein assets are locked. For example, Uniswap, a DeFi lending service founded in 2018, is now in version 4.0, but previous versions are still in operation. Not only is the locked value tracked slightly differently from version to version but to measure Uniswap's TVL one would have to take into account all active versions.

49 See <http://aave.com>.

Another complication comes from the rehypothecation of committed assets.[50] Normally, one would expect that when virtual assets are committed to a protocol, they are locked there and unavailable for any other use. However, there exist services that enable the creation of asset derivatives that rehypothecate collateral,[51] which results in duplicate (or more) counting of the same virtual asset value, unless the measurement specifically accounts for the possibility of rehypothecation.

(D) Calculation of mining and staking pool market shares

Mining technically refers to the process of creating new denominations of cryptoassets (eg a Bitcoin).[52] This has come to be seen as synonymous to adding ('finding') new blocks on a blockchain, because in the majority of the most popular cryptocurrencies a denomination of the cryptocurrency is created as reward whenever a new block is added to the respective blockchain. The reward is given in return for users committing the resources necessary to participate in the consensus mechanism that determines which new blocks should be added. This is an incentive mechanism to help the cryptoasset ecosystem run and grow, but it is not strictly necessary for the process of adding new blocks. In fact, it is mostly required when the resources that need to be committed to validating and adding new blocks are significant and would not likely be committed but for this reward,[53] as is the case with PoW cryptoassets.

An increasing number of cryptoassets employs alternative consensus mechanisms to determine which blocks should be added onto their respective blockchains.[54] The most common alternative is the proof of stake (PoS) consensus model, where the resource consumed in the process of adding new blocks can be the temporary escrowing of assets or space, rather than processing power. In PoS systems the reward comes only in the form of fees, as opposed to fees and tokens in PoW systems. As a matter of terminology, in cryptoassets, where finding new blocks does not also result in the creation of additional quantity of cryptoassets,

[50] For the practice of rehypothecation of cryptoassets generally, see Adam Levitin, 'Not Your Keys, Not Your Coins: Unpriced Credit Risk in Cryptocurrency' (2023) 101 Texas Law Review 877, 893–902. See also International Capital Market Association, 'What Is Rehypothecation of Collateral' (2024) at <https://www.icmagroup.org/market-practice-and-regulatory-policy/repo-and-collateral-markets/icma-ercc-publications/frequently-asked-questions-on-repo/10-what-is-rehypothecation-of-collateral/>.

[51] See eg EigenLayer <https://www.eigenlayer.xyz/>.

[52] Arvind Narayanan and others, *Bitcoin and Cryptocurrency Technologies: A Comprehensive Introduction* (Princeton UP 2016) 39; Carol R Goforth, 'The Lawyer's Cryptionary: A Resource for Talking to Clients About Crypto-Transactions' (2019) 41 Campbell Law Review 47, 88.

[53] Narayanan and others (n 52) 38–42. See also Miles Carlsten and others, 'On the Instability of Bitcoin Without the Block Reward' (2016) Proceedings of the 2016 ACM SIGSAC Conference on Computer and Communications Security 154.

[54] Paolo Tasca and Claudio J Tessone, 'A Taxonomy of Blockchain Technologies. Principles of Identification and Classification' (2019) 4 Ledger 1, 7–15.

the actors that perform this function are usually called nodes, validators, stakers, stakeholders, forgers, or other. They are the equivalent of miners in PoW systems.

While in theory, anyone participating in the mining or staking of cryptoassets can stand to profit from the rewards generated as part of the consensus process, in reality it takes large amounts of committed resources for rewards to accrue at an economically reasonable pace. This is because rewards are by and large proportional to the ratio of committed resources to global resources in the system. As a result, individual validators are unlikely to be profitable. To make mining/staking more viable they instead pool their resources together and form mining/staking pools, the purpose of which is to aggregate resources from multiple validators, use them to find new blocks, and then distribute the reward back to participating miners proportionately to the resources they contributed.[55] Pools are therefore a symptom of, and a business solution to, the requirements of the mining process and the expected returns.[56] The same applies to staking pools in the case of cryptoassets that set a staking threshold for participation in staking, which is so high that ordinary cryptoasset holders cannot meet.

i) Output and capacity: hashrate and block count

Output metrics are those that calculate market shares based on an appropriate standardized unit of production.[57] Capacity metrics are those that calculate market shares based on the rate at which resources can be committed to production output.[58] While productive capacity is not normally a common metric, it has become the metric of reference in cryptoasset mining that relies on PoW algorithms, probably due to Bitcoin's popularity, and it is often conflated with output. None is superior, but it is crucial to clarify what they measure and when they should be relied on.

Hashrate and block count. The relevant capacity-based metric for PoW cryptoassets is hashrate. Hashrate expresses the number of hashes per second, where hash is a cryptographic value that miners have to compute in order to find a new block and add it to the blockchain.[59] Finding blocks requires miners to solve a computationally difficult cryptographic problem, which involves trying

55 Narayanan and others (n 52) 124–30. Katalyse, 'Staking Pools—How They Work' *Medium* (8 March 2018). Other examples of pooling include Tezos delegation and the hybrid Decred PoW/PoS pooling system.

56 More accurately, it is a symptom of the fact that mining is probabilistic, which implies that give a certain amount of resources invested in mining the miner can expect proportional returns, but the time and variance of when they will get the return is unknown. Miners can reduce the wait time by pooling together resources thereby increasing the probability they will be among the successful miners sooner.

57 Gregory J Werden, 'Assigning Market Shares' (2002) 70 Antitrust Law Journal 67, 74.

58 ibid 83–85.

59 Antonopoulos (n 34) 228 et seq.

out different hash values until they find the one that fits.[60] Hashrate, therefore, shows the capacity of PoW miners to find new blocks. In PoS cryptoassets, capacity is measured on the basis of the scarce resource they rely on. For example, in Ethereum, the relevant 'stake' is ETH (ie the asset itself), whereas in Filecoin, the relevant stake is memory and storage space.

Comparison and nuances. On the other hand, the actual output of miners/stakers in blockchain networks is expressed in the new blocks they add onto the blockchain. The number of added blocks is usually referred to as *block count*. The more blocks a validator adds to a given blockchain, the larger its market share by output measured by block count.

Both hashrate and block count conceal an important aspect of pools, namely that pools should be thought as aggregators of the output and capacity of individual miners/stakers, and depending on the context it may be required to pierce their veil. This is because individual miners/stakers may control a large percentage within a pool, but also because they may hold large percentages at multiple pools at the same time.[61] In effect, while it could appear that pool capacity and output is distributed across various pools in the market, a large share of it can be concentrated in the hands of a single miner/stalker. The problem evokes the concern around common (or horizontal) ownership, whereby institutional investors own non-controlling stakes in multiple (non-dominant) firms raising fears of coordination among them.[62] The issue is discussed in more detail in section D, but for now suffice it to note that the aggregate hashrate or block count of pools may not necessarily be the correct focal point and instead the investigation should focus on the hashrate or block count of individual undertakings behind it.

Normally, one would prefer to measure market actors by the quantity they actually put out in the market (output), because this is the economic product that is made available for use/consumption, and that for which firms are remunerated by consumers. However, there may be circumstances under which market shares can be assigned on the basis of the ability to produce (capacity), rather than the production itself. This is when firms' relative abilities to produce are congruent with their relative abilities to sell, products are homogeneous, and the production capacity is rated.[63] In cryptoassets, for these conditions to be met the ability of validators to find blocks should be congruent with the blocks they find, blocks

[60] More accurately, miners have to find a nonce that results in a hash which satisfies the computational problem in the target block: Narayanan and others (n 52) 8–10.

[61] Matteo Romiti and others, 'A Deep Dive into Bitcoin Mining Pools: An Empirical Analysis of Mining Shares' (2019) arXiv:1905.05999.

[62] Einer Elhauge, 'Horizontal Shareholding' (2016) 129 Harvard Law Review 1267; Herbert Hovenkamp and Fiona Scott-Morton, 'Horizontal Shareholding and Antitrust Policy' (2018) 127 Yale Law Journal 2026. See contra Edward B Rock and Daniel L Rubinfeld, 'Antitrust for Institutional Investors' (2018) 82 Antitrust Law Journal 221; Menesh S Patel, 'Common Ownership, Institutional Investors, and Antitrust' (2019) 82 Antitrust Law Journal 279; Michael E Sykuta, 'The Case for Doing Nothing About Institutional Investors' Common Ownership of Small Stakes in Competing Firms' (2019) 13 Virginia Law and Business Review 213.

[63] Werden (n 57) 89.

should be undifferentiated, and mining hardware should come with standardized specifications.

While these conditions are commonly met in PoW cryptoassets, it is less common in PoS cryptoassets, where the conditions are relaxed. In PoW cryptoassets, hashrate and block count are by and large almost linearly correlated, because the probability of being the next successful node to add a block to the network is, on long-term average, constantly relative to hashing capacity, as the only way to add new blocks is to try out hash values until one fits,[64] and therefore, the more capacity one commands, the greater the probability of being successful. But in PoS cryptoassets, forging (ie the equivalent term of mining in PoS cryptoassets) is only partially informed by the committed resources. Depending on the implementation, other factors that are independent of the amount of the committed resources also inform the process of the stakeholder selection (eg age of stake), and therefore resources may not fully correlate to the probability of output.[65] As more consensus processes are devised and popularized, further removing output from capacity,[66] it bears keeping in mind that, unless there is a reason to prefer capacity, output is a more direct measurement of economic footprint.

Hashrate and block count are not complete substitutes for each other for additional reasons. They can yield further discrepancies firstly because finding blocks involves an element of luck (even when randomness is not coded into the consensus algorithm), and therefore the correlation between hashing capacity and added blocks is not complete; and secondly because some of the blocks that will be found as a result of the hashing process will not be validated but instead discarded, and therefore some of the hashing power will ultimately not correspond to any actual output. In that sense, block count can be a more accurate measurement of miners' output, albeit only by a small margin.

Moreover, they are not always interchangeable because hashrate is appropriate only for cryptoassets that rely on a PoW algorithm, whereas block count is a relevant metric in other cryptoassets as well (eg those that employ PoS). This is an important point for cross-asset comparisons, especially if a market is defined to include both PoW and PoS cryptoassets. For example, it would provide a meaningful measure of total captured share of the market to say that a stakeholder finds *x* per cent of blocks of a PoW cryptoasset and *y* per cent of blocks of a PoS cryptoasset, if those two cryptoassets are deemed to be in the same market, but it would be impossible to use hashrate because this measure could not encompass the PoS cryptoasset.

[64] Narayanan and others (n 52) 43–44. Blocks may differ in size and the transactions they contain may differ in number and value, but on average they can be thought as undifferentiated, and mining hardware commonly comes with specifications of capacity in hashrate.

[65] Zibin Zheng and others, 'An Overview of Blockchain Technology: Architecture, Consensus, and Future Trends' (2017) 2017 IEEE International Congress on Big Data (BigData Congress) 557.

[66] For an overview of consensus mechanisms, see Shehar Bano and others, 'SoK: Consensus in the Age of Blockchains' (2019) Proceedings of the 1st ACM Conference on Advances in Financial Technologies 183.

That said, hashrate can still be used across cryptoassets that rely on PoW, but caution should be exercised to correctly apportion hashrate figures to cryptoassets in case miners mine concurrently for multiple cryptoassets. A number of mining pools dynamically apportion their hash power to different cryptoassets ('merged mining'), and so one must ascertain how much of the reported capacity is allocated to each cryptoasset.

ii) Revenue and profits

Revenue from blocks and transaction fees. Market share calculation by revenue is common, as revenue shows the portion of the market captured by unit of currency spent by consumers, and therefore takes into account the price of goods, not just the units sold in the market. Revenue is mostly reliable when the price reflects the qualities and attributes of the good and is not the result of monopoly power, subsidies (eg freemium services) or other factors.[67]

In the mining/staking market, revenue can come from two sources: block reward and transaction fees. DLT products and services such as cryptoassets are free to choose whether validators will be compensated through block rewards or transaction fees, or both.[68] In calculating validators' revenue, one should ensure the inclusion of all applicable sources.

Block rewards—common in PoW cryptoassets—are new denominations of cryptoassets that are awarded by the blockchain network to miners for each block they successfully find. When miners find a block, they gain the right to include an extra transaction in the block which is equivalent to the denomination specified by the cryptoasset protocol, and which is made payable to the successful miner (although miners can choose someone else as the recipient of the block reward). For example, as of 2024 the Bitcoin block reward is 3.125 BTC, which means that for every block a miner adds to the Bitcoin blockchain, they earn 3.125 BTC as block reward (it will be halved in 2028).

Transaction fees are fees that are paid by cryptoasset spenders to validators to have a transaction included in a valid block. They are common both in PoW and in PoS cryptoassets and their purpose is to incentivize and reward miners. In most PoS cryptoassets, transaction fees are the only reward, whereas in PoW cryptoassets, they constitute an additional financial incentive toward miners to process transactions as a matter of priority when the network is congested (Figure 4.12).[69] In cryptoassets that issue block rewards, transaction fees tend to constitute a small percentage of the total revenue, but this may not always be the

[67] Werden (n 57) 76–78.
[68] These parameters are specified in the cryptoassets' protocols and whitepapers.
[69] Narayanan and others (n 52) 97–98.

case in the future.[70] For instance, block reward in Bitcoin is halved every 210,000 blocks, which means that as time passes, miners will turn to transaction fees to ensure sufficient compensation.

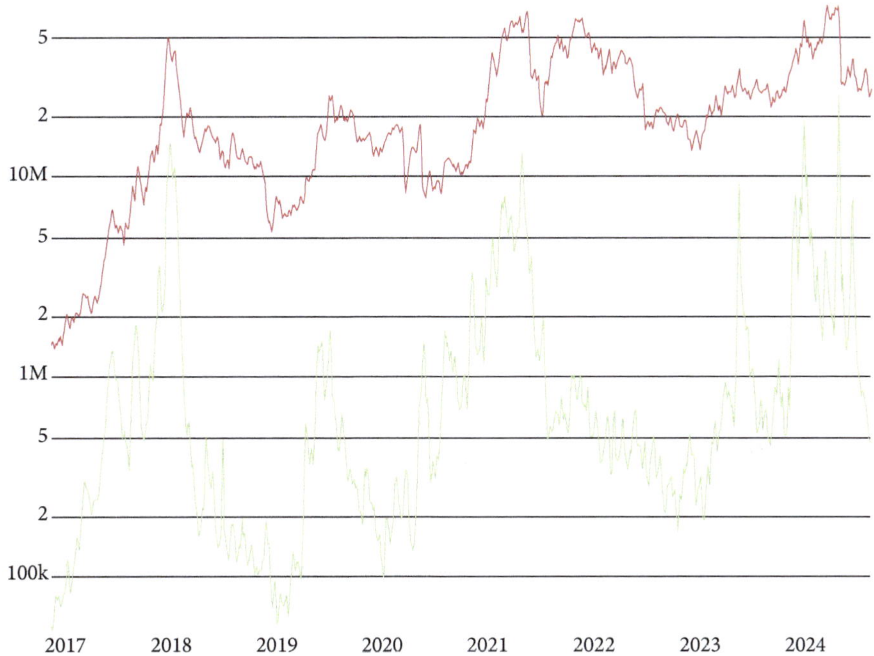

Figure 4.12 Miner revenue (in USD) from transaction fees (bottom line) and total miner revenue including fees and block rewards (top line). Total revenue rises when the native asset appreciates. Transaction fees rise also when the network is congested. Scale is logarithmic.
Source: Coin Metrics

Profits vs revenue. One interesting peculiarity of block rewards and fees as the source of validators' revenue is that neither the block reward size nor the fees are set by validators themselves. Block rewards are specified in the cryptoasset protocol and fees are set by spenders. As a result, the only way to increase revenue—assuming these are the only two sources—is to find more blocks or to process by priority transactions that come with higher fees. The fact that miners cannot use the pricing mechanism (but only output) to adjust revenue may be instructive about *profits* as a relevant metric of economic footprint. Even though profits are not normally considered a relevant metric, because they relate to internal-to-the-firm factors, such as efficiency and cost structure, as well as external-to-the-firm factors, such as taxation, they can sometimes be informative. For example, in 2018,

[70] David Easley, Maureen O'Hara, and Soumya Basu, 'From Mining to Markets: The Evolution of Bitcoin Transaction Fees' (2019) 134 Journal of Financial Economics 91.

Apple's share in the smartphone market was 19 per cent by unit sales (output), yet its market share by revenue was 51 per cent, and its market share by profits was closer to 90 per cent.[71] This means that even though Apple sells fewer smartphones than its competitors, it captures the majority of consumer spending, of which a large share is mark-up. The difference between revenue and profits may be attributable to innocuous factors, like increased efficiency, but it may also be an indication of the ability to price without regard to consumers or competitors, which in turn is an indication of market power.[72] Therefore, to the extent that market share is one of the proxies of market power, any measurement of market share, including by revenue and profit, that can be evidence of business conduct which shows disregard for consumers or competitors should be taken into account.

In the case of validators, since they have no control over the amount of fees, a prima facie conclusion would be that profitability hinges on efficiency and cost-reduction rather than mark-up and therefore it provides no evidence of exercise of market power.[73] However, this may not necessarily be true for collective mining pools, which distribute fees back to individual miners based on internal rules that can be shaped to increase profitability of the pool at the expense of profitability of the individual miners. In that case, sustained high profits that do not correspond to industry standard revenue-to-profit ratio or other innocuous explanations may be indicative of market power in the market for individual miners. An example of how this could happen is larger mining pools introducing higher joining fees during the hashing difficulty adjustment window. During this time, larger pools have an advantage over smaller pools because, with the difficulty adjusted upwards, larger pools are more likely to find blocks, and therefore miners may be more willing to (temporarily) switch to them. This is exacerbated in cryptoassets with less frequent block generation, because the laws of probabilities favour larger players.[74] It may therefore be worth looking at profit market shares as well, especially if there is a theory of market power or abuse of power behind the inquiry.

iii) Validator/miner/staker count

Definition of validator count. Mining and staking pools aggregate validator resources (the collective term to include mining and staking resources) to make the process economically more appealing to validators. In a pool arrangement

[71] Scott Bicheno, 'Apple iPhone: 19% of Shipments, 51% of Revenue, 87% of Profit' *Telecoms* (15 February 2018).

[72] See Hoffmann-La Roche (n 2) para 38; Case 27/76 United Brands Company and United Brands Continentaal BV v Commission ECLI:EU:C:1978:22, para 65.

[73] For a fuller discussion, see Chapter 4 section B.i.

[74] Adem Efe Gencer and others, 'Decentralization in Bitcoin and Ethereum Networks' in Sarah Meiklejohn and Kazue Sako (eds), *Financial Cryptography and Data Security*, vol 10957 (Springer 2018) 451–52.

validators offer their resources (hashing power in PoW cryptoassets; stake in PoS cryptoassets), and the pool offers the service of coordinating and managing the validators.[75] In this market one possible metric of pools' market share is by validator count, that is, the number of miners or stakers that commit their resources to one or more pools. In its most general sense, validator count represents the total number of validators belonging to each pool, but more precise counting may choose to include only active validators (eg validators that have contributed to the pool within a given time frame) or only validators that contribute over a certain threshold of capacity or apply other criteria as appropriate.[76]

Because validators can mine for multiple cryptoassets and multiple pools at the same time, a case of multihoming emerges, which affects the total validator count by which the validator count of a given pool should be divided. For example, in a market of four individual validators and two pools in which all four validators participate in both pools, the total individual validator count should be eight, not four, and the market share of each pool will be 50 per cent, even though each pool has signed up the total population of individual validators. Otherwise, we would end up with the paradox of two monopolists in the same market (both pools having 100 per cent of the total validators count in the same market).

Value and use of validator count as metric. The value of validator count as a metric may not be immediately apparent, since the goal of pools (and therefore their main metric of success in the market) is to aggregate as many resources as possible, regardless of the number of individuals contributing the resources. In that sense, a mining pool of a hundred miners and ten Thash/s (Terrahash/s) of total capacity is a 'bigger' player than a mining pool of a thousand miners and one Thash/s of total capacity. But validator count can become relevant in a number of contexts. For example, a merger between a pool with large capacity and few validators, and a pool with small capacity but many validators, would create a pool with large capacity and many validators. Depending on the market structure, this may be problematic, and yet it would not be captured in an assessment of the market share of the merging pools if we looked only at one metric (either capacity or validator count).

Moreover, validator count shows how many economic actors in a market are involved and/or affected, regardless of their size or importance. For some policy areas the number of individual independent actors in a market matters. For example, it can be linked to concentration rates. In the hypothetical example in Table 4.1, if we only look at the industry's capacity concentration rate based on number of mining pools the Herfindahl–Hirschman Index (HHI) is 3350 (high), whereas if we look at it based on individual miners it falls to 1395 (low). Whether it is more appropriate to calculate concentration rates based on pools or individual

[75] See n 52.

[76] Similar classifications of users (active users, unique users, total users) have been used in past cases, see eg Microsoft/Skype (n 17).

Table 4.1 An example of concentration rates measured by mining pool and by individual miners (capacity held constant). The basis of the calculation results in significantly different HHI figures.

Mining pool	Mining pool capacity	Number of miners in mining pool	Individual miner capacity
A	50 Ghash/s	2	25 Ghash/s
B	20 Ghash/s	4	5 Ghash/s
C	15 Ghash/s	10	1.5 Ghash/s
D	15 Ghash/s	10	1.5 Ghash/s
	HHI on pool basis 3350		HHI on miner basis 1395

validators depends on the purpose of each particular investigation, but it is worth noting that pools are not self-contained black boxes, but rather comprise individual potentially independent actors.

(E) Calculation of crypto-exchange and trading platform market shares

Crypto-exchanges are entities that enable trading between cryptocurrencies or between cryptocurrencies and fiat currencies or between other financial instruments as well (eg crypto-derivatives).[77] They also commonly incorporate a wallet function and thereby facilitate the transfer of cryptoassets between users. While the operation of crypto-exchanges resembles that of traditional exchanges, there are key differences that warrant caution as to how to properly perform market share analysis on crypto-exchanges.

Unlike traditional exchanges, which normally trade stocks or commodities, crypto-exchanges mostly trade currency pairs. This is peculiar, because fiat currencies are traded, for the most part, on a centralized global foreign exchange market, whereas cryptocurrency pairs and cryptocurrency-to-fiat currency pairs are traded on any number of crypto-exchanges, each with its own exchange rate.[78] Moreover, trading on traditional exchanges is performed by authorized intermediaries, whereas crypto-exchanges directly interface with end users. Lastly,

[77] Narayanan and others (n 52) 88–89; Xin Li and Chong Alex Wang, 'The Technology and Economic Determinants of Cryptocurrency Exchange Rates: The Case of Bitcoin' (2017) 95 Decision Support Systems 49, 50–51. Crypto derivatives exchanges are beginning to emerge, see eg Christine Kim, 'Markets Tech Firm to Launch Crypto Derivatives Exchange' *CoinDesk* (6 August 2018).

[78] On the determinants of exchange rates see Li and Wang, ibid.

exchanges are heavily regulated, whereas crypto-exchanges still operate largely unregulated, despite recent activity in that direction.[79] Taken together, these differences inform the relevance of applicable metrics and cast into doubt the reliability of some metrics, which may affect their influence on market share calculation.

Inapplicability of market capitalization and number of listed cryptoassets. Exchanges are characterized by a number of metrics. Some common metrics used for traditional exchanges seem unhelpful in the case of crypto-exchanges but are still worth mentioning. One is market capitalization. On traditional exchanges, market capitalization is the total number of issued shares of listed companies multiplied by their respective prices at a given time. For the vast majority of crypto-exchanges, there is no equivalent metric, since they do not list stocks or equivalent financial instruments. To say that the equivalent could be the aggregate market capitalization of their listed cryptocurrencies is also not quite the same, because unlike stocks, cryptocurrencies are traded on multiple crypto-exchanges and are therefore not associated with a single one; they can be created on demand; and there are no rules on which exchange they can be listed on (other than the rules drafted up by the crypto-exchanges themselves). Therefore, the aggregate market capitalization of listed cryptocurrencies may at first glance reflect a useful financial measure of size, but it is easy to manipulate.

The second one is the number of listed companies. Exchanges are sometimes ranked by the number of companies whose shares are traded on their platform, the idea being that the more the listed companies, the greater the economic importance of the exchange, everything else equal. The equivalent in crypto-exchanges could be the number of listed currency trading pairs (eg BTC–ETH), but this also does not correspond to any meaningful measurement, since trading pairs can be created arbitrarily on demand, and since they relate more to the scope of offered services, rather than the market size of a crypto-exchange.

Instead, trading volume, trade count, and trader count are more useful metrics for calculation of crypto-exchange market shares.

i) Trading volume

In exchange markets, trading volume is a common and influential metric.[80] It represents the total value of the assets traded on an exchange at a given time. The volume of stock trading, for example, is the total number of shares traded multiplied by their respective matching prices. Volume is relevant in market share

[79] See eg Securities and Exchange Commission, 'Statement on Potentially Unlawful Online Platforms for Trading Digital Assets' (7 March 2018). Antonio Brasse and Samuel Hyun, 'Cryptocurrency Exchanges and the Future of Cryptoassets' in H Kent Baker and others (eds), *The Emerald Handbook on Cryptoassets: Investment Opportunities and Challenges* (Emerald Publishing 2023).

[80] See eg Deutsche Boerse/NYSE Euronext (n 19).

calculation because the role of the exchange market is to enable the trading of assets, and volume shows what part of the total traded (exchanged) asset value is taking place on a given exchange. The equivalent in crypto-exchanges would be the aggregate value of all currency pair trades on a crypto-exchange at a given time, usually converted to US dollars as the common numeraire. Most crypto-exchanges advertise their traded volume, and most crypto-exchange rankings use volume as the main parameter to rank exchanges by market share.[81]

While volume is a useful metric, its measurement in the context of crypto-exchanges must be approached with caution. Crypto-exchanges are only lightly regulated, meaning that the reported volumes can be misleading, and the listed transactions manipulated (Table 4.2).[82] They can be misleading because crypto-exchange trading activity is only partly recorded on the blockchain, where anyone can see and validate transactions; the majority of transactions are consolidated internally and therefore the related reported volume depends on the veracity of the crypto-exchange.[83] For example, when a user wants to trade BTC for ETH on a crypto-exchange, the crypto-exchange updates the user's wallet with the new balances and records the transaction internally. The aggregate volume it reports is self-calculated and can be false. The incentive to lie is obvious: large trading volumes are usually associated with high liquidity and low spread, both of which are appealing to users.

Table 4.2 Reported transaction volume vs adjusted transaction volume (daily values in USD) based on data from Cryptorank (31 October 2024). Notice that reputable crypto-exchanges, such as Coinbase, do not misrepresent their volumes, while others report volumes multiple times larger than real volumes.

Crypto-exchange	Reported daily volume	Adjusted daily volume	Difference	Reputable
Coinbase	$2.3 bn	$2.3 bn	0%	Yes
Binance	$14.5 bn	$13.5 bn	7%	Yes
Poloniex	$542 m	$189 m	65%	No
Bithumb	$943 m	$301 m	68%	No

Source: Cryptorank

[81] See eg CoinMarketCap, 'Top Cryptocurrency Spot Exchanges' at <https://coinmarketcap.com/rankings/exchanges/>.

[82] Jialan Chen, Dan Lin, and Jiajing Wu, 'Do Cryptocurrency Exchanges Fake Trading Volumes? An Empirical Analysis of Wash Trading Based on Data Mining' (2022) 586 Physica A: Statistical Mechanics and its Applications 126405; Luke Vargas, 'Most Crypto Trading Volume May Be Fake, Study Says' Wall Street Journal (24 July 2023).

[83] Narayanan and others (n 52) 87.

Common techniques of manipulation include wash trading, where an investor simultaneously sells and buys the same financial instruments to create artificial activity on an exchange,[84] and 'painting the tape', where investors buy and sell among themselves to create the appearance of substantial trading activity.[85] Both practices are prohibited on traditional regulated exchanges, but inconsistently regulated on crypto-exchanges, thusly allowing fake volume reporting. To determine the credibility of self-reported volume data, investigations look at factors such as the ratio of visitors to declared volume relative to other exchanges (larger volume-per-user ratios can be suspect),[86] the patterns of trading volume (regular patterns can be suspect),[87] the effect of a transaction on the price of the traded currencies (big impact can be suspect),[88] the intra-exchange velocity (higher relative velocity can be suspect),[89] the level of activity and community engagement (low activity and engagement relative to claimed volume can be suspect),[90] and others (see eg Figure 4.13).

Given the state of the crypto-exchange market, there are a number of methods that investigators can employ to improve the reliability of volume metrics. One approach is to attempt to filter out suspect results. This approach requires intricate familiarity with the crypto-exchange market and perhaps arbitrary decisions—however it should fall within the capabilities of an antitrust investigator, and in any case adjusted volumes are also calculated by crypto-data analytics companies. A different way would be to calculate the average values from all available sources, after excluding high and low extremes, under the presumption that any tainted inputs will equally affect the market share of all actors. Lastly, investigators can choose to rely on meta-rankings, which employ methodologies that take into account a number of factors, both quantitative, such as volume, but also qualitative, such as reputation and activity tracking, and user base engagement.[91]

ii) Trade count

Another common metric that applies to many financial intermediaries, including exchanges, is the number of trades (:transactions) that are performed on their platform at a given time (only one side of the transaction is counted). In the context

84 Hacken (n 46).
85 Kenton (n 46).
86 Hacken (n 46).
87 ibid.
88 Sylvain Ribes, 'Chasing Fake Volume: A Crypto-Plague' *Medium* (10 March 2018).
89 Louis Baudoin, 'Further Hints of Fake Volume on Major Cryptocurrency Exchanges' LinkedIn (14 September 2018).
90 CCData, 'Exchange Benchmark Report' (2024).
91 ibid.

Trade History

Trade Size	Price (USD)	Time
0.0501	3419.60 ↗	16:48:18
0.0140	3419.60 ↗	16:48:15
0.1212	3419.59 ↘	16:48:13
0.0082	3419.60 ↗	16:48:05
0.0280	3419.60 ↗	16:48:02
0.1153	3419.60 ↗	16:48:02
0.0294	3419.60 ↗	16:47:57
0.1469	3419.60 ↗	16:47:53
0.0280	3419.60 ↗	16:47:51
0.0325	3418.94 ↘	16:47:43
0.0255	3419.42 ↘	16:47:43
0.0761	3419.60 ↗	16:47:41
0.0140	3419.60 ↗	16:47:41
0.0175	3419.60 ↗	16:47:40
0.0280	3419.71 ↗	16:47:36
0.0280	3419.72 ↗	16:47:33
0.5735	3421.42 ↗	16:47:30
0.2868	3421.42 ↗	16:47:30
0.0667	3420.12 ↘	16:47:28
0.8057	3421.62 ↗	16:47:27
1.0000	3421.16 ↗	16:47:22
0.8170	3421.14 ↗	16:47:27
0.6000	3421.14 ↗	16:47:25
0.0040	3420.24 ↗	16:47:25
0.4634	3420.23 ↘	16:47:24
0.0560	3418.95 ↗	16:47:23
0.0840	3418.95 ↗	16:47:19
0.0265	3418.94 ↘	16:47:18
0.0800	3418.94 ↘	16:47:18
0.0848	3418.95 ↗	16:47:12
0.0072	3441.57 ↗	13:14:34
0.1062	3441.57 ↗	13:14:30
0.0150	3441.57 ↗	13:14:30
0.2002	3441.57 ↗	13:14:22
0.0200	3441.48 ↗	13:14:22
0.0080	3441.21 ↗	13:14:22
0.1000	3441.01 ↗	13:14:22
0.2489	3441.00 ↗	13:14:22
0.4201	3440.88 ↗	13:14:22
0.0236	3440.88 ↗	13:14:15
0.0425	3440.87 ↗	13:14:14
0.1237	3440.87 ↗	13:14:13
0.0068	3440.87 ↗	13:14:13
0.0026	3440.87 ↗	13:14:12

Market Trades

Price(USDT)	Quantity(BTC)	Date
3271.27	0.4909	08:56:07
3271.27	0.4344	08:56:07
3271.27	0.5479	08:56:07
3271.27	0.4849	08:56:07
3271.33	0.8312	08:56:02
3271.33	0.7354	08:56:02
3271.33	0.8571	08:56:02
3271.33	0.7584	08:56:02
3271.33	0.9561	08:56:02
3271.33	0.8460	08:56:02
3273.28	2.5530	08:55:57
3273.28	2.2592	08:55:57
3273.28	2.9269	08:55:57
3273.28	2.5901	08:55:57
3273.36	1.2443	08:55:54
3273.36	1.1011	08:55:54
3273.36	1.0903	08:55:54
3273.36	0.9647	08:55:54
3273.36	1.2433	08:55:54
3273.36	1.1002	08:55:54
3273.99	0.7277	08:55:48
3273.99	0.6439	08:55:48
3273.99	0.6985	08:55:48
3273.99	0.6181	08:55:48
3271.38	0.5395	08:55:41
3271.38	0.4773	08:55:41
3271.38	0.6154	08:55:41
3271.38	0.5445	08:55:41
3268.97	1.5261	08:55:36
3268.97	1.3505	08:55:36

Figure 4.13 A side-by-side comparison of two crypto-exchanges, Coinbase on the left and Coinbene on the right. Coinbene is suspected of volume manipulation. Notice the regularity in Coinbene's price and time of trades compared to the more random values recorded on Coinbase.

of crypto-exchanges, this metric represents the total number of trades between cryptocurrencies and between cryptocurrencies and fiat currencies.

The number of trades as a metric for market share calculation shows how widely or frequently an exchange is used, regardless of the size of the transactions that take place on its platform. While normally not the most influential measure, trade count can provide insights into the nature and character of an exchange, which in turn can inform antitrust analysis. For example, an exchange that exhibits low transaction volume but high trade count is likely to be one that is preferred by smaller investors. This characteristic can be relevant in (anti-)concentration policy, where authorities have an interest to protect the market not only from concentration in terms of numbers, but from the exit of firms that have unique features or uniquely serve a certain part of the market (in this example small retail investors).[92]

Trade count suffers the same weakness as trading volume, namely that in the lightly regulated environment of crypto-exchanges, transactions can be easily fabricated and the numbers reported by crypto-exchanges can be misleading. Reports of crypto-exchanges employing bots that place buy-sell orders to artificially inflate the number of transactions are proliferating making trade count an unreliable metric.[93]

iii) Trader count

One less common metric of exchange activity is the number of trading participants, which represents the individuals who trade on an exchange through direct access to the trading platform.[94] Traditionally, this metric has not been indicative of exchanges' economic significance because it only measured the number of intermediaries that enable trading on the exchange, rather than end customers (investors) and the exchanges' economic footprint on the market. Limited exceptions, whereby private investors can directly trade on an exchange,[95] do not significantly change the utility of the metric.

However, the trading participant metric has greater value in the context of crypto-exchanges, because on crypto-exchanges users trade directly rather than

[92] An example of how firms' unique characteristics other than mere market size are taken into account in M&A can be found in the abandoned AT&T/T-Mobile merger, where the US Department of Justice expressed reluctance to allow AT&T to absorb T-Mobile, because T-Mobile was known as a small but disruptive player in the market. See *US DoJ v. AT&T* and *Deutsche Telecom*, 1:11-cv-01560 (31August 2011), at 12 et seq.

[93] Timothi Tam Coinfi, 'How Bots Are Manipulating Cryptocurrency Prices' *VentureBeat* (14 December 2017).

[94] For instance, CoinMarketCap reports weekly visits. Since anyone can be a trader, a visit to the exchange is a visit by a potential trader. See CoinMarketCap, 'Top Cryptocurrency Spot Exchanges' at <https://coinmarketcap.com/rankings/exchanges/>.

[95] London Stock Exchange, 'Direct Market Access' at<https://www.londonstockexchange.com/personal-investing/tools/direct-market-access>.

through brokers. In that sense, trading participant count shows the installed base of a crypto-exchange platform. It is not uncommon to use the number of users as an important metric in online platform markets as it is indicative of market adoption, especially if users are considered a homogeneous pool.[96]

The difficulty arises in terms of how to measure traders on crypto-exchanges. A simple approach would be to rely on the self-reported figures provided by the crypto-exchanges themselves. For instance, in its initial public offering prospectus submitted to the Securities and Exchange Commission (SEC), Coinbase reported over 43 million users.[97] However, not all crypto-exchanges report their user statistics, and even when they do, reliability concerns of the sort described previously remain.

Alternatively, and considering that blockchain transactions in permissionless blockchains are public, one would want to be able to infer the number of crypto-exchange users by looking into blockchain transactions and associating them with exchanges. This presents a number of difficulties. Firstly, it is most common that crypto-exchanges process transactions internally and then settle and post aggregate transactions on the blockchain, from which it is hard, if not impossible, to disentangle the individual transactions—and by extension the users behind them—that took place on the crypto-exchanges' platforms.[98]

Secondly, the parameter that is measurable in publicly posted transactions is the public key (address) with which transactions are signed. However, there is no one-to-one mapping between users as persons, user accounts, wallets, and keys. A user can have multiple accounts, each account may hold multiple wallets, and each wallet may hold multiple keys, or conversely, a number of users may be sharing an account, a wallet, or a key. As a result, it is impossible to calculate with accuracy the actual economic actors on any given crypto-exchange (a problem that in fairness is common on all online platforms).

Thirdly, a meaningful use of relative sizes would require knowing the total size of the market, that is, the total number of users, as well. While it is easier to calculate the total number of blockchain users, since no association with specific exchanges is needed, the mapping problem persists and not all of the addresses are economically relevant, meaning that they are used for transactions between two individuals and not simply as intermediate facilitators. Research has shown that

[96] For example, when Github was acquired by Microsoft, Github's market positioning was measured by the number of users (programmers) on its platform. See 'Microsoft to Acquire GitHub for $7.5 Billion' (Microsoft News Center, 4 June, 2018).

[97] Coinbase Global, Inc. Form S-1 Registration Statement under the Securities Act of 1933 (25 February 2021) at 2.

[98] Ivan da Silva Sendin, 'On Detecting Cold Storage Transactions on Bitcoin's Blockchain' (2018) Anais do XVIII Simpósio Brasileiro de Segurança da Informação e de Sistemas Computacionais 155.

there are 'about 460 million [Bitcoin addresses] as of December 2018. . . . [of these,] 172 million are economically relevant—they are controlled by people or services who currently own bitcoin. Of these, only 27 million actually hold bitcoin.'[99] Other estimates place the total number of addresses at around 35 million.[100] Services that attempt to work through these difficulties exist,[101] but their results are limited by what they can observe and extrapolate from there.[102]

[99] Chainalysis, 'Mapping the Universe of Bitcoin's 460 Million Addresses' (*Chainalysis Blog*, 7 February 2019), https://www.chainalysis.com/blog/bitcoin-addresses/.

[100] Michel Rauchs and others, 'Second Global Cryptoasset Benchmarking Study' (Cambridge Centre for Alternative Finance 2018).

[101] See eg Wallet Explorer at <http://www.walletexplorer.com>.

[102] For example, Wallet Explorer uses a common technique to better associate addresses (public keys) with wallets, by combining different addresses under the same wallet if they are spent in the same transaction. But on limitations see Sendin (n 98).

5
MARKET POWER

(A) **General** 115
(B) **Types of market power** 117
  i) Power over price: Mining/staking fees and cryptoasset price manipulation 117
    a) Definition and use 117
    b) Transaction fees and mining fees and rewards as price 118
    c) Mining and staking fees charged by pools as price 119
    d) Cryptoasset price manipulation 120
  ii) Power to exclude: Exclusion through delisting, governance, oversupply 123
    a) Definition and use 123
    b) Conventional exclusion in crypto markets 124
    c) Exclusion through governance 125
    d) Exclusion through oversupply 126
  iii) Architectural power: Controlling governance and monetization 126
    a) Definition and distinction from power over price and exclusionary power 126
    b) Expressions of architectural power: coercion, dependency, soft power 129
    c) Architectural power in the metaverse 130
  iv) Engagement power: exploitation and exclusion due to 'stickiness' 131
    a) Definition and use 131
    b) Engagement power vs power in aftermarkets 133
(C) **Factors limiting market power** 134
  i) Forking 134
  ii) DLT interoperability 135
  iii) Design and governance choices 137
  iv) Token effects and bootstrapping new DLT networks 140

(A) General

Market power is a fundamental concept in antitrust law since it serves as a virtually universal requirement for competition law to engage. Whether in the form of prohibiting monopolization and abuse of a dominant position, outlawing anticompetitive agreements, or controlling mergers, antitrust law by and large only challenges undertakings that enjoy an elevated degree of market power (usually in a defined market).[1] Understanding market power, therefore, becomes essential in applying competition law. Because the decentralized economy encompasses novel actors

[1] Eleanor M Fox, 'The Battle for the Soul of Antitrust' (1987) 75 California Law Review 917.

Antitrust in the Decentralized Economy. Konstantinos Stylianou, Oxford University Press.
 DOI: 10.1093/9780191925504.003.0005

and business practices, both the types of market power that one can encounter, and the factors that augment or limit market power merit special consideration.

The traditional conceptions of market power include power over price and the power to exclude competitors,[2] and in more general terms in EU case law, 'the power to behave to an appreciable extent independently of [an undertaking's] competitors, its customers and ultimately of consumers'.[3] Both power over price and power to exclude remain relevant in the decentralized economy, since price and the pricing mechanism still play an important role in the decentralized economy, and the exclusion of competitors undermines the competitive process as much in the decentralized economy as it does in conventional markets. But to those, one should add architectural power and engagement power. Architectural power emerges due to economic activity in the decentralized economy often assuming the form of ecosystem, and expresses an undertaking's ability to shape the market around it, whereas engagement power stems from the social production nature of the decentralized the economy, and it reflects the ability to attract and lock in the market's productive resources by exploiting stickiness, stickiness being the persistent behaviour even though the actor has choice.[4]

The type of market power does not change its legal treatment. But, to the extent that it is a condition to find anticompetitive conduct (unless direct evidence exists), the type of market power undertakings hold in any given investigation informs how competition authorities can meet their legal burden of proof of satisfying that condition. In other words, the choice of market power type indicates what is required to establish it.

In establishing market power, authorities will look at factors that enable it on the one hand, or limit it on the other, and attempt to reach a conclusion on balance. In Chapter 4, large market shares were discussed as indicating market power. In Chapter 6, high barriers to entry and expansion are discussed as another factor that promotes market power. This chapter, after introducing types of market power at play in the decentralized economy, discusses limitations of market power, which include forking, interoperability, design and governance choices, token effects, and bootstrapping of new Distributed Ledger Technology (DLT) networks.[5] The reader is advised to read this chapter in conjunction with Chapters 4 and 6 to gain the full picture of market power in the decentralized economy.

[2] *Ohio v. American Express Co.*, 585 U.S. 529, 549 (2018) ('Market power is the ability to raise price profitably by restricting output'); *United States v. E. I. du Pont de Nemours & Co.*, 351 U.S. 377, 391 (1956).

[3] United Brands Company and United Brands Continentaal BV v Commission ECLI:EU:C:1978:22, para 65; Case C-85/76 Hoffmann-La Roche & Co AG v Commission ECLI:EU:C:1979:36, para 38.

[4] See sections B.iii and B.iv, respectively.

[5] See section C.

(B) Types of market power

i) Power over price: Mining/staking fees and cryptoasset price manipulation

a) Definition and use

The paradigmatic expression of market power is power over price.[6] In its most basic form, this economic definition of market power expresses the ability to set price above marginal cost.[7] Since under perfect competition price equals marginal cost, the ability to price above that threshold signifies that the firm does not face perfect competition and therefore wields at least some market power. Evidently, market power is a matter of degree. A miniscule degree of market power would not be of concern to competition authorities, even though, technically, it fulfils the above definition. On the other end of the spectrum, the ability of a monopolist to price at the point on their demand curve where marginal cost equals marginal revenue, expresses complete market power. The degree of market power between those extremes is formalized in the Lerner index, which measures the proportional deviation of price at the firm's profit-maximizing output from the firm's marginal cost at that output.[8]

Construing market power as power over price can be an elegant approach but it comes with numerous limitations. It is elegant because, in theory, it is quantifiable (and therefore precise), and because price is a synthetic parameter that encapsulates a product's features, production costs, and supply and demand conditions. As a result, power over price can signal power over an essential aspect of competition in the market. However, the calculation of the Lerner index requires knowledge of marginal costs, a notoriously elusive metric, which renders the index ultimately impractical.[9] Moreover, even if marginal costs were known and the Lerner index could be calculated, one would still need to somehow determine an acceptable competitive price level against which the challenged price level would be compared—also an elusive task.[10] Additionally, the focus on price may disregard

[6] See n 2; European Commission Guidelines Guidance on the Commission's enforcement priorities in applying Article 82 of the EC Treaty to abusive exclusionary conduct by dominant undertakings (2009/C 45/02), para 10.

[7] William Landes and Richard Posner, 'Market Power in Antitrust Cases' (1981) 94 Harvard Law Review 937, 939. For a slightly different definition but in the same direction see *American Tobacco Co. v. United States*, 328 U.S. 781, 782 (1946) ('the material consideration in determining whether a monopoly exists is not that prices are raised and that competition actually is excluded, but that power exists to raise prices or to exclude competition when it is desired to do so').

[8] AP Lerner, 'The Concept of Monopoly and the Measurement of Monopoly Power' (1934) 1 The Review of Economic Studies 157.

[9] See Kenneth G Elzinga and David E Mills, 'The Lerner Index of Monopoly Power: Origins and Uses' (2011) 101 American Economic Review 558.

[10] Damien Geradin and others, 'The Concept of Dominance in EC Competition Law' (2005) SSRN 5.

other important elements of the competitive process, such as quality, variety, and innovation.[11] Lastly, not all products and services have a price tag making the power-over-price approach in those cases irrelevant. The proxy of price could be replaced by a different one—for example quality, where power could be expressed by how much a producer can reduce the quality of a product without losing so many customers as to make the reduction economically irrational[12]—but such solutions are deprived of the benefits that relying on price come with, namely that power over price is quantifiable and that price is a key composite parameter.

Those weaknesses notwithstanding, power over price continues to be monitored by competition authorities particularly in economic segments where products and services are homogeneous and therefore price mark-ups can more straightforwardly be linked to market power. In DLT markets, such economic segments are common either because they are integral to DLT technology (eg mining and staking), or because the identity of products and services is largely determined by their price (eg cryptoassets).

b) Transaction fees and mining fees and rewards as price

One of the first areas where power over price in DLT markets was studied was the ability of miners to charge supracompetitive fees for processing (ie validating and appending) transactions. For standard assumptions around how mining works, miners are unlikely to be able to exercise power over fees. Miners receive compensation in two forms, firstly block rewards, and secondly fees that transacting parties pay for prioritized processing of their transaction when the network is congested.[13] The more congested the network, the higher the incentive for transacting parties to pay fees. While miners cannot themselves set the level of fees (these are set by the transacting parties), they have an incentive to ignore transactions with low or no fees to induce transacting parties to pay higher fees. However, under conditions of free entry, this strategy is not profitable, because there will always be miners who are willing to process transactions with lower fees, as long as they can break even.[14] Whether miners break even depends on transaction fees, electricity costs, and the market price of the native mined asset.[15] It makes no economic sense to leave mining capacity idle and transactions unprocessed when the fees and rewards can still cover costs. As a result, the existence of miners willing to capture even small

[11] Commission Guidelines on the Application of Article 81(3) of the Treaty 2004/C 101/08, para 25.

[12] See Chapter 3 section C.i.

[13] Arvind Narayanan and others, *Bitcoin and Cryptocurrency Technologies: A Comprehensive Introduction* (Princeton UP 2016) 62–3.

[14] Gur Huberman, Jacob D Leshno, and Ciamac Moallemi, 'Monopoly without a Monopolist: An Economic Analysis of the Bitcoin Payment System' (2021) 88 The Review of Economic Studies 3011.

[15] Enrico Tedeschi and others, 'Mining Profitability in Bitcoin: Calculations of User-Miner Equilibria and Cost of Mining' in Rolando Martins and Mennan Selimi (eds), *Distributed Applications and Interoperable Systems*, vol 14677 (Springer Nature 2024).

profits will always drive fees down to competitive levels. This result holds even if incumbent miners collude, because entry of new miners who do not participate in the collusive arrangement and are willing to capture even small profits will again drive fees down.[16] It is evident that free entry is a key prerequisite. Under the assumption that mining profits are linearly correlated with mining power,[17] miner entry is a realistic assumption.[18] This is because miner costs are correlated with mining difficulty, and if difficulty increases to unprofitable levels for some miners, they will exit the market, thereby dropping the total hashing power, which will in turn drive difficulty back down, allowing and causing new miners to enter at a lower cost.

c) Mining and staking fees charged by pools as price

The mining fees as a reward for the mining process discussed above are distinct from the fees mining pools themselves charge to their members. Because the required resources to profitably mine are immense, individual miners are unlikely to be able to compete on their own and opt to combine their resources into mining pools.[19] For this 'risk-sharing' service,[20] mining pools charge a fee. Everything else equal, larger pools provide greater risk-sharing and can therefore charge higher fees.[21] Taken to its logical conclusion this trend would result in a monopolistic pool, which could exercise monopoly power over its members' fees. However, because miners can obtain the same risk-sharing benefits by spreading their resources across multiple pools instead of only just one, this concentration trend is undercut.[22] The trend is also exhausted at the point where the mining pool fee exceeds the risk-sharing benefit, and so there is an upper limit to how much a mining pool can charge.[23]

Similar results can be obtained for staking pools. Staking pools function similarly to mining pools, the difference being that the committed resource in staking

[16] Huberman, Leshno, and Moallemi (n 14).

[17] See R Bowden and others, 'Block Arrivals in the Bitcoin Blockchain' (2018) arxiv.1801.07447.

[18] Julien Prat and Benjamin Walter, 'An Equilibrium Model of the Market for Bitcoin Mining' (2021) 129 Journal of Political Economy 2415.

[19] Narayanan and others (n 13) 124–30.

[20] The term 'risk-sharing' used in the literature may be a misnomer. Because the likelihood of being the next successful miner to append a block is proportional to the committed computing power, any measure of committed computing power will eventually mine a block and reap the associated reward. However, for most individual miners the waiting time for this to happen is uneconomically long. Joining a mining pool ensures that miners get more frequent (but smaller) rewards, but it does not increase their chances based on their committed resources. Therefore, joining a mining pool affects the 'when' one gets their reward, not the 'if' and in that sense, mining pools do not technically reduce the risk of not getting one's reward.

[21] Lin William Cong, Zhiguo He, and Jiasun Li, 'Decentralized Mining in Centralized Pools' (2021) 34 The Review of Financial Studies 1191.

[22] ibid.

[23] Natkamon Tovanich and others, 'The Evolution of Mining Pools and Miners' Behaviors in the Bitcoin Blockchain' (2022) 19 IEEE Transactions on Network and Service Management 3633, 3641.

pool is most commonly a cryptoasset,[24] whereas in mining pools it is computing power. Because cryptoassets can be invested elsewhere outside of staking pools, staking them incurs an opportunity cost in the form of the yield of the alternative investment opportunities. Also, similarly to mining pools, as the total amount of committed resources (ie staked cryptoassets) increases in a blockchain network, so does the difficulty rate, and so does in turn the amount one needs to stake to become successful and reap rewards. This concomitantly increases the opportunity cost. Therefore, staking entities have an incentive to combine their resources leading to pool centralization and, in turn, higher market power of the resulting pool.[25] But at the same time, the exogenous opportunity cost serves an upper limit of profitable centralization.

d) Cryptoasset price manipulation

Power over price becomes even more relevant when the price is virtually synonymous with the underlying product or service, as is the case with cryptoassets. Cryptoasset prices reflect the market valuation of the cryptoasset's fundamentals, that is, its inherent value as determined by how the market (supply and demand) assesses it, but also by external factors, such as price manipulation.[26] Price manipulation is a common concern in financial markets, and while it is mainly dealt with by financial markets regulators, it also touches on competition law.[27] At the core of price manipulation practices that invite antitrust scrutiny is the economic power of the actor engaging in it. Classic schemes of 'long' manipulation, such as Accumulation-Lift-Distribution (ALD),[28] highlight the role of economic power over price. In ALD an actor with 'access to a relatively large amount of wealth' accumulates shares at a reasonably low price to 'build a dominant concentration of shares', while at the same time driving up prices, and once the accumulation has been complete and the manipulator controls supply, the manipulator starts slowly distributing the shares at the increased price and at a rate that does not cause other investors to sell their shares and cause a price collapse.[29] Similar schemes, where

[24] Disk space is another, less common staking resource. See eg Stefan Dziembowski and others, 'Proofs of Space' in Rosario Gennaro and Matthew Robshaw (eds), *Advances in Cryptology - Crypto 2015*, vol 9216 (Springer 2015).

[25] Ping He, Dunzhe Tang, and Jingwen Wang, 'Stake Centralization in Decentralized Proof-of-Stake Blockchain Network' (2020) SSRN.

[26] Bruno Biais and others, 'Equilibrium Bitcoin Pricing' (2023) 78 The Journal of Finance 967.

[27] See eg *In re Tether and Bitfinex Cryptoasset Litigation*, 1:19-cv-09236-KPF (2021) (*In re Tether and Bitfinex*), where the issue was the manipulation of the crypto-commodities market enabled by monopolization in the stablecoin market. See also *Pollock v. Citrus Associates of N.Y. Cotton Exchange*, 512 F.Supp. 711, 717 (1981) ('In sum, the legislative history of the CFTCA indicates that Congress intended that antitrust claims be allowed against brokers and traders operating in the commodity futures markets').

[28] Rajesh K Aggarwal and Guojun Wu, 'Stock Market Manipulation – Theory and Evidence' (2003) SSRN.

[29] Lawrence Robert Klein, Viktoria Dalko, and Michael H Wang (eds), *Regulating Competition in Stock Markets: Antitrust Measures to Promote Fairness and Transparency through Investor Protection and Crisis Prevention* (Wiley 2012) 71–72.

the price is artificially driven up, such that the manipulator can capture the margin between the artificial price and the price level that the market would otherwise set, have also been common in cryptoasset markets.[30] So-called 'pump and dump' schemes have afflicted various cryptocurrencies, including at some point even Bitcoin,[31] exploiting in particular the lacuna in financial regulation which could have otherwise prevented or minimized their occurrence and effect.

Admittedly, competition law may not be the most well-adapted tool to combat anti-competitive price-related power in cryptoasset markets, but this should not automatically rule out its application,[32] and at least provisionally price manipulation has been found to constitute antitrust harm in cryptoasset markets too.[33] One difficulty is the definition of the relevant market, and the assessment of power over the defined market. A single cryptoasset targeted for manipulation is not necessarily an antitrust market of its own, and power over a single cryptoasset does not necessarily mean market power.[34] If more than one cryptoasset is targeted, then the market is easier to define because the group of cryptoassets can collectively constitute a segment of the assets market: in *Bitfinex*, the argument was that the monopolization of the stablecoin market allowed Tether to monopolize the crypto-commodities market; while not all crypto-commodities' prices were affected, the effects on at least some where enough to lead the court to find antitrust harm in that market.[35]

Moreover, the traditional understanding of power over price refers to a producer's power over their own product. The price of financial products, however, including cryptoassets is a composite value determined by various market forces, and therefore it is difficult to measure an actor's power and its effect in isolation. That said, the transparency and auditability of many cryptoassets enables investigations not only into the price mechanics of the targeted cryptoasset, but

[30] Tao Li, Donghwa Shin, and Baolian Wang, 'Cryptocurrency Pump-and-Dump Schemes' (2018) SSRN.

[31] Neil Gandal and others, 'Price Manipulation in the Bitcoin Ecosystem' (2018) 95 Journal of Monetary Economics 86; Weili Chen and others, 'Market Manipulation of Bitcoin: Evidence from Mining the Mt. Gox Transaction Network' (2019) IEEE INFOCOM 2019 - IEEE Conference on Computer Communications 964; Timothy Peterson, 'To the Moon: A History of Bitcoin Price Manipulation' (2021) 13 Journal of Forensic and Investigative Accounting 254.

[32] For analysis on the applicability of competition law on price manipulation see Alan Schacter, 'The Availability of Antitrust Treble Damages for Commodities Market Manipulation' (1986) 54 Fordham Law Review 853; John Kern, 'Price Manipulation in the Commodity Futures Markets: A Reexamination of the Jurisdictions for Simultaneous Causes of Action under the CEA and the Sherman Act' (1987) 34 UCLA Law Review 1305; Shaun Ledgerwood and others, 'The Intersection of Market Manipulation Law and Monopolization under the Sherman Act: Does It Make Economic Sense' (2019) 40 Energy Law Journal 47.

[33] *David Leibowitz et al. v. iFinex, Inc et al.*, 1:19-cv-09236-KPF (2019) (*Bitfinex*) (the decision issued in this case is *In re Tether and Bitfinex* (n 27).

[34] See Chapter 3 sections B and C.

[35] *In re Tether and Bitfinex* (n 27) at 46 et seq. The argument was later amended: see *In re Tether and Bitfinex Crypto Asset Litigation Defendants' Memorandum of Law in Opposition to Plaintiffs' Motion for Leave to Amend*, 1:19-cv-09236-KPF (2023) at 37 et seq.

also into its surrounding market conditions, facilitating the gathering of required evidence for a demonstration of market power. In *Bitfinex*, the court provisionally accepted plaintiffs' argument that Tether had monopoly power over the crypto-commodities market not because of a showing of the traditional indicia of market power (such as high market shares, entry barriers, etc), but because of a showing of 'direct control over prices'.[36] Tether amassed the necessary power in the crypto-commodities market by first monopolizing the related stablecoin market. This is an interesting construct, because the court seemed to partly excuse the lack of evidence of high market shares in the neighbouring crypto-commodities market, because of evidence of high market shares in the main stablecoin market.[37] This theory is reminiscent of the *Tetra Pak* construct where the Commission and the Court of Justice accepted that abusive conduct can occur in neighbouring markets where the undertaking is not shown to be dominant, if it is shown to be dominant in a primary market that has 'associative links' with the neighbouring market.[38] In any case, the evidence that the court accepted in *Bitfinex* around 'direct control of prices' mainly stemmed from a single academic study, which argued that unbacked Tether inflated prices over a short period of time.[39] This study has been heavily criticized both on the grounds that the data and methodology were scarce and unverified and on the grounds that it does not sufficiently show causation, rather merely correlation.[40]

Thirdly, power over price is usually a cause for concern only when it persists; temporary market power is not normally considered a threat for the competitive process.[41] Price manipulation techniques, on the other hand, may only need to last for a few weeks to a few months to be effective,[42] and their effects are also short-lived. The transient acquisition of economic power to engage in price manipulation may not qualify as an antitrust concern.

One should note here, however, that seasonal exercise of market power has been deemed sufficient for competition law purposes when the market conditions are

[36] ibid at 52.

[37] ibid at 57 ('In any event, while Plaintiffs have not provided concrete allegations that the DigFinex Defendants [Tether] controlled a dominant share of the cryptocommodity market, as noted above, they have provided detailed allegations of how the DigFinex Defendants used their dominance of the closely related stablecoin market to manipulate prices in the cryptocommodity market').

[38] Commission decision of 24 July 1991 IV.31043 Tetra Pak II; Case T-83/91 Tetra Pak v Commission ECLI:EU:T:1994:246; Case C-333/94 P Tetra Pak v Commission ECLI:EU:C:1996:436. See also the discussion in Chapter 7 section C.ii.b. See also *In re Crude Oil Commodity Futures Litigation*, 913 F. Supp. 2d 41 (2012) (where defendants amassed a dominant position in physical crude oil and then dumped the commodity onto the market on certain dates with the view and effect to influence prices in the commodities futures market).

[39] John M Griffin and Amin Shams, 'Is Bitcoin Really Untethered?' (2020) 75 The Journal of Finance 1913. *Bitfinex* (n 33) paras 107 et seq.

[40] See eg Ganesh Viswanath-Natraj and Richard Lyons, 'Stable Coins Don't Inflate Crypto Markets' (*Centre for Economic Policy Research - VoxEU Column*, 17 April 2020).

[41] See eg *Lorain Journal Co. v. United States*, 342 U.S. 143 (1951).

[42] This is evidenced in the case studies discussed in n 31. See also the description and effects of the Tether scheme in *In re Tether and Bitfinex* (n 27).

such that the competitive game revolves around specific time segments.[43] As the Circuit Court ruled in *Crude Oil*, '[w]hile the duration of a monopoly may be "one measure" in determining whether a defendant possessed monopoly power, it is not dispositive'.[44] What matters most is whether the market conduct, no matter how short lived, can affect the competitive process or affect the structural operation of the market, based on the modus operandi of the specific market. The rationale can be extended to support the argument that, in financial products such as cryptoassets, market power can only be transient, because maintaining artificially high prices ad infinitum cannot be a profitable strategy; the price must fall for the manipulator to realize profits. Moreover, while the effects of a price manipulation scheme may be short-lived, the nature of trading markets is organized around short time intervals and punctuated by buy-and-sell movements.[45] As a result, even short-lived actions and conduct can affect the competitive conditions in the market.

ii) Power to exclude: Exclusion through delisting, governance, oversupply

a) Definition and use

The power to exclude competition from the market is recognized as the second key type of market power. As memorialized in *du Pont*, 'a monopoly involves the power to . . . exclude competition when the monopolist desires to do so'.[46] The power to exclude competition expresses dominant firms' ability 'to deter new competitors from entering an industry, to oblige rivals to exit, to confine them to market niches, or to prevent them from expanding'.[47]

The power to exclude is more open-ended than the power over price. The concept of power over price is by definition limited to controlling and affecting one element of competition, that of price; exclusionary power, on the other hand, can

[43] United Brands (n 3) (where the abusive practices revolved around the seasonal banana sales). See also Joined Cases T-374/94, T-375/94, T-384/94 and T-388/94 European Night Services Ltd (ENS) et al v Commission ECLI:EU:T:1998:198 (where the abusive practices were concentrated in the early morning and late evening hours as opposed to the entire day even though the relevant services were offered throughout the day).

[44] *In Re Crude Oil* (n 38), at 55.

[45] ibid. See also *Thompson's Gas & Electric Service, Inc., v. BP America Inc.*, 691 F.Supp.2d 860, 867 (where the relevant market was the propane market for a specific month and the District Court found that based on the features of that specific market '[e]ven assuming that "lasting structural change" and durability are necessary elements for a monopolization claim, Plaintiffs have adequately pled them').

[46] *United States v. E.I. du Pont de Nemours & Co.*, 353 U.S. 586, 592 (1957) (quoting *Transamerica Corp. v. Board of Governors*, 206 F.2d 163, 169 (1953)).

[47] Chiara Fumagalli, Massimo Motta, and Claudio Calcagno, *Exclusionary Practices: The Economics of Monopolisation and Abuse of Dominance* (CUP 2018) 1.

encompass any number of pricing or non-pricing practices that may disadvantage rivals. While exclusionary power can manifest itself in many forms, the core sources and effects of it are common. Fumagalli, Motta, and Calcagno argue that the source of exclusionary power hinges on 'the existence of scale economies and incumbency advantages (that is, an asymmetry between the dominant firm and the rival(s), for example in terms of established customer base, investment in a key infrastructure, exploitation of scale economies) that are found in a variety of industries'.[48] In turn, Krattenmaker, Lande, and Salop argue that the way exclusionary power works (regardless of its sources) is that it enables the dominant firm to raise its rivals' costs,[49] that is to place rival competitors 'at a cost disadvantage sufficient to allow the defendant firm to exercise monopoly power by raising its price'.[50] This is achieved by depriving competitors either of a key upstream input or of a key downstream channel. Depriving access to a key upstream input prevents rivals from producing the desired products or services, whereas depriving access to a key downstream channel prevents them from reaching downstream customers. Either way, competing becomes more costly. This, in turn, allows the dominant firm to raise its own price as well to match that of rivals, or, if it manages to cause rivals to exit the market, it faces less competition, and it can therefore again raise its own prices.[51] As it is obvious, exclusionary power is not fully disassociated from power over price, since the former can enable the latter.

b) Conventional exclusion in crypto markets

Exclusionary power in the decentralized economy can emerge both in traditional ways and in ways that are more idiosyncratic to its modus operandi. Among the traditional ways is the refusal of dominant banks to deal with crypto-exchanges thereby preventing customers of crypto-exchanges from adding fiat money from their bank accounts to their crypto-wallets.[52] The exclusionary power of banks stems from their incumbency advantage of serving as gatekeepers to the mainstream financial system; it consists in their ability to refuse an input to crypto-exchanges (in the form of an entry point for fiat money), thereby placing them at a disadvantage; and the method of delivery is simply refusal to interconnect. In another example, crypto-exchanges have often exercised their power to exclude cryptoassets from the market by delisting them from their platform. Delisting a cryptoasset from a major crypto-exchange can have dramatic consequences for its

[48] ibid 3.

[49] Thomas G Krattenmaker, Robert H Lande, and Steven C Salop, 'Monopoly Power and Market Power in Antitrust Law' (1987) 76 Georgetown Law Journal 241, 248–249; Thomas Krattenmaker and Steven Salop, 'Anticompetitive Exclusion: Raising Rivals' Costs to Achieve Power over Price' (1986) 96 Yale Law Journal 209.

[50] Krattenmaker and Salop, ibid 214.

[51] Krattenmaker, Lande, and Salop (n 49) 248 et seq.

[52] Natália de Lima Figueiredo, 'Banks *v* Cryptocurrency Exchanges: CADE's Investigation and the Search for a Villain' (2021) 9 Journal of Antitrust Enforcement 388.

price and liquidity,[53] which explains why crypto-exchanges have found themselves under criticism for doing so.[54] So called 'blockchain neutrality' has been offered as a response to such exclusionary conduct.[55] The exclusionary power here stems from crypto-exchanges' gatekeeper function in the trading world, and the method of delivery is the lack of support for a given cryptoasset.

c) Exclusion through governance

More interesting are iterations of exclusionary power that are idiosyncratic to the decentralized economy. One such manifestation of exclusionary power is through governance. Ferreira et al. model a situation whereby a conglomerate manufacturer of mining equipment optimized for a specific cryptoasset protocol, who is also is in the mining market, has an incentive to compete aggressively with other miners to support the cryptoasset protocol that their mining equipment is optimized for.[56] Faced with a protocol update, a choice presents itself as to which protocol version to mine for: the old one or the updated one. Protocol updates are not always a unanimous decision and the protocol version that wins is the one that will garner the greatest support from miners, since mining is performed on the basis of a protocol version and legitimizes the protocol. In that sense, choosing to mine on a certain version than another is an act of governance. In this situation a dominant conglomerate manufacturer/miner can exclude the miners who supported the competing protocol version. This model corresponds to accusations against Bitmain, the world's largest manufacturer of mining equipment, for the role it played in the Bitcoin Cash fork, which culminated in the *Bitmain* case.[57] The argument was that Bitmain, along with other defendants, anticompetitively diverted resources into the support of their preferred Bitcoin Cash protocol fork and at the expense of the competing fork Bitcoin SV (BSV). The source of Bitmain's exclusionary power is that it controlled the hardware used for mining and a large part of the mining activity as well, and it exercised this power by using its mining power to 'vote' for its preferred cryptoasset. The case was eventually thrown out and no statement of facts was issued.

[53] Notice of an Application to Commence Collective Proceedings Under Section 47b of the Competition Act 1998 Case No. 1523/7/7/22 (2022) (collective action claiming monetary losses of £12 billion from delisting). See also *Bit Global Digital Limited v. Coinbase Global, Inc.*, 5:24-cv-09019 (2024); Shivani Tanna and Elizabeth Howcroft, 'Binance to Convert Users' USD Coin into Its Own Stablecoin' *Reuters* (6 September 2022).

[54] Konstantinos Stylianou, 'What Will It Take to Regulate Crypto Exchanges?' *CoinDesk* (26 May 2019).

[55] Samuel Weinstein, 'Blockchain Neutrality' (2020) 55 Georgia Law Review 499.

[56] Daniel Ferreira, Jin Li, and Radoslawa Nikolowa, 'Corporate Capture of Blockchain Governance' (2023) 36 The Review of Financial Studies 1364.

[57] *United American Corp. v. Bitmain, Inc. et al.*, 530 F. Supp. 3d 1241 (2021). See commentary in Konstantinos Stylianou, 'What Can the First Blockchain Antitrust Case Teach Us About the Crypto-Economy?' (2019) Harvard Journal of Law and Technology (online).

d) Exclusion through oversupply

A question arises whether the ability to oversupply a cryptoasset effectively flooding the market and potentially excluding competing cryptoassets can be a reflection of exclusionary power. In *Bitfinex*, the applicant argued (among others) that Tether Holdings, a subsidiary of Digfinex, channelled $4.5 billion Tether tokens in the market between 2014 and 2018, thereby excluding competing cryptoassets.[58] Tether is a stablecoin, meaning that it pegs its value to a fiat currency (in this case the US dollar). Unlike other stablecoins, it maintains its peg by fully collateralizing the Tether tokens in circulation with reserves of US dollars.[59] The applicant alleged that Tether Holdings did not in fact maintain 1:1 collateral. Because Tether's pegging mechanism was not constrained by its technology, contrary to other stablecoins which maintained their pegging algorithmically, Tether Holdings could issue as many Tether tokens as it wished without the limitations of an algorithm's rules and without honouring its advertised 1:1 collateral. This conduct, plaintiffs argued, allowed it to monopolize the stablecoin market to the detriment of competing tokens and with it, and to also leverage that monopoly to monopolize the crypto-commodities market as well.[60] Tether's exclusionary power stemmed from a combination of factors: the unique position of stablecoins in the trading market allowing users to store value and exchange assets with minimal fees; Tether's technology which did not automatically constrain Tether issuance to collateral held; and the lack of regulation to make Tether's conduct illegal. In effect, this confluence of factors resulted in Tether commanding at its height up to 98 per cent of the stablecoin market.

iii) Architectural power: Controlling governance and monetization

a) Definition and distinction from power over price and exclusionary power

Definition. Architectural power refers to an undertaking's ability to shape the market around it. It was popularized in the context of business ecosystems and digital platforms, which constitute a group of actors and economic activities coalescing around a central sponsor who guides the multi-product or multi-actor system by determining the conditions of participation, the relationships among actors, and the general shape of the value proposition that will be offered to consumers.[61]

[58] See n 33.

[59] See <https://tether.to/en/understanding-tethers-peg-and-reserves/> (all links were last accessed on 1 September 2024).

[60] *In re Tether and Bitfinex* (n 27), at 59 et seq.

[61] Ron Adner, 'Ecosystem as Structure: An Actionable Construct for Strategy' (2017) 43 Journal of Management 39; Michael G Jacobides, Thorbjørn, Knudsen and Mie Augier, 'Benefiting from Innovation: Value Creation, Value Appropriation and the Role of Industry Architectures' (2006) 35 Research Policy 1200.

Such ecosystems and platforms are also common in the decentralized economy,[62] making architectural power relevant, although the decentralized nature of some of those ecosystems and platforms may undercut the kind of power concentration that has been common in conventional digital ecosystems and platforms.

Architectural power vs power over price and exclusionary power. Architectural power differs both from power over price and from power to exclude. It differs from power over price in that the priority is not to raise prices but rather to control the business environment in which products and services are commercialized.[63] Ultimately, this may allow the dominant actor to raise prices, but this is neither a necessary nor a direct outcome. Architectural power, by allowing the architect actor to regulate market relationships, enables them to dominate the market in more ways than just raising prices, chief among them by mandating the necessary market conditions to perpetuate their dominant position in existing market segments, and to facilitate their entry into new ones. Google's anti-forking policy in the Android ecosystem was a manifestation of such a strategy. The policy dictated that phone manufacturers who wanted to use the Google-sponsored version of Android (which comes with the suite of popular Google apps such as Gmail and Google Maps), must agree to not produce competing Android-based mobile operating systems (forks).[64] Both the basic and the Google-sponsored version of Android were free, and so Google's anti-forking policy was not aimed at raising the price of the Google sponsored-version or other affiliated free software; rather, the goal was to restrict entry of non-Google-sanctioned versions of Android thereby safeguarding the competitive positioning of the Google-sponsored Android version and of Google apps.[65]

Architectural power also differs from exclusionary power in that exclusion may be neither a priority nor a desirable outcome. In business environments that are conducive to the rise of architect firms, whose role is to structure techno-economic relationships that facilitate value creation, coöpetition rather than pure competition is the prevailing type of business relationship.[66] Coöpetition is the simultaneous pursuit of competition and cooperation between firms that are partly rivals and partly complements.[67] In this business environment, architectural power is

[62] See Chapter 3 section D.

[63] Michael G Jacobides and Ioannis Lianos, 'Ecosystems and Competition Law in Theory and Practice' (2021) 30 Industrial and Corporate Change 1199, 1217 et seq.

[64] Commission decision of 18 July 2018 AT.40099 Google Android, paras 155–171.

[65] ibid paras 1036 et seq.

[66] Dong Kyoon Yoo and others, 'Coopetition in a Platform Ecosystem: From the Complementors' Perspective' (2022) Electronic Commerce Research; Emily Bacon, Michael D Williams, and Gareth Davies, 'Coopetition in Innovation Ecosystems: A Comparative Analysis of Knowledge Transfer Configurations' (2020) 115 Journal of Business Research 307; Marta Riquelme-Medina and others, 'Coopetition in Business Ecosystems: The Key Role of Absorptive Capacity and Supply Chain Agility' (2022) 146 Journal of Business Research 464.

[67] Maria Bengtsson, Tatbeeq Raza-Ullah, and Vladimir Vanyushyn, 'The Coopetition Paradox and Tension: The Moderating Role of Coopetition Capability' (2016) 53 Industrial Marketing Management 19.

the ability of the dominant actor to shape relationships of participating actors in the ecosystem and extract a bigger share of the generated value to the expense of other actors.[68] The architect actor does not seek to exclude; quite the contrary, they invite participation onto their platforms so as to maximize value creation, but at the same time they may seek to exploit participating actors to capture more of that value. Various platforms, including Facebook, Amazon, and Apple, have both been accused of engaging in such strategies, through first onboarding and later exploiting partners on their platforms.[69]

The decentralized economy is replete with digital platforms and ecosystems as well, and so architectural power can be a concern. Facebook's cryptocurrency, Diem (formerly known as Libra), failed due to the intense regulatory scrutiny, part of which related to the market power that Facebook could exercise across the web of products and services it facilitated or offered.[70] The concern as summarized by the UK's Competition and Markets Authority is that:

> Facebook's position in social media, in particular its very extensive reach and social graph, make it an important partner for businesses in related markets, including those that rely on its 'free' developer tools and/or its advertising services. This means that Facebook may have the ability to exclude competitors in related markets. It may also have the incentive to do so, for example to protect its position in social media, or to gain additional profits from the most lucrative related markets by offering these products itself.[71]

Endorsing these observations, the Commission launched an antitrust investigation into Diem.[72] It feared that, because Facebook underpins a sprawling ecosystem of products and services and it also competes itself in some of those markets, a sponsored currency to intermediate transactions across the platform would give Facebook significant power over how said transactions would be structured. Introducing Diem in this business environment would allow Facebook to further shape it in ways that could make the system dependent on Diem.[73]

While it is true that architectural power can be a concern in decentralized ecosystems, their reliance on DLT networks necessarily invites a certain measure of sharing in the design and operation of the ecosystem. In (predominantly)

[68] Jacobides and Lianos (n 63) 1212.

[69] *FTC v. Facebook*, 1:20-cv-03590-JEB (2021), at 3; Scott Sher and Bradley Tennis, 'Exploiting Others' Investments in Open Standards' (2016) Competition Policy International.

[70] Pedro Aranguez-Diaz, 'A New Opportunity for Digital Competition: Facebook, Libra, and Antitrust' (2020) 50 Stetson Law Review 199, 221–224; Thibault Schrepel, 'Libra: A Concentrate of "Blockchain Antitrust"' (2020) 118 Michigan Law Review Online 160.

[71] Competition and Markets Authority, 'Online Platforms and Digital Advertising: Market Study Final Report' (2020), para 3.2.44.

[72] Mehreen Khan, Madhumita Murgia, and Javier Espinoza, 'Facebook Cryptocurrency Investigated by EU' (*Financial Times*, 21 August 2019).

[73] Jeffrey Waldron, 'Facebook Libra's Antitrust Problem' (*JIPEL Blog*, 1 April 2020).

decentralized markets, the dispersion of power across different actors can undercut the build-up or exercise of architectural power, without that meaning that architectural power is impossible. The dispersion of power follows from the fact that DLT and its associated governance is by nature a distributed decision-making technology.[74] The rules and norms, both on-chain and off-chain, that define how a given decentralized system works, also embed and reflect the architectural power of the stakeholders that enacted them. Because the rules and norms can be formalized or informal, architectural power can manifest in different ways: firstly, it can be expressed in formalized rules, whether embedded in code or in foundational documents, such as whitepapers and bylaws.[75] This would be the equivalent of the terms of service that conventional digital ecosystems and platforms impose on their partners, which reflect the sponsor's architectural power to dictate said terms. Secondly, it can be reflected in informal norms, such as unwritten voting procedures.[76] The ability to control and influence such procedures will result in influencing the governance process, and in turn the structure and shape of the system itself. It is unknown a priori how much control the undertaking architect will be willing to cede to the rest of the governance community, but one should at least acknowledge this mechanism as a source of potential limits to the architectural power the undertaking architect can hold.

b) Expressions of architectural power: coercion, dependency, soft power

Either way, architectural power can be expressed through coercion, dependency, or soft power. Coercion is the imposition of a stakeholder's will on their partners, such that it changes their intentions, dispositions, or actions.[77] The power to dictate governance terms is the paradigmatic manifestation of architectural power through coercion.

Dependency is the shaping of relationships between parties in such a way that one party ends up in a position of relative strength.[78] While dependency does not precipitate coercion, it amplifies the cost the weaker party will incur relative to the stronger party if agreement is not reached.[79] Some jurisdictions already recognize this kind of relational power and prohibit its abuse; examples include Germany,[80] France,[81] Korea,[82] and Japan.[83]

[74] See Chapter 1 sections D.ii and D.iii.

[75] Primavera De Filippi, Morshed Mannan, and Wessel Reijers, 'Blockchain Technology and the Rule of Code: Regulation via Governance' (2022) hal-03883249 22–28; Primavera De Filippi and Greg McMullen, 'Governance of Blockchain Systems' (Coalition of Automated Legal Applications 2018).

[76] De Filippi, Mannan, and Reijers, ibid 22–28; De Filippi and McMullen, ibid.

[77] See Max Weber, *The Theory of Economic and Social Organization* (Free Press 1947) 152.

[78] Mark S Granovetter, *Society and Economy: Framework and Principles* (Harvard UP 2017) 91 et seq; Samuel Bowles, *The New Economics of Inequality and Redistribution* (CUP 2012) 29–32.

[79] Bowles, ibid 29–32.

[80] Section 20 of the Competition Act.

[81] Article L. 420-2 of the French Commercial Code.

[82] Article 45(1)(6) of the Monopoly Regulation and Fair Trade Act.

[83] Article 2(5) of the Anti-Monopoly Act.

Soft power expresses a party's ability to co-opt partners by relying on influence and persuasion, rather than coercion. Because of the social production nature and governance dynamics of DLT products and services, there are often a number of competing influential stakeholders that can amass architectural power through soft power.[84] Decentralized ecosystems are often heavily influenced by 'sponsoring' institutions or otherwise powerful actors. To take Ethereum as an example, while Ethereum's architecture is co-shaped by the multitude of actors and stakeholders participating in its governance, the Ethereum Foundation is a particularly influential contributor, meaning that it can have a measure of architectural power within the Ethereum ecosystem.[85]

c) Architectural power in the metaverse

The metaverse presents an interesting market context for architectural power, because on top of governance as a process of building and exercising architectural power, new monetization and transaction methods can also affect architectural power. Metaverses can be sponsored both (a) by traditional centralized undertakings (eg Meta's metaverse), where governance's role is more limited since the architecture is controlled exclusively or predominantly by the sponsoring undertaking, and (b) built on top of token ecosystems (eg Decentraland), where governance's role is elevated in lack of a central authority. In metaverses built on top of token ecosystems, there are often two overlapping but distinct layers of governance, one that regulates the metaverse and one that regulates the token ecosystem, since the native token is also used in the metaverse. If the metaverse is seen as a miniature economy, the native token is the 'national' currency of that economy, and it can be used to make and enforce monetary and transactions policy, which directly influences the structure and operation of the system.[86] From inflation policy, to passive income through staking and airdrops, to transaction fees structure, to the ownership regime of assets on the metaverse, these decisions affect the architecture of what is and is not possible on the metaverse. As such, the ability to control these aspects of metaverses' governance translates into architectural power over it.

The power to control these aspects does not only become relevant on the metaverse, since monetary policy and transaction rules and methods are also exercised on token ecosystems that do not encompass a metaverse, but the metaverse gives participants a locus to expand their activity making these decisions and the power behind them more impactful.

[84] Marcella Atzori, 'Blockchain Technology and Decentralized Governance: Is the State Still Necessary?' (2015) SSRN 26–30.

[85] Mike Orcutt, 'Ethereum Thinks It Can Change the World. It's Running out of Time to Prove It' (2018) MIT Technology Review.

[86] Tascha Che, 'Public Blockchains Are the New National Economies of the Metaverse' *Wired* (9 February 2022).

iv) Engagement power: exploitation and exclusion due to 'stickiness'

a) Definition and use

Description. Engagement power is introduced here as a form of market power that emerges in decentralized markets on account of their social production nature and the role of governance in their development.[87] It is the ability to attract and lock in the market's productive resources by exploiting stickiness. Stickiness is the property that expresses an actor's persistent behaviour, even though the actor has choice.[88]

The social production nature of products and services in the decentralized economy means that their development relies on the coming together of various constituent actors and parts, managed and coordinated by a governance process.[89] If participating actors get increasingly embedded into the productive and governance process of a given product or service so that exiting becomes too costly, they may 'stick'. As new actors can join easily while participating actors find it hard to exit, the dominant product or service manages to coalesce even more productive elements around it.

From a market power perspective this has a dual effect: firstly, the dominant undertaking(s) that control the product or service can exercise power and control over other undertakings contributing to its production (intra-product engagement power); secondly, the dominant product or service (and controlling undertaking(s) behind it) can exercise power and control over other competing products or services in the market by starving them of productive resources, which tend to coalesce around the dominant product or service (inter-product engagement power). Inter-product engagement power is reminiscent of the concept of *unavoidable trading partner*, but whereas unavoidable trading partners are looked at from the demand side, inter-product engagement power is enjoyed by an undertaking vis-à-vis the supply side. The position of unavoidable trading partner means that 'customers . . . obtain part of their requirements from the undertaking in a

[87] See Chapter 1 sections D.ii and D.iii.

[88] 'Stickiness' in economics expresses a lag in response to an incentive, but more broadly it can describe organizational inertia due to a multitude of factors, such as organizational culture, habits, transition cost, etc. See Alexander Schmid, Jan Recker, and Jan vom Brocke, 'The Socio-Technical Dimension of Inertia in Digital Transformations' (2017) Proceedings of the 50th Hawaii International Conference on System Sciences 4796; Christopher A Sims, 'Stickiness' (1998) 49 Carnegie-Rochester Conference Series on Public Policy 317.

[89] Vangelis Papadimitropoulos, *Blockchain and the Commons* (Routledge 2023) ch 4; Richard Red, *Peer Production in the Crypto Commons* (2019); Sarah Manski and Michel Bauwens, 'Reimagining New Socio-Technical Economics Through the Application of Distributed Ledger Technologies' (2020) 2 Frontiers in Blockchain 29.

dominant position ("the non-contestable share"). The competitor of an undertaking in a dominant position is not therefore in a position to compete for the full supply of a customer, but only for the portion of the demand exceeding the non-contestable share ("the contestable share")'.[90] Similarly, but from the supply side, the position of having engagement power means that there will always be some part of the productive capacity of the market that will be dominated by the undertaking with engagement power, and competitors will only have the non-contestable share at their disposal for their productive activities.

Stickiness. Stickiness is the property that expresses an actor's persistent behaviour even though the actor has choice. It can be thought of as a variation of Hobson's choice, whereby only one outcome is possible even though technically there is free choice.[91] Stickiness is at the heart of engagement power as it creates mobility barriers around productive resources allowing dominant actors to keep resources and actors captive. In the context of DLT products and services, stickiness can have a number of causes. Firstly, it can stem from path dependency.[92] DLT products and services are hosted on a certain DLT network, processed and validated by a certain community of nodes, often facilitated by a native token, and often use or rely on smart contracts to fulfil their operations, which over the course of their lifetime can incur millions of transactions that represent governance decisions or transfers of value, and can develop further linkages with other smart contracts or external sources through oracles. To switch any of those components into a different network would entail migrating all dependencies (or starting anew).[93] Knowing this, the undertaking that controls the DLT system in question can exercise power and control over participating undertakings.

Economic reasons can also increase stickiness; the fact that the native token commonly represents for users a pathway to other uses, including investment opportunities, participation in the network's governance, participation in the native metaverse, etc, creates inertia, because users' decision to adopt a new token is not taken only in relation to one of the available services or applications in the system,

[90] Case T-286/09 RENV Intel Corporation v Commission ECLI:EU:T:2022:19, para 92. A slightly different definition of unavoidable trading partner can be found in *Google Search (AdSense)* (with further references to case law), whereby '[an]n undertaking which holds a very large market share for some time, without smaller competitors being able to meet rapidly the demand from those who would like to break away from that undertaking, is by virtue of that share in a position of strength which makes it an unavoidable trading partner and which, because of this alone, secures for it, at the very least during relatively long periods, that freedom of action which is the special feature of a dominant position'. See Commission decision of 20 March 2019 AT.40411 Google Search (AdSense), para 223.

[91] See Merriam-Webster Dictionary, 'Hobson's Choice'.

[92] See eg Roberto Moncada and others, 'Next Generation Blockchain-Based Financial Services' in Bartosz Balis and others (eds), *Euro-Par 2020: Parallel Processing Workshops*, vol 12480 (Springer 2021).

[93] Edward Castronova, 'Virtual Worlds: A First-Hand Account of Market and Society on the Cyberian Frontier' (2002)] SSRN 8–9, 38; Edward Castronova, 'On Virtual Economies' (2002) SSRN 23–28.

but also to the other uses it enables within the same system.[94] Metaverses are economic segments particularly prone to stickiness, because they represent entire worlds in which user activity develops—whether economic, social, or other—and therefore, while a metaverse technically only counts as one application, it encompasses numerous activities making switching out of it harder.

Stickiness can also stem from technical requirements; for instance, the validation process often relies on specialized investments (eg application-specific integrated circuit (ASIC) equipment), which constitutes sunk cost, and which further entrenches constituent productive components/actors into a given system.

b) Engagement power vs power in aftermarkets

Engagement power resembles power in aftermarkets, although with notable differences. Aftermarkets are markets for the supply of products or services needed for or in connection with what is typically a relatively long-lasting product or service that has already been acquired (primary market).[95] Power in aftermarkets stems from having locked in customers who have purchased a product in the primary market. Aftermarkets are a rigid construct as they require a) a primary durable and a secondary consumable good or service, b) without which the primary good or service cannot be used, c) a time delay between the purchase of the durable and the secondary good or service such that consumers do not make a single decision for the lifetime of the combination of the primary and secondary products or services, and d) secondary products or services that are priced by the producer of the primary good or service and are not free.[96] Despite these strict conditions aftermarkets were created to address the simple and intuitive concern that if customers are locked in the secondary market (eg by means of tying, exclusivity contracts, etc), the producer of the primary market product or service can exercise market power in the secondary market too. This is why competition authorities try to ensure either that there is 'effective competition in the primary market, which may discipline the market power of the producer of the primary product on the secondary market', or that customers are not artificially locked in the secondary market.[97]

Engagement power reflects a similar concern that actors may remain locked in an economic segment comprising multiple interdependent products and services, not because of their preferences or because of anticompetitive practices such as tying or exclusivity contracts, or forced incompatibility like in aftermarkets, but because of stickiness. Then, within the economic segment that a decentralized

[94] See eg Arash Negahban and Chih-Hung Chung, 'Discovering Determinants of Users Perception of Mobile Device Functionality Fit' (2014) 35 Computers in Human Behavior 75.

[95] Commission decision of 20 May 2009 rejecting the complaint in Case C-3/39.391 EFIM; Case T-296/09 European Federation of Ink and Ink Cartridge Manufacturers (EFIM) v Commission EU:T:2011:693, paras 60, 90, and 91.

[96] Commission decision of 04 March 2024 AT.40437 Apple – App Store Practices (music streaming), paras 363 and 466.

[97] ibid para 337.

product is produced, intra-product engagement power means that a dominant undertaking can exploit other co-producing undertakings that are 'stuck'.

Inter-product engagement power means that a dominant undertaking can exploit or exclude competitors by commandeering a non-contestable share of the market's productive resources, which 'stick' to the production of the dominant product. This, for instance, was a concern that JP Morgan raised against Tether, the largest stablecoin in the world, identifying 'the increasing concentration in tether over the past year as a negative for the stablecoin universe and the crypto ecosystem more broadly'.[98]

(C) Factors limiting market power

i) Forking

Forking is the process and result of a change in a DLT's protocol and data structure such that a new ledger develops out of the original one.[99] Forks are often divided in soft and hard; soft forks are those where the changes are backwards-compatible with nodes that have not been updated, whereas hard forks are those where the changes are not backwards-compatible because the nodes that have not been updated will reject the entries (usually blocks) following the changes.[100] Hard forks result in a new (or even multiple new) parallel version(s) of the original network. Because forks threaten to create or actually do create new versions of an existing network, they have the potential to exert competitive pressure both to the original network, but also to other networks. Multiple reasons concede to that.

Firstly, the creation of a parallel ledger/network that is substantially similar to the original one introduces a new competitor in the market, and indeed one that can serve as a close substitute. While sometimes one of the implicated ledgers will become obsolete, it is not uncommon that both the forked ledger and the original ledger will continue to coexist. The examples of Bitcoin XT and Bitcoin Cash are illustrative here, with Bitcoin XT forking from Bitcoin in 2014 but falling into disuse by 2017, whereas Bitcoin Cash forked from Bitcoin in 2016, becoming the 11th largest cryptocurrency by 2021, and consistently ranking in the top 50 cryptocurrencies since.[101] From a competition point of view, what is interesting is that the reasons usually leading to forking are grounded on disagreements around the introduction of innovations in the original network, and in that sense, forks

[98] Elijah Nicholson-Messmer, 'Stablecoin Tether's Market Dominance May Jeopardize Crypto, JPMorgan Says' *Bloomberg* (1 February 2024).

[99] Dylan Yaga and others, 'Blockchain Technology Overview' (National Institute of Standards Technology 2018) NISTIR 8202 29.

[100] ibid.

[101] See Katelyn Peters, 'A History of Bitcoin Hard Forks' *Investopedia* (22 March 2024).

not only serve as close competitors to the original network, but at the same time advance the industry by implementing variations and innovations rejected from the original network.[102]

Secondly, forks (or the threat thereof) can serve as a disciplining force to the original network since they take with them some of the resources that were committed to the original network, thereby weakening it. Even if the resulting fork proves to be a minor competitor, the original fork will still be weakened vis-à-vis other competitors in the market.

Thirdly, because DLTs are often the underlying infrastructure upon which other products and services develop, any change in the underlying ledger affects the products and services built on top. Forks emerge for a variety of reasons—to introduce updates, to correct security incidents, to account for disagreements in the development community—and as such, forks often affect core characteristics of the underlying DLT, which in turn affect the features and specifications of the products and services developed on top. Since not all participating actors in a DLT network and overlaid services and applications share the same interests, different stakeholder groups may form that push for competing outcomes (including rejecting a fork, adopting a fork, or proposing yet new forks),[103] creating fragmentation both in the ledger itself and in the ecosystem of products and services developed on top.[104] Depending on the scale, frequency, and justification of forks, this kind of activity may undermine the network's or ecosystem's health and undercut its market power. Crucially, even the technical possibility of effecting a fork and the threat of doing so may still impact the competitive positioning of the original DLT and its ecosystem, even if no forking takes place eventually.

ii) DLT interoperability

DLT interoperability is the ability of heterogeneous DLT systems and the data recorded on them to be reachable, verifiable, and referable by one another in a semantically compatible manner.[105] From this definition it follows that interoperability refers both to the actual technical mechanisms that enable cross-communication between networks, but also to semantic interoperability, which

[102] For a detailed account of the technological innovations and competitive dynamics that resulted from the landmark forking of Bitcoin see Jonathan Bier, *The Blocksize War: The Battle for Control over Bitcoin's Protocol Rules* (2021).

[103] Bruno Biais and others, 'The Blockchain Folk Theorem' (2019) 32 The Review of Financial Studies 1662.

[104] See relatedly Shurui Zhou, Bogdan Vasilescu, and Christian Kästner, 'What the Fork: A Study of Inefficient and Efficient Forking Practices in Social Coding' (2019) Proceedings of the 2019 27th ACM Joint Meeting on European Software Engineering Conference and Symposium on the Foundations of Software Engineering 350.

[105] Alex Pentland, Alexander Lipton, and Thomas Hardjono (eds), 'Interoperability of Distributed Systems', *Building the New Economy* (MIT Press 2020) 331.

expresses the ability of networks to exchange data with unambiguous shared meaning.[106] Understanding DLT interoperability on a multilayer basis is essential because it defines the degree to which networks, and by extension the products and services built on top, will be deemed substitutable.

Due to the high fragmentation across DLT networks in decentralized markets, interoperability has been a key desideratum since the early years. Interoperability allows users of different networks to interact, to use cross-chain functionalities, and to move their data between networks.[107] As a result, to the extent interoperability allows, products and services on different networks can become interchangeable, and therefore, the market power of each individual network is diminished.[108]

DLT interoperability generally takes two forms: either through solutions that connect two networks, or through networks which themselves are designed to serve as a platform for the development of other interoperable sub-networks on top.[109] A connection between networks is usually effectuated through so called 'bridges', which swap assets between networks or replicate assets on a receiving network while locking or burning them on the originating network, a process which is performed by centralized or decentralized custodians, smart contracts, or Decentralized Autonomous Organizations (DAO).[110] When assets are locked on one network and replicated on another it is often called 'wrapping' and it is a common way of using tokens of one network on another.[111] Bridges do not simply transfer tokens or value from one DLT network to another, but rather allow users to take full advantage of the target network's functionality similarly to native users. In fact, users can choose to transition completely to the target network leaving the original network behind, endowing bridges with the potential to achieve full substitutability between networks thereby increasing competitive intensity.

Interoperability can also be achieved through network which are designed with this purpose in mind. Such networks, sometimes called 'blockchains-of-blockchains' (BoB) serve as platforms on top of which other blockchains are built, each potentially serving a different use, but all compatible with each other.[112]

[106] See National Interoperability Framework Observatory, 'European Interoperability Framework' (2002).

[107] Wolfgang Kerber and Heike Schweitzer, 'Interoperability in the Digital Economy' (2017) 8 Journal of Intellectual Property, Information Technology and Electronic Commerce Law 39, 40.

[108] ibid 42.

[109] Rafael Belchior and others, 'A Survey on Blockchain Interoperability: Past, Present, and Future Trends' (2022) 54 ACM Computing Surveys 1; Ilham A Qasse, Manar Abu Talib, and Qassim Nasir, 'Inter Blockchain Communication: A Survey' (2019) Proceedings of the ArabWIC 6th Annual International Conference 1.

[110] Sung-Shine Lee and others, 'SoK: Not Quite Water Under the Bridge: Review of Cross-Chain Bridge Hacks' (2023) 2023 IEEE International Conference on Blockchain and Cryptocurrency (ICBC) 1, 2.

[111] Giulio Caldarelli, 'Wrapping Trust for Interoperability: A Preliminary Study of Wrapped Tokens' (2021) 13 Information 6.

[112] The technical definition of BoBs describes them as 'frameworks that provide reusable data, network, consensus, incentive, and contract layers for the creation of application-specific blockchains (customized blockchains) that interoperate between each other'. See Belchior and others (n 109) 19.

Popular blockchain ecosystems, such as Polkadot and Cosmos, provide such functionality. While the interoperability achieved through BoBs also results in increasing substitutability among the parallel blockchains, their competitive effect is broader: by providing ready infrastructure for interoperable pockets in the decentralized economy, they facilitate, normalize, and promote interoperability as an industry standard.[113] Moreover, if external to BoB blockchains become interoperable with one the parallel blockchains in the BoB system, the interoperability effect is propagated through the entire BoB.[114]

iii) Design and governance choices

The fact that products and services in the decentralized economy are intermediated by DLTs means that any design choices around the specific technology used in a given DLT network are bound to affect the network and its competitive positioning in the market. The effect can be ambivalent; as much as technological choices can act to increase market power, they can also act to reduce it (eg interoperability can reduce market power, and lack thereof when it is possible can increase it). This is true for any technology-intensive market, but in the decentralized economy technological choices can make market power more precarious because technology design choices often lie outside the control and influence of the actors affected by them, and they can also be motivated by non-market considerations that either ignore impact on market power or actively seek to limit it.

The social production nature of the decentralized economy brings into the decision-making process various stakeholder groups, whose objectives may reflect non-market considerations such as ideological, sociological, or cultural aspects that have to do with the ethos and purpose of the decentralized economy,[115] with the promotion of social good (however defined) and wealth redistribution,[116] with the role of technology in society,[117] with inclusion and representation,[118] and with social power dynamics.[119] Such considerations may often conflict with the

[113] See examples in Thomas Hardjono, Alexander Lipton, and Alex Pentland, 'Toward an Interoperability Architecture for Blockchain Autonomous Systems' (2020) 67 IEEE Transactions on Engineering Management 1298; Stefan Schulte and others, 'Towards Blockchain Interoperability' in Claudio Di Ciccio and others (eds), *Business Process Management: Blockchain and Central and Eastern Europe Forum*, vol 361 (Springer 2019). See also International Organization for Standardization, 'ISO/TC 307 Blockchain and distributed ledger technologies' (ISO/TC 307).

[114] Belchior and others (n 109) 19–20. For limitations on external interoperability see ibid 26.

[115] Nigel Dodd, 'The Social Life of Bitcoin' (2018) 35 Theory, Culture & Society 35.

[116] David Golumbia, *The Politics of Bitcoin Software as Right-Wing Extremism* (University of Minnesota Press 2016) chs 2 and 4.

[117] Toni Caradonna, 'Blockchain and Society' (2020) 43 Informatik Spektrum 40.

[118] Qiqi Gao and Jiteng Zhang, *Artificial Intelligence Governance and the Blockchain Revolution* (Springer 2024) ch 4.

[119] Malcolm Campbell-Verduyn, 'The Distributions of Distributed Governance: Power, Instability and Complexity in Polycentric Data Ordering' in Carolina Aguerre, Malcolm Campbell-Verduyn, and Jan Aart Scholte, *Global Digital Data Governance* (Routledge 2024).

conventional profit-maximizing objectives associated with the firm and can therefore undermine the attainment or maintenance of market power. At the same time, because the production process of DLT-based products or services is the confluence of undertakings that are often not centrally controlled or coordinated, undertakings can find themselves being affected by design choices that they oppose, that can limit their market power, but that have little or no control over.

Technological design choices in the Ethereum network showcase the above well. One such change concerns the effect the transition of Ethereum from a proof of work (PoW) blockchain to a proof of stake (PoS) blockchain had on miners.[120] Ethereum was initially created as a PoW blockchain, meaning that the process of validating transactions and adding blocks onto the blockchain was performed by miners through solving computationally difficult problems. Miners are a key stakeholder group in any PoW blockchain, because they control which transactions are posted on the blockchain, they maintain the security and integrity of the blockchain, and they decide the fate of forks by choosing to mine for the original or forked blockchain. Due to its centrality, mining has a large economic footprint; in the Ethereum blockchain, miners generated an average of $1bn in revenues per month in 2022.[121]

The PoW consensus mode in Ethereum was deemed to be prone to concentration, not conducive to scalability, and energy-intensive.[122] In response, the Ethereum developer community decided to transform Ethereum from a PoW blockchain to a PoS blockchain. In PoS blockchains, the committed resource for validation of transactions is stakers' native currency (in Ethereum's case, this is Ether), making the mining process obsolete. The technological design choice to make Ethereum a PoS blockchain rendered the entire economy of mining that was built to support Ethereum irrelevant.[123] The change was not the outcome of *competitive* rivalry between miners or between different stakeholders, but rather the response of the developer community to the perceived security, scalability, and sustainability concerns around the operation of Ethereum. As a result, large mining pools that had the power to influence Ethereum ecosystem's direction either exited the market, or switched their mining business to a different network, but in either case, they were disrupted as they lost their market power both relative to other miners and toward other stakeholders in the Ethereum economy.

Before Ethereum transitioned to PoS, another design choice was pushed to address the shortcomings of the mining process. As the mining process is

[120] Coin Metrics, 'Mapping Out the Merge: Understanding Ethereum's Move to Proof of Stake' (2022).

[121] See <https://www.theblock.co/data/on-chain-metrics/ethereum>.

[122] Coin Metrics (n 120) 6–9.

[123] Tobi Opeyemi Amure, 'What Ethereum 2.0 Means for Mining Coins' *Investopedia* (25 April 2024).

energy-intensive, specialized equipment, ASIC, emerged to make mining more efficient.[124] ASICs are expensive and because they are optimized for a particular consensus protocol, they have a sunk cost element to them.[125] The capital requirements required to invest in ASIC result in concentration of mining activities, which undermine decentralization and security credentials of DLT networks. In fact, one of the main motivations behind the creation of Ethereum in the first place was to avoid the kind of centralization that characterized Bitcoin mining; as Ethereum's founding whitepaper explained: 'the mining ecosystem has come to be dominated by ASICs . . . This means that Bitcoin mining is no longer a highly decentralized and egalitarian pursuit, requiring millions of dollars of capital to effectively participate in.'[126] Ethereum's solution was to use a consensus algorithm that was resistant to the kind of optimization ASICs effected.[127] When ASICs specifically designed for Ethereum emerged a few years later,[128] Ethereum's developers, concerned about the robustness of the blockchain network's resilience and decentralized character, implemented iterative improvements to limit the effectiveness of ASICs in the mining process.[129] Miners who relied on ASICs found themselves upended with every protocol upgrade. Their market position was not threatened by competitors—actual or potential—but rather by governance decisions aimed at maintaining the health of the network.

Interestingly, the forced obsolescence of PoW miners in Ethereum had spillover competitive effects for miners in other cryptoassets, as some of the miners in the Ethereum network transitioned to repurposing their equipment for mining in other cryptoasset networks. As more miners joined these alternative cryptoasset networks, existing miners therein found themselves facing a sudden and drastic increase in competition.[130] In either case, for both the miners forced to exit the Ethereum network, and for the miners in other networks that partly absorbed the former Ethereum miners, the competitive shock was precipitated by a technological choice that lied beyond their control.

[124] Jona Stinner, 'Inside the Black Box of Bitcoin Mining: A Theoretical Framework and Simulation Evidence' (2021) SSRN 7–8.

[125] Adam S Hayes, 'Cryptocurrency Value Formation: An Empirical Study Leading to a Cost of Production Model for Valuing Bitcoin' (2017) 34 Telematics and Informatics 1308, 1316.

[126] See Ethereum Whitepaper (last updated 14 March 2024) at https://ethereum.org/en/whitepaper/#mining-centralization.

[127] ibid.

[128] Rachel-Rose O'Leary, 'Ethereum ASICs Are Here: What the New Miners Mean and What's Next' *CoinDesk* (3 April 2018).

[129] Rachel-Rose O'Leary, 'Ethereum Developers Give "Tentative" Greenlight to ASIC-Blocking Code' *CoinDesk* (4 January 2019). Other solutions, like hard forks were also considered. See eg Marie Huillet, 'Ethereum Community Considers Hard Fork To Fight ASIC Miners' *CoinTelegraph* (3 April 2018).

[130] Eliza Gkritsi, 'Ex-Ethereum Miners Token Hop to Stay Alive After the Merge' *CoinDesk* (11 November 2022).

iv) Token effects and bootstrapping new DLT networks

Since most products and services in the decentralized economy constitute or rely on networks, it is only natural that network effects have an impact on building up and maintaining market power.[131] Network effects facilitate the build-up of market power by making larger networks more attractive to existing and new users. This creates the challenge for new and aspiring competitors of how to kickstart the process of onboarding users since users may prefer a more established network.

If there are mechanisms that help entrants bootstrap their networks, then these can mitigate the network effects accruing to more established networks. By doing so, these mechanisms can undercut the market power network effects accord established networks, making the market more contestable.

In DLT networks, the issuance of tokens can help overcome the initial obstacle of developing an installed base, which can then be augmented and maintained through network effects. The challenge new networks face is that users may have low incentives to join the network while it remains underdeveloped because the value of joining is low, or because they are uncertain about capturing it.[132] This creates a chicken-and-egg situation, which prevents networks from gaining critical mass.[133] Idiosyncraticities such as the ability to fork or to non-hierarchically effect design choices as mentioned previously may further drive away early adopters.[134]

The issuance of tokens overcomes this problem by creating both present and future value and utility for users in different ways.[135] Firstly, tokens can be bearers of monetary value, and can be used as transaction medium, exchange medium, or store of value.[136] Importantly, when there is promise or prospect of increase in value in the future, tokens can become even more attractive in the crucial early stages of a network's bootstrapping, thereby more effectively helping build installed base. Secondly, tokens can be used on the network to enable utility and functionality.[137] Users have an incentive not only to own tokens to unlock the

[131] See Chapter 6 section B.i.

[132] David P McIntyre and Mohan Subramaniam, 'Strategy in Network Industries: A Review and Research Agenda' (2009) 35 Journal of Management 1494.

[133] Marco Ardolino and others, 'A Business Model Framework to Characterize Digital Multisided Platforms' (2020) 6 Journal of Open Innovation: Technology, Market, and Complexity 10.

[134] Evan Miller, 'A Tale of Two Regulators: Antitrust Implications of Progressive Decentralization in Blockchain Platforms' (2021) 77 Washington and Lee Law Review Online 387, 391.

[135] Monetary incentives as a more general strategy to get platform sides on board has been explored among others in Thomas Eisenmann, Geoffrey G Parker, and Marshall W Van Alstyne, 'Strategies for Two-Sided Markets' (2006) 84 Harvard Business Review 92.

[136] Christian Catalini and Joshua Gans, 'Initial Coin Offerings and the Value of Crypto Tokens' (2018) National Bureau of Economic Research w24418.

[137] Monika di Angelo and Gernot Salzer, 'Tokens, Types, and Standards: Identification and Utilization in Ethereum' (2020) 2020 IEEE International Conference on Decentralized Applications and Infrastructures (DAPPS) 1. See also 'What Are You Token About? Blockchain Token Economics and Rights' *HackerNoon* (25 July 2017).

corresponding functionality, but to help enlarge the network thereby magnifying the network's functionality. Thirdly, tokens may be able to be traded in secondary markets, further increasing their value for users.[138]

This strategy has commonly been encapsulated in so-called Initial Coin Offerings (ICOs), whereby new networks/platforms sell a specified number of tokens to a select audience before the network/platform becomes fully available to the public at large.[139] ICOs have helped numerous platforms take off,[140] as investors are lured to ICOs with the promise of appreciation of their tokens in the future.[141] The return-on-investment in ICOs can be exceptionally high,[142] and while not all platforms manage to survive (the majority in fact fails), many have withstood competition and have grown to become major platforms, including Ethereum.

[138] Di Angelo and Salzer, ibid.

[139] Usman W Chohan, 'Initial Coin Offerings (ICOs): Risks, Regulation, and Accountability' in Stéphane Goutte, Khaled Guesmi, and Samir Saadi (eds), *Cryptofinance and Mechanisms of Exchange* (Springer 2019).

[140] See <https://coinmarketcap.com/ico-calendar/>.

[141] Jiasun Li and William Mann, 'Initial Coin Offering and Platform Building' (2018) SSRN.

[142] See Cryptorank, 'Average Return of ICO/IEOs by Sector' at <https://cryptorank.io/avg-roi-by-sector>.

6
BARRIERS TO ENTRY AND EXPANSION

(A) **General** 143
(B) **Network effects** 146
- i) Network effects in cryptoassets and CBDCs 148
  - a) Existence and measurement of network effects in cryptoassets 148
  - b) Switching and competition between cryptoasset and CBDC incumbents and competitors 151
- ii) Network effects in ICOs, dApps, and DLT platforms 152
- iii) Network effects in mining and staking pools 155

(C) **Economies of scale and scope** 157
- i) Economies in mining and validation 159
- ii) Economies in DLT applications and services 162
- iii) Assessing the impact of economies of scale and scope in DLT markets 164

(D) **Branding and economies of trust** 167

(A) General

While market shares, in providing a snapshot of the relative size of firms in a defined market, can be a useful indication of market power, they may be misleading if they can easily be eroded by competitive forces operating in the market. There are countless examples of products or services in the decentralized economy that once reigned supreme only to be superseded by competition shortly thereafter. To take just one notable example, the crypto-exchange market has seen dramatic changes in market share distribution, with Bitstamp, the world's longest-running exchange, climbing to the top three exchanges by volume between 2014 and 2016, but hovering closer to twentieth place only a decade later.[1]

Competitive forces that constrain firms may be actual, in that they are present in the market, or potential, in that they may materialize in the future. Barriers to expansion or entry express the difficulty by which such competitive forces can

[1] Compare Kaiko Research, 'The Shift Toward Transparency' (*Kaiko Blog*, 14 December 2022) and Garrick Hileman, 'Bitcoin Trading Volume Concentrating in Largest Exchanges' *CoinDesk* (15 March 2014).

Antitrust in the Decentralized Economy. Konstantinos Stylianou, Oxford University Press.

DOI: 10.1093/9780191925504.003.0006

emerge or be exercised. If barriers to expansion or entry are high, competitive constraints are weakened, and market power is easier to maintain. If, on the other hand, barriers to expansion or entry are low, then the exercise of market power by dominant firms is likely to be met with capacity expansion by existing competitors or to attract entry by new competitors, thereby constraining dominant firms and ultimately even eroding their market shares.

Definition and characteristics. The concept of barriers to entry originated in economics and for many years economists debated the proper definition.[2] The initial definition by Bain spoke of conditions that allow established firms, in the long run, to elevate their selling prices above the minimal average costs of production without inducing potential entrants to enter the industry.[3] For Bain, any factor that allowed sustained profitability could potentially be caught under his definition, making it arguably overinclusive. Stigler counter-proposed that entry barriers should be construed only as those that confer a cost advantage to incumbent firms that entrants do not enjoy.[4] It is this advantage that allows incumbents to sustainably elevate prices above cost and that serves as a barrier for entrants.

In antitrust circles, this debate is today somewhat moot, as it is now clear from the case law that Bain's definition has prevailed; any condition that accords an advantage to incumbents—whether of their own making or of potential entrants' making or owing to the structure of the industry—can be considered an entry or expansion barrier.[5] The Commission's Guidance notes that 'an undertaking can be deterred from increasing prices if expansion or entry is likely, timely and sufficient'.[6] Likely means that the expansion or entry must be sufficiently profitable for the competitor or entrant.[7] The history of the industry can be useful in assessing the likelihood of expansion or entry; frequent and successful expansion or entry in the past might be an indication that barriers to entry are low.[8] For instance, the myriad cryptoassets that historically have existed and exist today are a testament to the ease of entry in that market.

'Timely' means that expansion or entry must be sufficiently swift to deter or defeat the exercise of substantial market power.[9] While theoretically any expansion

[2] For an overview see Jeffrey Perloff and Dennis Carlton, *Modern Industrial Organization* (Pearson 2015) 76.

[3] Joe S Bain, *Barriers to New Competition: Their Character and Consequences in Manufacturing Industries* (Harvard UP 1956) 3.

[4] George Stigler, 'Barriers to Entry, Economies of Scale, and Firm Size', *The Organisation of the Industry* (Irwin 1968).

[5] For the European Union, see Commission Guidelines on the Commission's enforcement priorities in applying Article 82 of the EC Treaty to abusive exclusionary conduct by dominant undertakings (2009/C 45/02), paras 12, 16, 17. For the United States, see *Los Angeles Land Co. v. Brunswick Co.*, 6 F.3d 1422, 1427–28 (1993); *Rebel Oil Co., Inc. v. Atlantic Richfield Co.*, 51 F.3d 1421, 1439 (1995).

[6] Guidelines on enforcement priorities (n 5) para 16.

[7] ibid.

[8] Discussion paper on the application of Article 82 of the Treaty to exclusionary abuses (2005), paras 35–36.

[9] ibid.

or entry can have a constraining effect on dominant incumbents if they persist long enough, it is more relevant to look at short-term effects, because they are more observable and assessable.[10] There is no exact time period within which expansion or entry must occur; rather the appropriate time period depends on the characteristics of the market. In the domain of the decentralized economy, which is dominated by financial services, regulatory requirements can be a formidable obstacle to timely entry, as evidenced, for example, by the long road to approval of mainstream financial products incorporating cryptoassets, such as the Bitcoin Exchange-Traded Fund (ETF), which took a decade to gain approval by the US Securities and Exchange Commission (SEC).[11]

Sufficient means that expansion or entry must be of such magnitude as to be able to deter the exercise of market power by putatively dominant undertakings.[12] Small-scale entry in niche markets that is incapable of undercutting dominant incumbents will likely not be evidence of low barriers to expansion or entry. A common critique of the decentralized economy is that, despite its tremendous growth, it still represents only a fraction of the total economy and therefore decentralized economy products and services may not register as serious competitive alternatives to their mainstream economy counterparts. A far from perfect—but instructive—comparison, is between the global cross-border payment service Society for Worldwide Interbank Financial Telecommunication (SWIFT) and Ripple, a Distributed Ledger Technology (DLT) alternative (the comparison is imperfect, because, among other reasons, SWIFT only transmits messages with instructions to execute transactions, whereas Ripple actually transmits the funds as well). Ripple is cheaper, faster, and more complete, and has therefore emerged as a potential competitor to the established (and near-monopoly) SWIFT system. However, whereas Ripple processed 106 million transactions in Q4 2022, SWIFT handles around 46 million transactions daily.[13] Clearly, Ripple does not yet represent sufficient entry in cross-border payments.

Along those lines, barriers to expansion or entry that have been identified in the past include legal barriers (eg tariffs, quotas) and regulation; economies of scale and scope; privileged access to essential inputs; important technologies or an established distribution network; the established position of incumbents as a result of, for example, customer loyalty; network effects, especially when coupled with high switching costs; and significant investments, particularly sunk investments, that competitors or entrants would have to match.[14]

[10] Dennis W Carlton, 'Barriers to Entry' (2005) NBER Working Paper Series WP 11645 26.

[11] Suzanne McGee and Hannah Lang, 'The Decade-Long Journey to a Spot Bitcoin ETF' *Reuters* (10 January 2024).

[12] Carlton (n 10).

[13] Compare Ripple, 'Q4 2022 XRP Markets Report' (31 January 2023) at <https://ripple.com/insights/q4-2022-xrp-markets-report/> and SWIFT, 'Swift FIN Traffic & Figures' at <https://www.swift.com/about-us/discover-swift/fin-traffic-figures> (all links were last accessed on 1 September 2024).

[14] Guidelines on enforcement priorities (n 5) para 17; Discussion paper on exclusionary abuses (n 8) para 40; Brunswick (n 5) 1428.

Not all barriers to entry are equally influential in all industries. For the decentralized economy, network effects, economies of scale and scope, branding, and economies of trust have emerged as important determinants of ease of entry and expansion. This follows directly from the nature of the decentralized economy as digital, dominated by network products and services, and the particular ethos of the industry.

(B) Network effects

Definition. Network effects, sometimes referred to as demand-side externalities, have come to be one of the most influential parameters of competitive assessment in markets where the products or services offered are structured around networks. They were first studied in the 1970s to more accurately capture the value and growth of telecommunications networks,[15] but have since found application in numerous other industries and business models including PC software,[16] online platforms,[17] airline reservation systems, and ATMs[18] among others. Since markets in the decentralized economy are underpinned by distributed ledgers that are maintained by networks of actors, it is evident that network effects become relevant.

In network markets, the core claim is that the value of a product or service is linked to its userbase, so that when the userbase increases, the value of the product or service increases too, and when the userbase decreases, the value of the product or service decreases too.[19] More specifically, for every user added to the userbase of a product, value is created not just for the joining user but for existing users as well. As a result, each new user creates an externality in the form of value that is missed by the new user but captured by the network of existing users. Conversely, for every exiting user, value is lost not only for the exiting user, but also for existing users. The exact relationship between value and userbase can vary; it can be linear (proportional change),[20] logarithmic,[21] quadratic (Metcalfe's law),[22] or other. This

[15] Jeffrey Rohlfs, 'A Theory of Interdependent Demand for a Communications Service' (1974) 5 The Bell Journal of Economics and Management Science 16.

[16] *United States v. Microsoft Corp.*, 253 F.3d 34 (2001). Neil Gandal, 'Competing Compatibility Standards and Network Externalities in the PC Software Market' (1995) 77 The Review of Economics and Statistics 599.

[17] Jeffrey Church and Neil Gandal, 'Platform Competition in Telecommunications' in Martin Cave, Sumit Kumar Majumdar, and Ingo Vogelsang (eds), *The Handbook of Telecommunications Economics (Volume 2)* (North-Holland 2005).

[18] Nicholas Economides and Steven C Salop, 'Competition and Integration Among Complements, and Network Market Structure' (1992) 40 The Journal of Industrial Economics 105.

[19] Michael Katz and Carl Shapiro, 'Network Externalities, Competition and Compatibility' (1985) 75 American Economic Review 424.

[20] GM Peter Swann, 'The Functional Form of Network Effects' (2002) 14 Information Economics and Policy 417.

[21] Bob Briscoe, Andrew Odlyzko, and Benjamin Tilly, 'Metcalfe's Law Is Wrong—Communications Networks Increase in Value as They Add Members But by How Much?' (2006) 43 IEEE Spectrum 34.

[22] Robert Metcalfe, 'Metcalfe's Law After 40 Years of Ethernet' (2013) 46 Computer 26.

interlocking relationship makes products or services with large market shares potentially more attractive to users and therefore harder to displace.[23] For this reason, network effects can raise barriers to expansion or entry for other competitors in the market.

Implications. From this basic theorem, a number of important implications follow. Because for products or services that exhibit network effects, every new user makes the product or service more valuable, it creates incentives for other users to adopt that product or service over its competitors resulting in a snowball effect. As increasing returns accrue to the product or service due to network effects, the market may eventually tip in its favour (winner takes all).[24] Consequently—everything else equal and assuming homogeneity—dominant firms, or even monopolies, can be the natural outcome of markets that exhibit network effects. To secure this position, firms have an incentive to start developing their userbase as early as possible, which suggests that in markets with network effects there is a first-mover advantage.[25] Because in such markets firms often vie to secure an early foothold which in turn will allow them to gain dominance, it is said that in markets with network effects firms compete for the market, rather than in the market.[26] A further corollary of that is that the market may be locked in products or services that are intrinsically inferior to competitors, if competitors are latecomers.[27]

Limitations. While network effects give rise to competitive advantages that can shield firms from competition coming from expansion or entry of other firms, they are not insurmountable, and therefore it would be wrong to assume that firms aided by network effects are bound to emerge or remain dominant. If competitors (existing or potential) differentiate their offerings and if switching costs are low, users may turn away from the dominant network, particularly if the offerings of smaller competitors are superior.[28] If network effects have also locked the market in, user coordination may be necessary to enable transition to a different offering.[29] This means that if coordination mechanisms are available and accessible, network effects can be undercut. Network effects are also weakened if users can join multiple networks simultaneously (multihoming), since multihoming allows multiple networks to improve their competitive

[23] Oz Shy, 'A Short Survey of Network Economics' (2011) 38 Review of Industrial Organization 119, 131.
[24] Nicholas Economides, 'The Economics of Networks' (1996) 14 International Journal of Industrial Organization 673; Katz and Shapiro (n 19).
[25] Economides, ibid; Katz and Shapiro (n 19); Neil Gandal and Hanna Halaburda, 'Can We Predict the Winner in a Market with Network Effects? Competition in Cryptocurrency Market' (2016) 7 Games 16.
[26] ibid.
[27] ibid.
[28] Joseph Farrell and Paul Klemperer, 'Coordination and Lock-In: Competition with Switching Costs and Network Effects' in Mark Armstrong and Robert Porter (eds), *Handbook of Industrial Organization*, vol 3 (North-Holland 2007).
[29] ibid.

positioning (although not all at the same rate).[30] Lastly, the flipside of positive network effects can also be observed, whereby the loss of a user results in a supra-proportionate loss of value, which incites further losses and so on. Rapid decline is, therefore, the flipside of rapid growth that is enabled by network effects, and so the same forces that may propel a network to success may also cause its demise.

i) Network effects in cryptoassets and CBDCs

a) Existence and measurement of network effects in cryptoassets

Cryptoasset networks can exhibit network effects as their value proposition partly relies on a network of users and they have shown evidence of growing value as they became more popular.[31] A showing of strong network effects in cryptoasset networks would affect both how cryptoassets compete with each other, but also whether cryptoassets and Central Bank Digital Currencies (CBDC) can compete with fiat money, as fiat money can itself exhibit network effects for the same reasons and are the incumbent product/service.

Network effects in cryptoassets were first studied to establish valuation formulas which could then be used to predict price growth.[32] The most commonly tested hypothesis was that the price growth of Bitcoin could be explained on the basis of Metcalfe's Law, which stipulates that the value of a network grows at a rate proportional to the square of the number of users.[33] For reasonable projections of userbase growth, one could use Metcalfe's Law to predict realistic prices of Bitcoin into the future.

From there, a number of observations followed painting a more mixed picture on the applicability of network effects in cryptoassets. First, there is the question of how to measure network effects. To be able to determine whether the value of a product or service changes in response to its userbase, the first step is to establish what is meant by *value* and *userbase*. Because network effects occur when the price changes in response to userbase, value must be understood to mean value for users, that is, value as perceived by the users of the cryptoasset network. The most common proxy for value is token price. Token price expresses value in conventional monetary terms (ie value in fiat currency) and is the value that users as

[30] Toker Doganoglu and Julian Wright, 'Multihoming and Compatibility' (2006) 24 International Journal of Industrial Organization 45.

[31] Ernie GS Teo, 'Emergence, Growth, and Sustainability of Bitcoin: The Network Economics Perspective', *Handbook of Digital Currency* (Elsevier 2015).

[32] Timothy Peterson, 'Metcalfe's Law as a Model for Bitcoin's Value' (2018) 7 Alternative Investment Analyst Review 9.

[33] ibid.

market participants collectively assign to a given cryptoasset by deciding to buy and sell at that price level.

While an appropriate measure, the monetary value of cryptoassets is not the only utility they have for users. Another proxy that has been proposed is transaction value, which expresses the value of the sum of native units transferred per point in time.[34] Transaction value as a proxy sees cryptoassets as means of transaction, the assumption being that as a cryptoasset network becomes more valuable to users, they will use it more frequently and/or they will transfer greater value through it. Therefore, transaction value can also be indicative of the utility users draw from the network. Transaction count can also be instructive as it expresses the number of transactions that take place on a network per point in time.[35] Similar to transaction value, transaction count sees value as a function of users' engagement with the network, but it may be more accurate than transaction value if value can be manipulated more easily.

Userbase is also open to different interpretations.[36] Similar to traditional online platforms and networks, the appropriate period within which it is measured should be established. The measurement would count all unique (user) addresses that have been active at least once over the chosen time frame from the time of measurement,[37] and it is usually between one and six months. Userbase can also be measured on the basis of (user) addresses with non-zero balance on their account. This proxy represents the sum count of unique addresses holding any amount of native units on the cryptoasset network. The utility of this proxy lies in that it excludes all economically non-active addresses, the assumption being that addresses with zero balance are dormant (similar to bank accounts with zero balance).

Considering the different ways that exist by which network effects can be measured, there is not a uniform observation that either proves or disproves network effects on cryptoasset networks. Studies that cover the period up until the end of 2017 and use token price and total active addresses as proxies for value and userbase respectively seem to prove the existence of network effects in Bitcoin,[38] although not without disagreement.[39] Later and more nuanced studies present a more inconsistent picture, with network effects characterizing some cryptoassets but not others,[40] reverse network effects also present, and no winner-take-all dynamics

[34] Konstantinos Stylianou and others, 'Cryptocurrency Competition and Market Concentration in the Presence of Network Effects' (2021) 6 Ledger 81, 88–89.

[35] ibid.

[36] ibid.

[37] See eg Xing-Zhou Zhang, Jing-Jie Liu, and Zhi-Wei Xu, 'Tencent and Facebook Data Validate Metcalfe's Law' (2015) 30 Journal of Computer Science and Technology 246.

[38] Peterson (n 32); Ben Van Vliet, 'An Alternative Model of Metcalfe's Law for Valuing Bitcoin' (2018) 165 Economics Letters 70; Ken Alabi, 'Digital Blockchain Networks Appear to Be Following Metcalfe's Law' (2017) 24 Electronic Commerce Research and Applications 23; Gandal and Halaburda (n 25).

[39] Jamil Civitarese, 'Does Metcalfe's Law Explain Bitcoin Prices? A Time Series Analysis' (2018) SSRN.

[40] Stylianou and others (n 34); Tiam Bakhtiar, Xiaojun Luo, and Ismail Adelopo, 'Network Effects and Store-of-Value Features in the Cryptocurrency Market' (2023) 74 Technology in Society 102320.

potentially attributable to differentiation among cryptoassets.[41] Reverse network effects are interesting, because if the network which benefits from network effects raises prices, users will turn to competitors initiating a negative feedback loop.[42] Therefore, network effects can act pro-competitively, too. See Figure 6.1.[43]

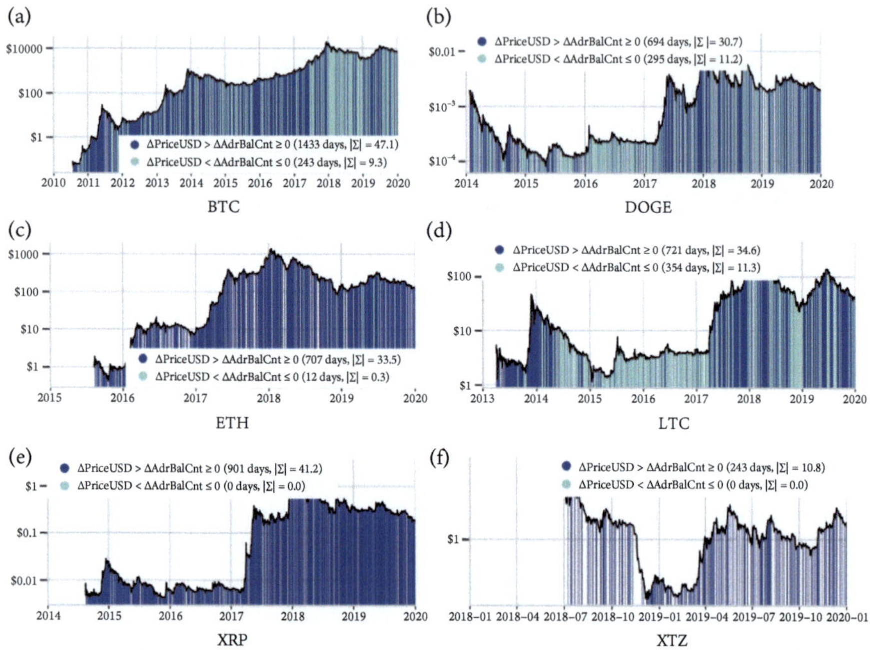

Figure 6.1 Network effect observations and distribution in six cryptocurrencies. Blue bars indicate positive network effects, green bars indicate negative network effects, and white bars indicate no network effects; userbase measured by total addresses with non-zero balance, value measured by USD token price.
Source: Stylianou et al (n 34)

For CBDCs, empirical evidence is scarce, and the literature is ambivalent, since the results of network effects depend on how strong they are, how differentiated competitors are, and whether the market is oligopolistic or competitive.[44]

These findings are important for competition policy, because they moderate and qualify the competitive implications of network effects without denying their

[41] Stylianou and others (n 34).
[42] Youming Liu and others, 'The Potential Competitive Effects of CBDC on Deposits, Payments and Bank Business Models' in Konstantinos Stylianou, Marios Iacovides, and Björn Lundqvist (eds), *Fintech Competition: Law, Policy, and Market Organisation* (Bloomsbury-Hart 2023) 137–38.
[43] Armstrong builds his model with this assumption in mind in Mark Armstrong, 'Competition in Two-Sided Markets' (2006) 37 The RAND Journal of Economics 668.
[44] Liu and others (n 42) 137–38.

existence. Differentiation among competitors, multihoming, and switching, as well as reverse network effects, dampen the overall strength of network effects. This is not to deny any relevance of network effects in cryptoassets. It just cannot automatically be assumed that because cryptoassets are based on networks, network effects are necessarily the dominant factor that predicts their competitive positioning; instead a case-by-case examination may be required.

b) Switching and competition between cryptoasset and CBDC incumbents and competitors

As mentioned, the existence of network effects does not inexorably suggest an insurmountable competitive advantage; if switching to different networks is low-cost and easy, then the advantage accorded by network effects is attenuated. While switching is a factor that becomes relevant in assessing network effects across the industry, it becomes particularly influential when network effects accrue to an incumbent network. The particular concern is that users will not be willing to switch to alternative networks because the incumbent network enjoys an established size, reputation, and other potential cost advantages such as economies of scale, even if alternative networks may present a better value proposition.[45] For that reason, the combination of network effects and entrenched incumbents poses considerable antitrust policy challenges.

In the context of cryptoassets, and particularly stablecoins, the most obvious incumbent is fiat money, but—further—CBDCs, to the extent they represent a digital version of fiat money can also be considered incumbent; and Bitcoin can be seen as the incumbent cryptocurrency relative to alternative cryptocurrencies (altcoins).[46] CBDCs present a particularly potent competitor because they can support additional features on top of those of traditional fiat money, such as programmability, native interest accrual, and online as well as offline functionality, etc. How one models these parameters, as well as the strength of network effects and differentiation with competitors, influences their competitive appeal.[47] The problem that arises is the lack of incentives users might have to switch from fiat money or CBDCs to alternative forms of money (in this case cryptoassets, and particularly stablecoins) or from Bitcoin to altcoins, if they cannot be certain that the alternative will be as reliable or featureful as fiat money or Bitcoin.[48]

[45] Israel Kirzner, *The Meaning of Market Process: Essays in the Development of Modern Austrian Economics* (2nd edn, Routledge 2001) 163ff.

[46] Daniel Schwarz, 'Central Bank Digital Currencies and Competition Laws: Recognising the Importance of Competition Laws in the CBDC Ecosystem' (2023) 02/23 Butterworths Journal of International Banking and Financial Law 107.

[47] Max Fuchs, 'CBDC as Competitor for Bank Deposits and Cryptocurrencies' (2022) MAGKS Joint Discussion Paper Series in Economics No. 10-2022; Philippe Bacchetta and Elena Perazzi, 'CBDC as Imperfect Substitute to Bank Deposits: A Macroeconomic Perspective' (2022) Swiss Finance Institute Research Paper N°21-81.

[48] Lawrence White, 'Does a Superior Monetary Standard Spontaneously Emerge?' (2002) 12 Journal des Économistes et des Études Humaines; William J Luther, 'Cryptocurrencies, Network Effects, and Switching Costs' (2016) 34 Contemporary Economic Policy 553; Fuchs (n 47); Schwarz (n 46) 108.

That said, there are a number of factors that can facilitate switching. Coordination among users can help overcome the initial inertia that characterizes users locked in fiat money or in Bitcoin.[49] If users switch en masse concurrently, or if there is a credible commitment mechanism whereby users commit to start using cryptoassets instead of fiat money in the future, then the utility of cryptoassets can grow fast enough to convince users to switch. In lack of coordination, the existence of benefits that are unrelated to the size of the network, can still serve as powerful incentives for users to switch.[50] Cryptoasset features such as fast, anonymous, cheap electronic transfers, or the fact that they (ostensibly) constitute an alternative economic order compared to government-controlled fiat money, or the fact that at least some cryptocurrencies can serve simultaneously as both means of exchange and store of value, are examples of private benefits that one can derive from cryptoassets and that do not depend on the size of the network. Compatibility between cryptoassets and complementary tools, such as wallets, and multihoming both on the side of users and on the side of complementary tools, such as crypto-exchanges, can further facilitate switching.[51]

Moreover, rational first-mover adopters who see an opportunity in adopting cryptoassets can help counter the initial inertia of adoption, inciting more users to follow.[52] The opportunity can consist in filling a niche market, or more pertinently for cryptoassets, in investing early in hopes that their initial investment will appreciate in the future. Unlike conventional networks where early adopters derive minimal value from the under-developed network, cryptoassets, which promise future appreciation or enhanced security as the network grows, can use this bootstrapping method to their advantage. See Table 6.1.[53]

ii) Network effects in ICOs, dApps, and DLT platforms

Cryptoassets often develop ecosystems around them, where the native cryptoasset is the token that facilitates (eg as transaction medium, utility token, governance token, etc) the creation of further services, applications and products. Initial Coin Offerings (ICO) are sometimes used to enable such ecosystems, whereby the issuing institution sells DLT-based assets to initially fund the creation of a platform ecosystem whereon asset-holders will then be able to spend their assets or sell their

[49] William J Luther, 'Getting Off the Ground: The Case of Bitcoin' (2019) 15 Journal of Institutional Economics 189.

[50] Malavika Nair and Nicolás Cachanosky, 'Bitcoin and Entrepreneurship: Breaking the Network Effect' (2017) 30 Review of Austrian Economics 263.

[51] Christian Catalini and Katherine Tucker, 'Antitrust and Costless Verification: An Optimistic and a Pessimistic View of Blockchain Technology' (2018) 82 Antitrust Law Journal 861.

[52] Nair and Cachanosky (n 50).

[53] Christian Catalini and Joshua Gans, 'Some Simple Economics of the Blockchain' (2016) National Bureau of Economic Research W22952 13–20. See also Chapter 1 section D.iii.

Table 6.1 Competition among fiat currencies, CBDCs, stablecoins, and cryptocurrencies, based on network effects, differentiation among them, and switching ease/costs between them.

	Switching				Differentiation				Network effects			
	Fiat	**CBDC**	**Stablecoins**	**Cryptos**	**Fiat**	**CBDC**	**Stablecoins**	**Cryptos**	**Fiat**	**CBDC**	**Stablecoins**	**Cryptos**
Fiat	-	o	*	*	-	o	o	*	-	Fiat	Fiat	Fiat
CBDC	o	-	o	*	o	-	o	*	Fiat	-	CBDC	CBDC
Stablecoins	*	o	o	o	o	o	o	*	Fiat	CBDC	Compete	Compete
Cryptos	*	o	o	o	*	*	*	*	Compete	Compete	Compete	Compete

Legend

Switching
*denotes high switching costs
o denotes low switching costs
- denotes no application

Differentiation
*denotes high differentiation
o denotes low differentiation
- denotes no application

Network effects
Fiat/CBDC denotes which asset is the incumbent vis-à-vis the other asset
Compete denotes there is no incumbent and there are competing network effects
- denotes no application

assets onwards.[54] Similarly, Decentralized Apps (dApps) are applications or services that, instead of relying on the server-client model, they run on DLT networks and their operation is therefore decentralized. Depending on their functionality they can either rely on an existing DLT platform network or serve as platforms themselves for further dApps to run on.[55] As with other network platforms, ICOs, dApps, and generally DLT-based platforms can exhibit network effects.

At a basic level they can exhibit direct network effects similar to those described in cryptoasset networks. Direct network effects arise because of the value platforms users draw from the ability to interact with each other, such that the more users join the platform the greater the utility for all. The interaction can be in the form of trading on ICO networks or using the available applications of dApp networks (eg dApp social networks).[56] Additionally, because dApps enable the creation of new services and applications, such networks can exhibit indirect network effects as well. Indirect network effects arise when the userbase of a network incites the creation of complementary products and services in a two-sided (or multi-sided) market fashion.[57] As a result, the more users exist on one side, the more inviting the other side becomes too. Consider the example of decentralized oracles, whose purpose is to feed real-world data to DLT services and applications.[58] The more sources of real-world data they can employ on one side, the more DLT services and applications can use them on the other side.

An additional way by which value increases in ICO networks (or other predominantly finance-oriented networks) is the information sharing or observation of conduct among participants, especially if the network facilitates transparency.[59] A common problem in bootstrapping investor networks is investors' reluctance to join absent expert certification. Traditionally, a trustworthy underwriter solves this problem. In ICOs, the function of the underwriter can be substituted with the 'wisdom of the crowd', such that the growing number of joining users (:investors) signals a worthy opportunity. Moreover, ICOs often promise increasing prices of the issued tokens to encourage early adoption.[60] This method, coupled with the expectation for price appreciation across all tokens as the ICO network becomes more valuable, helps kick-start network effects in the early stages.

[54] Jiasun Li and William Mann, 'Initial Coin Offering and Platform Building' (2018) SSRN; Usman W Chohan, 'Initial Coin Offerings (ICOs): Risks, Regulation, and Accountability' in Stéphane Goutte, Khaled Guesmi and Samir Saadi (eds), *Cryptofinance and Mechanisms of Exchange* (Springer 2019).

[55] Aija Leiponen, Llewellyn DW Thomas, and Qian Wang, 'The dApp Economy: A New Platform for Distributed Innovation?' (2022) 24 Innovation 125.

[56] An example of a dApp social network is Steemit.

[57] Jeffrey Church, Neil Gandal, and David Krause, 'Indirect Network Effects and Adoption Externalities' (2008) 7 Review of Network Economics 337.

[58] Chainlink is a notable oracle example.

[59] Yannis Bakos and Hanna Halaburda, 'Overcoming the Coordination Problem in New Marketplaces via Cryptographic Tokens' (2022) 33 Information Systems Research 1368; Rowena Gan, Gerry Tsoukalas, and Serguei Netessine, 'Decentralized Platforms: Governance, Tokenomics, and ICO Design' (2023) 69 Management Science 6667.

[60] See US Securities and Exchange Commission, 'Framework for "Investment Contract" Analysis of Digital Assets' (8 March 2023) at <https://www.sec.gov/corpfin/framework-investment-contract-analysis-digital-assets>.

iii) Network effects in mining and staking pools

Mining and staking are responsible for the processing and validation of the transactions proposed for inclusion on DLT networks. Control over mining and staking, therefore, amounts to control over what is recorded on the network ledger. Strong network effects in mining and staking would suggest that the effective control of any given network could eventually become the prerogative of a single mining or staking entity.[61] Overall, while factors that tend to support network effects in mining and staking can be identified, these economic activities are also characterized by forces that resist full centralization.

At a basic level, mining and staking should not normally give rise to network effects (Figure 6.2). Nodes' success rate in appending and validating blocks is proportional to their mining or staking power.[62] When miners or stakers come together to form mining or staking pools, their individual success rate does not increase, and therefore the addition of new miners or stakers to the pool should not make the pool more valuable to existing users.

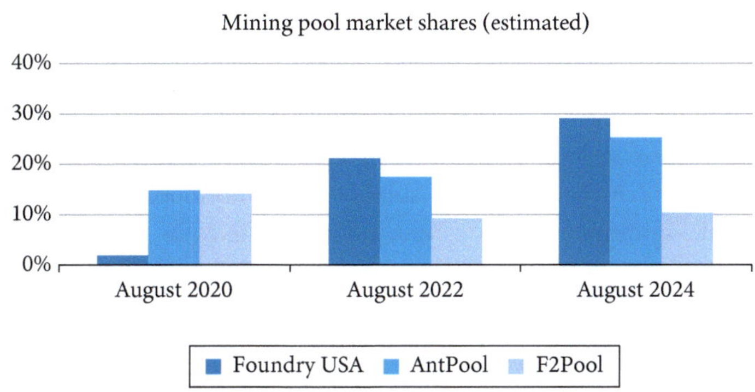

Figure 6.2 Market shares of major mining pools. Despite some concentration, mining does not appear to be a winner-take-all market on account of network effects.
Source: Data from BTC.com, Hashrate Index, Cryproslate

Success rate, however, is not the only aspect of value users draw from participating in pools. While pool size may not normally increase profitability, it increases the frequency by which users get rewarded for participating in the pool

[61] Without suggesting that network effects are a contributory factor, the mining market is characterized by a long tail oligopolistic market structure. See eg <https://hashrateindex.com/hashrate/pools> which shows dominance by a small number of pools and a long tail of smaller pools.

[62] Jacob D Leshno and Philipp Strack, 'Bitcoin: An Axiomatic Approach and an Impossibility Theorem' (2020) 2 American Economic Review: Insights 269. But see José Parra-Moyano, Gregor Reich, and Karl Schmedders, 'A Note on the Non-Proportionality of Winning Probabilities in Bitcoin' (2023) 64 Computational Economics 1697.

(sometimes this is referred to as risk-sharing, the risk being the inability of sole miners to find blocks within reasonable timeframes).[63] This is because, as mentioned, the likelihood of finding the next block is proportional to capacity, and so the larger the share of a pool relative to total capacity in the network, the more frequently it will be finding new blocks, and the more frequently it will be collecting block rewards and distributing it to its members. For that reason, frequency of payments through risk-sharing (as distinguished from size of payments) can be the source of network effects in mining and staking pools. This would suggest that users have an incentive to join the biggest pool further reinforcing its size advantage.

There can be other sources of network effects in mining pools. For instance, bigger mining pools may be able to supra-proportionately increase their ability to detect transactions in the memory pool with higher pay-offs, or to front-run transactions.[64] In that case, the addition of every new user to the pool creates externalities that extend beyond the capacity the user contributes. The precise mechanism by which the mining process can deviate from the axiom that mining success is proportional to mining capacity is less important than the fact that such mechanisms exist, which in turn open the door to network effects.[65]

On the other hand, there are a number of factors that constrain network effects in pools. This suggests that network effects can be strong enough to drive pools' initial success and maintain it at a certain level, but, since they are not inexhaustible, it is unlikely that they will result in (near-) monopoly situations. Among the important limitations that constrain network effects in mining and staking pools are governance, user preferences, fees, and risk-sharing across, rather than within, pools.

Governance is an unquantifiable but powerful factor. Because validators, such as miners and stakers, are responsible for what gets recorded on the ledger, there is a strong sense that this function should not be vested in a single entity, since this would allow it to act arbitrarily and even fraudulently.[66] These concerns are not exclusive to traditional permissionless DLT networks; even private or semi-open networks, such as Ripple and Hedera, often opt for multi-stakeholder governance acknowledging the benefits of decentralized validation.[67] Under this light, when a

[63] Lin William Cong, Zhiguo He, and Jiasun Li, 'Decentralized Mining in Centralized Pools' (2021) 34 The Review of Financial Studies 1191.

[64] See eg Christof Ferreira Torres, Ramiro Camino, and Radu State, 'Frontrunner Jones and the Raiders of the Dark Forest: An Empirical Study of Frontrunning on the Ethereum Blockchain' (2021) Proceedings of the 30th USENIX Security Symposium 1343.

[65] For more methods of manipulating the mining process see nn 82, 83, and accompanying text.

[66] Roman Beck, Christoph Müller-Bloch, and John Leslie King, 'Governance in the Blockchain Economy: A Framework and Research Agenda' (2018) 19 Journal of the Association for Information Systems 1020; Johannes Rude Jensen, Victor von Wachter, and Omri Ross, 'How Decentralized Is the Governance of Blockchain-Based Finance: Empirical Evidence from Four Governance Token Distributions' (2021) arXiv:2102.10096.

[67] Hedera claims that numerous 'collusion-resistant organizations lead the Hedera network' and RippleNet, which is Ripple's global payments network, claims that it 'is democratically governed by

validator (which can be an individual or a mining or staking pool) reaches capacity levels that would allow them to unilaterally control the validation process, at least some (other) validators are likely to choose to compete rather than join, with the view to better distribute power across the network. Therefore, while it may be economically rational to join the bigger validator, validators may choose to refrain on the grounds of the considerations of wider dispersion of validation power to prevent controlling monopolies. Such (non-economic) decisions can undercut network effects that could otherwise arise.

Moreover, while pools allow more frequent payments to participating users, practicality and costs place an upper limit to how frequent payments will become. Most large pools gravitate towards daily or twice-daily payments, as it is doubtful that even more frequent payouts would increase the value of the pool to users. At the same time, larger pools tend to have higher fees,[68] so what users get in higher frequency of payments, they lose in lower payments. This is explained by standard oligopoly theory, whereby firms that command a larger share of the market are seen to have respective market power which they exercise through higher prices, and has been empirically validated and modelled for mining pools too.[69] Depending on individual preferences, the point where preferred frequency of payments meets the highest fee a user is willing to pay to the pool, is the point where network effects are exhausted. See Table 6.2.

Lastly, the risk-sharing benefit miners and stakers enjoy by pooling together their resources into a pool, they can also get by diversifying across different pools.[70] This kind of multihoming, that is, mining or staking for different pools, undercuts the incentive behind all miners or stakers joining the same pool, since in both cases pooling occurs. As a result, network effects can be obtained across and not only within pools, which may prevent pool centralization.

(C) Economies of scale and scope

Economies of scale and scope refer to production economies that allow firms to produce at lower costs as production grows (scale) or diversifies (scope).[71] Economies of scale are associated with firm size and materialize when production costs rise proportionately less than output when output increases. Diseconomies

the RippleNet Committee—a group of global, industry-leading financial institutions'. See respectively <https://hedera.com/council> and <https://ripple.com/ripplenet-committee/>.

[68] Cong, He, and Li (n 63).
[69] ibid.
[70] ibid.
[71] Aubrey Silberston, 'Economies of Scale in Theory and Practice' (1972) 82 The Economic Journal 369; Stigler (n 4).

Table 6.2 Factors cutting in favour and against concentration in the mining/staking market based on network effects and economies of scale and scope.

Factors cutting in favour concentration	Factors cutting against concentration
• Under certain conditions larger pools may be able to detect more profitable transactions. • Larger pools can provide more frequent and stable payouts (but there is a low ceiling to this benefit). • Larger pools may have more resilient cost structure to weather volatility. • Larger pools enjoy higher scale economics on expensive capital costs. • Larger pools may have better vertical integration prospects.	• Larger pools are technically not more successful in mining/staking. • Larger pools on average charge higher (internal) fees. • Larger pools may be perceived as a threat to the decentralized nature of the DLT industry.

of scale are also possible, whereby production passes the optimum point and costs per additional unit begin to increase. Economies of scope arise when the cost of producing two or more products jointly is lower than when they are produced independently. Economies of scale and scope can serve as barriers to expansion or entry—albeit not uncontroversially—because they give a cost advantage to large established firms compared to smaller firms or new entrants.[72] This has been well recognized in antitrust law.[73]

Typically, economies of scale are divided into real and pecuniary economies: real economies are those that refer to actual production economies owing to size, whereas pecuniary economies derive from the better deals and enhanced perception larger firms can achieve in the market.[74] Examples of real economies are the initial fixed costs and capital, labour specialization, technological advancements, advertising, and information. Examples of pecuniary economies are lower interest rates on finance products, bulk discounts, and enhanced bargaining power. Some assets can realize both economies of scale and scope. For example, information can be reused both across the production of multiple units of the same product (scale) and across different products (scope).[75]

72 Kip W Viscusi, Joseph E Harrington, and John M Vernon, *Economics of Regulation and Antitrust* (4th edn, MIT Press 2005) 168–72.

73 Case 27/76 United Brands Company and United Brands Continentaal BV v Commission of the European Communities ECLI:EU:C:1978:22, para 122; Commission decision of 13 May 2009 COMP/37.990 Intel, paras 859 et seq; Commission decision of 29 May 2018 M.8084 Bayer/Monsanto, para 178; *Brunswick* (n 5); *Rebel Oil* (n 5).

74 Ramesh Chandra and Roger Sandilands, 'The Role of Pecuniary External Economies and Economies of Scale in the Theory of Increasing Returns' (2006) 18 Review of Political Economy 193.

75 Robert Wilson, 'Informational Economies of Scale' (1975) 6 The Bell Journal of Economics 184.

Despite the occasional reference in case law and the theoretical recognition in antitrust analysis, economies of scale and scope have traditionally not been a determinative factor. Two difficulties beset their use. First, virtually every economic activity involves a measure of economies of scale or scope, since very few input assets are exclusively committed to and consumed in the production of only one unit of output. As input assets are spread over more units of output (both quantity and type) economies of scale and scope are realized. Therefore, it is not a matter of whether economies of scale and scope generally exist, but rather a matter of identifying, and ideally quantifying, the particular types of economies of scale and scope in a given industry. In DLT markets, economies can be realized either in the same way as they do in other markets, or through the exploitation of particular DLT features, which makes them harder to recognize but imperative to consider. Secondly, the cost advantage that economies of scale or scope accord does not automatically result in industry structure conducive of anticompetitive outcomes. Whether economies of scale and scope indeed serve as a formidable barrier to entry and expansion depends on the minimum efficient scale, the size of the market, and other factors. These are examined in turn below.

i) Economies in mining and validation

Traditional economies with application in DLT markets. Mining exhibits both economies that resemble those encountered in traditional markets, and economies that are realized due to the unique features of DLT. Among the traditional economies, those relating to capital and specialization are commonly encountered. Capital investments can become significant sources of economies of scale and scope where large fixed costs are spread over multiple units and types of output. In proof of work (PoW) mining, the initial investment in mining equipment is spread over the mining of multiple blocks (scale) and it is also common for miners to mine for different DLT ledgers/networks thereby spreading the capital cost across multiple networks (scope).[76] Scope economies are limited, however, by the fact that mining is commonly performed using Application-Specific Integrated Circuits (ASICs), which are customized chipsets that specialize in one mining algorithm, and therefore do not perform as well in other mining contexts. Also,

[76] Yonatan Sompolinsky and Aviv Zohar, 'Bitcoin's Underlying Incentives' (2017) 15 ACM Queue 29; Aljosha Judmayer and others, 'Merged Mining: Curse or Cure?' in Joaquin Garcia-Alfaro and others (eds), *Data Privacy Management, Cryptocurrencies and Blockchain Technology*, vol 10436 (Springer International Publishing 2017).

mining equipment itself, being a form of computer equipment, is noted to exhibit economies of scale, because the increase in power is larger than the increase in cost of producing more powerful equipment.[77]

Moreover, larger miners are more resilient and less likely to go out of business when mining rewards drop or when mining difficulty rises, and therefore they utilize the capital equipment over a longer period of time allowing greater economies of scale.[78] Contestability can theoretically ease the effect of this factor, but it is as of yet an untested hypothesis.

Specialization of labour makes production more efficient and can therefore increase output for the same cost. Larger mining pools have been known to develop specialized mining equipment, which significantly improves the chances of finding blocks for the same (or similar) variable costs (eg electricity).[79] For instance, Bitmain, historically the largest ASIC manufacturer in the world, also operates two popular mining pools, Antpool and BTC.com.

Idiosyncratic DLT economies. The less visible but interesting economies in mining are those that emerge due to the strategic (but legal) exploitation of the nature and operation of the DLT itself.[80] At a basic level, because validation rewards are in principle proportional to the contributing capacity, the validation process should not give rise to economies.[81] That said, there are various ways of strategic manipulation by larger miners. These, while instructive, are merely indicative of the broader observation that the mining process can and is manipulated by larger miners. The current methods of strategic manipulation may be superseded in future protocol releases, but the principle may remain that larger miners can find ways to earn supra-proportionate rewards. Supra-proportionate reward means a mining revenue share that exceeds the capacity share that the miner is contributing in the blockchain network. Normally, mining rewards are in principle proportionate to the mining capacity; economies of scale emanating from strategic manipulation allow larger miners to secure revenue shares that are higher than their capacity share.

[77] Sompolinsky and Zohar (n 76); Michael Bedford Taylor, 'The Evolution of Bitcoin Hardware' (2017) 50 Computer 58.

[78] See Shaurya Malwa, 'As Bitcoin Bellyflops to $54K Only Five Mining Rigs Remain Profitable, Says F2Pool' *CoinDesk* (5 July 2024).

[79] Taylor (n 77).

[80] Strategic exploitation is used herein to refer to methods that take advantage of consensus protocols to deliver results that are unintended (dishonest) by the protocol design, but which are still legal. There are numerous other methods that can achieve unanticipated results, but which are illegal. While the boundaries are yet unclear, examples of potentially illegal methods can be found in Aron Laszka, Benjamin Johnson, and Jens Grossklags, 'When Bitcoin Mining Pools Run Dry' in Michael Brenner and others (eds), *International Conference on Financial Cryptography and Data Security* (Springer 2015); Benjamin Johnson and others, 'Game-Theoretic Analysis of DDoS Attacks Against Bitcoin Mining Pools' in Rainer Böhme and others (eds), *International Conference on Financial Cryptography and Data Security* (Springer 2014).

[81] See nn 62, 63.

One way larger miners can achieve that is by minimizing the chances of mining orphaned blocks.[82] Orphaned blocks are blocks that have been validly mined but do not end up being included in the longer and only valid blockchain (commonly due to network latency), and therefore the accompanying reward is lost and the mining capacity that has been committed to their mining wasted. Because the decision on which block will be confirmed in the longer chain and which will be orphaned is up to miners, larger miners have more influence on this decision and can therefore minimize the chances of mining blocks that will end up becoming orphaned and wasteful.

Another method of strategic manipulation to generate economies of scale is through 'selfish mining'.[83] In selfish mining, exploitative miners that represent at least 30 per cent of total mining capacity keep the blocks they find hidden from the main blockchain and create an initially private fork. The rest of the miners continue to mine on the public chain, while the selfish miners on their own private fork. When the public blockchain approaches the selfish miners' private fork in length, the selfish miners reveal blocks from their private chain to the public, establish a longer, and therefore now valid, blockchain, causing some of the other miners to join them, further increasing their revenues.

Moreover, larger miners may be more likely to identify first transactions that yield high rewards relative to payload, because they can achieve more widespread connectivity in the network and therefore are more likely to be able to choose first which of the pending transactions they will process. This would allow them to compile blocks that contain more lucrative transactions. Technical advancements may complicate the picture and mitigate the effect of size here; there are various sophisticated methods to increase the maximal extractable value (MEV) of mining, with entities called searchers undertaking the role of finding and ordering lucrative transactions to feed to miners.[84] In this process, miner size does not necessarily accord an advantage in selecting lucrative transactions, because the relevant task of finding and selecting transactions is performed by searchers.

[82] Nick Arnosti and S Matthew Weinberg, 'Bitcoin: A Natural Oligopoly' in Avrim Blum (ed), *10th Innovations in Theoretical Computer Science Conference*, vol 124 (Schloss Dagstuhl 2018).

[83] Ittay Eyal and Emin Gün Sirer, 'Majority Is Not Enough: Bitcoin Mining Is Vulnerable' in Rainer Böhme and others (eds), *International Conference on Financial Cryptography and Data Security* (Springer 2014); Nicolas T Courtois and Lear Bahack, 'On Subversive Miner Strategies and Block Withholding Attack in Bitcoin Digital Currency' (2014) arXiv:1402.1718.

[84] See Financial Conduct Authority, 'Review of Maximal Extractable Value and Blockchain Oracles' (2024) Research Note 02/2024.

ii) Economies in DLT applications and services

Economies can also be realized in applications and services that are built on top of the consensus layer undertaken through mining and/or validation. These types of economies may be grounded either in the way the consensus layer operates, or in the way the application or service itself operates, but in either case, the economies assist the economic activity of the application or service, not the underlying consensus mechanism.

A key source of economies grounded on the operation of the consensus layer but benefiting the content layer on top relates to security and trust. One of the main functions of the consensus process in DLT networks is to serve as a secure way of recording valid transactions. The novelty of DLTs lies in replacing a centralized authority charged with ensuring the integrity and functionality of the system with a distributed group of nodes, which performs the same function through a secure consensus process. In both PoW and PoS consensus models, the more the committed resources (computational work or stake) that are required in the process of validation, the more secure the system becomes,[85] and the harder it is for attackers to compromise it.[86] This generates economies of scale in the form of security and by extension trust. Because DLT applications and services often function as platforms or intermediaries, whose success heavily relies on designing and maintaining a robust reputation system,[87] this type of 'economies of trust' becomes critical.[88] This is even more true considering the predominantly finance-oriented nature of applications and services in the decentralized economy. As the validator base of applications and services grows larger, so does their security and by extension their reputation for being trustworthy, and they can attract more people more easily. See Figure 6.3.[89]

[85] Carl Worley and Anthony Skjellum, 'Blockchain Tradeoffs and Challenges for Current and Emerging Applications: Generalization, Fragmentation, Sidechains, and Scalability' (2018) 2018 IEEE International Conference on Internet of Things (iThings) 1582, 1584; Mauro Conti and others, 'A Survey on Security and Privacy Issues of Bitcoin' (2018) 20 IEEE Communications Surveys & Tutorials 3416, 3435.

[86] Arthur Gervais and others, 'On the Security and Performance of Proof of Work Blockchains' (2016) Proceedings of the 2016 ACM SIGSAC Conference on Computer and Communications Security 3.

[87] Michael Luca, 'Designing Online Marketplaces: Trust and Reputation Mechanisms' (2017) 17 Innovation Policy and the Economy 77; Hemang Subramanian, 'Decentralized Blockchain-Based Electronic Marketplaces' (2017) 61 Communications of the ACM 78.

[88] See also below in section D.

[89] Catalini and Gans (n 53) 13.

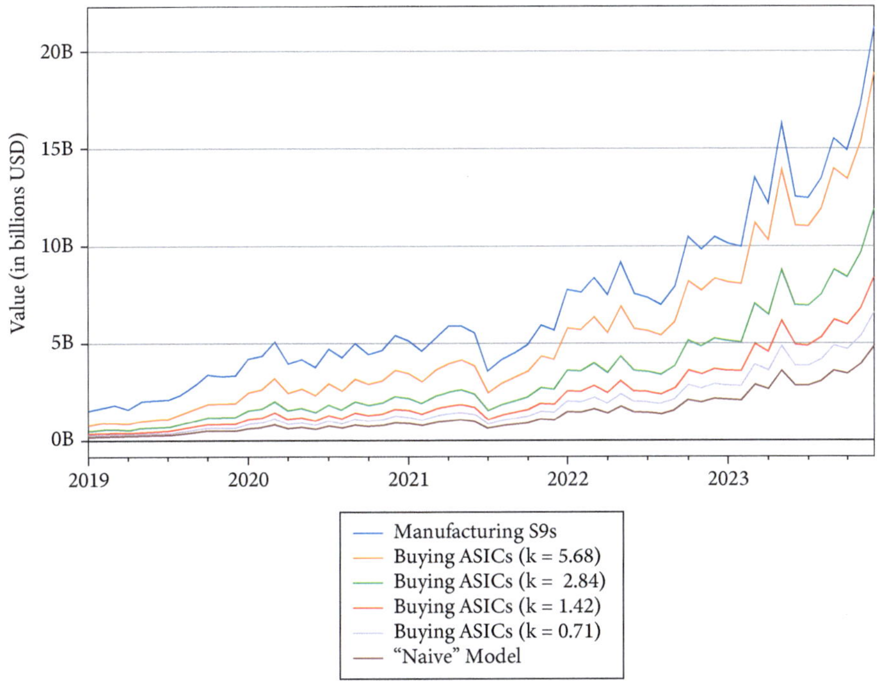

Figure 6.3 Total cost of a one-hour attack of the Bitcoin network under different assumptions around procuring the necessary mining equipment. It is evident that the cost is virtually prohibitive under all assumptions making the Bitcoin network extremely secure, and therefore reliable in the eyes of users and investors.
Source: Coin Metrics

On the other hand, size can also give rise to diseconomies of scale. As DLT networks grow larger, they may take longer to validate transactions, either because of the higher volume that validators have to process, or because some of the transactions will be de-prioritized as higher volume pushes up transaction fees, which not all users will be willing to pay (putting aside the design features of each network which is the predominant factor that affects speed).[90]

Economies that are grounded in the way the application or service itself operates can often be similar to those arising when the application or service is offered in traditional markets, or they can be more idiosyncratic to the DLT context. For example, it is well documented that larger exchanges or banking institutions exhibit economies of scale and scope on account of more efficient information

[90] Scalability of blockchain networks, namely the ability to grow larger while maintaining performance is a key concern. See Soohyeong Kim, Yongseok Kwon, and Sunghyun Cho, 'A Survey of Scalability Solutions on Blockchain' (2018) 2018 International Conference on Information and Communication Technology Convergence (ICTC) 1204.

gathering and use, more robust risk profiles, and more efficient deployment of technology.[91] There is no reason to believe that crypto-exchanges and other DLT financial institutions cannot benefit from the same factors. Furthermore, larger crypto-exchanges maintain deeper orderbooks minimizing spread,[92] and they can more easily and credibly develop complementary services such as their own token with which they can offer additional financial services.[93]

Economies that are more idiosyncratic to DLTs implicate again the consensus layer, and have been observed in decentralized finance (DeFi) applications such as decentralized exchanges (DEX). Unlike most crypto-exchanges, which are centralized and settle most trades off-chain (ie on the exchange platform rather than on the underlying asset ledgers), DEX execute and settle transactions on-chain and therefore need to record them on the ledger by going through the applicable consensus process. Larger nodes comprising the DEX can exert greater influence on the consensus process, preferencing transactions that will help them achieve better trading deals, for instance through arbitrage or front-running.[94] While some of the ways by which better deals can be achieved may be banned on traditional exchanges (eg front-running) and soon on crypto-exchanges as well, the exploitation of the underlying consensus layer can, as a matter of fact, allow the realization of economies.

iii) Assessing the impact of economies of scale and scope in DLT markets

The mere existence of factors that can give rise to economies does not inexorably mean that economies constitute formidable barriers to expansion or entry, or that they grant a significant competitive advantage. It is almost impossible to find production lines that do not benefit at all from economies of scale, scope, or both. Instead, where economies become relevant is across two dimensions: (a) determining what level of production meets the minimum efficient scale or scope, and

[91] Shaofang Li and Matej Marinč, 'Economies of Scale and Scope in Financial Market Infrastructures' (2018) 53 Journal of International Financial Markets, Institutions and Money 17; Amélie Charles and others, 'Stock Exchange Mergers and Market Efficiency' (2016) 48 Applied Economics 576; Joseph P Hughes and Loretta J Mester, 'Who Said Large Banks Don't Experience Scale Economies? Evidence from a Risk-Return-Driven Cost Function' (2013) 22 Journal of Financial Intermediation 559; David C Wheelock and Paul W Wilson, 'Do Large Banks Have Lower Costs? New Estimates of Returns to Scale for U.S. Banks' (2012) 44 Journal of Money, Credit and Banking 171.

[92] Clara Medalie, 'Bid-Ask Spread as an Indicator of Crypto-Market Liquidity' *Medium* (27 April 2020).

[93] For example, Binance, the world's largest crypto-exchange, also issues BNB, a native token used to pay for fees when trading on Binance, usually at a discounted rate.

[94] Philip Daian and others, 'Flash Boys 2.0: Frontrunning in Decentralized Exchanges, Miner Extractable Value, and Consensus Instability' (2020) 2020 IEEE Symposium on Security and Privacy (SP) 566.

(b) determining the share of the market that corresponds to that level. For either of those dimensions to become influential in antitrust policy, they would need to reflect a considerable measure of economies. If economies account for only marginal benefits, they likely will not rise to the level of constituting barriers to expansion or entry.

The minimum efficient scale tells us the level of production (regarding both scale and scope) at which long run average costs are minimized. Firms that can achieve minimum efficient scale produce at the lowest possible cost, and any further increase in size or diversity of output does not yield further reductions in production. In other words, this is the level where economies are exhausted.[95] If economies are exhausted at a production level that is attainable by numerous firms, then economies are not a high barrier to expansion or entry, whereas if relatively large investments are required to achieve minimum efficient scale then fewer firms (or perhaps even just one) will be able to achieve the most efficient level of production, meaning that a competitive advantage will accrue to an oligopolistic (or monopolistic) group of market actors.[96]

The share of the market required for minimum efficient scale tells us how many firms in a defined market can achieve that level. Sometimes, even if the necessary investment is low and numerous firms can afford it, the market is simply not big enough to accommodate all of them. Firms that will be limited to smaller than required market shares will not be able to operate at the optimal scale and will therefore operate at a competitive disadvantage. This also means that if the market can only accommodate one or a small number of firms that can fully exploit economies of scale and scope, then monopoly or oligopoly will be the most economical structure of production. It also means that because the production will be taking place at the tail end of the cost curve, production will be most efficient.[97] However, as the

[95] Richard Schmalensee, 'Economies of Scale and Barriers to Entry' (1981) 89 Journal of Political Economy 1228, 1230.

[96] Vinod K Gupta, 'Minimum Efficient Scale as a Determinant of Concentration: A Reappraisal' (1981) 49 The Manchester School 153; Stephen Davies, 'Minimum Efficient Size and Seller Concentration: An Empirical Problem' (1980) 28 The Journal of Industrial Economics 287.

[97] This is an intuitive point that expresses antitrust law's focus on efficiency. In *Beef Industry Development Society* the question was whether an agreement among beef producers to increase sustainability of production but which at the same time required limiting production was anticompetitive. Advocate General Trstenjak observed that the agreement would artificially keep inefficient producers in business, whom the market would otherwise reject. In his words: 'In the first hypothetical situation (without the BIDS agreements), the selection function of competition would generally mean that the most efficient processors on the market stay, or the processors who best meet the demands of their customers and ultimately of consumers. If the stayers are selected in the second hypothetical situation (with BIDS agreements) not through the market mechanisms, but through an arrangement between the processors, this affects the selection function of competition . . . Under the BIDS arrangement, a processor cannot therefore decommission its inefficient processing plants and remain on the market with the efficient processing plants'. See Opinion of AG Trstenjak in Case C-209/07 Beef Industry Development and Barry Brothers ECLI:EU:C:2008:467, para 81.

size of the market and the factors that feed into production costs and economies change, so does the most efficient industry structure.

It is difficult to assess those two dimensions in DLT markets because of their volatility. An estimation of minimum efficient scale is only meaningful if the production parameters that inform the analysis remain relatively stable and are representative of a firm's (or industry's if one is to extrapolate from there) operation. Similarly, to determine whether economies are likely to favour a concentrated or unconcentrated industry structure, the size of the market that the industry covers would have to be known. The idiosyncratic features of the decentralized economy cause dramatic fluctuations in production and market metrics, making it hard to find a representative scale and scope of operation to use as a yardstick. Both the mining/validation industry segment, which represents the consensus layer, and the applications and services segment are susceptible to this type of indeterminacy.

The mining/validation industry segment expands and contracts often and significantly, in response to demand for DLT products and services, the assigned or perceived value of such products and services, and network adjustments to account for security. When DLT products and services are in high demand, more capacity is required to perform the consensus function necessary to run them. As a corollary, consensus protocols adjust the difficulty rate to ensure that the network remains secure (otherwise, increased validation capacity could facilitate compromise of the consensus process). Because the above factors have been noted to be volatile, so is the output of the mining/validation industry segment, which represents its size.[98]

Figure 6.4 shows that the profitability of Bitcoin miners relative to the committed resources has been erratic. Because part of validators' reward comes in the form of block rewards (eg a Bitcoin denomination for every block mined), which they use to pay for their costs, the real value of tokens in fiat money matters. As the exchange rate of tokens to fiat money fluctuates dramatically, so do production costs,[99] which, again, makes the calculation of economies challenging, or at the very least hard to generalize to the whole industry segment.

[98] See Chapter 4 section D.

[99] Mick Roche, 'Bitcoin's Supply Reduction: What Does Bitcoin's Fourth Halving Mean, and Why Does It Matter?' *ZodiaMarkets* (18 April 2024).

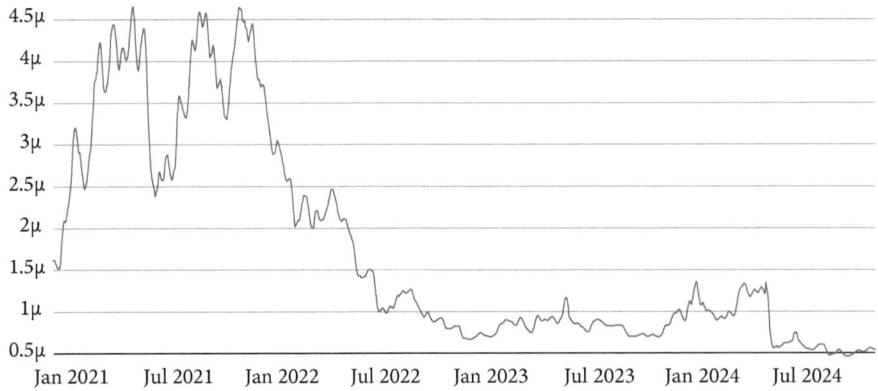

Figure 6.4 Miner revenue (in USD) per hash. Hash rate represents the estimated number of hashes per second the bitcoin network performs in 24-hour increments and therefore shows the committed resources to the network. Miner revenue expresses the total revenue from block rewards and miner fees. It is evident that the revenue rate relative to committed resources fluctuates widely, which makes it hard to estimate (minimum) efficient scales of operation in the mining industry.
Source: Coin Metrics

The applications and service segment is not immune to the indeterminacy of economies either. This is both because DLT applications and services rely on the consensus layer, and so the production realities of the consensus layer are embedded into the applications and services layer, but also due to the volatility of their own production realities. For example, crypto-exchanges, much like regular exchanges, can exhibit economies of scale relating to bid–ask spread and the price impact of trades,[100] but these are tied to the volume exchanged on their platforms. With vast fluctuations in exchange volume and the costs of processing the trades, the calculation of economies is an inaccurate exercise.

(D) Branding and economies of trust

Strong reputation and branding are also commonly examined as barriers to entry.[101] Brand identity can shield a product or service from competition by creating market inertia around it as consumers and users may be unwilling to try

[100] Torsten Schaper, 'Organising Equity Exchanges' (2012) 10 Information Systems and e-Business Management 43.

[101] Commission decision of 13 May 2009 COMP/37.990 Intel, paras 867 et seq; Commission decision of 27 June 2017 AT.39740 Google Search (Shopping), para 312.

alternatives.[102] Usually aided by large advertising investments and imperfect information that hinders switching, branding establishes and perpetuates product differentiation and conditions of monopolistic competition around the benefiting product or service.[103]

In exceptional cases, strong branding can endow a product or service with 'must-have' status, meaning that the product or service is so essential to consumers and users that it always needs to be featured in the relevant market. In *Intel*, the Commission found the company possessed must-have status 'resulting from its investment in product differentiation and its installed base'. The Commission concluded that 'Intel's must-stock status provides it with significant leverage over its OEM customers because a switch to an all- or majority-AMD product line-up would be unrealistic for them'.[104] In *Google Search*, the Commission similarly found that 'because of the strength of the Google brand, users trust in the relevance of search results provided by Google. Consequently . . . a significant number of users are unlikely to multi-home even if Google were to degrade the quality of its general search service', a finding that was mirrored by the District Court in the *Google Search Advertising* case in the United States too.[105]

Strong reputational effects can also be noticed in markets of the decentralized economy, although the degree to which they amount to a barrier to entry would have to be empirically tested in concreto. They are particularly pronounced as regards the feature of trust, which plays a major role in DLT product and service adoption due to the early (and to some extent continuing) concerns around the legitimacy, safety, and security of the blockchain industry.[106] Therefore, products or services that are perceived as trustworthy can build an insurmountable advantage to them, especially combined with first-mover advantages.[107]

The branding effects of trust have been determinative in the exchanges market. Coinbase, for instance, heavily relied on trust as a differentiating factor against competition when it went public.[108] Despite the fact that Coinbase fees have

[102] See David Aaker, 'Win the Brand Relevance Battle and Then Build Competitor Barriers' (2012) 54 California Management Review 43; Richard Schmalensee, 'Brand Loyalty and Barriers to Entry' (1974) 40 Southern Economic Journal 579.

[103] Intel (n 101) paras 867–869. See also Steven Salop, 'Information and Monopolistic Competition' (1976) 66 The American Economic Review 240.

[104] Intel (n 101) para 870.

[105] Google Shopping (n 101) para 312. *U.S. v. Google, Inc.*, 1:20-cv-03010-APM (2024), paras 130–133.

[106] Martin Fleischmann and Björn Ivens, 'Exploring the Role of Trust in Blockchain Adoption: An Inductive Approach' (2019) Hawaii Proceedings of the International Conference on System Sciences. See also PricewaterhouseCoopers, 'Global Blockchain Survey 2018' (2018), at 4 ('Blockchain, by its very definition, should engender trust. But in reality, companies confront trust issues at nearly every turn'); Zeynep Gurguc and William Knottenbelt, 'Cryptocurrencies: Overcoming Barriers to Trust and Adoption' (2018) Imperial College London Consultants.

[107] Richard Schmalensee, 'Product Differentiation Advantages of Pioneering Brands' (1982) 72 The American Economic Review 349.

[108] Coinbase Global, Inc. Form S-1 Registration Statement under the Securities Act of 1933 (25 February 2021), at 89.

historically been among the highest in the industry,[109] Coinbase userbase has grown exponentially over the last decade,[110] as Coinbase built a reputation for the most secure, trusted, and law-compliant exchange in the market.[111] As a result, Coinbase became the preferred exchange for risk-averse institutional investors, whose trading grew to even surpass that of retail investors since 2019.[112] For the same reasons of trust and compliance, Coinbase has become the preferred custodian of Bitcoin ETFs, sparking fears of concentration in that segment of the market.[113]

Trust plays a role in the cryptoasset market as well, as it constitutes one of the main parameters for adoption.[114] For instance, while Bitcoin may not be the fastest or most versatile cryptocurrency available, its consensus mechanism has never been compromised and it is commonly ranked as the top cryptocurrency on numerous dimensions.[115] The trust users show in Bitcoin creates positive feedback to the point where Bitcoin is now a must carry cryptoasset.

[109] Bailey Reutzel, 'Coinbase Review: A Crypto Exchange for New Investors and Traders' *CNBC* (30 January 2023).

[110] 'Coinbase Usage and Trading Statistics' (*Backlinko*, 11 June 2024).

[111] 'Coinbase Strategy Teardown: How Coinbase Grew into the King Midas of Crypto' (2021) CB Insights Research Report.

[112] Coinbase SEC Form S-1, at 6 and 24–28.

[113] Yueqi Yang and Olga Kharif, 'Coinbase at the Center of Bitcoin ETF Draws Envy and Risks' *Bloomberg* (15 January 2024).

[114] Venkata Marella and others, 'Understanding the Creation of Trust in Cryptocurrencies: The Case of Bitcoin' (2020) 30 Electronic Markets 259.

[115] Besides market capitalization and security, Bitcoin ranks toward the top also in liquidity and (low) volatility. See also Muhammad Habib ur Rehman and others, 'Trust in Blockchain Cryptocurrency Ecosystem' (2020) 67 IEEE Transactions on Engineering Management 1196; Felix Irresberger, Kose John, and Fahad Saleh, 'The Public Blockchain Ecosystem: An Empirical Analysis' (2020) SSRN.

PART III
OFFENCES

7
ABUSE OF DOMINANCE AND MONOPOLIZATION

(A) General 173
(B) Defining and extending the concepts of abuse and monopolization in the decentralized economy 174
  i) The standard merit-based definitions and tests of abuse and monopolization 175
  ii) Abuse and monopolization in the decentralized economy: beyond merit 178
(C) Types of abuse and monopolization: Introducing governance abuse 183
  i) The standard classifications of abuse and monopolization and their links to applicable legal tests 183
  ii) Governance abuse 186
    a) Description and function of governance abuse 186
    b) Relevant markets in governance abuse 191
(D) Specific abuse and monopolization practices 194
  i) Refusal to deal and the essential facilities doctrine: Access to DLT networks, products, services, and consortia 194
  ii) Discrimination, self-preferencing, neutrality 204
    a) Discrimination in Article 102(c) TFEU and Robinson Patman Act: Application to delisting, AMMs, and MEV 206
    b) Self-preferencing: Filling the gaps of traditional discrimination 213
    c) Blockchain neutrality 216

(A) General

The abuse of dominance or monopolization offence aims at putting a backstop to how dominant firms can use their market power. While having market power is not per se illegal, it rarely sits well with antitrust authorities. 'Bigness' is often seen as an anathema in competition policy, because, even if it remains in check, it still has the potential to distort the competitive fabric of markets, let alone when abused.[1] This is not only due to the economic effects attributed to it (such as

[1] Adi Ayal, 'The Market for Bigness: Economic Power and Competition Agencies' Duty to Curtail It' (2013) 1 Journal of Antitrust Enforcement 221; Barak Orbach and Grace Campbell Rebling, 'The Antitrust Curse of Bigness' (2012) 85 Southern California Law Review 605.; Naomi R Lamoreaux, 'The Problem of Bigness: From Standard Oil to Google' (2019) 33 Journal of Economic Perspectives 94.

Antitrust in the Decentralized Economy. Konstantinos Stylianou, Oxford University Press.
 DOI: 10.1093/9780191925504.003.0007

industry concentration, higher entry barriers, too-big-to-fail concerns, threats to innovation, etc), but also due to political effects (such as political influence and a distortive role in democracy).[2] At the same time, when bigness is meritorious, one should not be punished for finding success. The offence of abuse of dominance or monopolization is tasked with striking the fine balance between tolerating and even encouraging meritorious success which may result in substantial market power, and preventing its undue acquisition, maintenance, or exercise. But, since 'the means of illicit conduct and the means of legitimate competition are myriad',[3] the difficulty lies in how to devise legal standards to tell the difference.

The features of Distributed Ledger Technology (DLT) markets, and of the decentralized economy more generally, further complicate the discovery of which conduct is abusive or monopolistic and why. A key reason for that is that the concept of abuse and monopolization developed under certain neoclassical economic assumptions about how firms and markets operate, which may not fully apply in the decentralized economy, which is partly influenced by its grassroots pedigree, social production, and ethos that at times diverges from purely economic considerations.[4] Secondly, due to the central role of governance in the production process of DLT products and services, a concept of governance abuse may need to be recognized. Thirdly, even traditional types of abuse or monopolization, such as refusal to deal and anticompetitive discrimination, while still applicable in the decentralized economy, require adaptations.

(B) Defining and extending the concepts of abuse and monopolization in the decentralized economy

The exact meaning of what conduct constitutes abuse of dominance or monopolization has eluded authorities and scholars since the inception of competition laws.[5] This is somewhat expected, since competition laws are abstract, and markets are characterized by multifarious business practices. To devise therefore a universally accepted or applicable definition or legal test to distinguish between legitimate competition and abusive or monopolizing conduct is next to impossible. Considering that the decentralized economy opens up yet more types of business conduct, it makes the inquiry even more challenging, particularly because in the new economic context of the decentralized economy we may not know what we should be looking for (the 'unknown unknowns', in Rumsfeld's parlance).[6] This

[2] Ayal, ibid; Orbach and Campbell Rebling, ibid; Lamoreaux, ibid.

[3] *United States v. Microsoft Corp.*, 253 F.3d 34, 58 (2001).

[4] See Chapter 1 section D and below, section B.

[5] See the comprehensive note by OECD, 'Competition on the Merits' (2005) DAF/COMP(2005)27 21–23.

[6] United States Department of Defense, 'Defense.gov News Transcript: DoD News Briefing – Secretary Rumsfeld and Gen. Myers' (12 February, 2002). Archived from the original on 6 April 2016, at

section summarizes current conceptualizations of what constitutes abuse of dominance or monopolization, and also discusses extensions thereof that are necessary to account for newfound conduct enabled by the technological novelties of the decentralized economy.

i) The standard merit-based definitions and tests of abuse and monopolization

Definitions. The concepts of abuse and monopolization aim to tell apart conduct that is considered normal legitimate competition, from anticompetitive illicit competition[7] ('normal competition' is the terminology used in EU competition law as the flipside of abuse of dominance).[8] These are not defined in the black letter of the law; instead, it is courts that have interpreted them. The definitions courts have come up with broadly fall under two groups: those that are circular and therefore unhelpful, and those that juxtapose abusive and monopolistic conduct with conduct that reflects competition on the merits. There are numerous definitions in the first group, which, albeit technically good law, do not provide much guidance. For example, EU and US courts have ruled that normal competition (and therefore not abuse or monopolization) consists in practices that do not 'unfairly tend to destroy competition',[9] 'are not directed at smothering competition',[10] do not 'substantially fetter competition',[11] or do not 'hinder the maintenance of the degree of competition still existing in the market or the growth of that competition'.[12] These formulations are circular because they define legitimate competition as practices that cannot or do not harm competition, but the whole point of the inquiry is to define what harms competition.

The remaining (non-circular) definitions understand abuse or monopolization as conduct that departs from *competition on the merits*. There are numerous variations of what merit means. In *Irish Sugar* the Court of Justice (CoJ) noted that 'Article 86 of the Treaty [now 102 TFEU] prohibits a dominant undertaking from eliminating a competitor and thereby reinforcing its position by having recourse to means other than those within the scope of *competition on the merits*' (emphasis

<https://web.archive.org/web/20160406235718/http://archive.defense.gov/Transcripts/Transcript.aspx?TranscriptID=2636> (all links were last accessed on 1 September 2024).

[7] OECD (n 5) 17–18.; Alison Jones and Brenda Sufrin, *EU Competition Law* (5th edn, OUP 2014) 378–81.

[8] See most recently Case C-333/21 European Superleague Company ECLI:EU:C:2023:1011, para 125 (with references to additional case law).

[9] *Spectrum Sports, Inc. v. McQuillan*, 506 U.S. 447, 458 (1993).

[10] *Berkey Photo, Inc. v. Eastman Kodak Co.*, 603 F.2d 263, 275 (1979).

[11] Case C-6/72 Europemballage Corporation and Continental Can Company v Commission ECLI:EU:C:1973:22, para 26.

[12] Case 85/76 Hoffmann-La Roche & Co. AG v Commission ECLI:EU:C:1979:36, para 91.

added).[13] In *AKZO*, the CoJ offered a slight variation of competition on the merits by ruling that 'Article 86 [now 102 TFEU] prohibits a dominant undertaking from eliminating a competitor and thereby strengthening its position by using methods other than those which come within the scope of *competition on the basis of quality*' (emphasis added).[14] In the recent landmark *Servizio Elettrico Nazionale* decision, the CoJ summarized the concept of abuse as follows:

> [I]n order to establish whether a practice constitutes abuse of a dominant position, it is sufficient for a competition authority to prove that that practice is capable of *impairing an effective competition structure* on the relevant market, unless the dominant undertaking concerned shows that the exclusionary effects that could result from the practice at issue are *counterbalanced or even outweighed by positive effects for consumers* (emphasis added).[15]

The first part follows the kind of circular definitions mentioned earlier, while the second part conditions acceptable conduct on producing positive effects for consumers.

In the United States, the Supreme Court elaborated on merit ruling in *Grinnell* that monopolization is 'the willful acquisition or maintenance of [monopoly power] as distinguished from growth or development as a consequence of a *superior product, business acumen, or historic accident*' (emphasis added).[16] And in a similar vein in *Aspen Skiing*, the district court instructed the jury that the question of monopolization revolved around the distinction 'between practices which tend to exclude or restrict competition on the one hand and the success of a business which reflects only *a superior product, a well-run business, or luck, on the other*' (emphasis added).[17] Looked at from the opposite side, in *Olympia Equipment*, the Seventh Circuit ruled that 'conjoined with other evidence, *lack of business justification* may indicate probable anti-competitive effect' (emphasis added).[18]

From the above definitions it follows that competition law understands illicit conduct as conduct deviating from pro-competitive considerations. The case of *Professional Engineers*, even though it did not concern a monopolization tactic but rather an unreasonable restraint of trade, expresses this obsession with competition-only parameters as bluntly as a court can express itself.[19] The issue in

[13] Case T-228/97 Irish Sugar plc v Commission ECLI:EU:T:1999:246, para 111.

[14] Case C-62/86 AKZO Chemie BV v Commission ECLI:EU:C:1991:286, para 70. See also British Airways, where the CFI stated that 'the protection of the competitive position of an undertaking which . . . occupies a dominant position must, at the very least, in order to be lawful, be based on criteria of economic efficiency': Case T-219/99 British Airways plc v Commission ECLI:EU:T:2003:343, para 280.

[15] Case C-377/20 Servizio Elettrico Nazionale SpA and Others v Autorità Garante della Concorrenza e del Mercato and Others ECLI:EU:C:2022:379, para 48.

[16] *United States v. Grinnell Corp.*, 384 U.S. 563, 570–71 (1966).

[17] *Aspen Skiing Co. v. Aspen Highlands Skiing Corp.*, 472 U.S. 585, 596 (1985).

[18] *Olympia Equipment Leasing Co. v. Western Union Telegraph Co.*, 797 F.2d 370, 378 (1986).

[19] *National Society of Professional Engineers v. United States*, 435 U.S. 679 (1978).

that case was an association's canon of ethics prohibiting competitive bidding by its members. The rationale the association offered was that the ban was put in place to minimize the risk that competition would produce inferior engineering work endangering the public safety. The Supreme Court emphatically rejected this goal as pertinent to antitrust law. It ruled that the 'petitioner's attempt to [justify the ban] on the basis of the potential threat that competition poses to the public safety and the ethics of its profession is nothing less than a frontal assault on the basic policy of the Sherman Act'.[20]

From definitions to legal tests. The above understandings of abuse and monopolization are admittedly still too abstractly phrased to be of specific guidance. This is why they have further been translated into legal tests for use in specific abuses or monopolization practices. Different practices can be decided upon based on different tests, even though the concept of abuse and monopolization is ostensibly objective and static. The two main tests that are currently in use are the no economic sense test—preferred in the United States—[21] and the as efficient competitor test—preferred in the European Union.[22] The 'no economic sense' test holds that conduct should be unlawful if it makes no economic sense absent its tendency to eliminate or lessen competition.[23] For example, in *Matsushita* the Supreme Court ruled that '[t]o survive petitioners' motion for a summary judgment, respondents must establish that there is a genuine issue of material fact as to whether petitioners entered into an illegal conspiracy that caused respondents to suffer a cognizable injury. If the factual context renders respondents' claims implausible, that is, claims that make no economic sense, respondents must offer more persuasive evidence to support their claims than would otherwise be necessary'.[24]

The as efficient competitor test asks whether the challenged conduct is likely to exclude rivals that are at least as efficient as the dominant firm, and if the answer is positive, then the conduct constitutes illicit competition, and if the answer is negative, then the conduct is considered lawful. For instance, in *AKZO*, the CoJ found prices below average total costs as abusive if they are determined as part of a plan for eliminating a competitor, since '[s]uch prices can drive from the market undertakings which are perhaps as efficient as the dominant undertaking but which, because of their smaller financial resources, are incapable of withstanding the competition waged against them'.[25]

[20] ibid at 695.

[21] See eg *Matsushita Electric Industrial Co. v. Zenith Radio Corp.*, 475 U.S. 574 (1986); *United States v. Aluminum Co. of America*, 148 F.2d 416 (1945).

[22] Commission Guidelines on the Commission's enforcement priorities in applying Article 82 of the EC Treaty to abusive exclusionary conduct by dominant undertakings (2009/C 45/02), para 25; AKZO (n 14); Commission decision of 13 May 2009 COMP/37.990 Intel. See also Richard A Posner, *Antitrust Law* (2nd edn, University of Chicago Press 2001) 194.

[23] OECD (n 5) 27; Gregory J Werden, 'The No Economic Sense Test for Exclusionary Conduct' (2005) 31 Journal of Corporate Law 293.

[24] *Matsushita* (n 21) 575.

[25] AKZO (n 14) para 72.

The above definitions and tests, and their many variations,[26] remain all applicable in the decentralized economy as well, but so does the challenge of translating actual business conduct into proxies of merit, and even more pertinently for the decentralized economy, the question whether merit and its proxies should be the only basis around which definitions of abuse and monopolization are developed considering the decentralized economy's alternative and often subversive origins and character that may not fully subscribe to metrics developed for the mainstream economy. The following section expands on this.

ii) Abuse and monopolization in the decentralized economy: beyond merit

The problem. The above definitions make clear that normal legitimate competition is to be assessed on the grounds of competition-related merit, which encompasses either improvements in quality or efficiency, or reduction in prices, or is the result of business ingenuity, innovation or technical, economic, or managerial progress. It is against these proxies that courts have traditionally assessed business conduct. But with merit being the standard of assessment, there is an implicit assumption that the challenged conduct *can* indeed be a reflection of merit, otherwise there is nothing to assess the conduct against. This approach creates the following problem: how does one assess merit in economic contexts that materially differ from the ones courts and authorities are familiar with, especially if such economic contexts encompass *competitively neutral* conduct, which neither necessarily promotes nor undermines competition-related merit parameters such as quality, efficiency, pricing, or progress? The decentralized economy can indeed raise this challenge, because DLT-based products and services are partly defined by governance and social production processes that reflect considerations alien to merit or competition, and which were either absent or less determinative in traditional markets.[27]

Considerations beyond merit. The social production and governance of decentralized economy products and services brings together various stakeholders with diverging interests which may but do not necessarily serve merit considerations. They are not always geared towards progress and improvement; instead, they may reflect ideological, sociological, or cultural considerations that have to do with the ethos and purpose of a decentralized economy,[28] with the promotion of social good (however defined) and wealth redistribution,[29] with the role

[26] See OECD (n 5).

[27] See Chapter 1 sections C.ii and C.iii.

[28] Nigel Dodd, 'The Social Life of Bitcoin' (2018) 35 Theory, Culture & Society 35.

[29] David Golumbia, *The Politics of Bitcoin Software as Right-Wing Extremism* (University of Minnesota Press 2016) chs 2 and 4.

of technology in society,[30] with inclusion and representation,[31] and with social power dynamics.[32] Writing in the early days of the industry about Bitcoin, which back then was synonymous with the industry, Kostakis and Giotitsas theorized that '[Bitcoin] creators' intention was to create a currency that is rid of debt in the spirit of various politico-economical critiques of the credit system' and that 'as a piece of software [it] is imbued with ideas drawn from a certain political framework'.[33] Bauwens, Kostakis, and Pazaitis go further and claim that DLT infrastructures enable a new form of capitalism, 'distributed capitalism', which 'purport[s] to offer individual autonomy from both big business and the state. In this model, the aspects of autonomy and large-scale participation are celebrated and supported by P2P infrastructures, though individual profit-maximization is still the primary motive'.[34] Along the same lines, Golumbia argues that 'Bitcoin can be seen as a technical object that is structured to an unusual extent by politics . . . Bitcoin's real utility and purpose (and that of the cryptocurrency movement in general) can be better understood as a "program" for recruiting uninformed citizens into a neoliberal and (nominally) anti-government political discourse'.[35] Synthesizing the influences DLT networks are subject to what Alston et al call 'polycentric, in that they are subject to the social rules that emanate from multiple decision centers, social rules which include institutions articulated through the formal collective choice mechanisms of specific organizations, as well as norms emanating from the cultural groups that exist within and around these organizations'.[36] While the influences can relate to objective and economic considerations, such as how to improve a network's speed or scalability, and therefore be well reflected in merit-based conceptions of abuse or monopolization, they can also encompass non-economic considerations that traditional undertakings—the usual subjects of competition law—are not normally associated with. For instance, an entire sub-segment of the cryptocurrency market, the so-called *memecoins*, with market capitalization in the tens of billions, is motivated by such varied purposes as criticizing the industry itself by targeting speculation, expressing internet culture, expressing community

[30] Toni Caradonna, 'Blockchain and Society' (2020) 43 Informatik Spektrum 40.

[31] Qiqi Gao and Jiteng Zhang, *Artificial Intelligence Governance and the Blockchain Revolution* (Springer 2024) ch 4.

[32] Malcolm Campbell-Verduyn, 'The Distributions of Distributed Governance: Power, Instability and Complexity in Polycentric Data Ordering' in Carolina Aguerre, Malcolm Campbell-Verduyn, and Jan Aart Scholte, *Global Digital Data Governance* (Routledge 2024).

[33] Vasilis Kostakis and Chris Giotitsas, 'The (A)Political Economy of Bitcoin' (2014) 12 tripleC 431, 435.

[34] Michel Bauwens, Vasilis Kostakis, and Alex Pazaitis, *Peer to Peer: The Commons Manifesto* (University of Westminster Press 2019) 37.

[35] David Golumbia, 'Bitcoin as Politics: Distributed Right-Wing Extremism' in Geert Lovink, Nathaniel Tkacz, and Patricia de Vries (eds), *An Intervention in Digital Economy* (Institute of Network Cultures 2015) 120.

[36] Eric Alston and others, 'Blockchain Networks as Constitutional and Competitive Polycentric Orders' (2022) 18 Journal of Institutional Economics 707, 707.

sentiment, or commenting on viral events,[37] none of which at first glance relate to merit proxies. Even more established products are sometimes defined by non-economic considerations. For example, Bitcoin's governance is known to prioritize immutability and a rigid adherence to the fundamental principles of blockchains, even if that means foregoing objective improvements such as in terms of speed or scalability, and Ethereum, even though it is more open to flexible consensus, is known to sometimes adopt controversial decisions that go against the spirit of blockchain's immutability but serve fairness and reputation, as exemplified in the decision to hard fork Ethereum after the 2016 DAO incident.[38]

Analogy with standard-setting processes (and limits thereof). None of these considerations are automatically excluded for the purview of competition law, but to be taken into consideration under a traditional understanding of abuse or monopolization they would have to be linked to merit as the only available standard as per above. In fact, such economic activity that comprises open-market governance and decision-making is not completely foreign to competition law and its merit-based standard, but previous experience may be of limited value in the decentralized economy context. Perhaps the closest arrangement to the open market governance model described here is standard-setting consortia, with which competition law has had frequent encounters in the past.[39] Similar to DLT decision-making and production, standard-setting consortia bring together independent players that jointly develop outputs and doing so is an economic activity. This activity can be (and has been) the subject of abuse of dominance or monopolization. But the standard-setting process is materially different in two respects:

> Firstly, in standard-setting mechanisms the express goal (and the reason why competition law tolerates such collaboration among otherwise horizontal competitors) is merit-based, that is, to achieve efficiencies and progress that would either be impossible, slower, or more costly absent the collaboration.[40] Therefore, standard-setting already by nature reflects a merit-based conception of normal competition. There is no such express expectation in the development, governance, or decision-making processes of products and services of the decentralized economy. While merit considerations certainly feed into governance and

[37] Yathukulan Yogarajah, '"Hodling" on: Memetic Storytelling and Digital Folklore Within a Cryptocurrency World' (2022) 51 Economy and Society 467; Adrian Stencel, 'What Is a Meme Coin? Dogecoin to the Moon!' (2023) hal-04360574.

[38] Primavera De Filippi, Morshed Mannan, and Wessel Reijers, 'Blockchain Technology and the Rule of Code: Regulation via Governance' (2022) hal-03883249 35.

[39] See eg James Anton and Dennis Yao, 'Standard-Setting Consortia, Antitrust, and High-Technology Industries' (1995) 64 Antitrust Law Journal 247; Björn Lundqvist, 'Competition Law as the Limit to Standard-Setting' in Josef Drexl and Fabiana Di Porto (eds), *Competition Law as Regulation* (Edward Elgar 2015).

[40] David Teece and Edward Sherry, 'Standards Setting and Antitrust' (2003) 87 Minnesota Law Review 1913. See also the European Telecommunications Standards Institute, 'Guidelines for Antitrust Compliance' (Version adopted by Board #133, 10 June 2021).

decision-making processes, the decentralized economy is, as mentioned, more eclectic in its origins, composition, culture, goals, and interests, such that merit considerations cannot be said to be as universal as in traditional standard setting activities.

Secondly, standard-setting is highly prescriptive based on detailed contracts and even government involvement.[41] The fact that the activities and relationships among firms are regulated through contractual agreements leaves only little room for competition law to apply, and when it does, the assessment of the conduct is heavily influenced by the contractual rights and obligations, which, as mentioned, already reflect merit goals.[42] Contrary to that, DLT products and services can often be grassroots, and can emerge and expand spontaneously without a commitment to adhere to a specific goal, interest, process, or structure. Whatever processes, protocols, and whitepapers exist that regulate and shape the blockchain product or service may not be legally binding, often lack detail, and may be subject to continuous change. In this context, the economic activity that develops is more unconstrained and competition law has a bigger role to play as a backstop regulator, which brings back the issue of the suitability of the merit standard to assess this type of economic activity. This factor is relaxed in enterprise level DLT activity to the extent that contractual relationships may be playing a more defining role.

Commonness and industry modus operandi as alternative non-merit considerations. It is not that the kind of alternative considerations ascribed to the decentralized economy and DLT markets are completely absent from traditional business conduct, but they were less pronounced, and the modern economic analysis of competition law has so forcefully emphasized merit in the form of efficiencies, welfare, and progress that any alternative consideration has been overshadowed by merit or subsumed under it. When new economic settings arise where business conduct is materially informed by non-merit considerations, an exclusive focus on merit may not capture how normal competition works in such economic settings. While admittedly courts do not differentiate normal competition based on the particular market in question, the very concept of normal competition implies a measure of how things are habitually ('normally') done in a given market. In that sense, conduct that is detrimental to competition is conduct that deviates from how competition is normally supposed to work in a given market. But this does not invariably need to be tied to merit. Therefore, assessing what normal competition means in the decentralized economy—a realm of economic activity that comprises

[41] Colin Scott, 'Standard-Setting in Regulatory Regimes' in Martin Cave, Martin Lodge, and Robert Baldwin (eds), *The Oxford Handbook of Regulation* (OUP 2010) 108–11. On government involvement see eg American National Standards Institute, 'United States Standards Strategy' (2023).

[42] See eg Gregory Sidak, 'The Frand Contract' (2018) 3 Criterion Journal on Innovation 1.

open-market governance, decision-making, and social production—may benefit from taking into account how such processes are supposed to commonly work, how they actually commonly work, and whether the aberrant conduct upsets those dynamics. Merit considerations do remain relevant, but complementary—no longer the only determinative considerations.

Reliance on this element of commonness of conduct and processes is grounded on the assumption or belief that common practices and processes are attuned to the needs and features of a certain market, and they reflect a modus operandi that the market gravitates towards.[43] Market actors do not operate in vacuum but rather their conduct is shaped by market characteristics and by other actors.[44] Where the existing merit-based standard may be less informative, either because the particular market context does not operate on the basis of merit, or because the modus operandi of the particular market context is novel and unfamiliar to competition law enforcers, the commonness criterion can fill the gap.

Resistance to commonness. It should be noted that enforcers have resisted arguments to that effect. In *Google Search*, Google explained that it was standard practice for search engines to compete in the market 'by showing *their* results, not results from other services [since] users do not expect search services to provide results from other services' (emphasis in the original), an argument that was rejected by the Commission.[45] In *British Airways*, the Commission similarly rejected an argument by British Airways that the kind of discrimination it engaged in was common in the market.[46] On the other hand, in *Tampa Electric*, the Supreme Court appeared to consider common business models by acknowledging that in utilities markets long-term exclusive supply contracts may be necessary.[47]

Evidently, this element of commonness sits uneasily in standard competition law enforcement. But it can be informative in economic contexts that defy the principles on which standard competition law tools were developed. In the end, factoring in the usual ways by which a certain non-traditional market works is still permitted by the textual interpretation of current standards. In *Irish Sugar* the CoJ stated that 'it is necessary to consider all the circumstances'[48] in determining whether a practice constitutes abuse or is legitimate competition, a phrasing that was repeated in many other cases.[49] The totality of circumstances can and should

[43] Konstantinos Stylianou, 'Can Common Business Practices Ever Be Anticompetitive? Redefining Monopolization' (2020) 57 American Business Law Journal 169, 197 et seq.

[44] Michael Porter, *The Competitive Strategy: Techniques for Analyzing Industries and Competitors* (Free Press 2004); Jay B Barney, 'Types of Competition and the Theory of Strategy: Toward an Integrative Framework' (1986) 11 Academy of Management Review 791; Richard R Nelson, 'Why Do Firms Differ, and How Does It Matter?' (1991) 12 Strategic Management Journal 61.

[45] Commission decision of 27 June 2017 AT.39740 Google Search (Shopping), para 657.

[46] British Airways (n 14) para 59.

[47] *Tampa Electric Co. v. Nashville Coal Co.*, 365 U.S. 320 (1961).

[48] Irish Sugar (n 13) para 114.

[49] Google Shopping (n 45); Case C-280/08 P Deutsche Telekom v Commission EU:C:2010:603, para 175.

include a consideration of the decision-making and production processes of the decentralized since these reflect priorities that deviate from those of the traditional firm, which merit-based standards had in mind.

(C) Types of abuse and monopolization: Introducing governance abuse

Abuse of dominance and monopolization practices usually follow one of two classifications: exploitative or exclusionary, and pricing or non-pricing. As will be shown, these distinctions are less determinative than their widespread mentions in soft law and case law might suggest. They do point, however, to an important implication, which is that they inform—although still not consistently—the choice of the appropriate legal test on how to distinguish abusive or monopolizing conduct from legitimate competition (see section B). The reason why this is a discussion worth having in the context of the decentralized economy is because there occurs conduct that should amount to abuse or monopolization which, however, may not be sufficiently caught by existing tests and distinctions and for which an expanded typology is required. This is the case with so-called *governance abuses*, which consist in conduct that manipulates the governance process underlying decentralized products or services. Governance abuses do not squarely fall under the exploitative/exclusionary distinction, and they can be effectuated through either pricing or non-pricing methods, without, however, the associated tests being sufficient.

i) The standard classifications of abuse and monopolization and their links to applicable legal tests

Exploitative practices are those that extract rent from consumers or take advantage of them in other ways that would not have been possible without substantial market power;[50] exclusionary practices are those that hinder the maintenance of the degree of competition in the market or the growth of that competition, thereby indirectly harming consumers.[51] Pricing abuses are those that are harmful to competition by employing the pricing mechanism,[52] whereas non-pricing practices encompass a variety of other methods to harm consumers or the competitive process.

[50] Robert O'Donoghue and A Jorge Padilla, *The Law and Economics of Article 102 TFEU* (3rd edn, Hart Publishing 2020) 294 et seq.

[51] Hoffmann-La Roche (n 12) para 91.

[52] John Temple Lang and Robert O'Donoghue, 'Defining Legitimate Competition: How to Clarify Pricing Abuses Under Article 82 EC' (2002) 26 Fordham International Law Journal 82; Kathryn McMahon, 'A Re-Evaluation of the Abuse of Excessive Pricing' in Pınar Akman, Or Brook, and Konstantinos Stylianou (eds), *Research Handbook on Abuse of Dominance and Monopolization* (Edward Elgar 2023).

The two types of classifications mentioned before are not hard-coded into competition law. The non-exhaustive listing of conduct that amounts to abuse in Article 102 TFEU seems to hint to a distinction between exploitative (Article 102(a) TFEU—unfair pricing and trading conditions) and exclusionary practices (Article 102(b) TFEU—limiting production, markets, or technical development), but the discriminatory practices described in Article 102(c) TFEU can be either, and the tying practices described in Article 102(d) TFEU are also exclusionary, which causes the classification to break down. Besides, even if the classification held up, the wording of Article 102 TFEU does not reserve different treatment of for each type of practice, and so the distinction seems moot. At the same time, US antitrust law barely recognizes exploitative practices, because its approach is that a monopolist can only charge whatever the market can bear and therefore there can be no exploitation,[53] and US antitrust doctrine is very reluctant to interfere with the pricing mechanism of the market. As a result, US antitrust law focuses almost exclusively on exclusionary practices, making the distinction irrelevant. Therefore, the distinction between exploitative and exclusionary practices seems to be purely of pedagogic value; it does not per se inform the legal treatment of the conduct, rather it simply serves to emphasize *why* the conduct runs afoul of competition law's goals.

The distinction between pricing and non-pricing practices is also not mentioned in the black letter of the law. The classification was explicitly introduced in the Commission's guidance on enforcement priorities in applying Article 102 TFEU as a way to determine the application of the correct legal test for finding abuse of dominance.[54] For pricing abuses, the Commission indicates that it will 'only normally intervene where the conduct concerned has already been or is capable of hampering competition from competitors which are considered to be as efficient as the dominant undertaking',[55] thereby endorsing the as efficient competitor test.

In that sense, the distinction between pricing and non-pricing abuses has the practical implication of linking certain abusive practices to a certain legal test. In the *Google Shopping* case, the General Court (GC) confirmed this link: to defendants' argument that the Commission failed to prove that Google's conduct drove out of the market equally efficient competitors, the GC stated that 'the Commission is correct in maintaining that it was not required to prove this. The use of the as-efficient-competitor test is warranted in the case of pricing practices'.[56] But despite the seeming clarity, the pricing/non-pricing distinction has suffered

[53] *Berkey Photo* (n 10) 297.
[54] Commission guidance on enforcement priorities (n 22).
[55] ibid para 23.
[56] Case T-612/17 Google and Alphabet v Commission (Google Shopping) ECLI:EU:T:2021:763, para 538.

many setbacks both on the grounds that it is unnecessary, and on the grounds of inconsistent application. Lianos et al characterize the distinction as a 'conceptual anomaly' in the framework of Article 102 TFEU, since price and non-price abuses can lead to similar foreclosure effects.[57] Meanwhile, the CoJ has refused to consistently endorse it across all pricing practices, notably in *Tomra*[58] and *Post Danmark II*,[59] where the CoJ, even though it confirmed that 'the application of the as-efficient-competitor test consists in examining whether the pricing practices of a dominant undertaking could drive an equally efficient competitor from the market',[60] it acknowledged that there is no obligation to base *all* pricing practices (in that case, rebates) on the as-efficient-competitor test, leaving margin for deviation.[61] The US Supreme Court has also ruled that 'there is no reason to distinguish between price and non-price components of a transaction'.[62]

Two insights derive so far: first, based on the discussion in sections B.i and C.i, it becomes apparent that despite efforts to establish one universally applicable test to assess conduct, different types of conduct may need to be assessed on the basis of different tests.[63] This, of course, creates a fragmentation risk, which has not gone unnoticed.[64] Secondly, albeit inconsistently, there is a tendency to condition applicable tests to the type of abuse or monopolization in question. As such, if new types of abuse or monopolization emerge in the decentralized economy, they may necessitate modifications in existing tests to account for the potentially special features of the new conduct. In section B.ii it was already argued that in determining what conduct should amount to abuse or monopolization, the modus operandi of the industry needs to be taken into account in an effort to move away from an exclusive focus to merit-based considerations. In section C.ii below, the concept of governance abuse is developed and is linked to how the modus operandi of the industry feeds into the legal test of determining governance abuse.

[57] Ioannis Lianos, Valentine Korah, and Paolo Siciliani, *Competition Law*, vol 1 (OUP 2019) 889.

[58] Case C-549/10 P Tomra Systems and Others v Commission EU:C:2012:221.

[59] Case C-23/14 Post Danmark A/S v Konkurrencerådet EU:C:2015:651.

[60] ibid para 56.

[61] ibid para 57.

[62] *Pacific Bell Telephone Company v. Linkline Communications Inc.*, 129 S Ct 1109 (2009), para 10.

[63] Mark S Popofsky, 'Defining Exclusionary Conduct: Section 2, the Rule of Reason, and the Unifying Principle Underlying Antitrust Rules' (2006) 73 Antitrust Law Journal 435, 437; Douglas Melamed, 'Exclusive Dealing Agreements and Other Exclusionary Conduct–Are There Unifying Principles' (2006) 73 Antitrust Law Journal 375; Andrew I Gavil and others, *Antitrust Law in Perspective: Cases, Concepts, and Problems in Competition Policy* (3rd edn, West Academic Publishing 2017) 596–600.

[64] John Vickers, 'Abuse of Market Power', Discours lors de la 31ème Confèrence de l'Association Europèenne pour la Recherche en Èconomie Industrielle (Berlin 2004) at 6.

ii) Governance abuse

a) Description and function of governance abuse

Description. Governance abuse describes practices that compromise or manipulate the decision-making process of DLT-based products and services. That is, the element of abuse or bad conduct manifests itself in the governance process. Decision-making process means both the consensus mechanism itself, that is, the way by which DLT networks determine which transactions are to be added onto the ledger, as well as the mechanisms by which decisions are taken regarding the product or service features and operation, including any voting procedures. It should also be understood to encompass both the technical (eg coding of protocols) and non-technical (eg capacity or voting manipulation) aspects of decision-making processes.[65]

Governance abuse is a newly emerging form of abuse because the market context in which it can arise did not exist in traditional markets. In traditional abuse of dominance and monopolization analysis, the firm is regarded as a black box. The particular mechanics of how corporate decisions are taken in the production process are immaterial as long as the conduct can be imputed to the firm, and any internal-to-the-firm malfeasance is the subject matter of corporate law, not competition law.[66] In that sense, firms' internal decision-making processes are not the subject of abuse or monopolization claims in themselves; it is the outcome of the processes as they manifest themselves as business conduct in the market that competition law is after.

The situation is different with DLT products and services, because of their social production and distributed nature of decision-making. While it is possible that a DLT product or service is developed entirely within the boundaries of a single undertaking, the majority of DLT networks (even enterprise DLTs) bring together undertakings from the open market. The DLT decision-making and operation processes ('governance') bind together the participating undertakings, but these still operate in the open market environment. Because the decision-making and operation processes are diffused across market participants, distorting these processes is equal to distorting the market in which governance takes place. The fact that the participating undertakings may all be working toward the common goal of enabling and offering the product or service does not detract from their functioning as independent undertakings capable of manipulating the competitive

[65] For the elements of the governance process see Chapter 1 section D.iii.

[66] There are, of course, exceptions, whereby antitrust law is also involved in the internal decision-making process of the firm, notably with criminal liability of cartel executives, director disqualification, and horizontal shareholding. But these areas represent a minority of antitrust practice. See Florence Thépot, *The Interaction Between Competition Law and Corporate Governance: Opening the 'Black Box'* (CUP 2019).

positioning of other undertakings and their offerings in the governance market or the product or service market linked to the underlying governance.

Real-world application. An example, based on real-world events,[67] of what can amount to governance abuse and why existing definitions and tests may fail to recognize it can be instructive here: a dominant undertaking that manufactures specialized mining equipment (application-specific integrated circuit (ASIC)) takes out a flash loan to acquire sufficient voting rights to steer the Decentralized Autonomous Organization (DAO) entrusted with managing a decentralized finance (DeFi) smart contract to pass a proposal for a protocol update that would optimize its validation process for the dominant undertaking's ASIC chips, thereby extending its dominance. Flash loan is a type of uncollateralized loan that lets users borrow assets with no upfront collateral as long as the borrowed assets are paid back within the same blockchain transaction.[68] As a result, large amounts can be borrowed, which can and often are used to influence voting processes that distribute voting rights based on the amount of committed assets. Flash loans are not illegal and are common practice in decentralized markets. DeFi products are usually developed on the basis of smart contracts that control their operation, and the smart contracts in turn are often managed, governed, and updated through DAOs. The reason why DAOs are used is to prevent centralized control over the smart contract (whereas with DAOs voting rights are distributed to a larger base) and by extension over the DeFi product or service.

In this example, the DAO's governance is taken over by the dominant undertaking to impose a design choice in the validation process of the DeFi product, which will result in the adoption of the dominant undertaking's ASICs. Note that (a) the dominant undertaking makes use of legitimate tools (ie flash loan); (b) plays by the rules of the DAO governance process; and (c) the optimization for the dominant firm's ASICs is not a purely economic decision, because the question of whether protocols of decentralized products or services are designed to be conducive or resistant to ASIC efficiencies goes directly to the heart of what it means for DLT products and services to avoid exposure to unidimensional sources of influence. Conduciveness or resistance to ASICs in general or a specific ASIC in particular has to do with the decentralization ethos of the industry and the tensions

[67] The example is a combination of two cases. In the *Platypus Finance* case, hackers removed $8.5m from Platypus Finance, a DeFi service, but they were acquitted by the French court, which ruled that the exploit of the flawed smart contract was non-fraudulent. The hackers used flash loans in support of their attack. See Louis Adam, 'Piratage de La Plate-Forme de Cryptomonnaies Platypus: Les Deux Accusés Relaxés Par La Justice' *Le Monde* (1 December 2023). In a separate incident, Bitmain, the world's largest manufacturer of mining equipment, was accused of manipulating Bitcoin Cash's governance at the expense of the competing Bitcoin SV cryptocurrency, because its mining equipment was more optimized for Bitcoin Cash. See *United American Corp. v. Bitmain, Inc. et al.*, 530 F. Supp. 3d 1241 (2021).

[68] Dabao Wang and others, 'Towards A First Step to Understand Flash Loan and Its Applications in DeFi Ecosystem' (2021) Proceedings of the Ninth International Workshop on Security in Blockchain and Cloud Computing 23.

between polycentricity and hierarchical authority that characterize the industry's decision-making.[69] The fact that the dominant undertaking stands to gain from the DeFi product switching to its ASIC chips cannot fully mask the additional perceived roles and considerations of the consensus mechanism.

The traditional merit-based conceptualization of abuse and the associated tests to detect it may be of limited help here. Indeed, if one were to apply the preferred merit-based understanding of abuse and the no economic sense test, the question would revolve around whether increasing one's influence in the voting process by buying up assets that give voting rights does not make sense absent its tendency to reduce competition in the voting process. One can argue that it does not make sense: the argument would be that reducing competition in the voting process is the only reason why one would build up their voting stake, which would imply that the conduct fails the test and is illicit. But this is not a helpful conclusion because all voting processes are a zero-sum game—every vote that is gained by one side is lost by another—and if one knew in advance that they would not be able to overtake competition, they would not seek to increase their influence over voting in the first place. An economic sense test seems to be overinclusive with regard to voting. On the other hand, one can argue that the conduct makes economic sense: the argument would be that increasing voting power by buying voting rights through a flash loan makes economic sense because it constitutes merit-based competition. But because this conduct emerges in the context of a governance process, a conclusion cannot be reached solely on the usual economics-oriented understanding of merit-based competition. As explained, governance in the decentralized economy is a confluence of diverse forces, some of which are merit driven, but some have socio-political or other idiosyncratic motivations linked to the nature of the decentralized economy (these may often be competitively neutral). Because these diverse forces are inextricably intertwined, it is impossible to include the merit-oriented ones but exclude the non-merit ones in the assessment of governance conduct. Competition law necessarily needs to account for any non-merit considerations in determining whether the element of abuse or the element of bad conduct in monopolization is present.

Operationalizing governance abuse. To incorporate additional non-merit considerations into governance abuse or monopolization tests it was suggested above that the commonness of business practices can play a role. A study into the habitual role, use, function, and context of the challenged governance conduct is essential in

[69] See David Rozas and others, 'When Ostrom Meets Blockchain: Exploring the Potentials of Blockchain for Commons Governance' (2021) 11 SAGE Open 215824402110025; Primavera De Filippi and Xavier Lavayssière, 'Blockchain Technology: Toward a Decentralized Governance of Digital Platforms?' in Anna Grear and David Bollier, *The Great Awakening: New Models of Life Amidst Capitalist Ruins* (Punctum Books 2020) 196–201; Stephen DiRose and Mo Mansouri, 'Comparison and Analysis of Governance Mechanisms Employed by Blockchain-Based Distributed Autonomous Organizations', *2018 13th Annual Conference on System of Systems Engineering (SoSE)* (IEEE 2018) 199.

understanding and appreciating its purpose and effects. The logistics of integrating commonness into legal tests as a heuristic are described in detail elsewhere.[70] In short, the commonness test suggest that the commonness of a business practice in the market in which it occurs should be examined before considering the question of whether the practice is supported by legitimate business justifications and efficiencies. It comprises two steps. The first step is to ask whether the practice under question is *designed* to harm competition—which is not the same as being likely to harm competition. This step ensures that certain practices, no matter how common, will not qualify as normal competition given their pernicious nature as signalled by the fact that their success is predicated on harming competition. If it is not designed to harm competition, then the test asks whether the business practice under scrutiny is common in the market in which it occurs. If the practice is common and not designed to harm competition, then it should be considered normal competition and therefore not be deemed illegal monopolization without requiring a showing of business justifications or efficiencies, as is required under the current tests. If it is not common, then the examiner may revert to another test of choice.

What is important to address here is the sources one would have to look at to determine commonness in governance in the decentralized economy. In other words, where can competition authorities look to assess the usual meaning and function of the challenged practice in the context it emerges? This can be a tricky and onerous task, because the social production nature of the decentralized economy, of which governance forms part, is often characterized by unwritten, informal, and malleable norms, whose detection and interpretation may be elusive.

At the very least, a key source to be consulted is the written (enacted) rules of governance of the product or service in question.[71] These can be founding whitepapers, bylaws, and any procedural rules that define governance participants, role allocation, powers and responsibilities, proposal and voting processes, validation, reporting, and accountability.[72] However, not all DLT products and services have well-developed enacted rules; many rely on customary (interactional) norms that are harder to detect and specify, but to the extent possible, these should be consulted too. Such informal norms may reflect deviations from the written rules, or they can constitute separate practices altogether, which are indicative of what is common and acceptable, common but unacceptable, uncommon but acceptable, or uncommon and unacceptable. Obviously, common and acceptable practices

[70] Stylianou (n 43).

[71] See Project Liberty and BlockchainGov, 'Interim Report on Blockchain Governance Practices: Insights' (2023) 9.

[72] On sources and structures of governance see Yue Liu and others, 'Defining Blockchain Governance Principles: A Comprehensive Framework' (2022) 109 Information Systems 102090; Jersain Zadamig Llamas Covarrubias and Irving Norehem Llamas Covarrubias, 'Different Types of Government and Governance in the Blockchain' (2021) 10 Journal of Governance and Regulation 8.

provide the strongest indication that they form part of legitimate governance even though they are not enshrined in enacted rules. Norms that are deemed unacceptable should not be counted as legitimate competition even if they are common, since they are clearly misaligned with the industry's best practices (in the commonness test, such practices would count as designed to harm competition and would therefore fail the test).[73]

Flash loans to increase voting capacity would fall under the category of unwritten practices that are commonly fed into governance, and the inquiry would turn on deciphering the market's and community's sentiment on their habitual role, use, function, and context in governance. It is in this assessment that such non-merit parameters would need to be considered.

There is also the issue of how the different sources should be weighed against each other. Because governance is a multi-stakeholder process influenced by formal or informal written or unwritten rules and customary practices, there is often lack of coordination and reconciliation, and as a result there emerges an incohesive picture of how governance is supposed to work in the studied context.[74] It is impossible to offer a universally applicable ranking of source authoritativeness and prioritization, and it cannot even be asserted that written rules overrule unwritten norms as more formal—if anything, governance seems to be more about actual practice than black-letter provisions, as exemplified by deviations in landmark moments of the decentralized economy's development.[75]

One last consideration that comes into the picture, to which the answer also seems elusive for now, concerns the evolution of governance rules and norms. DLT governance is protean, especially to the extent that it is informed by customary practices (as opposed to written rules, which may be more stable), and this should be accounted for when attempting to identify the content and zeitgeist of DLT governance practices that are challenged under competition law. It seems right to apply the commonness test to assess governance dynamics at the time the challenged practice occurred, and not at the time of the investigation. While this sounds reasonable, competition law has in the past been affected by time sequence problems, and so it is worth raising awareness about this potential pitfall. For instance, when assessing tying and specifically the question of whether the two tied products are separate, the test 'focuses on historic consumer behaviour, likely before integration'

[73] See Stylianou (n 43) 209–11.

[74] See Nadine Kathrin Ostern and Guido Perscheid, 'Solve for Blockchain: Toward A Framework for Navigating Blockchain Tensions' (2021) 11 ICIS 2021 Proceedings 1.

[75] Perhaps the most famous governance conflict was the DAO hack incident, which, after a decentralized autonomous organization built on Ethereum was hacked, created two factions in the Ethereum community on how to deal with the hack. One option was to fork the Ethereum blockchain to 'undo' the results of the hack, a move that would violate blockchain's basic premise of immutability. The other option would be to do nothing as per the blockchain's normal operation, acknowledging that the hack exploited a vulnerability in the DAO code. The first option was preferred in the end. See Vikram Dhillon, David Metcalf, and Max Hooper, 'The DAO Hacked' in Vikram Dhillon, David Metcalf, and Max Hooper, *Blockchain Enabled Applications* (Apress 2017).

and therefore risks ignoring consumer behaviour and preferences post integration.[76] So, even if two products would eventually naturally 'merge' into one, the tying test would treat them as two at the time of the tying and condemn the practice. To avoid such discontinuities, the investigation into governance abuse should aim to ascertain governance patterns at the time of the conduct.

b) Relevant markets in governance abuse

In governance abuses, there are two sets of relevant markets: the governance market(s) and the DLT product or service market(s). The governance market encompasses the economic activity around the governance that gives shape to and supports the DLT product or service. It includes the consensus-building process (eg mining), protocol development, and any other process that feeds into a DLT network's governance structure. While the economic activities included in governance markets may be disparate, their collective output can be seen as a unified one, that of providing the decision-making, consensus-building, and validation infrastructure necessary for products and services that are built on top. To appreciate this point consider how miners, even though they perform an economic activity distinct from protocol development, determine the protocol's fate and therefore the underlying governance: protocols provide the instructions on how DLT network work, including their consensus mechanisms, but the actual performance of the consensus is performed by miners. When there is a protocol update (or a fork), miners choose whether to adopt the update or not by continuing to mine on their preferred version of the protocol. As a result, miners 'vote' on governance choices through a choice of their own on where they channel their mining capacity. Together, protocol developers and miners offer governance, a distinct market worth monopolizing (by either a dominant developer or dominant miner or other dominant undertaking in the governance market).

Since the governance market can be distinct from the product or service market, there are three possibilities in terms of how those two markets can relate to each other:

a) The undertaking abuses its dominance (monopolizes) in the governance market to maintain or enhance its dominance (monopoly) in that same market. In this paradigmatic case of abuse of dominance or monopolization, where market power, anticompetitive conduct, and effects take place in the governance market, the DLT product or service market is unaffected. The dominant undertaking's goal is to control the governance market for what it is, not as a proxy to control the DLT product or service market. For example, a mining pool may want to monopolize the Bitcoin mining market to

[76] *Microsoft (US)* (n 3) 77.

maximize profits from mining without any interest in influencing Bitcoin's features and market positioning through using its mining power to control Bitcoin's governance process. Note that the effects of the conduct need not be limited to the market where the conduct occurs; for instance, in *Apple Music Streaming*, market power and conduct occurred in the OS/app distribution market, whereas the effects occurred in the music streaming market.[77]

b) The undertaking abuses its dominance in the governance market to acquire, maintain or enhance power in the DLT product or service market. In this case, market power and conduct occur in the same market but the effects occur in a different market. This is a form of leverage whereby the undertaking uses its power in one market to influence an adjacent market (or markets) in which it is not necessarily dominant.[78] The adjacent market(s) can be either horizontal or vertical to the main market. The *Bitfinex* case provides a good application of this leverage theory: in *Bitfinex* defendants leveraged their monopoly in the stablecoin market through unbacked issuance of the stablecoin Tether contrary to Tether's assurances that each Tether was backed by a US Dollar, in order to monopolize the cryptocommodities market.[79] The unbacked issuance would be the governance abuse since it contravened the stated and central tenet of Tether's operation that it is 1:1 backed by US Dollars. The ultimate goal was to manipulate the pricing mechanism in the cryptocommodities market and profit from the artificially raised prices. The District Court found that the distortion of the price mechanism in the cryptocommodities market was sufficient to show monopolization without need for a showing of high market shares.[80]

c) The undertaking engages in anticompetitive conduct in the governance market, in which it is *not* dominant, in order to a) either strengthen its power in that market or b) to maintain or strengthen its power in the DLT product or service market, in which it is dominant. This scenario stretches the theory of abuse of dominance or monopolization, because the anticompetitive conduct does not take place in the market where the undertaking has market power. This construct was allowed in *Tetra Pak*, where Tetra Pak was found to have engaged in abusive conduct in a neighbouring market (the market for non-aseptic products) even though it was not separately found dominant in that market, on account of two conditions: firstly, it was found dominant in the primary market (the market for aseptic products), and secondly, there were 'associative links' between the two markets, which allowed Tetra Pak

[77] Commission decision of 4 March 2024 AT.40437 Apple – App Store Practices (music streaming).

[78] Classic leverage cases of this type are the Microsoft cases, see Commission decision of 24 March 2004 COMP/C-3/37.792 Microsoft; *Microsoft (US)* (n 3); Google Shopping (n 45).

[79] *In re Tether and Bitfinex Cryptoasset Litigation*, 1:19-cv-09236-KPF (2021), at 48–49 and 55–57.

[80] ibid.

to exploit its overall market power.[81] Following *Tetra Pak*, as long as there are associative links between the governance market and the DLT product or service market (and the undertaking is dominant in the DLT product or service market), then it can be found to engage in abusive conduct in the governance market even in lack of dominance in that market. The GC and CoJ did not give a definition of associative links or associated markets, but the CoJ noted that 'in the case of distinct, but associated, markets . . . application of Article 86 [102 TFEU] to conduct found on the associated, non-dominated, market and having effects on that associated market can only be justified by special circumstances'.[82] While it is likely that associative links between the governance market and the overlaid DLT product or service market exist, since the governance process determines the competitive features of the overlaid DLT product or service and they can therefore constitute *special circumstances*, one should acknowledge the exceptional nature of the associated markets arrangements and ensure that the links are substantial and proven.

d) In *Tetra Pak*, the GC may have not *required* a *separate* finding of dominance in the neighbouring market, but it still emphasized the fact that Tetra Pak's market share of that market still indicated dominance. Moreover, associative links between the primary and the neighbouring market were essential in the theory and so was the fact that Tetra Pak was dominant in the primary market. It stands to reason that if any of these conditions were missing, no liability could have been found. But the GC also noted that 'Article 86 [102 TFEU] of the Treaty prohibits any abuse by one or more undertakings of a dominant position within the common market or in a substantial part of it. . . . It gives no explicit guidance as to the requirements relating to where on the product market the abuse took place'.[83] This phrasing does not even seem to require associative links between the two markets. Can it be stretched to mean that an undertaking which is not dominant in the governance market but is dominant in the DLT product or service market can be found to engage in abusive conduct in the governance market, even if there are no associative links between the governance market and the DLT product or service market?

Regardless of whether the anticompetitive conduct and its effects take place in one or more markets, establishing that the conduct in question is abusive/monopolistic still remains a requirement. There is a risk particularly when multiple markets are involved that, because an undertaking is dominant in one market and increases

[81] Commission decision of 24 July 1991 IV.31043 Tetra Pak II; Case T-83/91 Tetra Pak v Commission ECLI:EU:T:1994:246; Case C-333/94 P Tetra Pak v Commission ECLI:EU:C:1996:436.

[82] Tetra Pak (CoJ) (n 81) para 27.

[83] Tetra Pak (GC) (n 81) para 113. Upheld by the CoJ in Tetra Pak (CoJ) (n 81) para 24.

its power in another related market, it is automatically assumed that this is illicit competition. This would be incorrect; authorities still need to prove that the specific actions of an undertaking in the governance market constitute *abuse* or *bad conduct*.

(D) Specific abuse and monopolization practices

i) Refusal to deal and the essential facilities doctrine: Access to DLT networks, products, services, and consortia

Refusal to deal is an offence whereby an undertaking that controls an input in an upstream market, which is essential for competitors on a downstream market, refuses to deal with downstream competitors with the effect of eliminating effective competition.[84] In the United States, a more limited essential facilities doctrine reflects the same concept.[85] The United States generally places a high premium to undertakings' freedom to deal,[86] and accordingly the Supreme Court has been 'very cautious in recognizing such exceptions [to said freedom to deal], because of the uncertain virtue of forced sharing and the difficulty of identifying and remedying anticompetitive conduct by a single firm'.[87] Despite the significant academic attention that refusal to deal has received, few cases have resulted in a finding that an undertaking's refusal to deal was anticompetitive. That said, this theory of harm can apply in DLT markets under two forms:

a) off-chain refusal to deal, where the refusal involves a DLT product or service, but the refusal is not effectuated on the DLT infrastructure. For example, between 2018 and 2020, the Brazilian competition authority, CADE, investigated the refusal of several major domestic banks to link user bank accounts with the accounts of cryptocurrency trading companies, effectively making it harder or near impossible for those companies to receive funds into user accounts or to allow users to withdraw their funds into a regular bank account; as a result, the cryptocurrency trading companies were effectively shut out

[84] See generally Gregory Werden, 'The Law and Economics of the Essential Facility Doctrine' (1987) 32 St. Louis University Law Journal 433; Barry Doherty, 'Just What Are Essential Facilities?' (2001) 38 Common Market Law Review 397; Csongor István Nagy, 'Refusal to Deal and the Doctrine of Essential Facilities in US and EC Competition Law: A Comparative Perspective and a Proposal for a Workable Analytical Framework' (2007) 32 European Law Review 664.

[85] See *Verizon Communications Inc. v. Law Offices of Curtis v. Trinko LLP*, 540 U.S. 398 (2004); *Aspen Skiing* (n 17); *Lorain Journal Co. v. United States*, 342 U.S. 143 (1951). See also *MCI Communications Corp. v. AT&T, 708 F.2d 1081* (1983).

[86] *United States v. Colgate & Co.*, 250 U.S. 300 (1919).

[87] *Verizon* (n 85) 408.

from the mainstream financial system.[88] Off-chain refusal to deal does not present particular challenges in DLT markets, because the mechanics of the refusal are not affected by DLT's nature. In the previous example, banks' denial to link user bank accounts with cryptocurrency user accounts was qualitatively no different from denying to link user bank accounts with non-DLT accounts, such as user accounts held in another bank. For the most part, conventional refusal to deal analysis would suffice here.

b) on-chain refusal to deal, where the refusal is effectuated on DLT infrastructure, meaning that a DLT-based product or service is integral in bringing about the refusal. For example, in 2022, Binance, the largest cryptoasset exchange in the world, stopped listing USDC, the second largest stablecoin in the world.[89] Without suggesting that this case meets all the conditions for anticompetitive refusal to deal, both the service and infrastructure that executed the refusal (ie the cryptoasset exchange) and the product that was refused access to the service (ie the stablecoin) were DLT-based. Such cases may require additional consideration as analyzed below, but the general principles and conditions of refusal to deal still apply.

The refusal to deal offence requires a number of strict conditions to be established. In the European Union, the main conditions were set in a triptych of landmark cases, *Bronner*,[90] *Magill*,[91] and *IMS*,[92] and further elaborated on in additional cases. In the United States, the key cases are *Verizon*, *Aspen Skiing*, and *Lorain Journal*.[93] The conditions laid out in this body of case law are applicable in the decentralized economy too, with important considerations emerging around the nature of requests for access to DLT products and services, and justifications for

[88] Natália de Lima Figueiredo, 'Banks *v* Cryptocurrency Exchanges: CADE's Investigation and the Search for a Villain' (2021) 9 Journal of Antitrust Enforcement 388. See also a similar claim against Apple, whereby Apple was accused of entering into anticompetitive agreements with horizontal competitors to exclude from the App Store (and by extension from the Apple ecosystem) services that offered decentralized payments. While the case was argued under section 1 Sherman Act, it was in essence a claim about Apple's unilateral decision to block certain functionality on payment apps. Unsurprisingly, the section 1 claim failed. See *Lamartine Pierre et al v. Apple, Inc., Class Action Complaint*, 5:23-cv-5981 (2023).

[89] Shivani Tanna and Elizabeth Howcroft, 'Binance to Convert Users' USD Coin into Its Own Stablecoin' *Reuters* (6 September 2022). In 2019, Binance delisted another cryptocurrency, BSV, which led to a collective proceedings claim submitted to the Competition Appeal Tribunal in the UK, but that case was argued under Article 101 TFEU and the Chapter I prohibition in s. 2 Competition Act 1998. See Notice of an Application to Commence Collective Proceedings Under Section 47b of the Competition Act 1998 Case No. 1523/7/7/22 (2022).

[90] Case C-7/97 Oscar Bronner GmbH & Co. KG v Mediaprint Zeitungs- und Zeitschriftenverlag GmbH et al ECLI:EU:C:1998:569. In its 2025 *Android Auto* decision, which came out while this monograph was in press, the CoJ distinguished *Bronner* where the input/infrastructure to which access is sought was not developed solely for the needs of the dominant undertaking's own business but with a view to enabling third-party undertakings to use it. See Case C-233/23 Alphabet and Others v Autorità Garante della Concorrenza e del Mercato ECLI:EU:C:2025:110, and a brief analysis in Addendum on pages 259–60.

[91] Joined Cases C-241/91 P and C-242/91 P Radio Telefis Eireann (RTE) and Independent Television Publications Ltd (ITP) v Commission ECLI:EU:C:1995:98.

[92] Case C-418/01 IMS Health GmbH & Co. OHG v NDC Health GmbH & Co. KG. ECLI:EU:C:2004:257.

[93] See n 85.

refusals to join permissioned DLT networks. For completeness, the rest of the conditions are adapted to the context of the decentralized economy too:

There is refusal: An application to the question of what counts as transaction in DLT products and services. This obvious requirement means that the challenged undertaking refuses to deal with another undertaking either completely, or only under unreasonable terms. The latter has come to be known as constructive refusal to supply,[94] which the Commission has scoped out to include 'unduly delaying or otherwise degrading the supply of the product or involve the imposition of unreasonable conditions in return for the supply'.[95] The particular commercial and technical particularities of each case are to be taken into account and in fact they should be considered in combination to determine the conditions under which the essential input is supplied.[96]

A question arises in DLT-based markets on whether the refusal to supply/deal must refer to refused *transactions* with the requesting party. In all of the case law on refusal to supply, servicing the requesting party (or denying to do so) involved getting into a transactional relationship with it; in cases of access to physical infrastructure, the transaction reflected the agreement to share the infrastructure, and in cases of access to intellectual property (IP), the transaction reflected the licensing of the IP. But consider the listing of cryptoassets on crypto-exchanges (and the refusal to do so). If a cryptoasset is publicly available, the act of listing it does not require any active involvement on the side of the asset and therefore a request; the exchange reads and writes on the asset's ledger and displays on its platform information about the asset. Does this process of reading/writing on a public ledger amount to transactions, which can be requested and refused? In *Bit Global*, the company argued that Coinbase delisted wBTC, a popular cryptoasset maintained by Bit Global, upon launching its own competing version, called cbBTC, and Bit Global argued that this constituted refusal to deal based on FTC's Section 5 Policy Statement, which identifies 'discriminatory refusals to deal which tend to create or maintain market power' as a violation of the FTC Act.[97] Assuming that listing cryptoassets on exchanges is a transaction (more on that below in section D.ii.a), in this case there was a request from Bit Global to Coinbase to continue listing wBTC. But for cryptoassets that are not maintained by a single or 'main' protocol foundation or institution, it is unclear that there is a valid acting source which can lodge a request (which may be refused resulting in a refusal to deal). This, however, seems to be a question of imputability, that is, which entity can act on behalf of an

[94] Commission decision of 25 July 2001 COMP/C-1/36.915 Deutsche Post AG - Interception of cross-border mail, para 103.

[95] Commission guidance on enforcement priorities (n 22) para 79.

[96] Commission decision of 22 June 2011 COMP/39.525 Telekomunikacja Polska, paras 107 et seq.

[97] *Bit Global Digital Ltd. v. Coinbase Global, Inc.*, 3:24-cv-09019-AMO (2024), para 118. See also FTC, Policy Statement Regarding the Scope of Unfair Methods of Competition Under Section 5 of the Federal Trade Commission Act Commission File No. P221202, at 16.

undertaking, rather than a question of whether a refusal to deal offence has been established.

The GC in *Google Shopping* came close to providing an answer, but sidestepped the issue. The challenged conduct was Google's demotion of search results of competing comparison shopping services to favour its own. The GC recognized that Google's conduct did resemble refusal to supply, but distinguished the offence on two grounds: it noted that refusal to supply 'implies (i) that it is express, that is to say, that there is a "request" or in any event a wish to be granted access and a consequential "refusal", and (ii) that the trigger of the exclusionary effect—the impugned conduct—lies principally in the refusal as such, and not in an extrinsic practice such as, in particular, another form of leveraging abuse'.[98] By focusing on the element of request, it forewent the question of whether granting the request would amount to a transaction between Google and the requesting comparison shopping services. Moreover, by implying that in that case the exclusionary effect came about through other conduct besides the refusal (even if there were any), it provided the basis to rely on a separate type of abuse (in this case self-preferencing; see section D.ii).

In the end, *Google Shopping* did not answer whether a simpler set of facts, namely the unilateral refusal to include a product or service in one's offerings with exclusionary effects, could amount to refusal to deal with a requesting undertaking. It is true that the wording of the offence (refusal to *supply* or refusal to *deal*) implies some sort of transactional relationship. But the exclusionary effect can be the same even if there is no transactional relationship, and absent additional harmful conduct which could establish a different offence (eg self-preferencing), the conduct would escape antitrust enforcement. It may therefore be fair to say that refusal to deal requires a request (to be refused), but that the request does not necessarily have to establish a transactional relationship if granted.

Another way to overcome this limitation is to rely on collective boycotts if the refusal is implemented by horizontal competitors. While boycotts can consist in refusing a transactional relationship,[99] such a relationship is not necessary as the particular mechanics of how the boycott is implemented are immaterial as long as the object or effect is exclusionary. For example, in *Pre-insulated Pipes* a group of competitors leveraged industry norms and standards to delay the introduction of new technologies that would cause them to drop prices.[100] Similar cases in the United States have also run into antitrust law.[101] In *Bitmain*, an argument by which miners, protocol developers, and exchanges conspired in favour of a cryptocurrency with the effect of plaintiff, who supported a competing

[98] Google Shopping (GC) (n 56) para 232.
[99] See eg Case C-18/12 Město Žamberk v Finanční ředitelství v Hradci Králové ECLI:EU:C:2013:95.
[100] Commission decision of 21 October 1998 COMP IV/35.691/E-4 Pre-insulated Pipe cartel.
[101] *Allied Tube v. Indian Head, Inc.*, 486 U.S. 492 (1988); *Fashion Originators' Guild of America v. FTC*, 312 U.S. 457 (1941).

cryptocurrency, sustaining financial damage was presented as group boycott, but failed on multiple grounds.[102] Admittedly, group boycott offences are not a unilateral refusal to deal, but rather require an anticompetitive arrangement to be in place between competitors, but the effect is similar to unilateral refusal to deal, and can be relied on when the conditions of a refusal to supply offence are not met.

In the United States, lack of regulation and a pre-existing trading relationship. The US experience, notoriously engraved in *Verizon*, also tells us that where a regulatory framework exists that compels access, any failures resulting from such regime should not suffice to establish a refusal to deal claim.[103] Instead, it is for regulators to resolve the issue. This can become relevant in the decentralized economy due to its finance focus. Financial markets are normally heavily regulated, and while crypto markets have so far remained at the periphery of regulation this is quickly changing. *Verizon* is in line with the United States' general resistance to apply antitrust law in highly regulated economic segments, contrary to the EU approach, which sees regulation and competition law and two separate instruments.[104]

More limiting yet, is how *Aspen Skiing* and *Verizon* have been interpreted by lower courts to almost always require a pre-existing trading relationship between the refusing party and the party seeking access. In *Novell*, where the issue concerned access to certain aspects of Microsoft Windows by WordPerfect, the circuit court ruled that to prevail in refusal to deal claim plaintiffs must show '(1) "a pre-existing voluntary and presumably profitable course of dealing between the monopolist and rival"; and (2) discontinuation of that course of dealing that "suggest[s] a willingness to forsake short-term profits to achieve an anti-competitive end"'.[105] While other courts have disagreed that *Aspen Skiing* formulated a general rule that a pre-existing trading relationship must exist, and instead suggested that this requirement was tied to the specific facts of the case,[106] the general consensus is that after *Verizon*, some type of profit sacrifice based on pre-existing conduct must be shown to success in a refusal to deal claim.[107]

Most commonly, the refusal concerns an input in one market to be used in an another vertically related market. In most cases where a refusal to deal was found to be anticompetitive, the refused product or service was in a separate market in vertical relationship with the product or service that required it; in other words, it served as an input.[108] The reason for that requirement is that competition law

[102] *Bitmain* (n 67).
[103] *Verizon* (n 85).
[104] See the relevant discussion in Chapter 1 section C.
[105] *Novell, Inc. v. Microsoft Corp.*, 731 F.3d 1064, 1074–76 (2013).
[106] *Viamedia, Inc. v. Comcast Corp.*, 951 F.3d 429 (2020).
[107] See eg *New York v. Facebook, Inc.*, 549 F. Supp. 3d 6, 25–28 (2021); Erik Hovenkamp, 'The Antitrust Duty to Deal in the Age of Big Tech' (2022) 131 Yale Law Journal 1483.
[108] Oscar Bronner (n 90) (publication and distribution of newspapers); Joined Cases 6-7/73 Istituto Chemioterapico Italiano SpA and Commercial Solvents Corporation v Commission ECLI:EU:C:1974:18 (production of raw material and derivatives). See contra in the United States, eg

may tolerate a lawful monopoly in the market of the refused good or service, but the monopoly over the input should not be used to affect other adjacent markets. Furthermore, there seems to be consensus that for a finding of anticompetitive refusal to supply, the dominant undertaking must also be present in the downstream market, and therefore compete with the requesting undertaking.[109] Where this is not the case, at the very least a finding that effective competition in the downstream market is eliminated is still required; for instance in *Glaxo Greece* the CoJ noted that 'with regard to a refusal by an undertaking to deliver its products in one Member State to wholesalers which export those products to other Member States, such an effect on competition may exist not only if the refusal impedes the activities of those wholesalers in that first Member State, but equally if it leads to the elimination of effective competition from them in the distribution of the products on the markets of the other Member States'.[110]

The refused input is indispensable, non-duplicable, and there are no alternatives: This is the core of anticompetitive refusal to deal. The elements of indispensability and non-duplicability are linked. Indispensable means essential for 'carrying on that [the requesting undertaking's] business',[111] 'inasmuch as there is no actual or potential substitute in existence for that facility',[112] in other words, as long as the input is non-duplicable. This in turn means that the creation of the refused products or services by the requesting undertaking 'is not economically viable for production on a scale comparable to that of the undertaking which controls the existing product or service'.[113] Put differently, that duplication is 'prohibitively expensive and would not make any commercial sense' but this does not mean that alternatives have to be equally advantageous.[114] In *Bit Global*, which revolved around a claim of refusal to deal on the grounds of Coinbase delisting wBTC

Aspen Skiing (n 17) (where the product to which access was sought was downhill skiing facilities, the same as the one offered by the competitors seeking access).

[109] See Commission guidance on enforcement priorities (n 22) para 76 ('Typically competition problems arise when the dominant undertaking competes on the "downstream" market with the buyer whom it refuses to supply. The term "downstream market" is used to refer to the market for which the refused input is needed in order to manufacture a product or provide a service. This section deals only with this type of refusal.'). See also Herbert J Hovenkamp and Phillip E Areeda, *Antitrust Law: An Analysis of Antitrust Principles and Their Application* (Wolters Kluwer 2013) s 771a. See also Case T-504/93 Tiercé Ladbroke SA v Commission ECLI:EU:T:1997:84, para 130 ('in the absence of direct or indirect exploitation by the sociétés de courses of their intellectual property rights on the Belgian market, their refusal to supply cannot be regarded as involving any restriction of competition on the Belgian market').

[110] Joined Cases C-468/06 to C-478/06 Sot. Lélos kai Sia EE and Others v GlaxoSmithKline AEVE Farmakeftikon Proïonton, formerly Glaxowellcome AEVE ECLI:EU:C:2008:504, para 35.

[111] Bronner (n 90) paras 38–45. The element of indispensability does not apply where the input/infrastructure was developed with a view to enabling third-party undertakings to use it. *See Android Auto* (n 90).

[112] Commission decision of 3 July 2001 COMP D3/38.044 NDC Health/IMS Health (Interim measures), para 70.

[113] IMS Health (CoJ) (n 92) para 28.

[114] Commission decision of 27 August 2003 COMP/37.685 GVG/FS, para 109; Bronner (n 90) paras 43 and 44; IMS Health (CoJ) (n 92) para 28.

from its platform, Coinbase counterargued that it only accounted for 1 per cent of wBTC's transaction volume and therefore other venues not only existed, but they likely represented equally good alternatives.[115]

For IP goods or services in the European Union, the refusal prevents the creation of a new product or service in the vertically related market: This requirement applies in situations where the refusal to deal concerns goods or services protected by intellectual property. In *IMS*, which concerned the replication of a data presentation structure to represent sales of pharmaceutical products, the CoJ stated that:

> [I]t is clear from that case-law that, in order for the refusal by an undertaking which owns a copyright to give access to a product or service indispensable for carrying on a particular business to be treated as abusive, it is sufficient that three cumulative conditions be satisfied, namely, that that refusal is preventing the emergence of a new product for which there is a potential consumer demand, that it is unjustified and such as to exclude any competition on a secondary market.[116]

The case law the CoJ cited, and the *IMS* case itself all involved IP rights. Therefore, in situations where the refusal involves intellectual property, one requirement for a finding of anticompetitive refusal to deal is that the refusal blocks the creation of a new product or service that has never before been offered or that it is not offered by the undertaking which refuses to supply. The rationale according to the CoJ is that 'in the balancing of the interest in protection of the intellectual property right and the economic freedom of its owner against the interest in protection of free competition, the latter can prevail only where refusal to grant a licence prevents the development of the secondary market to the detriment of consumers'.[117]

Due to the digital and technical nature of DLT-based products and services, it is tempting to assume that an IP component will always be present in refusal to deal cases. This, however, would be misguided. The determinative element is whether access is requested specifically to the IP component; it is not enough to request access to a physical resource which embeds IP that makes it work. Nearly all modern production equipment embeds a logical layer that endows it with functionality, and if that was sufficient, then all refusal to supply cases in digital markets would need to meet this condition. To illustrate, a mining pool that refuses to mine for a certain asset, refuses access to its equipment even though the equipment runs on software. But a metaverse platform that refuses to share interoperability specifications, refuses access to its IP, the component in question being the specifications as embedded in the relevant software.

[115] Defendant's Opposition to Ex Parte Emergency Motion for Temporary Restraining Order and Preliminary Injunction in case *Bit Global Limited v. Coinbase Global, Inc., 3:24-cv-09019-AMO* (2024), at 1.

[116] IMS Health (CoJ) (n 92) para 38.

[117] ibid para 48.

In any case, if access to IP is at the core of the request, the CoJ in *Microsoft* lowered the 'new product' threshold by noting that 'the circumstance relating to the appearance of a new product, as envisaged in *Magill* and *IMS Health* ... cannot be the only parameter which determines whether a refusal to license an intellectual property right is capable of causing prejudice to consumers within the meaning of Article 82(b) EC [now 102(b) TFEU]. As that provision states, such prejudice may arise where there is a limitation not only of production or markets, but also of technical development'.[118] Arguably, the numerous unique conditions that surrounded the *Microsoft* case (the nature and effects of interoperability, Microsoft's internal documents evidencing a scheme, the nature of digital markets and particularly network effects, and others), may have played a role in the CoJ's willingness to relax the requirement for a wholly new product or service.

The refusal results in elimination of effective competition: Because, in principle, undertakings are free to dispose of their assets as they wish, the obligation to open them up to competitors is only justified if the repercussions entail extreme damage to the competitive fabric of the market. This is why refusals to deal are only anticompetitive if they threaten the 'elimination or substantial reduction of competition to the detriment of consumers in both the short and the long term'.[119] If the downstream market remains competitive even after the refusal, then the forced sharing not only offers little, but it also imposes an onerous requirement onto the dominant undertaking and undermines its success incentives. While the CoJ has at times suggested that the elimination of *all* competition is the applicable standard,[120] *Microsoft* concluded that it is enough that the refusal is likely to eliminate all *effective* competition on that market,[121] at least when equally efficient competitors are taken into account. Also, the elimination of a single competitor is not necessarily the same as the elimination of effective competition.[122]

There are no objective justifications for the refusal. An application to refusals to join permissioned DLT networks: In *Bronner*, Advocate General (AG) Jacobs clearly stated that 'an undertaking which occupies a dominant position in the provision of an essential facility . . . and which refuses other companies access to that facility without objective justification ... infringes Article [102] if the other conditions of that Article are met'.[123] In *Aspen Skiing*, the Supreme Court engaged in an extensive discussion around the circumstances of Ski Co.'s, the refusing

[118] Case T-201/04 Microsoft Corp. v Commission ECLI:EU:T:2007:289, para 647.

[119] Opinion of AG Jacobs in Case C-7/97 Oscar Bronner GmbH & Co KG v Mediaprint Zeitungs- und Zeitschriftenverlag GmbH & Co KG, Mediaprint Zeitungsvertriebsgesellschaft mbH & Co KG and Mediaprint Anzeigengesellschaft mbH & Co KG ECLI:EU:C:1998:264, para 51. Competition need only be hindered, not eliminated, where the input/infrastructure was developed with a view to enabling third-party undertakings to use it. *See Android Auto* (n 90).

[120] IMS Health (n 92) para 38; Bronner (n 90) para 40.

[121] Microsoft (GC) (n 118) paras 563.

[122] Opinion of AG Jacobs in Bronner (n 119) para 51. *Verizon* (n 85) 408.

[123] Opinion of AG Jacobs in ibid para 48. For what can constitute an objective justification in cases where the input/infrastructure was developed with a view to enabling third-party undertakings to use it, *see Android Auto* (n 90).

undertaking's, reasons to terminate access to its ski slopes, a necessary input for competitors. It concluded that Ski Co. departed significantly from previous business practices, forewent profits by terminating access, and did not convince the jury that 'its conduct was justified by any normal business purpose'.[124]

There is no specific list of acceptable objective justifications, but some that can be of relevance in products and services of the decentralized economy might include: capacity limitations on the side of the dominant undertaking[125] (but not if the undertaking artificially constrains capacity);[126] safety;[127] the fact that the dominant undertaking wishes to enter or expand into the vertically related market where the competitor is active;[128] or if the refusal to deal 'is necessary to allow the dominant undertaking to realise an adequate return on the investments required to develop its input business, thus generating incentives to continue to invest in the future, taking the risk of failed projects into account'.[129]

An idiosyncratic key objective justification for refusal in DLT markets can be the maintenance of a ledger's permissioned nature. A common distinction between DLT networks is between permissioned and permissionless. Permissioned networks are those that are open only to actors that meet certain criteria and are not meant to be accessible by the general public; permissionless networks are those that are open to the general public, and anyone can join as long as they comply with the network's technical specifications. Some permissioned DLT networks are enterprise networks, and therefore they reflect and enable the operation of business activity which needs to be separated from the open market. Other permissioned DLT networks are formed in the frame of business consortia and membership is limited to the consortium. Yet other DLT networks are structured as permissioned to support and effectuate a governance model and/or safeguard and secure the consensus process.

Permissioned enterprise networks should be treated similarly to other assets of undertakings. Everything else equal, the fact that an operation is performed on a DLT network as opposed to a different type of technology does not change the rationale or mechanics of the refusal to supply offence. Therefore, simply stating that an enterprise DLT network is designed to be permissioned, does not automatically exclude it from the scope of the refusal to supply doctrine.

124 *Aspen Skiing* (n 17) 608.

125 Commission decision of 19 April 1977 IV/28.841 ABG/Oil Companies operating in the Netherlands.

126 Commission decision of 14 January 1998 IV/34.801 FAG - Flughafen Frankfurt/Main AG, paras 85–86.

127 ibid para 77.

128 See Commission guidance on enforcement priorities (n 22) para 89: 'The Commission will . . . consider claims by the dominant undertaking that its own innovation will be negatively affected by the obligation to supply, or by the structural changes in the market conditions that imposing such an obligation will bring about, including the development of follow-on innovation by competitors'.

129 ibid.

In the case of permissioned DLT networks formed by consortia, one would have to look more closely into what is being requested, namely, access to the DLT technology developed by the consortium or the right to join the consortium in order to co-develop the DLT technology. The latter is not a refusal to supply issue, because what is being requested is not an input but membership in a club that develops an input. That said, it can still constitute anticompetitive exclusion similar, for example, to exclusion from a standard-setting organization.[130] The former, namely refusal to supply access to the DLT network that the consortium develops, can constitute refusal to supply, since the DLT nature of the network should make no difference to its nature as an input and to the characterisation of the conduct.

However, the distinction is less clear than it initially looks. Some DLT consortia are formed on an indefinite basis to initially develop but also to continuously evolve and maintain DLT networks and technologies, and so participation in the consortium means both membership in the consortium and access to the technology it develops. For example, the USDF is a closed-group consortium that brings together numerous traditional banks with the purpose of developing a DLT-based digital dollar in the form of tokenized deposits (distinct from a potential Federal Reserve Central Bank Digital Currency (CBDC)).[131] Joining USDF means both membership to the development of the tokenized deposits shared ledger, and access to the ledger itself. Other consortia have closed membership, but the underlying DLT technology is open to anyone. This would be the case of the Ethereum Enterprise Alliance, which is a group of stakeholders tasked with the development and promotion of the Ethereum ecosystem, and while membership in the alliance is controlled, the development of the Ethereum ecosystem is open to anyone.[132]

The third justification for structuring a DLT network as permissioned, namely as part of its governance or consensus model, is perhaps the most genuine justification for refusal to supply access. This is because restricted access is part of the design of the network and opening it up would force it to adopt a different architectural and business model. Competition law is generally inimical to dictating design choices and only under exceptional circumstances does it mandate them.[133] In *Slovak Telekom*, which concerned granting access to assets that the company had developed for itself, the CoJ noted that an obligation to conclude a contract with a competitor 'is especially detrimental to the freedom of contract and the right to property of the dominant undertaking, since an undertaking, even if dominant,

[130] See also in the similar context of professional associations *Kreuzer v. American Academy of Periodontology*, 735 F. 2d 1479 (1984) ('[W]e wish to make clear in the strongest possible terms that the antitrust laws do not bar the formation of associations with membership limited to classes of similarly situated persons and dedicated to the joint pursuit of their common interests. It is only in that rare instance when such membership limitations have the effect of unreasonably restraining trade that the concerns of the antitrust laws are triggered'. ibid at 1496).

[131] See <https://usdfconsortium.com/>.

[132] See <https://entethalliance.org/>.

[133] Pablo Ibáñez Colomo, 'Product Design and Business Models in EU Antitrust Law' (2021) SSRN.

remains, in principle, free to refuse to conclude contracts and to use the *infrastructure it has developed for its own needs*' (emphasis added).[134] The CoJ concluded that an obligation to grant access to infrastructure that an undertaking has developed for the needs of its own business should be granted 'only where such access is indispensable to the business of such a competitor, namely where there is no actual or potential substitute for that infrastructure'.[135] Permissioned DLT networks fall under that category of infrastructure that is developed for use, not by one, but still by a closed group of undertakings, which co-develop the network, and therefore only if elimination of competition in the market is threatened can access be mandated.

ii) Discrimination, self-preferencing, neutrality

Discriminatory treatment is a broad category of conduct that sits in the gaps and margins of other practices that may constitute illicit competition. In the European Union it is separately codified in Article 102(c) TFEU, and in the United States in Robinson–Patman Act of 1936 (R–P Act). Article 102(c) TFEU prohibits 'applying dissimilar conditions to equivalent transactions with other trading parties, thereby placing them at a competitive disadvantage' whereas the R–P Act bans 'discriminat[ion] in price between different purchasers of commodities . . . and where the effect of such discrimination may be substantially to lessen competition or tend to create a monopoly'.[136] A newer theory of harm, under the name self-preferencing, was introduced recently by the Commission in the *Google Shopping* case,[137] which extends the scope of anticompetitive discriminatory treatment in ways that are particularly relevant for DLT markets. A step further yet, *Google Shopping* can be read to suggest a broader neutrality concept, which, applied in DLT markets, can give rise to a so-called blockchain neutrality obligation, which, while far from established, is aligned with a push for a level playing field in digital markets.[138] The R–P Act has today fallen in disuse, but references to it will still be made as it the Federal Trade Commission has recently re-discovered it as a potential tool.[139]

[134] Case C-165/19 P Slovak Telekom, a.s. v Commission ECLI:EU:C:2020:678, para 46.

[135] ibid para 49.

[136] 15 U.S. Code § 13a.

[137] Google Shopping (n 45).

[138] The Digital Markets Act is the strongest expression of this trend. While unrelated to DLT markets, it is technology agnostic and so it equally applies to any market as long as the actors and activities fall within its scope. See Regulation (EU) 2022/1925 on contestable and fair markets in the digital sector, OJ L 265.

[139] See Christopher Finnerty, 'The FTC's "New" Tool: Greater Enforcement of the Robinson-Patman Act' (*K&L Gates U.S. Policy and Regulatory Alert*, 13 July 2022). See also Federal Trade Commission, 'Policy Statement Regarding the Scope of Unfair Methods of Competition Under,' P221202 (10 November 2022).

The literature usually distinguishes between primary-line discrimination and secondary-line discrimination.[140] Primary-line discrimination occurs when the results of the discrimination occur in the market in which the dominant firm is active and therefore directly harms its (horizontal) rivals. The obvious incentive for primary-line discrimination is that rivals of the dominant firm are disadvantaged. Secondary-line discrimination occurs when the results of the discrimination are produced in a market in which the dominant firm is not active, potentially distorting competition in that market. At first glance, secondary-line discrimination does not benefit the dominant firm, since the disadvantaged parties are in a market wherein the dominant firm is not active.[141] However, it may still indirectly benefit it by weakening a rival's downstream customers which may be reflected in the rival's performance, or by enabling strategic behaviour; for example, the dominant firm may want to enter the neighbouring market, but because the number of active firms is regulated, it first needs to drive out of the market one of the existing firms.

Discrimination can also be a component in other theories of harm beyond the scope of Article 102(c) or the R–P Act. For instance, primary-line discrimination often occurs in the context of predatory pricing or loyalty rebates.[142] Reliance on discrimination as the main theory of harm usually arises in cases that may not meet the conditions of other theories of harm, but which can still distort competition or run afoul of more specialized objectives of competition law, such as the protection of the common market's integrity in cases where the discrimination take place on the basis of the nationality of the dominant firm's customers.[143] Interestingly, even though competition law is usually seen to protect consumers/buyers as the weaker party, the R–P Act has often been used as defence against dominant buyers instead of dominant sellers.[144]

[140] For more detailed treatment of the different types of discrimination, see eg Lang and O'Donoghue (n 52) 83.

[141] Opinion of AG Wahl in Case C-525/16 MEO—Serviços de Comunicações e Multimédia SA EU:C:2017:1020, paras 76–77; Case C-525/16 MEO—Serviços de Comunicações e Multimédia SA v Autoridade da Concorrência, EU:C:2018:270, paras 13 and 35.

[142] For instance, for rebates, see Case T-219/99 British Airways plc v Commission ECLI:EU:T:2003:343; Case C-95/04 P British Airways plc v Commission ECLI:EU:C:2007:166; for predatory pricing, see *Brooke Group Ltd. v. Brown & Williamson Tobacco Corp.*, 509 U.S. 209 (1993).

[143] Because of the limited scope of the R–P Act, discrimination cases can be brought under the more flexible section 5 of the Federal Trade Commission Act. See FTC Unfair Methods Policy Statement (n 139), at 13–14.

[144] See eg *Abbott Labs. v. Portland Retail Druggists Association, Inc.*, 425 U.S. 1, 11, 96 S.Ct. 1305 (1976) ('[The Robinson–Patman Act] was intended, in part, to protect small competitors from discriminatory pricing in favor of larger purchasers, who would have the power to impose higher prices with their stronger brand names.'); *FTC. v. Fred Meyer, Inc.*, 390 U.S. 341, 349, 88 S.Ct. 904, 908 (1968) ('[T]he Robinson–Patman Act was enacted in 1936 to curb and prohibit all devices by which large buyers gained discriminatory preferences over smaller ones by virtue of their greater purchasing power.'). In the European Union, many cases are grounded on the goal of competition law to protect the internal market from fragmentation. See eg Case C-27/76 United Brands Company and United Brands Continentaal BV v Commission ECLI:EU:C:1978:22; Case C-7/82 Gesellschaft zur Verwertung von Leistungsschutzrechten bmH (GVL) v Commission ECLI:EU:C:1983:52.

It is important to note that mere discrimination, in the sense that an undertaking treats different customers differently even if they are similarly positioned, does not per se amount to a competition law offence. As the CoJ ruled in *Post Danmark I*, 'the fact that the practice of a dominant undertaking may . . . be described as "price discrimination", that is to say, charging different customers or different classes of customers different prices for goods or services whose costs are the same or, conversely, charging a single price to customers for whom supply costs differ, cannot of itself suggest that there exists an exclusionary abuse'.[145] The full conditions (analysed below) of an alleged type of offence must be met.

DLT markets, being nascent and malleable, are good candidates for discriminatory practices. Discriminatory treatment of customers allows undertakings both to weaken competition as per above, and to maximize producer surplus by segmenting high-paying and low-paying customers.[146] Moreover, it can allow firms to differentiate themselves in the market by reserving for themselves preferential treatment compared to their rivals thereby finding it easier to promote to customers their own products and services. In the emerging markets of the decentralized economy this can be particularly effective in securing first mover advantages and early market lock-in.

In the following paragraphs, the general conditions for anticompetitive discrimination are discussed first, with a particular focus on whether and how they can apply to DLT markets. Then, self-preferencing is introduced as a form of anticompetitive discrimination, and lastly, the expanded blockchain neutrality concept is presented, which may be gaining traction.

a) Discrimination in Article 102(c) TFEU and Robinson Patman Act: Application to delisting, AMMs, and MEV

Transactions: Meaning of, and application to different types of tokens. Article 102(c) TFEU speaks of 'applying dissimilar conditions to equivalent transactions with other trading parties, thereby placing them at a competitive disadvantage' and the R–P Act discrimination 'in price between different purchasers of commodities . . . in commerce'. Anticompetitive discrimination, therefore, presupposes *transactions* between trading parties, although the scope of the R–P Act is limited to commodities. This severely limits the R–P Act's application in the decentralized economy, since it is service-driven, although it should be noted that at least some cryptoassets in at least some jurisdictions have been classified as commodities.[147]

[145] Case C-209/10 Post Danmark A/S v Konkurrencerådet EU:C:2012:172, para 30.

[146] Jonathan Baker, 'Competitive Price Discrimination: The Exercise of Market Power Without Anticompetitive Effects (Comment on Klein and Wiley)' (2003) 70 Antitrust Law Journal 643; Hal Varian, 'Price Discrimination' in Richard Schmalensee and Robert Willig (eds), *Handbook of Industrial Organization*, vol 3 (North-Holland 2007) ch 10.

[147] In the United States, the Commodity Futures Trading Commission considers at least Bitcoin and Ethereum commodities. See Commodity Futures Trading Commission, 'Digital Assets Primer: December 2020', at 23–24, 29–30, at <https://www.cftc.gov/media/5476/DigitalAssetsPrimer/download>.

What counts as transaction between trading parties for the purposes of anti-competitive discrimination is not a matter that has received significant attention in case law, because in the majority of cases it was undisputed that the discriminatory treatment was grounded on commercial transactions.[148] The issue, however, is of relevance to DLT markets, because various practices that appear discriminatory may not even involve transactions, which would therefore preclude the application of Article 102(c) TFEU or the R–P Act. For instance, if listing and delisting cryptoassets on a crypto-exchange does not constitute a transaction, then demoting or eliminating cryptoassets from an exchange would not amount to anti-competitive discrimination under Article 102(c) TFEU even if there is, in essence, discriminatory treatment among cryptoassets (the R–P Act would be inapplicable here anyway as the transaction would involve a service, not the purchase of commodities). It should be noted, however, that the non-application of the discrimination offence in Article 102(c) or the R–P Act does not rule out a finding of abuse of dominance or monopolization based on the general prohibition contained in Article 102 TFEU and section 2 Sherman Act.

In the most basic sense, a transaction is a transfer of value, and since competition law applies only to economic activities, transactions of interest to competition law can only be those where the transfer carries *economic* value.[149] The value does not have to be monetary, but it must be economic. In *GVL*, the Commission noted that the dispositive element to conclude that the relationship between a collecting society (GVL) and artists can give rise to transactions within the meaning of Article 102(c) TFEU, was that GVL's service 'is provided only in return for valuable consideration, i.e. GVL's administrative share of the royalties collected. The sole decisive factor is the fact that GVL's activity, namely the provision of services, corresponds to a material consideration moving from the artist'.[150]

As such, transactions that involve monetary value tokens (such as Bitcoin) would count, but so would transactions that involve utility or securities tokens, because those too carry economic value in the form of the functionality a utility token gives access to or the right that a securities token carries. Transactions that carry other types of data that are common in DLT markets, such as personal data (decentralized identity verification services), insurance, supply chain, real estate, legal smart contracts, etc, can also fall under the definition of transactions here, because the data in those services generate value for the involved parties and are therefore economic in nature.

[148] In fact, in *GZS*, the CoJ concluded that discriminatory treatment of different mail categories (which does not readily resemble transactions) amounted to a violation of 102(c) [then 86(c)] without addressing the question whether the sender was a trading partner of the dominant undertaking or not. See Joined cases C-147/97 and C-148/97. Deutsche Post AG v Gesellschaft für Zahlungssysteme mbH (GZS) and Citicorp Kartenservice GmbH ECLI:EU:C:2000:74.

[149] See Chapter 2 section B.

[150] Commission decision of 29 October 1981 IV/29.839 GVL, para 49.

Trading parties and business relationships: Centralized and decentralized partners, and interactions with smart contracts and AAMs. Moreover, the transaction should take place between *trading parties*, meaning that the economic exchange must be performed in the context of trade (or commerce in the parlance of the R–P Act). What constitutes 'trading party' has been interpreted exceptionally broadly by EU institutions. In *DPAG - Interception*, the Commission initially defined trading partner as 'a voluntary commercial relationship between two undertakings' and it further noted that this relationship does not need to be direct.[151] In that case, because Deutsche Post AG (DPAG) was the monopoly postal services provider in Germany, the Commission found that 'the postal monopoly imposes upon foreign senders a commercial if not directly contractual relationship with DPAG. The sender in the UK that contracts with the BPO to have his mailings sent to Germany knows beforehand that the mail will be delivered by DPAG to German addressees. The actions of DPAG in the German market for incoming cross-border letter mail directly affect the commercial activities of the UK senders. At the very least, there is an indirect relationship between the UK senders contracting with the BPO and DPAG. Under these circumstances, the Commission finds that the senders must be regarded as trading partners of DPAG within the meaning of Article 82(c) [now 102(c)]'.[152]

The reference to relationship between *undertakings* and *trading partners* might sound somewhat limiting in the context of DLT markets where activity can be distributed, automated, and commonly involving lay actors. This, however, should not detract from the applicability of the provision because, despite these characteristics of decentralized economy actors, the definition of undertaking is broad enough to encompass many of those players and activities as long as they perform economic/commercial activity.[153] In that sense, an undertaking that reserves discriminatory treatment in transactions with a centralized crypto-exchange (CEX) and with a decentralized one (DEX), still differentiates between two trading partners, even though the decentralized exchange cannot be reduced to a single controlling entity. Here, there is a question of imputability, that is, who will be the trading partner in the decentralized operation to whom the transaction will be attributed, but there is no question as to the existence of a trading partner.

In *BDkEP*, the Commission also confirmed that a trading relationship does not require the existence of a contract.[154] In that case, Deutsche Post AG (DPAG) argued that the parties it allegedly discriminated against were either end consumers or mere intermediaries of their respective clients and therefore not contracting partners of DPAG. The Commission disagreed stating that 'there is no

[151] Interception of cross-border mail (n 94) para 130.
[152] ibid.
[153] See also Chapter 2 section B.
[154] Commission Decision of 20 October 2004 COMP/38.745 on the German Postal Legislation Relating to Mail Preparation Services, paras 91–92.

Commission or Court precedent . . . to support DPAG's view that "*trading partners*" should be construed in a narrow way as "contracting parties". Mere business contacts between the dominant undertaking and its "trading partners" are generally considered to be sufficient' (emphasis in original).[155] This is a useful clarification in the context of the decentralized economy, because trading relationships or contacts in the decentralized economy are often not underpinned by express contracts (which, if it were a requirement, would preclude the applications of the provisions at hand). In fact, unlike conventional digital markets where services and applications are almost always offered on the basis of express terms of service (ToS), which have been repeatedly deemed to constitute legally binding adherence contracts,[156] trading relationships and interactions in the decentralized the economy are often not explicitly linked to written terms and conditions resulting in vagueness around their legal status.[157] Even when transactions are made through smart contracts, which are at the core of DEX, not all smart contracts are legally binding contracts.[158] The legacy of the decentralized economy's subversive origins still today colours its relationship with the law.

In all, mere business contacts or a direct or indirect commercial relationship that includes consideration seem to suffice to constitute a transaction between trading parties. It is unclear whether the element of consideration is to be understood in its contract law sense, or if the Commission simply wanted to emphasize the quid pro quo nature of trade.[159] Considering the broader formulations of 'mere business contacts' and 'voluntary commercial relationship' and that an actual contract is not required, it seems unlikely that bi-directional promises are required. That said, at the very least, business *contact and/or relationship* is required, even indirect, and it is proper to understand such contact/relationship as interactive, that is to say that the parties are aware of the fact that they are establishing a business contact/relationship, even if they do not know with whom it is ultimately, because, for example, the formation takes place through intermediaries.

While this does not invariably preclude automatic means of relationship formation (eg algorithmic trading), an element of interaction between the software

[155] ibid para 92.

[156] For helpful overviews see Mark A Lemley, 'Terms of Use' (2006) 91 Minnesota Law Review 459; Jennifer Femminella, 'Online Terms and Conditions Agreements: Bound by the Web' (2003) 17 St. John's Journal of Legal Commentary 87; Juliet Moringiello, 'Signals, Assent, and Internet Contracting' (2005) 57 Rutgers Law Review 1307.

[157] See eg Mikołaj Barczentewicz and Natasha Vasan, 'Transaction Execution on Ethereum Decentralized Exchanges (DEX) From a Legal Perspective' (2024) SSRN.

[158] Mateja Durovic and Franciszek Lech, 'The Enforceability of Smart Contracts' (2019) 5 Italian Law Journal; Riccardo De Caria, 'The Legal Meaning of Smart Contracts' (2018) 26 European Review of Private Law 731; Vimal Dwivedi and others, 'Legally Enforceable Smart-Contract Languages: A Systematic Literature Review' (2022) 54 ACM Computing Surveys 1; Kristin B Cornelius, 'Standard Form Contracts and a Smart Contract Future' (2018) 7 Internet Policy Review (online).

[159] On the meaning of consideration in contract law see Jack Beatson, Andrew Burrows, and John Cartwright, 'Consideration And Promissory Estoppel' in Jack Beatson, Andrew Burrows, and John Cartwright, *Anson's Law of Contract* (OUP 2020).

clients or the software and a user would still have to be shown. It is perhaps because of this requirement that the *Google Shopping* case was not litigated under a theory of anticompetitive discrimination, but rather as self-preferencing (see section D.ii.c): the ranking of search results and their presentation were the outcome of Google's algorithm, and the pages that appeared on the list did not have a business relationship with Google.[160] In that sense, listing/delisting cryptoassets on platforms, to the extent that the platform's actions are unilateral and unidirectional, is unlikely that it would count as transactions between trading parties. This does not mean that the conduct cannot otherwise be deemed anticompetitive discrimination in the broad sense—it would just have to be examined either under the self-preferencing theory of harm or the blockchain neutrality doctrine (see below), and failing both, it could be examined under the general prohibition contained in Article 102 TFEU or section 2 of the Sherman Act.

On the other hand, interaction with smart contracts should count as trading relationship to the extent that there is awareness and intentionality. Smart contracts are deployed on DLT networks and are 'called' by clients to perform their programmed function. For instance, automated market maker (AMM) services, which are used to swap, lend, or borrow assets, rely on smart contracts which implement algorithms to calculate swapping, lending, borrowing rates and link assets to one another. Unlike a situation like Google's result ranking, which is performed without any involvement by the ranked pages, AMM smart contracts are deployed with the purpose of being interacted with by third parties. This is true even if the actor interacting with a smart contract might not be targeting that specific smart contract; for example, when a service is instructed to look for the best exchange rate on the market, it pings various AMMs and automatically chooses the one offering the best exchange rate. The process is concealed from the user, but there is still awareness and intentionality on the side of the user to interact with the winning AMM.

Discrimination among trading partners: Criteria for similar/different transactions. The fact that Article 102(c) TFEU and the R–P Act apply only to discriminatory transactions vis-a-vis trading partners also implies that the discrimination must generate its effects between trading partners of the dominant undertaking, and not simply between the dominant undertaking and its trading partners.[161] In other words, Article 102(c) TFEU and the R–P Act do not apply in situations when the dominant undertaking discriminates between its own products and services and those of its trading partners. This means that if the crypto-exchange Binance reserves preferential treatment on its platform for its own cryptoasset, BNB, at the

[160] See Pınar Akman, 'The Theory of Abuse in Google Search: A Positive and Normative Assessment under EU Competition Law' (2017) 2017 Illinois Journal of Law, Technology and Policy 301, 330–31.

[161] MEO (CoJ) (n 141) para 25; O'Donoghue and Padilla (n 50) 779; Herbert Hovenkamp, *Federal Antitrust Policy: The Law of Competition and Its Practice* (4th edn, West Academic Publishing 2011) 629.

expense of other cryptoassets, this conduct will not be caught by Article 102(c) TFEU or, if BNB is deemed a commodity, by the R–P Act.

The next requirement for Article 102(c) TFEU is that the transactions are equivalent and treated differently (or that they are different and treated similarly),[162] or for the R–P Act that a seller of a commodity discriminates in price between different purchasers of commodities of like grade and quality. What constitutes equivalent transaction and different treatment is assessed on a case-by-case basis, but it should be obvious that equivalent does not mean identical,[163] and the degree of difference in treatment needs to be non-negligible.[164] As AG Trstenjak noted, there is different treatment between transactions 'if amongst trading parties there is no relation between the respective values of the benefit and the consideration'.[165] For the R–P Act, like grade and quality are assessed on the basis of functional interchangeability.[166]

A good example here is the method of selecting which transactions will be included in a block by validators/miners, based on the maximal extractable value (MEV). MEV refers to the maximum value that can be extracted from block production through fees by including, excluding, and changing the order of transactions in a block.[167] From the pool of candidate transactions for the next block, validators will want to include those that, when put in a specific order, will result in the largest total fee amount. While two transactions may be identical in terms of size and the fee they yield separately, they may produce different total fee yield when combined with other transactions in a given block. They are therefore identical when taken separately, but different when taken in context, and therefore a validator would have a reason to differentiate between them as regards the order in which they would process them.

It is apparent that the particular technological and commercial realities of the transactions need to be taken into account to be able to assess whether they are equivalent and whether they are treated differently. In the words of AG Wahl, 'as is clear from the case law, account must be taken of all of the prevailing conditions on the market in order to determine whether transactions are equivalent'.[168] The CoJ, endorsing AG Wahl's view, listed a number of relevant parameters, including 'the undertaking's dominant position, the negotiating power as regards the tariffs, the conditions and arrangements for charging those tariffs, their duration

[162] Case 13/63 Italian Republic v Commission ECLI:EU:C:1963:20, para 6.

[163] O'Donoghue and Padilla (n 50) 969.

[164] Opinion of AG Wahl in MEO (n 141) paras 108–110.

[165] Case C-52/07 Kanal 5 Ltd and TV 4 AB v Föreningen Svenska Tonsättares Internationella Musikbyrå (STIM) upa. ECLI:EU:C:2008:703, para 109.

[166] Frederick Rowe, 'Price Differentials and Product Differentiation: The Issues under the Robinson-Patman Act' (1956) 66 Yale Law Journal 1, 15–18.

[167] See Ethereum Development Documentation: Maximal Extractable Value (MEV), at <https://ethereum.org/en/developers/docs/mev/>.

[168] Opinion of AG Wahl in MEO (n 141) para 57. Confirmed by the CoJ in MEO (n 141) para 31.

and their amount, and the possible existence of a strategy aiming to exclude from the downstream market one of its trade partners which is at least as efficient as its competitors'.[169] In DLT markets, the technological characteristics of transactions will also heavily weigh in that assessment. But, technological differences (which are almost inevitable) should not be used to obscure what may otherwise be commercially and/or functionally similar transactions. For instance, the most widely circulated stablecoin, USDT, is issued on different networks, most commonly Tron and Ethereum. While minor differences between these networks exist, the basic features of USDT are the same on all networks. To establish discrimination between treatment of USDT on Ethereum and USDT on Tron, one would have to substantiate how potential differences matter instead of simply invoking that they were issued on different networks.

Competitive disadvantage. The final requirement is that the discrimination results in a competitive disadvantage for the trading partner (purchaser) that has been discriminated against. As mentioned, this presupposes that the undertakings benefiting or losing out from the discrimination are in competition with one another.[170]

How closely the undertakings need to compete and what the nature of the competitive disadvantage needs to be are unclear, with some evidence pointing to a flexible approach from EU institutions, and potentially less so from US institutions.[171] Either way, *MEO* highlighted that the nature of the competitive disadvantage must be such as 'to lead to a distortion of competition' between the involved undertakings.[172] In DLT markets, it seems appropriate to interpret distortion of competition in a way that includes dimensions of competition that are idiosyncratic to the technology, particularly governance aspects. For example, discrimination that has no bearing on cost or pricing, but that can corrupt voting, mining, or staking processes should in principle count (the R–P Act would not be applicable in this example, because it only concerns price discrimination). DLT networks can compete for governance (including voting), mining or staking resources, which are directly tied to key performance measures, such as security or liquidity, and therefore their ability to compete in the market. That said, not every discriminatory interference that affects a DLT product's or service's governance or other functions will amount to the kind of abuse prohibited by Article 102(c) TFEU. Certain choices on DLT networks can be *inherently* discriminatory—for example, a mining pool choosing to mine blocks of a fork and not of the original ledger seemingly discriminates

[169] ibid.

[170] See n 161. See also Commission Decision of 23 July 2004 COMP/A.36.568/D3 Scandlines Sverige AB v Port of Helsingborg, para 256 ('It has not been established that the ferry-operators and the cargo operators compete on the same market as concerns the transportation of goods').

[171] O'Donoghue and Padilla (n 50) 976–82; Rowe (n 166) 18, where the author notes that '[t]he "injury" requirement has evolved into an almost automatic inference from the differential itself'.

[172] MEO (CoJ) (n 141) para 27.

against otherwise similar transactions, but this process is also how miners indicate support for a new ledger, and without any aggravating circumstances it should be considered normal competition.

b) Self-preferencing: Filling the gaps of traditional discrimination

From the previous exposition, it may transpire that the strict conditions of Article 102(c) TFEU and the even stricter conditions of the R–P Act can be difficult to meet in DLT markets. This does not mean that discriminatory conduct which does not meet the conditions of Article 102(c) TFEU or of the R–P Act is always legal.[173] Self-preferencing has emerged—in the European Union at least—as a form of anticompetitive discrimination that goes beyond Article 102(c) TFEU, and which can even be more applicable in DLT markets. The United States has tiptoed around similar concepts but without any concrete developments. In lack of judicial activism of the kind seen in the European Union, reliance on standard antitrust violations, such as tying, is often seen as the preferred way of addressing discrimination that is not caught by the R–P Act whether exclusively under section 2 of the Sherman Act[174] or in conjunction with the Clayton Act, which made it unlawful to sell a good on the condition that the user of the good not deal in the goods of a competitor.[175] Some legislative action has been initiated but a bill has yet to be passed. Specifically, the American Innovation and Choice Online Act (AICOA) would make it illegal for platforms to 'preference the products, services, or lines of business of the covered platform operator over those of another business user on the covered platform in a manner that would materially harm competition'.[176] Since platforms are defined as 'a website, online or mobile application, operating system, digital assistant, or online service that ... (B) facilitates the offering, advertising, sale, purchase, payment, or shipping of products or services, including software applications',[177] it can include DLT platforms that offer DLT-based products and services. In the meantime, and until legislation is enacted, self-preferencing has only been elevated to a distinct offence in the European Union.

In the European Union, self-preferencing was introduced as a separate and self-standing theory of harm in the *Google Shopping* case, where the Commission found that Google engaged in self-preferencing vis-à-vis its own comparison shopping service compared to those of competitors.[178] Not every case of showing preferential

[173] See eg Lucy MR Chambers, 'Vertical Agreements in Fintech Markets' in Konstantinos Stylianou, Marios Iacovides, and Björn Lundqvist, *Fintech Competition: Law, Policy, and Market Organisation* (Hart Publishing 2023) 194–95.

[174] See eg Erik Hovenkamp, 'Platform Exclusion of Competing Sellers' (2024) 49 Journal of Corporate Law 299.

[175] Herbert Hovenkamp, 'Antitrust and Self-Preferencing' (2023) 38 Antitrust 5. See also s 3 of Clayton Antitrust Act of 1914.

[176] American Innovation and Choice Online Act, S.2992 - 117th Congress, s 3(a)(1).

[177] ibid s 2(9)(B).

[178] Google Shopping (n 45).

treatment to one's own products or services, however, will amount to anticompetitive self-preferencing as understood in *Google Shopping*. The Commission, and the GC's subsequent upholding of the Commission's decision,[179] drew specific contours around this offence. Self-preferencing was found to violate Article 102 TFEU because (cumulative conditions): (a) Google promoted its own listings in ways that did not make available to competitors; (b) Google demoted results from competitors; (c) traffic flow and diversion were instrumental for the success or failure of Google's competitors; (d) there was no credible alternative to making up for the diverted traffic; (e) the conduct was capable of extending Google's dominant position.[180] In a similar case, *Amazon Buy Box*, Amazon was found to favour its own retail offers by placing them in Buy Box, a side frame which features products and sellers more prominently to users.[181] Because the Amazon Buy Box case was ended with commitments, the Commission did not have to reach a final conclusion on the legal characterization of Amazon's conduct, but the analysis is still instructive. The conditions identified in *Google Shopping* and *Amazon Buy Box* are evidently case-specific, but one can abstract out and identify the main elements of self-preferencing that are of relevance in DLT markets.

Actively harmful conduct. Firstly, conduct that may be deemed self-preferencing cannot be merely passive; rather active steps that are *intended to harm competitors* are needed. This follows from the Commission's and the GC's insistence that what made Google's conduct abusive was not simply the promotion of its own services, but the active demotion of competitors' services.[182] In *Amazon Buy Box*, the conduct consistent in Amazon implementing 'artificial settings that favour Amazon Retail's offers in the ranking (and thus display) of offers by the [Amazon] algorithm'.[183] If the artificial settings were not in place, Amazon's offers would be ranked equally alongside other sellers with whom Amazon had a most-favoured nation clause agreement. What may count in DLT markets as conduct that is intended to harm competitors is undefined, but it is evident that intent cannot be overlooked. While the GC explained that proof of anticompetitive intent is not necessary to establish a violation of Article 102 TFEU, it can still 'be taken into account in order to determine that a dominant position has been abused'.[184]

Establishing intent behind the positive conduct to harm competitors may be tricky due to the DLT product and services' (decentralized) governance, the competing interests (and therefore intents) of involved actors, and the sometimes protean nature of DLT products and services, and by extension the intent behind

[179] Google Shopping (GC) (n 56).
[180] Google Shopping (n 45) paras 341–342. Google Shopping (GC) (n 56) paras 187, 212.
[181] Commission decision of 20 December 2022 AT.40462 Amazon Marketplace and AT.40703 Amazon Buy Box.
[182] Google Shopping (GC) (n 56) paras 345 et seq.
[183] Amazon Buy Box (n 181) para 174.
[184] Google Shopping (GC) (n 56) para 256. See also Commission decision of 15 October 2014 AT.39523 Slovak Telekom, para 369.

them).[185] A In traditional competition law, where undertakings are regarded as black-box corporate entities with central management, intent can be traced back to the undertaking's decision-makers. While many DLT products and services can be offered by such undertakings, many others take the shape and direction that their community gives them, and it may not always be apparent which direction that is or what motivated it. Moreover, since the involved stakeholders can be separate independent undertakings, they can pursue different interests and may even oppose the conduct that was adopted in the end. While in the context of traditional undertakings this is irrelevant, because competition law treats undertakings as a black box and internal disagreements do not matter; in DLT markets decision-making and development are the confluence of separate independent undertakings and each can count as an independent decision-making centre. In those cases, the *prevailing intent* must be determined. In any case, in determining intent, the supporting evidence can span anything from technical documentation, communications, interviews, etc, much like in non-DLT markets.[186]

Transactions not necessary. Secondly, unlike the prohibition in Article 102(c), self-preferencing does not seem to necessitate transactions between trading partners (no matter how broadly the term has been defined by the Commission and the CoJ/GC as explained above). The Commission did not treat Google's conduct as a discrimination under Article 102(c) or as a refusal to supply, obviating the need to show transactions between Google and competing comparison shopping services. A step further, the GC on appeal noted that Google does in essence refuse to supply an essential facility, that is, its general results page, but what was missing to characterize this conduct as a refusal to supply offence was a 'request' on the side of competing comparison shopping services, which Google would expressly refuse to satisfy.[187] The GC thereby implicitly rejected the idea that competing providers and Google have 'business contacts' or a 'voluntary commercial relationship' as required by case law to establish transactions between trading partners.[188]

The lack of the requirement for business contacts or voluntary commercial relationships opens the door for the applicability of self-preferencing in a vast array of situations in DLT markets that may be prone to discriminatory treatment: (a) listing, delisting, and promoting cryptoassets. A crypto-exchange that also issues its own cryptoasset has an incentive to award preferential treatment to its cryptoasset on its platform, through, for example, lower transaction fees; (b) metaverse ecosystems: an undertaking builds a metaverse wherein it promotes

[185] For a more complete discussion of governance, decision-making, and conflicting interests in DLT-based products and services see section C.ii.a and also Chapter 8 section E.iv and Chapter 1 section D.iii.

[186] See eg Slovak Telekom (n 184) paras 389–390. Commission decision of 15 June 2005 COMP/A.37.507/F3 AstraZeneca, para 789.

[187] Google Shopping (GC) (n 56) paras 219–234.

[188] See discussion in nn 151–160 and accompanying text.

its own DLT offerings over third parties; (c) transaction ordering: a DLT platform for tokenized real-world assets prioritizes mining/validation of own/affiliated transactions.

No indispensability requirement. Lastly, the combination of elements (c) and (d) above, coupled with the GC's rejection that Google's conduct amounted to refusal to supply, means that the product or service provided by the undertaking that discriminates does not have to be indispensable to the competing undertakings in the sense of the refusal to supply offence. The GC noted in relation to Google's conduct that 'all or, at the very least, most practices capable of restricting or eliminating competition ("exclusionary practices") are liable to constitute implicit refusals to supply, since they tend to make access to a market more difficult. Nonetheless, [the refusal to supply doctrine as per *Bronner*] cannot be applied to all of those practices without disregarding the spirit and the letter of Article 102 TFEU, the scope of which is not limited to abusive practices relating to "indispensable" goods and services within the meaning of that judgment'.[189] While the product or service that enables the discrimination does not need to be indispensable it still has to be essential (point (c) above) and hard to replicate (point (d) above). This point was clearly spelled out in *Amazon Buy Box*: in the legal assessment of the Amazon's Buy Box policy, the Commission observed that '[i]n view of the importance of the Featured Offer for the visibility of offers and the ability of sellers to generate transactions ... Amazon's artificial settings that favour Amazon Retail's offers in the ranking (and thus display) of offers by the [Amazon] algorithm, is capable of distorting competition on its e-commerce platforms'.[190] Generally, the Commission placed great emphasis on how important the Buy Box is to sellers and to competition on Amazon's platform.[191]

c) Blockchain neutrality

Part of the appeal of the DLT technology has been its potential to serve as an infrastructure generative technology upon which other technologies, products, services, and markets will be developed.[192] Reminiscent of the role of the internet (on which DLT applications and services run in turn), there have been calls to replicate a neutrality and openness regime that ostensibly characterized the early internet.[193]

[189] Google Shopping (GC) (n 56) para 234.

[190] Amazon Marketplace (n 181) para 174.

[191] ibid para 173 ('Sales through the Buy Box represent the vast majority of all transactions on each of Amazon's e-commerce platforms').

[192] Itzhak Aviv, 'The Distributed Ledger Technology as Development Platform for Distributed Information Systems' in Harish Sharma and others (eds), *Proceedings of the International Conference on Intelligent Vision and Computing (ICIVC 2021)*, vol 15 (Springer 2022); Karim Jabbar and Pernille Bjørn, 'Growing the Blockchain Information Infrastructure', *Proceedings of the 2017 CHI Conference on Human Factors in Computing Systems* (ACM 2017); Florian Glaser, Florian Hawlitschek, and Benedikt Notheisen, 'Blockchain as a Platform' in Horst Treiblmaier and Roman Beck (eds), *Business Transformation through Blockchain* (Springer 2019).

[193] Samuel Weinstein, 'Blockchain Neutrality' (2020) 55 Georgia Law Review 499. On blockchain neutrality as a feature of the network see Hanna Halaburda and Daniel Obermeier, 'Decentralization

The concept of 'blockchain neutrality' is ill-defined but broadly refers to a desideratum that 'regulators . . . promote vigorous blockchain competition [and] ensure open access and non-discrimination on dominant blockchain networks'.[194]

While the limiting principles around blockchain neutrality have not been clearly laid out, one cannot help but draw parallels with the host of quasi-regulatory antitrust rules adopted or proposed to ensure a certain measure of neutrality in digital markets (eg Digital Markets Act, the proposed AICOA). While these instruments have different conditions and requirements to engage but they share common motivations and underlying rationales, namely that the regulated entity or activity exists in a highly non-contestable market, that the regulated service serves as infrastructure or bottleneck intermediary, and that their conduct frequently harms partners and competitors. The rules emerged with the realization that oligopolistic structures are common in digital platform markets and instilling more contestability could not be left up to the market mechanism or to antitrust law enforcement since the problem was generalized. If there were to emerge a blockchain neutrality rule, it would have to be in relation to blockchain networks that are non-contestable, that serve as infrastructure for other products or services to be developed upon, and that they are found to distort competition in ways that standard competition law enforcement does not have the resources to correct.

vs. Blockchain Neutrality: The Unequal Burden of Ethereum's Market Mechanism on dApps' (2024) SSRN.

[194] Weinstein (n 193) 505.

8
ANTICOMPETITIVE AGREEMENTS AND RESTRAINTS OF TRADE

(A) General 219

(B) Aggravating and mitigating collusion factors in DLT markets 221

(C) Meaning of collusion (agreements, restraints of trade, concerted activity) 224

(D) Impermissible contacts and information exchange on private and public DLT networks and DLT markets 228

- i) Meaning and role of contact between undertakings 228
- ii) Private contacts and information exchange on private (permissioned) DLT networks 231
- iii) Public sharing of information in DLT markets 235

(E) Illicit coordination vs legitimate cooperation in DLT markets 239

- i) Can DLT cooperative activities be exempt from competition law? 240
- ii) Coordination and cooperation in DLT markets as ancillary restriction and objective necessity 242
- iii) Cooperation in DLT markets as standard-setting or joint venture 245
- iv) The by object/effect and per se/rule of reason treatment and its determinants in the decentralized economy 252

(A) General

Competition law aims to safeguard the competitive process in the market,[1] and it therefore seeks to encourage rivalry rather than cooperation among undertakings. The Court of Justice (CoJ) early on ruled that 'each economic operator must determine independently the policy which he intends to adopt on the common market including the choice of the persons and undertakings to which he makes offers or sells'.[2] This is because, as the Supreme Court explained, '[c]oncerted activity inherently is fraught with anticompetitive risk. It deprives the marketplace of the

[1] For a discussion on the goals of competition law and further references see Konstantinos Stylianou and Marios Iacovides, 'The Goals of EU Competition Law: A Comprehensive Empirical Investigation' (2022) 42 Legal Studies 620.

[2] Joined Cases 40–48, 50, 54 to 56, 111, 113, and 114–173 Coöperatieve Vereniging 'Suiker Unie' UA and others v Commission EU:C:1972:70, para 174.

Antitrust in the Decentralized Economy. Konstantinos Stylianou, Oxford University Press.
 DOI: 10.1093/9780191925504.003.0008

independent centers of decisionmaking that competition assumes and demands'.[3] Undertakings, on the other hand, may often have the incentive to substitute competition for cooperation (whether competition on price, output, quality, or other parameter), as this can increase profits and reduce risk. To prevent undertakings from 'cozying up' to each other, competition law prohibits collusion. Collusion is a general term used to describe situations where undertakings do not act independently in the market. In EU competition law, collusion occurs when undertakings enter into agreements or engage in concerted practices that are prohibited under Article 101 TFEU. In US antitrust law, collusion occurs when undertakings enter into contracts, combinations in the form of trust or otherwise, or conspiracies in restraint of trade or commerce prohibited by section 1 of the Sherman Act.[4]

At the heart of collusive arrangements is contact between undertakings to devise a common course of action. Every technology that engenders new forms of communication naturally adds to the tools undertakings have at their disposal to align their conduct with one another, and this is true for Distributed Ledger Technology (DLT) markets as well. In fact, collusive activity is the most common antitrust risk that lawyers identify as DLT facilitating, because by its very nature, DLT is a collaborative distributed database,[5] and it is a claim that also commonly appears in litigation, although with limited success for now.[6]

While it is true that the collaborative nature of the production of DLT products and services diverges from competition law's basic premise that undertakings (should) act independently in the market, the mere use of DLT infrastructure is not sufficient to raise suspicion of illicit conduct. There are numerous conditions that need to be met to establish collusion both under EU competition law and under US antitrust law, and the sections below explain how the analysis can reflect the particular features of the decentralized economy for each condition. Particular areas of difficulty are establishing awareness of contact between undertakings on DLT networks—a prerequisite of collusive arrangements—the role of public sharing of information in DLT markets, the possible favourable treatment of DLT activity as ancillary restriction or objective necessity, standard-setting, or joint venture, and

[3] *Copperweld v. Independence Tube*, 467 U.S. 752, 768-9 (1984).

[4] Section 1 of the Sherman Act, 15 U.S.C. § 1.

[5] Robert Schwinger, 'Can Blockchain Participants Act in Restraint of Trade?' (2021) New York Law Journal; Brad Finney, 'Blockchain and Antitrust: New Tech Meets Old Regs' (2018) 19 Transactions: The Tennessee Journal of Business Law 709; Evan Miller, 'Antitrust Live: The New Blockchain Era of Antitrust' (2022) 24 Columbia Science and Technology Law Review 106.

[6] See eg *United American Corp. v. Bitmain, Inc. et al.*, 530 F. Supp. 3d 1241 (2021) (the claim was that miners, protocol developers, and exchanges conspired to control of the Bitcoin Cash blockchain. The case was dismissed); *Lamartine Pierre et al. v. Apple, Inc.*, 5:23-cv-5981 (2023) (the claim was that Apple conspired with competing payment services to exclude crypto-payment services from Apple's iOS platform. The case was dismissed); Notice of an Application to Commence Collective Proceedings Under Section 47b of the Competition Act 1998 Case No. 1523/7/7/22 (2022) (the claim was that a number of exchanges entered into an anticompetitive agreement to delist BSV. The case is pending).

finally the question of how to construe the object, purpose, and effects of DLT activity.

(B) Aggravating and mitigating collusion factors in DLT markets

While undertakings can attempt to collude in any market, collusion is more likely in certain market contexts than others. As will be shown below, this can be because the market structure and available technologies make collusion (a) easier, (b) more sustainable/stable, or (c) less detectable.[7] When conditions that facilitate collusion are in place, competition authorities may wish to be more vigilant.

Transparency and immutability. A main determinant of success in collusive arrangements is the ability of undertakings to effectively coordinate around a common plan. Markets with increased transparency are more susceptible to collusive outcomes, because firms can more easily observe and contact their competitors with a view to agree on a common market strategy.[8] Under normal market conditions, firms do not and should not publicly disclose information of strategic importance, because such information can be seen as an attempt to contact or influence competitors and engage them in a joint scheme.[9] However, in product or service markets underpinned by DLT infrastructure a large amount of (potentially strategic) information is available to all participating actors, and in the case of public DLT networks, to the public at large as well. For instance, in cryptoassets enabled by permissionless blockchains, the blockchain ledger records the full history of all transactions and transacting parties, data on miners and validators (who usually sign their activity), and even open-ended messages that are added as metadata in transactions.[10] The shared ledger can therefore serve not only as a means of communication, but also as an accurate reflection of industry actors and relations. As a result of the increased transparency, concerns around the possibility that DLTs will be used to facilitate collusion in the market have been raised.[11]

[7] For a good overview and discussion see Edward J Green, Robert C Marshall, and Leslie M Marx, 'Tacit Collusion in Oligopoly' in Roger D Blair and D Daniel Sokol (eds), *The Oxford Handbook of International Antitrust Economics*, vol 2 (OUP 2015).

[8] Peter Møllgaard and Per Baltzer Overgaard, 'Market Transparency and Competition Policy' (2001) Econstor Working paper No 6-2001; Matthew Bennett and Philip Collins, 'The Law and Economics of Information Sharing: The Good, the Bad and the Ugly' (2010) 6 European Competition Journal 311, 320–27. See also *In re Text Messaging Antitrust Litigation*, 782 F.3d 867 (2015), where Judge Posner discusses collusion in oligopolistic markets and how independent matching of competitors' conduct should be illegal.

[9] See section C.

[10] On the information that can be included in a block, see Andreas M Antonopoulos, *Mastering Bitcoin: Programming the Open Blockchain* (2nd edn, O'Reilly Media 2017) 195 et seq. Miner signatures are often used to decipher which miner mined each block.

[11] Almudena Arcelus, Mihran Yenikomshian, and Noemi Nocera, 'Mitigating Antitrust Concerns When Competitors Share Data Using Blockchain Technology' (2021) Harvard Journal of Law and Technology (online).

On the other hand, while transparency may help firms to coordinate, the fact that transactions are observable and permanently recorded on the ledger also means that activity on the ledger leaves a permanent trail, which can be audited by competition authorities.[12] Most collusive rings go to great lengths to keep their activities hidden both from outsider firms and from competition authorities, to protect the integrity and the continuing operation of the ring. To the extent that DLTs are immutable ledgers of transactions and activity, they raise the risk of discovery and evidence collection and might therefore not be an ideal means of collusion.

Transparency plays a role on the demand side too and has the opposite effect to that on the supply side. Under conditions of demand-side transparency, consumers/users can observe deviations from the collusive behaviour, and can act to reward the deviator, making deviation more lucrative.[13] As a result, deviation becomes more likely and, in turn, collusion becomes less stable. Everything else equal, and at least when it comes to public DLT networks, users indeed have full and ready access both to the consensus mechanism and to the transactions themselves, and can therefore detect anomalies more easily than in traditional markets, where even basic market parameters like price are often hard to observe on a large scale.

Deviation detection and deterministic punishment. Moreover, the prospects of collusion are determined by how easy it is for members to detect deviation from the common plan, and by how easy and effective punishment of the deviating conduct can be.[14] Deviation from the collusive arrangement is in firms' *selfish* interest, because doing so will result in them capturing a larger market share. At the same time, it is not in their *collective* interest, because each deviation undermines the collective success. Whether firms will opt to serve their own selfish interests or the collective interests of the collusive group will depend on the probability of getting caught if they deviate and on the magnitude of the punishment. To the extent that DLT products and services rely on a transparent infrastructure, in that participants can observe strategic information on the common ledger, it can be argued that DLT enhances detection of deviating market conduct. Moreover, the deterministic nature of smart contracts ('if this, then that'), which are prevalent in the decentralized economy, can ensure both that participants can quickly adapt their behaviour to that of other participants, and that deviating behaviour is punished automatically according to pre-agreed rules. Combined, these two characteristics suggest that collusion in blockchain markets can be easier, more stable, and more effective, because deviation is harder and more costly.

12 ibid.

13 Møllgaard and Overgaard (n 8). See also Christian Schultz, 'Transparency and Tacit Collusion in a Differentiated Market' (Center for Economic Studies & IFO Institute for Economic Research 2002).

14 George Stigler, *The Theory of Price* (4th edn, Pearson 1987) 226–27; Bennett and Collins (n 8) 320–27.

Automation of collusive activity and detection, and oligopolies by design. Lastly, the number of firms participating in a collusive arrangement and the total number of firms present in the market are influential parameters as well, with smaller numbers being more conducive to successful collusion. As the number of members in a collusive scheme increases, they each stand to make less collusive profit because it is shared among more firms, while at the same time deviation becomes more profitable as it will result in capturing the share of more firms.[15] Both factors introduce instability into the collusive scheme. At the same time, transparency and deviation detection become easier among a small number of firms that can closely observe each other. The impact of large number of participants in the success of collusive schemes can be ameliorated in DLT markets, because both collusive activity as well as detection can be automated, which can bring about the desired results regardless of number of participants.

In oligopolistic markets, where the number of firms in the market is low, collusive arrangements are further aided by the fact that firms know that their every action has a considerable effect upon their competitors, which means that they are more likely to choose strategies that are optimal for the group rather that individually.[16] Further, because oligopolies can be more easily preserved in markets where new entrants cannot undermine the prospects of the collusive scheme, entry barriers also become a contributing factor. When entry is easy, any attempt to raise or maintain higher prices would invite new firms into the market causing profitability across the industry to shrink, and making the collusive arrangement less enticing.

While many DLT markets are populated by a large number of actors, oligopolistic clusters exist, where collusion can become a concern. For example, the governance system of blockchain protocol EOS comprises only a fixed number of twenty-one validators, who are chosen through voting that is supposed to represent anyone with a stake in the EOS ecosystem.[17] Yet, in 2018, and despite the nominal 'free and democratic election process within EOS', patterns of 'irregular block producer voting' emerged.[18] The irregular voting was the result of existing block producers (validators) coordinating to continue to vote each other to remain in their position and avoid being voted out.[19] This kind of coordination was enabled partly by the small-sized and tightly knit validator community, which in fact was, by design, limited to twenty-one members. While each validator position

[15] Marc Ivaldi and others, 'The Economics of Tacit Collusion' (2003) IDEI WP 186.

[16] See FT Dolbear and others, 'Collusion in Oligopoly: An Experiment on the Effect of Numbers and Information' (1968) 82 The Quarterly Journal of Economics 240. Chamberlin also describes how sellers in an oligopolistic market can, without engaging in explicit collusion, reach a higher price for a cooperative solution. See Edward Chamberlin, *The Theory of Monopolistic Competition* (8th edn, Harvard UP 1962).

[17] Yuheng Huang and others, 'Characterizing EOSIO Blockchain' (2020) arXiv:2002.05369.

[18] Block.one, 'Statement: EOS Public Blockchain Governance' *Medium* (1 October 2018).

[19] Ana Berman, 'EOS Developer Acknowledges Claims of "Collusion" and "Mutual Voting" Between Nodes' *CoinTelegraph* (2 October 2018).

was contestable, the number of positions could not be increased, and therefore the market for EOS validation was protected by absolute technological entry barriers.

As should be obvious from the above exposition, the deployment of DLT and the transition to decentralized DLT-based market structures does not necessarily increase the risk of collusion, let alone conclusively contribute to it.

(C) Meaning of collusion (agreements, restraints of trade, concerted activity)

Collusion, whether in the form of agreement, concerted practice, or restraint of trade, requires (a) impermissible *contact* between undertakings and (b) unlawful *coordination* between undertakings. Without contact—proven or presumed—conduct is considered independent and therefore outside the scope of Article 101 TFEU and section 1 of the Sherman Act, and without coordination, there is no potentially illicit arrangement to go after. DLT markets complicate both those conditions, because the technology itself is predicated on collaborative production, which at first glance necessitates contact and implies coordination. The case law presents a far more nuanced picture and it is necessary to untangle it first in order to appreciate how collusion works in DLT markets. This section sets out the key elements of contact and coordination, which will then be applied in DLT markets in sections D and E.

(Express) agreements. Express or explicit agreements are the 'obvious' way by which an unlawful arrangement can be concluded. Article 101(1) TFEU prohibits *agreements* whose object or effect is the prevention, restriction, or distortion of competition. Section 1 of the Sherman Act prohibits any *contract* in restraint of trade. EU courts have been more formalistic about defining the concept of agreement as distinct from concerted practices, but in US case law the different forms unlawful restraints can take under the scope of section 1 of the Sherman Act (contract, combination, or conspiracy) are handled together and so they are examined below under concerted practices and activity. In any case, in both EU and US law, courts are clear that the form of the collusive arrangement is immaterial; it is the content of the arrangement that matters.[20]

In *Bayer,* the General Court (GC) defined agreement as 'a concurrence of wills between at least two parties, the way in which it is manifested being unimportant so long as it constitutes the faithful expression of the parties' intention'.[21] That the way in which the agreement is manifested is unimportant has led to Article

[20] Commission decision of 23 April 1986 IV/31.149 Polypropylene, paras 21, 105; *American Tobacco Co. v. United States,* 328 U.S. 781, 809 (1946); *United States v. Paramount Pictures, Inc.*, 334 U.S. 131, 142–43 (1948).

[21] Case T-41/96 Bayer v Commission EU:T:2000:242, para 69.

101(1) TFEU to apply in a wide range of situations that qualified as agreements, including gentleman's agreements,[22] oral agreements,[23] constitutions of associations,[24] guidelines that are adhered to by their intended parties,[25] and commercial correspondence.[26]

Since the form is immaterial, the main determinative feature of agreements is the existence of *an expression* of concurrence of wills which reflects the parties' *joint intention*.[27] This presupposes offer and acceptance of an arrangement; unilateral offers, announcements, and mere negotiations do not qualify as agreements, since there is no consensus,[28] although they may amount to concerted practice (see below).[29] Tacit acquiescence, though, can be enough to indicate acceptance.[30]

Further, since offers and acceptance are expressions of joint intention, the offer must be made with an *intent* to enter interdependent obligations (ie conditional upon the participation of the other party),[31] and the acceptance must be performed under the condition that the offeree is *aware* of the offeror's offer and intent, and assents to the interdependent obligations.[32] While intent is subjective, that is, when one must establish that the undertakings in question themselves had the necessary intent, it can be objectively presumed, meaning that external indicia can be used to infer intent based on what can be reasonably foreseen.[33] In the words of Advocate General (AG) Szpunar in *Eturas*, if it can be found that 'it is highly probable . . . that a reasonably attentive and prudent economic operator would have become aware . . . of the related restriction, [it can be concluded] that the high probability of that inference justifies the application of a rebuttable presumption'.[34]

[22] Case T-53/03 BPB plc v Commission EU:T:2008:254, para 82.

[23] Case 28/77 Tepea v Commission EU:C:1978:133, para 41.

[24] Commission decision of 30 March 1984 IV/30.804 Nuovo CEGAM, para 13.

[25] Commission decision of 14 December 1999 IV/34.237/F3 Anheuser-Busch Incorporated - Scottish & Newcastle, para 59.

[26] Case C-260/09 P Activision Blizzard Germany GmbH v Commission ECLI:EU:C:2011:62, para 82.

[27] Joined Cases T-305/94 and others, Limburgse Vinyl Maatschappij NV and others v Commission (PVC II) ECLI:EU:T:1999:80, para 715. The agreement does not even have to be complete or have specified all aspects of the arrangement. See Case T-240/07 Heineken Nederland v Commission EU:T:2011:284, para 45.

[28] Joined Cases C-2/01 P and C-3/01 P Bundesverband der Arzneimittel-Importeure eV and Commission v Bayer AG ECLI:EU:C:2004:2, para 101; Case E-3/97 Jan and Kristian Jæger AS/Opel Norge AS (1998) OJ C 263, para 36.

[29] Case T-202/98 Tate & Lyle v Commission ECLI:EU:T:2001:185, para 54.

[30] See eg Case C-338/00 P Volkswagen AG v Commission ECLI:EU:C:2003:473, para 65.

[31] Bayer (n 21) para 67; Case T-7/89 SA Hercules Chemicals NV v Commission ECLI:EU:T:1991:75, para 256.

[32] Oliver Black, 'Agreement: Concurrence of Wills, or Offer and Acceptance?' (2008) 4 European Competition Journal 101, 112–13.

[33] Case C-49/92 P Commission v Anic Partecipazioni SpA ECLI:EU:C:1999:356; Case C-74/14 'Eturas' UAB and others v Lietuvos Respublikos konkurencijos taryba ECLI:EU:C:2016:42, paras 38 et seq.

[34] Opinion of AG Szpunar in Case C-74/14 'Eturas' UAB and others v Lietuvos Respublikos konkurencijos taryba ECLI:EU:C:2015:493, para 56.

Concerted practices and activity. Arrangements between two or more parties that have not reached the point of an *expression* of joint intention, may qualify as concerted practices, which are also prohibited by Article 101(1) TFEU, or combinations or conspiracies, which are prohibited by section 1 of the Sherman Act. The term *concerted activity* will be used to reflect both EU and US law. Concerted activity is not mutually exclusive with agreements in the sense that authorities do not need to specify whether the facts of a case amount to an agreement or a concerted activity, as long as they can prove either.[35] The CoJ has noted that agreements and concerted practices are 'forms of collusion having the same nature and are only distinguishable from each other by their intensity and the forms in which they manifest themselves'.[36]

Concerted practices in EU case law have been defined as 'a form of coordination between undertakings which, without having reached the stage where an agreement properly so-called has been concluded, knowingly substitutes practical cooperation between them for the risks of competition'.[37] The CoJ explained that the intentional substitution of cooperation for competition can take place through 'any direct or indirect contact between . . . operators, the object or effect whereof is either to influence the conduct on the market of an actual or potential competitor or to disclose to such a competitor the course of conduct which they themselves have decided to adopt or contemplate adopting on the market'.[38] Along similar lines, the Supreme Court in *Monsanto* ruled that, falling short of conclusively establishing an agreement, plaintiffs under US antitrust law must provide 'direct or circumstantial evidence that reasonably tends to prove that [participants] had a conscious commitment to a common scheme designed to achieve an unlawful objective'.[39]

Like agreements, a mutual understanding between the concerting undertakings is necessary. In *Cimenteries* the GC emphasized that 'the concept of concerted practice does in fact imply the existence of *reciprocal contacts*' (emphasis added) but active participation in devising the concerted practice is not necessary—even passive acceptance of a competitor's future intentions is enough.[40] Parties do not have to achieve a 'meeting of minds' or a 'common course of conduct'[41] —rather the concerted activity may arise out of coordination which becomes apparent from the behaviour of the participants.[42] On this point, the Supreme Court requires a

[35] See n 20.
[36] Anic (n 33) para 131.
[37] Case 48/69 ICI v Commission EU:C:1972:70, para 64; Case C-8/08 T-Mobile Netherlands BV v Raad van Bestuur van de Nederlandse Mededingingsautoriteit EU:C:2009:343, para 26.
[38] Suiker Unie (n 2) para 174.
[39] *Monsanto Co. v. Spray-Rite Service Corp.*, 465 U.S. 752, 764 (1984).
[40] Joined Cases T-25/95 and others Cimenteries CBR and Others v Commission ECLI:EU:T:2000:77, para 1849.
[41] Case T-587/08 Fresh del Monte v Commission EU:T:2013:129, para 300.
[42] ICI (n 37) para 65.

showing that participants 'had a unity of purpose or a common design and understanding, or a meeting of minds in an unlawful arrangement'.[43]

Further, since the undertakings in question must *knowingly* substitute cooperation for competition,[44] or consciously commit to a common scheme,[45] it is necessary to demonstrate the involved undertakings were aware of the contact and each other's intention to substitute competition with cooperation. Similar to agreements, this knowledge can be objectively deduced from external indicia if it cannot be subjectively established.[46]

Despite the commonalities with agreements, because concerted activity lacks the element of the mutually communicated expression of intent to engage in the anticompetitive scheme (the 'agreement'), they require, on top of contact between parties, evidence of subsequent conduct in line with the anticompetitive scheme, and a causal link between the contact and the conduct.[47] When the undertakings taking part in the concerted action remain active on the market, it can be presumed, subject to proof to the contrary, which the economic operators concerned must adduce, that the causal link between contact and conduct exists.[48]

From the previous exposition it emerges that the establishment of a collusive arrangement, regardless of the form it takes, requires a showing of contact and coordination between undertakings. Both merit particular attention in the context of blockchain. Because under conventional market conditions, (competing) undertakings are not expected to be in contact with one another regarding their market intentions and conduct, communication along those lines is considered suspicious. However, the collaborative nature of DLT networks, products, and services, turns this premise on its head (section D). Moreover, the consensus-based nature of the DLT governance and/or production blurs the line between what constitutes acceptable consensus building as part of the normal modus operandi of the DLT technology, and what constitutes prohibited coordination among (competing) undertakings (section E).

[43] *American Tobacco* (n 20) 810.

[44] See nn 32–34.

[45] *Monsanto* (n 39).

[46] See Odudu Okeoghene, *The Boundaries of EC Competition Law – The Scope of Article 81* (CUP 2008) 69.

[47] T-Mobile (n 37) para 51; Case C-286/13 P Dole Food Company and Dole Fresh Fruit Europe v Commission ECLI:EU:C:2015:184, para 126; *Interstate Circuit v. United States*, 306 U.S. 208, 223 (1939).

[48] Case C-199/92 P Hüls v Commission ECLI:EU:C:1999:358, paras 161–163; T-Mobile (n 37) para 51.

(D) Impermissible contacts and information exchange on private and public DLT networks and DLT markets

As mentioned in the previous section (section C), the form in which collusion manifests is immaterial. While obviously express (written or oral) agreements count, so do formations of associations, guidelines as long as they are adhered to by members, and even correspondence. This broad scope is necessary in the context of the decentralized economy as numerous aspects of the economic activity within are regulated by norms, rules, and customs which are new to the economy (and by extension to competition law). The formation of foundations to support the development of cryptoassets, whitepapers, voting procedures and governance rules and norms—whether written or customary, and the exchange of information and messages on public or private blockchains can all, in principle, serve as the basis on which collusive activity can develop. The specific conditions under which this can happen are discussed below.

i) Meaning and role of contact between undertakings

Contact in agreements. As seen, direct or indirect contact between undertakings is a necessary precondition for the formation of agreements or concerted activity.[49] The element of contact is thornier in concerted activity than in agreements. This is because, to form an agreement, undertakings need to communicate offer and acceptance between them; this exchange encapsulates contact into itself, since without contact, the communication of an offer and of an acceptance is impossible. Therefore, in agreements, a showing of contact is usually intertwined with the showing that offer and acceptance have been communicated.

Contact in concerted activity. In concerted activity, in lack of offer and acceptance that would demonstrate contact, the current standard both in EU and US law is that contact may be *inferred* by undertakings' conduct when the conduct has *no plausible explanation other than contacts* between the undertakings.[50] In other words, where contact cannot be proven directly, it can be reverse-constructed through the conduct of the suspected undertakings in the market. For example, in *ICI* a number of dyestuffs producers were found to have engaged in a concerted practice to raise prices. In inferring contact from price announcements, the CoJ found concerted activity reasoning that:

[49] Suiker Unie (n 2) para 174.

[50] Joined Cases C-89/85 and others A. Ahlström Osakeyhtiö and others v Commission ECLI:EU:C:1993:120, para 71; *Interstate* (n 42).

> although a general, spontaneous increase on each of the national markets is just conceivable, these increases might be expected to differ according to the particular characteristics of the different national markets. Therefore, although parallel conduct in respect of prices may well have been an attractive and risk-free objective for the undertakings concerned, it is hardly conceivable that the same action could be taken spontaneously at the same time, on the same national markets and for the same range of products.[51]

In *Suiker Unie*, the exchange of telex documents that included statements of export plans were deemed to be sufficient contact to establish concerted action, because 'had it not been for the concerted action, some of the undertakings concerned would have been forced to sell more sugar within the common market'.[52] On the other hand, in *Woodpulp/Ahlström*, the CoJ rejected the Commission's finding that a group of wood pulp producers who preannounced their prices as members of a trade association engaged in price fixing.[53] The CoJ concluded that, even though producers preannounced prices, prices were similar, and set in close temporal proximity, this line of conduct was not attributable to the contacts between association members, but rather to the industry's unique features, especially that paper producers adjusted their future production based on the wood pulp prices they could anticipate, and that there were many different types of wood pulp, which required producers and customers to know each other's plans before committing.[54]

In the United States, courts draw inference as to the existence of concerted activity by relying on a set of *plus factors*, which, in addition to parallel conduct, tend to support the exclusion of the hypothesis of independent conduct.[55] These can include acting against one's own economic interests[56] and coordinated pricing.[57] In *Interstate*, the Supreme Court inferred concerted activity among a number of distributors from a combination of factors, such as strong motive for concerted action, risk of substantial loss if action was not coordinated, and the fact that the circulated proposals were under consideration by the others, concluding '[i]t taxes credulity to believe that the several distributors would, in the circumstances, have accepted and put into operation with substantial unanimity such far-reaching changes in their business methods without some understanding that all were to

[51] ICI (n 37) paras 108–109.
[52] Suiker Unie (n 2) para 599.
[53] Woodpulp/Ahlström (n 50).
[54] Woodpulp/Ahlström (n 50) paras 102–105.
[55] *Williamson Oil Co. v. Philip Morris USA*, 346 F.3d 1287 (2003); *City of Tuscaloosa v. Harcros Chemicals, Inc.*, 158 F.3d 548 (1998). William Kovacic and others, 'Plus Factors and Agreement in Antitrust Law' (2011) 110 Michigan Law Review 393; Christopher Leslie, 'The Probative Synergy of Plus Factors in Price-Fixing Litigation' (2021) 115 Northwestern University Law Review 1581.
[56] *Pan-Islamic Trade Corp. v. Exxon Corp.*, 632 F.2d 539, 559 (1980).
[57] *Monsanto* (n 39).

join, and we reject as beyond the range of probability that it was the result of mere chance'.[58]

Information in contact: What type of information is relevant. Implicit in the construct that contact can be inferred from conduct is the notion that the contact must carry some information that can influence the conduct. Otherwise, there can be no meaningful link between them. While not all information sharing between undertakings is impermissible (indeed, undertakings routinely exchange information), the threshold for which information can contribute to concerted practices is low: it must simply be 'capable of removing uncertainties concerning the intended conduct of the participating undertakings'.[59]

In turn, this assessment revolves around three factors: the content of the information, the market conditions, and any benefits to consumers. Regarding the content of the information, 'sensitive information concerning . . . competitors' strategic policies in terms of prices, capacity and technological development' has been deemed as sufficient to give rise to concerted activity,[60] and so has information about market entry.[61] Market conditions are also taken into account to assess whether the exchanged information pertains to 'normal competition'. Such market conditions include 'the nature of the products or services offered, the size and number of the undertakings involved and the volume of that market',[62] but also more broadly the structure of the market, including the level of transparency, the turnover rate of supply contracts, and the needs and demands of consumers.[63] The needs and demands of consumers, and generally any offsetting benefits of the information exchange are also taken into account. For example, in *Container Shipping*, the Commission explained that 'genuine public pricing announcements can help customers to make a more informed choice and reduce customers' search costs. However, efficiencies are less likely to result from the publication of future pricing intentions . . . because companies which announce their pricing intentions may revise them before consumers actually purchase based on that information'.[64] In a helpful summary, Bennett and Collins classify individualized, private, future pricing or quantity information as the most problematic, and aggregated, public, historic information as the least problematic.[65]

To sum up, impermissible contact between undertakings requires communication whereby information to knowingly (:with intent) engage (:offer and

[58] *Interstate* (n 47) 223.
[59] T-Mobile (n 37) para 43. For a discussion on how to assess the relevance and risk of different types of information for antitrust purposes see Bennett and Collins (n 8) 328 et seq.
[60] Case T-758/14 Infineon Technologies AG v Commission ECLI:EU:T:2016:737, para 174.
[61] Cimenteries (n 40) paras 1849 et seq.
[62] T-Mobile (n 28) para 33. Case 172/80 Gerhard Züchner v Bayerische Vereinsbank AG ECLI:EU:C:1981:178, para 14.
[63] Woodpulp/Ahlström (n 50) paras 102–120.
[64] Commission decision of 7 July 2016 AT.39850 Container Shipping, para 157.
[65] Bennett and Collins (n 8) 333.

acceptance) in interdependent illicit conduct is exchanged. If communication cannot be proven, it can be inferred based on conduct and plus factors, if conduct has no plausible explanation other than contacts between the undertakings.

ii) Private contacts and information exchange on private (permissioned) DLT networks

Private communication among undertakings is rarely looked upon favourably. Undertakings are supposed to compete in the public arena of the market, and therefore private communication is inherently suspicious. This is why it is of influence to determine whether the context of communication is private or not.

Contact awareness in private DLTs. There is no clear demarcation of where non-private settings end and private settings begin, but it appears from the case law that private settings are those where the exchange stays exclusively or predominantly between the participating undertakings. In-person meetings, the exchange of messages whether on paper or electronically, and phone calls have all been deemed means of private communication.[66] The US *LIBOR* cases are instructive.[67] LIBOR (London Inter-Bank Offered Rate) is an interest rate average that is calculated and published by Thomson Reuters based on the estimates submitted by sixteen leading banks on what they expect they would be charged if they borrow from other banks.[68] The cases concerned illicit backchannel communication among bank representatives who discussed rates via emails, text messages, and other documents prior to submission; even though the exchanged messages were shared among numerous people, the communication was considered private, as only the final LIBOR rate became publicly available, not the process by which banks settled on their submitted rate.[69] Platforms designed specifically for information sharing or communication between undertakings also count as fora wherein contact can be achieved; for example, in *Airline Tariff Publishing*, the US Department of Justice went after a number of airlines which founded the Airline Tariff Publishing Company (ATPCO) to disseminate actual current and future prices.[70] The information appeared on a communication system developed by ATPCO for that purpose.

66 For in person meetings see eg ICI (n 37) and T-Mobile (n 37). For messaging see eg Commission decision of 4 February 2015 AT.39861 Yen Interest Rate Derivatives.

67 *In re Libor-Based Financial Instruments Antitrust Litigation*, 935 F. Supp. 2d 666 (2013) (*LIBOR I*); *In re Libor-Based Financial Instruments Antitrust Litigation*, 11 MDL 2262 (NRB) (2015) (*LIBOR II*).

68 ICE Benchmark Administration Limited (IBA) is the authorized and regulated administrator of LIBOR. See <https://www.theice.com/iba/libor> (all links were last accessed on 1 September 2024).

69 *LIBOR I* (n 67).

70 *United States v. Airline Tariff Publishing Co.*, 1994-2 Trade Case (CCH) 61, 659 (1977). See also Eturas (n 33).

Private DLT networks can be thought of as private contexts. Private DLT networks, often in the form of permissioned blockchains, limit membership to a select number of participants based on set criteria. This is common in enterprise DLT networks which bring together participating undertakings working together on a joint endeavour, and while membership count can be high, undertakings have prior business relationships and entry is controlled. Because membership is closed, it can be presumed that the participating actors know if not the exact identity, at the very least the essential characteristics of the other actors and therefore their position and role in the market. For instance, several financial institutions around the world are building DLT networks together with peers, which allow private transfers, remittances, and settlement among participating actors.[71] Trickier is the issue of whether it can be assumed that participants know that any information shared within the private network will be picked up by all other participants, unless extra precautions are taken (eg a communication is exclusively addressed to a specific recipient). If the answer is positive, and the information carries an offer for agreement, this would satisfy the element of contact awareness, namely that actors are aware they have been approached with an offer. In *Eturas*, AG Szpunar noted that the contact awareness presumptions must take into account the characteristics of the technical system in place.[72] In that case, messages were sent to a communication/announcements platform of a booking system, and so the presumption that any information shared thereon is monitored and acknowledged was reasonable. However, DLT networks, even though they can carry messages in the transactions posted on the ledger, are not communications platforms; they are programmable databases. It would be inaccurate to blanketly assume that, because a permissioned network is more tightly knit than public networks, participants take note or should take note of all messages circulated within, especially if the network underpinning the offered product or service is not one geared specifically toward message exchange as the platform in *Eturas*.[73] If, however, it can be shown that participants use the DLT network as a means of communication, then the *Eturas* presumption can hold.

Showing intent in private DLTs and smart contracts. Next, even if it is assumed that mere participation in a private DLT network suffices to establish contact awareness, it may still not be sufficient to presume that participants are aware of the potentially anticompetitive character of some shared information or that they subscribe to it. Instead, that participants intend to contribute to a common anticompetitive objective and that they are aware of the conduct planned by the other participants, or that they could have reasonably foreseen that conduct and were

[71] See eg Esli Spahiu, Paolo Spagnoletti, and Augusto Sposito, 'Building a Blockchain-Based Platform for Interbank Collaboration' (2024) 28 International Journal of Electronic Commerce 269.

[72] See nn 32–34 and 46.

[73] Eturas (n 33).

ready to accept the risk, is something that will need to be proven.[74] In other words, it cannot be automatically assumed that the originator(s) and the recipient(s) of the communication intend or at least accept the exchange.[75] If, however, a private DLT network has been set up with the purpose of facilitating anticompetitive conduct, then its existence can be equated with meetings among competitors where anticompetitive conduct is discussed, and where mere participation can result in liability, since both the character of the information exchange and the relevant intent can be presumed to be anticompetitive.[76]

How smart contracts and automation affect intent. Notice should be taken of the fact that DLT activity can be largely automated, for example, through smart contracts. Smart contracts are deterministic software deployed on a ledger that automatically executes pre-programmed actions once pre-programmed conditions are met and records the output on the ledger. For the purposes of establishing intent, smart contracts can therefore be seen as algorithms, and despite the automation, the human factor remains decisive:[77] if undertakings programme smart contracts to engage in contact with counterparts with the intent to enter reciprocal obligations, then intent can be ascribed to the undertaking. Contrariwise, if undertakings do not have the specific intention to use the smart contract in that way, then the element of intent should be considered absent (and be investigated in other actions), even if the effect of the smart contract's operation results in concerted activity.[78] This is clearly problematic, because the result in the market is the same, but, similarly to tacit coordination, which is also problematic from a purely economic point of view,[79] it is an outcome that lies beyond the law's scope because in these cases, undertakings are not knowingly and jointly pursuing the outcome.[80] Lastly, if different undertakings knowingly use the same smart contract as an intermediary to facilitate collusion, such that they develop a hub-and-spoke arrangement, then anticompetitive intent can also be ascribed not only to the undertakings that serve as spokes, but potentially also to the undertaking that deploys the smart contract that serves as the hub (see below).[81]

[74] Case T-99/04 AC-Treuhand AG v Commission ECLI:EU:T:2008:256, paras 122, 127, and 130.

[75] See Cimenteries (n 40).

[76] See Cimenteries (n 40); T-Mobile (n 37).

[77] Ariel Ezrachi and Maurice E Stucke, 'Artificial Intelligence & Collusion: When Computers Inhibit Competition' (2017) 2017 University of Illinois Law Review 1775; Lea Bernhardt and Ralf Dewenter, 'Collusion by Code or Algorithmic Collusion? When Pricing Algorithms Take Over' (2020) 16 European Competition Journal 312.

[78] This scenario is often called Predictable Agent. See Ezrachi and Stucke (n 77) 1783.

[79] See Michael Blechman, 'Conscious Parallelism, Signalling and Facilitating Devices: The Problem of Tacit Collusion under the Antitrust Laws' (1979) 24 New York Law School Law Review 881. See also *Bell Atlantic Corp. v. Twombly*, 550 U.S. 544 (2007).

[80] See Alessio Azzutti, Wolf-Georg Ringe, and Siegfried Stiehl, 'Machine Learning, Market Manipulation, and Collusion on Capital Markets: Why the "Black Box" Matters' (2021) 43 University of Pennsylvania Journal of International Law 79, 119 et seq.

[81] It is correct to say that the elements of awareness, knowledge, and intent apply in hub-and-spoke arrangements as much as in direct communication arrangements. See Peter Whelan, 'Trading

It should be noted that some networks, while not fully private, may still exercise control over membership.[82] Such permissioned networks will often set a list of criteria for membership, but they are open to anyone who fulfils the set criteria. Semi-private networks, therefore, may fall anywhere along the spectrum between fully private and fully public. If the above-mentioned presumptions are tenuous even in fully private networks, they should be used even more cautiously in hybrid environments. Conclusions can only be reached tied to the specific facts of each semi-private/public network.

Direct and hub-and-spoke DLT structures: Application to interoperability blockchains and cross-border CBDC infrastructure. Contact in DLTs can be direct or indirect. Indirect contacts occur when an undertaking separate from the colluding ones intermediates or facilitates the exchange, whether by technical means or otherwise.[83] The use of DLT does not per se render communication between parties indirect—the DLT infrastructure is simply the shared medium through which parties communicate. When the information exchange is indirect, the intermediate party can also be held liable for participating in the anticompetitive scheme even if it does not itself perform the anticompetitive conduct, as long as it intended to contribute to the common scheme.[84] For instance, in *Yen Interest Rate Derivatives*, a number of banks that jointly set Japanese Yen LIBOR rates were found to be engaging in anticompetitive agreements. Part of the communication was done directly, but part of it was facilitated through ICAP, which is an interdealer broker that 'distributes quotes to the market participants ... [with the view] to bring two counterparties together, which then enter into a trade directly once they have agreed upon the specific terms of the trade'.[85] The Commission found that ICAP was liable for attempting to influence certain Japanese Yen LIBOR panel banks by 'disseminating misleading information to them ... and/or directly contacting them'.[86] The Commission followed the principle for intermediary liability laid out by the GC in *Treuhand*, by which an intermediary can be held liable if they 'intended, through its own conduct, to contribute to the common objectives pursued by the participants as a whole and that it was aware of the substantive conduct planned or implemented by other undertakings in pursuance of those objectives, or that it could reasonably have foreseen that conduct and that it was ready to accept the attendant risk'.[87]

Negotiations Between Retailers and Suppliers: A Fertile Ground for Anti-Competitive Horizontal Information Exchange?' (2009) 5 European Competition Journal 823, 833 et seq.

[82] Imran Bashir, *Mastering Blockchain: Distributed Ledger Technology, Decentralization, and Smart Contracts Explained* (2nd edn, Packt 2018) 65.
[83] Eturas (n 33).
[84] See Treuhand (n 74); Case T-36/05 Coats Holdings Ltd v Commission ECLI:EU:T:2007:268.
[85] Yen Interest Rate Derivatives (n 66) para 98.
[86] ibid para 166.
[87] Treuhand (n 74) para 130.

While the standard structure of DLT networks would have participants communicate directly with one another, indirect hub-and-spoke structures are also possible, whereby private networks communicate through a common intermediary. This structure is preferred when the private 'zones' or spokes form distinct agglomerations of undertakings, which however seek to transact with other agglomerations. This is a common structure for *interoperability blockchains*, which are used to bridge blockchain networks:[88] the spokes are separate blockchain networks each developing their own services, and the hub is the central chain that allows them to interconnect. This is not to suggest that interoperability blockchains are suspicious, or that they meet the conditions set out in *Treuhand* by default; those would have to be proven in concreto. Hub-and-spoke structures are also recommended for *cross-border Central Bank Digital Currency (CBDC) transactions*, whereby national CBDCs form the spokes and a central intermediary that exchanges one national CBDC for another to enable the transaction forms the hub.[89] While it is unlikely that CBDC hub-and-spoke schemes will be used to facilitate collusion, this structure can be mirrored by other private cross-border transaction mechanisms, and so it is worth highlighting it.

iii) Public sharing of information in DLT markets

To the extent that the setting in which information is exchanged is not private, it can be considered public. As mentioned, there is no clear dividing line between private and public, and so considerations pertinent to both settings are likely to come into the picture more often than not (this means that section D.ii should be consulted even for public sharing of information).

In the previous version of the Commission's Guidelines on Horizontal Cooperation Agreements, it was stated that 'exchanges of genuinely public information are unlikely to constitute an infringement of [competition law]', with genuinely public information being understood as 'information that is generally equally accessible (in terms of costs of access) to all competitors and customers'.[90] The new version takes a more cautious approach clarifying that 'the fact that an undertaking discloses commercially sensitive information through a public announcement . . . does not in itself exclude the possibility that the announcement may constitute a concerted practice within the meaning of Article 101(1)'.[91]

[88] Examples include Provenance and Cosmos.

[89] Bank for International Settlements, 'Breaking New Paths in Cross- Border Retail CBDC Payments' (2023) BIS Innovation Hub-Project Icebreaker.

[90] Guidelines on the applicability of Article 101 of the Treaty on the Functioning of the European Union to horizontal co-operation agreements (OJ C 11), para 92. See also OECD, 'Information Exchanges Between Competitors under Competition Law' (2010) DAF/COMP(2010)37 296.

[91] Commission Guidelines on the applicability of Article 101 to horizontal co-operation agreements (2023/C 259/01), para 398.

Strategically sensitive information on public DLTs. Public or permissionless DLT networks are those where membership is open to anyone. This means that membership in these networks is open to an indefinite number of actors, as long as they comply with the technical specifications, and information is or can be received by all nodes.[92] On many DLT networks, financial transactions are recorded and pricing details (eg commissions, interest rates, etc) also abound, which can normally constitute sensitive strategic information. While in conventional markets this can be problematic, such information can still be considered 'genuinely public information' in DLT networks because public visibility of transactions and the state of the network is integral to how transactions are processed and settled on DLT networks.[93] This, naturally, does not apply to information that is non-essential information for the operation of the DLT networks and the processing of transactions.

Contact awareness, calls for action, and announcements on public DLTs. While in public DLTs it is common that all information is visible to all participants, and therefore the information can be deemed to be shared among all participants, it cannot be readily presumed that participants understand that they are the intended recipients of all communications including communication containing intent for illicit conduct. Public information that is shared indiscriminately by default does not have specific intended recipients, and therefore, specific reciprocal contacts may not be fulfilled simply by the fact that a member of a public network imparts information or even an offer for illicit conduct, and other members receive that information. Specific ascent to the offer would have to be shown on the side of the receiving part. The same goes for public information that is observed (not shared) among competitors, resulting in copying competitors' conduct; absent any other incriminating circumstances, parallelism resulting from observing competitors is currently not illegal.[94] However, general public sharing of information or offers can constitute *preparatory acts*, which in some jurisdictions may be outlawed.[95]

Moreover, because the information is shared in a public context, recipients may not realize that the initiator of the communication intends to establish *interdependent* illicit obligations, and instead such communication may be treated as a unilateral announcement that does not give rise to the required collusive consensus. For instance, when miners publicly announce that they intend to support with their mining operations one fork over another, and other miners follow their

[92] Efficiency and practicality reasons may explain why not all nodes see all of the information circulating on the network as a matter of actual practice, but in truly permissionless networks they have the ability to access the information if so desired.

[93] Falk Schöning and Myrto Tagara, 'Blockchain: Mind the Gap! Lessons Learnt from the Net Neutrality Debate and Competition Law Related Aspects' (2018) 3 Concurrences 1, 3.

[94] *In Re Messaging* (n 8).

[95] See eg Article 1A of the Greek Competition Law 3959/2011.

lead, it is unlikely that an interdependent understanding has been achieved among them.[96] This is because the announcement itself and the ensuing conduct are performed independently of the conduct of other miners—each is acting rationally and separately.

The answer can change if additional evidence from market structure and miner conduct indicates that such an announcement and the ensuing conduct are intertwined—for instance, if miners in the market habitually follow the lead of a certain miner who acts as leader, and that miner is aware of their function and effect in the mining market.[97] In a similar incident whereby the largest crypto exchange Binance was hacked in May 2019, a call was circulated in various fora for miners to coordinate to undo the hacking transaction.[98] The 'reorg' as it was called would require a sufficient number of miners to agree (under the coordination of the CEO of Binance) to rewind the blockchain ledger to the status before the hacking thusly artificially changing the market. The proposal ultimately failed, but from a competition law point of view, this call was problematic. Miners represent the productive capacity of DLT networks and participate as actors in DLT networks' governance processes, and therefore they provide a service to DLT networks under conditions of competition.[99] Coordination of mining activity robs the market of the independent decision-making that each miner (or mining pool) as a separate undertaking is expected to perform in the market. While in this case, the coordination was motivated by a desire to offer a potential solution to a security breach incident, similar conduct can result in illicit coordination that competition law detests. In *United American Corp.*, plaintiffs alleged that a number of mining pools, investors, crypto-exchanges, and protocol developers colluded to divert mining resources to their preferred cryptocurrency at the expense of others.[100] Part of the coordination campaign was performed on public for a, such as blogs, corporate announcements, and social media, showing the potential of such mechanisms to establish contact between competitors.[101]

[96] See Commission Decision of 6 August 1984 IV/30.350 Zinc Producer Group, where the issue was whether a 'price leadership' practice constituted collusion. The Commission noted: 'The situation prevailing in this case seems to have been more characteristic of that which could give rise to what is known in economic theory as "barometric price leadership". This does not remove from undertakings the ability to "determine independently the policy which (they intend) to adopt on the common market". Under such circumstances, parallel pricing behaviour in an oligopoly producing homogeneous goods will not be in itself sufficient evidence of a concerted practice. However, sufficient evidence may result from parallel pricing in combination with other indications, such as contacts between undertakings on desirable price changes prior to price changes, or the exchange of information which reinforces contacts to this kind'. Ibid, paras 75–76.

[97] ibid. See also Polypropylene (n 35).

[98] See Christine Kim, 'What a Bitcoin "Reorg" Is and What Binance Has to Do With It' *CoinDesk* (8 May 2019).

[99] See Chapter 2 (B)ii).

[100] See *Bitmain* (n 6); Konstantinos Stylianou, 'What Can the First Blockchain Antitrust Case Teach Us About the Crypto-Economy?' (2019) Harvard Journal of Law and Technology (online).

[101] Alex Lielacher, 'Fallout: Everyone's a Loser after Bitcoin Cash Split' *Brave New Coin* (4 December 2018).

Third-party information sharing and data analytics. Since the information shared on public blockchains is available to everyone who taps into the network, one question that arises revolves around whether the offering or procurement of strategically significant information about competitors from third parties can count as contact between undertakings. Numerous data analytics companies aggregate and disseminate information on blockchain activity, some of which can be competitively relevant. The added value of such companies is not in the information itself, since the information is available to all, but in the ease of obtaining it, as well as in any processing (eg cleaning the data), aggregation, and analysis these companies may offer. On the one hand, the Commission has maintained a strict policy against the exchange of information even if it is otherwise public. In *Hasselblad*, the Commission opined that 'the fact that it is possible, although bothersome and time-consuming, to obtain price lists with the help of third parties such as dealers in no way detracts from the assessment that the exchange of price information brings about an artificial change in the conditions of competition'.[102] This approach would suggest that the sharing of strategic information (not just on prices) through an intermediary might still constitute impermissible contact even when the information is otherwise available, especially if the intermediary curates the information. The decision can turn around whether the information reduces competitive uncertainty and risk among undertakings; if the answer is positive, then sharing of publicly available information can still fall under the ambit of competition law. On the other hand, the CoJ in *Woodpulp II* adopted a much more permissive stance.[103] As seen previously, the case concerned the sharing of pricing information in the concentrated wood pulp market through announcements, but also through a network of buyers, suppliers, and traders, all of which created conditions of a high degree of transparency in the market.[104] The CoJ concluded that the exchange of information, unilaterally and through third parties, did not amount to impermissible contact among competing suppliers and that the parallelism of prices observed in the market was explicable on the grounds of the unique structure and conditions of the market, especially that paper producers adjusted their future production based on the wood pulp prices they could anticipate, and that there were many different types of wood pulp, which required producers and customers to know each other's plans before committing.[105] These unique market conditions make *Woodpulp II* an oddity, and competition authorities are likely to not automatically excuse sharing of publicly available information. But *Woodpulp II* does highlight that the industry context matters and so to the extent that aggregation, analysis, and sharing of publicly available network and transaction data

[102] Commission Decision of 2 December 1981 IV/25.757 Hasselblad, para 51.
[103] See n 50.
[104] Woodpulp/Ahlström (n 50) paras 80–88.
[105] ibid para 126.

does not reduce competitive uncertainty and risk among undertakings, it can escape scrutiny by authorities.

(E) Illicit coordination vs legitimate cooperation in DLT markets

Impermissible contact alone is not enough to substantiate collusive activity. It must also be shown that the contact invites illicit coordination between the involved undertakings. In conventional markets, competition law mandates a vision whereby the norm is independent activity among undertakings and reciprocal contacts are seen as the vehicle that enables the artificial prevention, restriction, or distortion of competition. But in DLT markets, this vision breaks down because various segments of DLT markets operate by nature cooperatively and rely on formal or informal consensus mechanisms that necessitate contact between undertakings.[106] This is true in protocol development, governance, mining, and validation, among other core functions. These functions are by nature cooperative, in the sense that, even though they can technically be performed by a single undertaking, doing so would defeat the purpose of employing DLTs. As a result, both contact and cooperation are part of the standard modus operandi of DLT markets, and the question becomes how to distinguish between coordination that is prohibited by competition law and cooperation that forms the industry's standard functions. There are various avenues by which this conundrum can be approached:

i) **Cooperative DLT activity as part or not of the competitive process.** Firstly, one should inquire as to whether the cooperative functions and activity in DLT markets are exempt from the application of competition law altogether if it can be deemed that they do not form part of the *competitive* process that competition law is tasked with safeguarding;
ii) **Cooperative DLT activity as ancillary restriction or objective necessity.** Next, to the extent that the cooperative functions and activity in DLT markets falls within the scope of competition law, the question arises as to whether the cooperative aspects can be seen as *ancillary restraints or objective necessity*, which are permitted under competition law;
iii) **Cooperative DLT activity as standard-setting or joint venture.** A different way to justify the cooperative activity in DLT markets is to consider it *standard-setting or joint venture*, which enjoy special protections under competition law;
iv) **Application of the by object/effect or per se/rule of reason analysis in cooperative DLT activity.** If none of the above are applicable, then one would

[106] See Chapter 1(D)ii) and also Peder Østbye, 'Who Is Liable for Collusion in Cryptocurrency Protocol Development?' (2019) SSRN 15.

resort to the usual assessment of *by object/effect* (EU) and *per se/rule of reason* (US) to determine the legality of cooperative activity, albeit with necessary adapations to take into account the special features of DLT markets.

These options are considered in sequence below.

i) Can DLT cooperative activities be exempt from competition law?

Since competition law is concerned with the competitive process, the activities that fall within its ambit must be capable of affecting the process of competition. This raises the reasonable question of whether the cooperative activities that underpin the operation of DLT products, services, and networks are of the kind that competition law was designed to capture. If not, then they are incapable of affecting the competitive process and should be immune from competition law.[107]

This question arose in the *LIBOR* series of cases in the United States.[108] As mentioned earlier, LIBOR is a composite benchmark calculated based on the estimates submitted by leading banks on what they expect they would be charged if they borrow from other banks.[109] The LIBOR-setting process is cooperative, but participating banks are expected to act independently when submitting an interest rate based on their expert knowledge of market conditions, which remains confidential until all submissions have been received, at which point the LIBOR is computed and published, along with all individual submissions.[110] The ex ante confidentiality and ex post transparency were meant to serve as 'safeguards ensuring that LIBOR would reflect the forces of competition in the London interbank loan market'.[111]

The *LIBOR* ligation concerned the alleged manipulation of LIBOR rate by some of the participating banks, which communicated with each other prior to submitting their daily estimates in an effort to artificially suppress their own and ultimately the composite LIBOR rate.[112] The District Court found the banks' conduct was not anticompetitive because 'the process of setting LIBOR was never intended to be competitive. Rather, it was a cooperative endeavor wherein otherwise-competing

[107] Note here that whether cooperative DLT activities are of competitive nature is a related but distinct question to whether they constitute economic/commercial activity, which was discussed in Chapter 2(B)i).

[108] See n 67.

[109] ICE Benchmark Administration Limited (IBA) is the authorized and regulated administrator of LIBOR. See <https://www.theice.com/iba/libor>.

[110] 'Second Consolidated Amended Complaint', Mayor & City Council of Baltimore & City of New Britain Firefighters' & Police Benefit Fund, Texas Competitive Electric Holdings Company LLC v. Credit Suisse Group AG et al., In re: LIBOR-Based Financial Instruments Antitrust Litigation, No. 1:11-md-2262 (S.D.N.Y. Sept. 10, 2013) at 24 para 62 (Doc. 406).

[111] ibid para 65.

[112] *LIBOR I* (n 67).

banks agreed to submit estimates of their borrowing costs'.[113] The District Court concluded that the LIBOR-setting process and the alleged collusion 'occurred *in an arena in which defendants never did and never were intended to compete*'[114] (emphasis added), and therefore any injury plaintiffs suffered 'would have resulted from defendants' misrepresentation, not from harm to competition'.[115]

The Circuit Court disagreed.[116] It conceded that the banks were engaged in a joint process, but crucially also that the banks circumvented the rules put in place to prevent collusion in the frame of that process.[117] The cooperative nature of the rate-setting could not shield banks from liability any more than the cooperative nature of standard-setting can shield member undertakings of the standard-setting organization, since as the Supreme Court has warned 'members of such associations often have economic incentives to restrain competition and . . . the product standards set by such associations have a serious potential for anticompetitive harm'.[118] Banks are competitors and the specific machinery they may have employed (in this case, the LIBOR) to tamper with the pricing mechanism in the market is immaterial.[119]

Can cooperative activities required by the modus operandi of DLTs be considered as occurring in an arena in which participants do not intend to compete? On the one hand, such economic activities as the consensus mechanism in DLT networks responsible for the recording and validation of transactions on the ledger, the iterative protocol development process, the voting mechanisms embedded in DLT networks' governance are all activities that require *by design* the input of multiple actors. And if one were to follow *LIBOR* to the end, the District Court further opined that fixing LIBOR is not price-fixing, since the prices actually paid were not fixed by the conspiring banks; they were merely influenced by the corrupted LIBOR rates.[120] By the same logic, cooperative economic activities in the production of DLT products and services (such as consensus-building, validation, governance voting, etc) are not the end-product themselves, they merely feed into it during the production process, and therefore, these activities can be shielded.

But, as the Circuit Court correctly counter-argued, collusion (ie illicit cooperation) is prohibited because it alters the market *process* and market structure even if the outcome remains the same.[121] Market outcomes should be left only up to

[113] ibid para 688.
[114] ibid para 689.
[115] ibid.
[116] *In re LIBOR-Based Financial Instruments Antitrust Litigation, Docket Nos. 13-3565-cv (L) et al.* (2016).
[117] ibid at 31.
[118] *Allied Tube & Conduit Corp. v. Indian Head, Inc.*, 486 U.S. 492, 500 (1988).
[119] *United States v. Socony-Vacuum Oil Co.*, 310 U.S. 150, 223 (1940).
[120] *LIBOR I* (n 67) para 689 ('LIBOR is an index intended to convey information about the interest rates prevailing in the London interbank loan market, but it does not necessarily correspond to the interest rate charged for any actual interbank loan').
[121] See *LIBOR II* (n 67) para 89.

competitive forces (or regulation). Not only can the processes of protocol development and decision-making, validation consensus mechanism, or governance voting plausibly affect the competitive outcome in the market, but the economic actors involved in the process can themselves have competing interests, even if they have the same goal, that is, the development of the product or service in question. Therefore, both the process of development and the outcome belong in the competitive arena, and their corruption by means of cooperation between participating actors can itself be brought under the scope of competition law. This does not mean that such activities constitute illicit cooperation, but only that they are not exempt from the scope of competition law.

ii) Coordination and cooperation in DLT markets as ancillary restriction and objective necessity

Definitions in EU and US law. In EU law, the doctrine of ancillary restrictions covers any restriction which is directly related and necessary to the implementation of a main operation.[122] Directly related means that the restriction 'is subordinate to the implementation of that operation and which has an evident link with it'.[123] Ancillary restrictions can escape antitrust liability if they are objectively necessary for the implementation of the main operation and if they are proportionate to it.[124] They are objectively necessary if 'without the restriction, the main operation is difficult or even impossible to implement'.[125]

US antitrust law has a similarly sounding doctrine of *ancillary restraint*, but its function is different. While the EU ancillary restriction must be objectively necessary, and once deemed ancillary to a lawful main operation, it is automatically lawful, the US ancillary restraint is a restraint that is 'subordinate and collateral to a separate, legitimate transaction . . . in the sense that it serves to make the main transaction *more effective* in accomplishing its purpose',[126] and therefore it does not have to be objectively necessary. This is why when a restraint is deemed ancillary under US antitrust law it is still assessed under the rule of reason; it is not automatically equated with a lawful restraint. In the words of the Ninth Circuit, '[t]he proper function of ancillarity in antitrust analysis "is to remove [in some instances] the per se label from restraints otherwise falling within the category"'.[127] However, closer to the EU meaning of ancillary restriction, US antitrust law has

[122] Case T-112/99 Métropole télévision (M6) and Others v Commission ECLI:EU:T:2001:215, para 104. See also Case T-111/08 MasterCard and Others v Commission EU:T:2012:260.

[123] Métropole télévision (n 122) para 105.

[124] ibid para 106.

[125] ibid paras 107–109.

[126] *Rothery Storage & Van Co. v. Atlas Van Lines, Inc.*, 792 F.2d 210, 224 (1986).

[127] *Aydin Corp. v. Loral Corp.*, 718 F.2d 897, 901 (1983) (quoting Robert Bork, 'Ancillary Restraints and the Sherman Act' (1959) 15 ABA Antitrust Section Proceedings 211, 212).

recognized exceptions for restraints that are necessary for the emergence of a new product or service, which are discussed below.

Back to ancillary restrictions in EU competition law, the GC noted in *MasterCard*, 'only those restrictions which are necessary in order for the main operation to be able to function *in any event* may be regarded as falling within the scope of the theory of ancillary restrictions. Thus, considerations relating to the indispensable nature of the restriction *in the light of the competitive situation* on the relevant market are not part of an analysis of the ancillary nature of the restriction' (emphasis added).[128] In other words, the necessity must be objective for the operation of the system under any conditions, not simply in the particular context in which the restriction arises, and not just for its commercial success but rather for its very existence.[129] In that case, MasterCard claimed that a multilateral interchange fee (MIF), as a default charge levied by an issuing bank to an acquiring bank when making payment to it in the absence of agreement between them, was indispensable for the operation of the MasterCard network. The claim was rejected by the GC, whose decision was affirmed by the CoJ stating, that 'the fact that that operation is simply more difficult to implement or even less profitable without the restriction concerned cannot be deemed to give that restriction the "objective necessity" required in order for it to be classified as ancillary'.[130]

As mentioned, in US antitrust law, while the doctrine of ancillary restraints does not have the same effect as the doctrine of ancillary restrictions in EU competition law, exceptions exist regarding agreements that are necessary for the emergence of a new product or service. In *Broadcast Music*, the Supreme Court found that blanket copyright licenses, which give licensees the right to perform all of the compositions owned by the member-creators behind the licence for a standard fee, are not a violation of section 1 of the Sherman Act, even though they prevent creators from negotiating individual prices for their works, and therefore resemble price-fixing.[131] The Supreme Court reasoned that blanket licences were a new type of product compared to the alternative of negotiating with individual creators, and indeed 'an obvious necessity if the thousands of individual negotiations, a virtual impossibility, were to be avoided'.[132] Therefore, to the extent that an agreement is necessary for the existence of a new product or service that cannot exist as a unilateral offering, it may be excused.

It is evident that the scope of ancillary restrictions (European Union) or exceptions for a new product (the United States) is very limited. Those doctrines exempt only restrictions without which a main activity which is not caught by the prohibition

[128] MasterCard (n 122) para 89.
[129] Métropole télévision (n 122) para 115.
[130] Case C-382/12 P MasterCard and Others v Commission EU:C:2014:2201, para 91.
[131] *Broadcast Music, Inc. v. Columbia Broadcasting System, Inc.*, 441 U.S. 1 (1979).
[132] ibid at 20.

against collusion could not be implemented or proceed,[133] or activities that result in a new product of service, which without the restriction they would be impossible.[134]

Some function-services in DLT markets can match these conditions when they are so essential to the operation of a DLT product or service, that the DLT product or service in question would not exist without them. Consensus mechanisms and automated market makers (AMM) can be such services.

Consensus protocols. Consensus mechanisms control, inter alia, how miners and validators interact with one another to confirm which transactions are valid to be added to the network's ledger. In the process of consensus-forming, information on transactions and the state of the network is exchanged among consensus participants. Such information is conventionally of strategic importance in the competitive process and the sharing of that kind of information among consensus participants could constitute coordination of the kind that can be caught under competition law. However, both consensus mechanisms and the associated information exchange are an integral part of DLT, without which the technology cannot exist. Unlike MIFs, which only *facilitate* the operation of the credit card network, consensus mechanisms constitute the essential trust and verification process in decentralized networks, which in centralized networks is performed by a single operator (eg the MasterCard corporation). Consensus mechanisms therefore can, in principle and as long as they are proportionate, qualify as an ancillary restriction that is objectively necessary to the existence of DLT products and services, which in this context would constitute the main operation.

Note that the exception of ancillary activity applied here covers the technical operation of consensus on the chain (ie the rules and processes that are coded into the consensus function of a DLT product or service), not any surrounding activity among consensus-building stakeholders. Such surrounding activities, which can consist in negotiations, meetings, voting, calls to action, etc, can seek to influence the technical or non-technical aspects of the consensus process, and may themselves be deemed to constitute illicit cooperation if they meet the relevant conditions.[135]

Automated Market Makers (AMMs). Another key function-service in DLT markets are AMMs. AMMs are at the heart of decentralized finance (DeFi) as they enable decentralized exchanges (DEX).[136] Conventional centralized exchanges rely on order books to match buy and sell orders: buy and sell orders are recorded on a central order book, and matched against each other, thereby setting the exchange rate between the traded assets. This method perfectly captures supply (sell) and demand (buy) dynamics that competitive markets are used to. DEX on

[133] MasterCard (CoJ) (n 130) para 93.
[134] *Polk Bros., Inc. v. Forest City Enterprises, Inc.*, 776 F.2d 185 (1985).
[135] See sections D.ii and D.iii.
[136] Prominent examples of such services are Uniswap, SushiSwap, and Balancer.

the other hand use *pools* of liquidity: each traded asset forms its own so-called pool, and every traded asset pair is associated with the corresponding pool pair.[137] Evidently, since there is no order book, the exchange rate between assets in each asset pair pool is set by the AMM and it is adjusted dynamically while at the same time calculating transaction fees. This type of functionality is reminiscent of price-fixing as the AMM intermediates between traders and sets the rate at which they will exchange their assets.[138] Yet, even if it is, this kind of price setting function performed by the protocol is essential in establishing the relative exchange rate between pools in lack of an order book that would otherwise be used to match trades. In that sense, automated market maker DEX offerings cannot exist without such mechanisms, making them objectively necessary. It would still have to be ascertained that the main activity of DEX is legitimate and that the price-setting function of the protocol is proportionate.

Moreover, both consensus mechanisms and market maker mechanisms can be regarded as restrictions that engender new products or services and therefore serve consumer interests (as per *Broadcast Music*). In *Wallace*, the plaintiff argued that the GNU General Public License (GPL) violates section 1 of the Sherman Act because users who use this license to develop and distribute Linux software must give away their software for free and under the same licence, effectively fixing the price at zero and making other competing products and services unattractive to consumers.[139] Putting aside the substantive price-fixing issues, the Court of Appeals refused to call GPL and the people who use it a conspiracy arrangement, because GPL 'is a cooperative agreement that facilitates production of new derivative works, and agreements that yield new products that would not arise through unilateral action'.[140] Similarly, consensus and market maker mechanisms can be seen as cooperative arrangements that the involved individuals cannot offer by themselves unilaterally: blockchain is built on the premise of decentralized consensus and DEX are built on the premise of (automatic) rate-setting, neither of which can be offered without the collaborative input of network participants.

iii) Cooperation in DLT markets as standard-setting or joint venture

Standard-setting and joint ventures are collaborative schemes among industry players which aim at facilitating joint technical progress. Standard-setting involves

[137] See Sirio Aramonte, Wenqian Huang, and Andreas Schrimpf, 'Trading in the DeFi Era: Automated Market Maker' (2021) BIS Quarterly Review; Guillermo Angeris and others, 'An Analysis of Uniswap Markets' (2019) arXiv:1911.03380.

[138] A similar argument was made with regard to transportation platforms as price-fixers; see *Meyer v. Kalanick*, 174 F.Supp.3d 817 (2016); *Swink v. Uber Technologies, Inc.*, 4:16-cv-01092 (2016).

[139] *Wallace v. International Business Machines Corp.*, 467 F.3d 1104 (2006).

[140] Ibid at 1107.

industry actors coming together to agree on product, service, or process specifications that are meant to be implemented by participating organizations to facilitate the development and interoperability among their offerings. Joint ventures (often referred to as research and development, or R&D, agreements) can take a wide array of forms and may encompass diverse purposes ranging from basic research all the way to commercial production.[141] Cooperation in DLT markets that can be shown to perform standard-setting functions, especially by formalized industry associations, or that constitutes joint venture under the conditions set down by the law and the case law, is likely to not be deemed anticompetitive. While there are examples of such legitimate activity, caution still needs to be applied.

Since standard-setting and joint ventures openly involve collaboration among potential competitors, they can clearly constitute agreements or concerted activity of the kind that falls under competition law. The harms associated with standard-setting and joint ventures range from reduction of competitive intensity among participating actors, exclusionary effects against actors who do not participate in the collaborative scheme, delayed or sub-optimal outcomes due to hold-up, and the risk of covert cartelization behind the moniker of standard-setting or joint venture.[142] At the same time, both standard-setting and joint ventures are linked to benefits for producers and consumers alike, including faster and cheaper development of new products, services, and technologies, the sharing of risk, the development of synergies, and the realization of economies of scale and scope.[143] For this reason, authorities and governments are generally willing to tolerate the dangers of standard-setting and joint ventures in exchange of the long-term and broad benefits that they are thought to induce.[144]

Specifically, EU competition law establishes a safe harbour for standard-setting activities as long as they have as their primary objective the definition of technical or quality requirements with which current or future products, production processes, value chain due diligence processes, services or methods may comply, and they are voluntary, non-discriminatory, participation is open, and results are accessible to members and third parties.[145]

[141] Guidelines on horizontal cooperation agreements (n 91) para 52 ('R&D agreements vary in form and scope. They include agreements under which one party finances R&D carried out by another party ("paid-for" R&D); agreements covering the joint improvement of existing products and technologies, and agreements concerning the development of products and technologies that would create an entirely new demand. The R&D cooperation may take the form of a cooperation agreement or a joint venture, namely a jointly controlled company'). See also Jonathan Turner, *Intellectual Property and EU Competition Law* (OUP 2010) paras 2.154 et seq.

[142] Guidelines on horizontal cooperation agreements (n 91) paras 439–445, 218–221. See also James Anton and Dennis Yao, 'Standard-Setting Consortia, Antitrust, and High-Technology Industries' (1995) 64 Antitrust Law Journal 247, 249–51; Carl Shapiro and Robert D Willig, 'On the Antitrust Treatment of Production Joint Ventures' (1990) 4 Journal of Economic Perspectives 113, 114–17; Joseph F Brodley, 'Joint Ventures and Antitrust Policy' (1982) 95 Harvard Law Review 1521, 1530–34.

[143] Joseph Farrell and Garth Saloner, 'Standardization, Compatibility, and Innovation' (1985) 16 The RAND Journal of Economics 70; Shapiro and Willig (n 142); Brodley (n 142) 1527–30.

[144] On the historical development of case law in the area see Shapiro and Willig (n 142) 118.

[145] Guidelines on horizontal cooperation agreements (n 91) paras 448–462.

It also creates a presumption of legality for joint ventures when they are focused on research and are far removed from the stage of production, and even more so when they involve non-competitors.[146] The rationale is that such joint ventures are unlikely to have restrictive effects on competition within the meaning of Article 101(1) TFEU, while at the same time they bring about efficiency gains by combining complementary skills and assets, thus resulting in improved or new products and technologies. US antitrust law also reserves lenient treatment to Standard Setting Organizations (SSO) and joint ventures by extending rule of reason treatment, as opposed to the per se illegality treatment that was previously often applied to collaborative activities among competitors.[147]

DLT standard-setting organizations. Based on the above, where collaborative activities in DLT markets can be labelled as standard-setting or can constitute a research-oriented joint venture, they will enjoy more lenient treatment. Some collaborative activities and organizations in DLT markets clearly engage in standard-setting activities.[148] Enterprise Ethereum Alliance, for instance, aims at driving the use of Enterprise Ethereum and Mainnet Ethereum blockchain technology as an open-standard for use by any interested undertaking.[149] Upon joining, members agree to the organization's Antitrust Policy and Guidelines, which, among others, requires members to not 'hinder competition by non-Participants', to not 'coerce or discriminate against Participants', and generally to not 'act in restraint of trade or engage in anticompetitive conduct'.[150]

The International Swaps and Derivatives Association (ISDA), another prominent organization which predates the popularization of blockchain technology, also develops and maintains, through its members, standard documentation for derivatives (including those embodied on blockchains), which are considered authoritative and are being followed and implemented widely in the market. ISDA's competition policy, recognizing the antitrust concerns around cooperative activities, underscores that members 'must at all times be mindful of and comply with their responsibilities under competition law, not only in formal ISDA meetings but also in any social environment surrounding any ISDA gathering'.[151]

Such activities closely match what is traditionally understood as standard-setting. In fact, they are performed by organizations set up for that purpose,

[146] ibid paras 56 et seq.
[147] National Cooperative Research and Production Act of 1993 (CRPA), 5 U.S.C. §§ 4301, sec 4302.
[148] For a detailed list of industry consortia see Global Blockchain Business Council, 'Industry Consortia List' at <https://gbbcouncil.org/wp-content/uploads/2021/11/GBBC-Consortia-List_Updated-November-2021.pdf>.
[149] See <https://entethalliance.org/about/>.
[150] Enterprise Ethereum Alliance Antitrust Policy and Guidelines, sec 4(c)(d)(g) respectively (2022) (policy document on record with author).
[151] International Swaps and Derivatives Association, 'Member Competition Policy' at <https://www.isda.org/membership/member-competition-policy/>. See also By-laws of International Swaps and Derivatives Association (11 April 2019) at <https://www.isda.org/a/u0SME/ISDA-By-Laws-April-11-2019.pdf>.

which, at least in the United States is a requirement to benefit from the statutory lenient treatment reserved for standard-setting: the US Cooperative Research and Production Act of 1993 (CRPA) defines standards development activity as 'any action taken by a standards development organization for the purpose of developing, promulgating, revising, amending, reissuing, interpreting, or otherwise maintaining a voluntary consensus standard, or using such standard in conformity assessment activities, including actions relating to the intellectual property policies of the standards development organization',[152] and in turn, it defines standards development organizations as 'a domestic or international organization that plans, develops, establishes, or coordinates voluntary consensus standards using procedures that incorporate the attributes of openness, balance of interests, due process, an appeals process, and consensus in a manner consistent with the Office of Management and Budget Circular Number A–119'.[153] The statutory provision for the application of the rule of reason in SSO activities does not preclude the application of the rule of reason in standard-setting activities outside of SSOs—courts and scholars had already gravitated towards a rule of reason approach regardless of the CRPA. In the European Union, pursuant to the Commission's Guidelines on Horizontal Cooperation Agreements, the protections extended to standard-setting are not reserved only for registered or certified SSOs.

Protocol development as standard-setting? The possibility of enjoying the safeguards around standard-setting even outside the frame of organizations set up for that purpose raises the question of whether protocol development (of cryptoassets, consensus mechanisms, DeFi market makers, etc) as a collaborative activity among actors can benefit from the more lenient provisions associated with standard-setting. In the *LIBOR* litigation, where the issue was the alleged price-fixing resulting from the coordinated manipulation of interest rate submissions, plaintiffs relied on case law involving the manipulation of standard-setting[154] or similar index-setting processes.[155] Their argument was that LIBOR-setting, as a cooperative activity among competitors whose outcome is followed by the industry, resembles standard-setting activities, the manipulation of which was recognized in the case law to have resulted in antitrust harm.

Standard-setting safeguards should not be extended where the rationale of the relevant rules is not served by the activity in question.[156] The process of standard-setting is tolerated by competition authorities because of the expectation that it will result in socio-economic benefits that would not materialize had collaboration

[152] CRPA (n 147) sec 4301(a)(7).
[153] ibid sec 4301(a)(8).
[154] *LIBOR I* (n 67) 693–94.
[155] *Allied Tube* (n 118); *In re Rail Freight Fuel Surcharge Antitrust Litigation*, 587 F.Supp.2d 27 (2008).
[156] Cf Nicolo Zingales and Olia Kanevskaia, 'The IEEE-SA Patent Policy Update under the Lens of EU Competition Law' (2016) 12 European Competition Journal 195.

between competitors been prohibited under normal competition law. The main socio-economic benefit that emerges from the standardization efforts of industry players is the creation of shared and interoperable specifications which promote *economic interpenetration across the industry*, which would otherwise not arise, or arise with considerable delay.[157] Standards facilitate the emergence of markets, where interoperability is key to realizing the full potential of the relevant products and services, or where one unified platform (the standard) is needed to allow the emergence of complements.[158] Where development efforts around specifications of DLT technologies are not designed to or do not have the potential to enjoy industry-wide adoption or to serve as platforms, the standard-setting protections do not seem justified. For example, the development of yet another cryptoasset protocol, consensus mechanism, or market-making mechanism for DeFi, do not bear the hallmarks of standard-setting, since they neither rely on the contribution of cross-industry expertise and support nor are they designed to serve as a common industry-wide platform. They may market themselves as having the aspiration of doing so, but unless the process of development is such as to address the obstacles that standard-setting is expected to resolve (ie a market failure due to lack of coordination), their development likely does not deserve the protection of standard-setting safe harbours.

And even if those activities did resemble standard-setting, the lenient treatment of standard-setting is extended only when it is likely that the resulting process and outcomes will do more good than harm. The Commission's Guidelines on Horizontal Cooperation Agreements notes that standard-setting will not normally restrict competition within the meaning of Article 101 TFEU when participation in the process is unrestricted, the procedure is transparent, compliance with the standard is non-mandatory, and access to the standard is provided under fair, reasonable, and non-discriminatory terms.[159] Similar conditions are advanced by the US Standards Development Organization Advancement Act, which specifies that for SSOs to benefit from rule of reason treatment when specifying technical standards, they are required inter alia, to provide opportunities to participate, to balance interests so that standards development activities are not dominated by any single group, and to provide access to essential information regarding the proposed standards.[160] These restrictions are put in place to make sure that the standard-setting process is such that will likely result in pro-competitive and pro-market

[157] See Guidelines on horizontal cooperation agreements (n 91) para 439.

[158] Joseph Farrell and Timothy Simcoe, 'Four Paths to Compatibility' in Martin Peitz and Joel Waldfogel, *The Oxford Handbook of the Digital Economy* (OUP 2012) 36–38; Richard Gilbert, 'Competition Policy for Industry Standards' in Roger D Blair and D Daniel Sokol (eds), *The Oxford Handbook of International Antitrust Economics*, vol 2 (OUP 2015) 555.

[159] See n 145.

[160] Standards Development Organization Advancement Act amending the CRPA, sec 102(5). See Standards Development Organization Advancement Act of 2004, Pub. L. 108–237, title I, §102, 22 June 2004, 118 Stat. 661.

outcomes that will offset any losses from the lack of competition between the partaking actors during the development of the standard. While some projects in DLT markets are developed in the frame of recognized SSOs, many are take place in the open market, and while they are open to participation and their results are also freely available, their processes are often not designed, meant, or de facto such as to bring together parties with competing interests from across the industry—they rather usually constitute efforts of a homogeneous group that aims to develop the next 'big thing'. This is why they are often organized as foundations in support of a specific project, rather than an industry-wide solution.

Joint ventures in DLT markets. Because the term joint venture has a looser meaning, it can apply to a wide array of collaborative activities in DLT markets. Most joint ventures seen in DLT markets are set up to deliver a combination of new logical infrastructure (eg protocols) and physical infrastructure (eg transactions transmission facilities), and they often involve a combination of undertakings that fall inside and outside the DLT industry—and less often even government players in their commercial capacity.[161]

Joint ventures become relevant vis-à-vis collusion in two ways: firstly, because joint ventures can assume their own legal personality, the activity of its members can be subsumed under and ascribed to the joint venture thereby ceasing to be activity of separate undertakings that can collude with one another; secondly, under conditions laid down in the law, joint ventures can enjoy more lenient treatment regarding their competitive effects.

Joint ventures can assume legal personality in different ways. Many opt for formal contractual formation of the legal entity that will be the joint venture vehicle, but joint ventures can also emerge as *partnerships*—even unbeknownst to their members. Before the decentralized economy, open-source software development projects had attracted the label of informally formed joint venture partnerships.[162] This 'spontaneous' formation of partnerships becomes of particular interest in the decentralized economy, due to the prevalence of social production, whereby individuals participate in the development of products and services often without realizing that their involvement can be characterized by the law as formation of partnership. In the US case of *Van Loon*, which concerned the legal designation of a cryptocurrency mixer service, Tornado Cash, as an *entity* for the purposes of the International Emergency Economic Powers Act, a group of blockchain software developers, community members that participated in governance voting

[161] Examples include Partior, a joint venture between the Development Bank of Singapore, JPMorgan, and state-owned investment fund Temasek; and AllUnity, a joint venture between Deutsche Bank and trading house Flow Traders. See also Antoine Babinet and David Dubois, '"Archipels" Case: EU's First Merger Control Analysis of a Private Blockchain Consortium' (2021) 12 Journal of European Competition Law & Practice 630.

[162] Stephen Mauer, 'The Penguin and the Cartel: Rethinking Antitrust and Innovation Policy for the Age of Commercial Open Source' (2012) 2012 Utah Law Review 269.

processes, and infrastructure providers was deemed to have formed such an entity, even though participants were otherwise unknown to and unaffiliated with each other.[163] The Department of Treasure defined entity to encompass 'a partnership, association, trust, joint venture, corporation, subgroup, or other organization'.[164] The District Court ruled that participants in Tornado Cash formed an entity noting that '[t]he record sufficiently supports [the Office of Foreign Assets Control] determination that the founders, the developers, and the Tornado Cash DAO [Decentralized Autonomous Organizations] have acted jointly to promote and govern Tornado Cash and to profit from these activities'.[165] The possibility of participants in the social production process of the decentralized economy forming single economic units—to use the terminology of EU competition law—such as joint venture partnerships, becomes even more acute in the case of DAOs, which assume the institutional function of market organizations but whose operation is controlled and performed by smart contracts.[166] The unassuming process of forming DAOs and the heavy focus on technical automation obscures the fact that legally they can constitute joint venture partnerships, whether statutory, common law, or more recently, 'contractarian'—a term proposed to mean partnerships formed through informal contracts while avoiding the legal implications of statutory or common law partnerships.[167]

To be sure, the formation of a joint venture scheme (intentional or not) does not automatically move the ratione personae focus of competition law away from the members of the joint venture and onto the joint venture itself. Whether the subject of competition law will be the joint venture as a single economic unit or its individual members separately revolves around the question of whether the conduct of individual members can be ascribed to the joint venture. This depends, in EU competition law, on whether the parent undertakings exercise decisive influence over the joint venture,[168] and in US antitrust law whether the intra-enterprise conspiracy doctrine is satisfied.[169] If the veil of the joint venture can be pierced, then competition law will apply to the joint venture's members and collusion among them is possible.

Regardless of how joint ventures are formed, once recognized as such by competition law, they can enjoy more lenient treatment. In EU competition law,

[163] *Van Loon v. Department of Treasury*, 2023 WL 5313091 (2023). See also *Symbiont.io Inc. v. Ipreo Holdings, LLC*, 2021WL 3575709 (2021).

[164] See 31 C.F.R. §§ 510.305, 578.305.

[165] *Van Loon* (n 163) at 15.

[166] Carla Reyes and Christine Hurt, 'The Contractarian Joint Venture' (2024) Alabama Law Review (forthcoming).

[167] ibid.

[168] Case C-588/15 LG Electronics Inc and Koninklijke Philips Electronics NV ECLI:EU:C:2017:679, paras 78–79. See also Guidelines on horizontal cooperation agreements (n 91) para 12. See also Chapter 2 section C.i.

[169] *American Needle, Inc. v. National Football League*, 130 S. Ct. 2201, IV (2010). See also Chapter 2 section C.i.

this ranges from a presumption that they satisfy the Vertical Block Exemption Regulation (in the case of R&D joint ventures) to simply a recognition that below certain market shares they are unlikely to harm competition and that they may satisfy Article 101(3) TFEU, depending on their type (eg production joint ventures, commercialization joint ventures, etc).[170] In US antitrust law, the more lenient treatment means that their activity will be assessed based on rule of reason,[171] but the benefit or the rule of reason is not extended when the scheme involves (among other restrictions) 'exchanging information among competitors relating to costs, sales, profitability, prices, marketing, or distribution of any product, process, or service if such information is not reasonably required to carry out the purpose of such venture'.[172]

The above discussion points to two key conclusions: firstly, that joint ventures can emerge more commonly than assumed in the decentralized economy; and secondly, that the protections or benefits that competition law may extend to joint ventures are not automatic but rather the challenged conduct must first be attributed to the joint venture as opposed to its members and secondly the joint venture must not be of the kind that competition law considers may still pose dangers to the competitive process.

iv) The by object/effect and per se/rule of reason treatment and its determinants in the decentralized economy

So far, the previous sections discussed the possibility that various types of cooperative activity in DLT markets may (a) be exempted altogether as lying beyond the regulatory scope of competition law; (b) be justified as ancillary restraints or objective necessities; or (c) be treated more leniently as standard-setting or joint ventures. Despite these carveouts, it is likely that the bulk of cooperative activity that may constitute anticompetitive agreements or concerted activity will not benefit from them, and instead the standard analysis of agreements/restraints or concerted activity will apply. The standard analysis recognizes that not all agreements/restraints or concerted activity are illegal. Article 101 TFEU prohibits only those agreements and concerted practices that are *by object or by effect anticompetitive*, and section 1 of the Sherman Act prohibits only those restraints that are *unreasonable*.[173] To determine reasonableness, US antitrust law draws a similar distinction

[170] Guidelines on horizontal cooperation agreements (n 91). See generally Luis Silva Morais, *Joint Ventures and EU Competition Law* (Hart Publishing 2013).

[171] For a summary of the rule of reason application in joint ventures see Joseph Kattan, 'Antitrust Analysis of Technology Joint Ventures: Allocative Efficiency and the Rewards of Innovation' (1993) 61 Antitrust Law Journal 937.

[172] CRPA (n 147) sec 4301(b).

[173] *United States v. American Tobacco Co.*, 221 U.S. 106, 181 (1911) (reaffirming the earlier case of *Standard Oil Co. v. United States*, 221 U.S. 1 (1911) on the same matter).

to EU competition law between per se anticompetitive (equivalent to by object) and anticompetitive by the rule of reason (RoR, equivalent to by effect).[174]

There is nothing in DLT markets that detracts from this standard approach and so it remains in toto. However, how it applies in DLT markets will need to take into account their special characteristics.

The function and meaning of the by object/per se and by effects/RoR distinction. By object/per se anticompetitive agreements are those whose nature and purpose are inimical to competition, and courts declare them as anticompetitive without a detailed examination of their effects on the market. Agreements that are not by object/per se anticompetitive are examined by looking at their effects on the market (or, in the United States, by applying the RoR, which has a similar function). The distinction serves to provide legal certainty and economization of resources. By labelling certain types of agreements as by object/per se anticompetitive, undertakings know with certainty to steer clear of them, and competition authorities save resources by not performing a full analysis of their potential anticompetitive effects, namely how and to what extent such agreements harm competition.[175]

The distinction is far from clear both in the European Union[176] and in the United States, where the Supreme Court even introduced an intermediate category of review called 'quick look', which is reserved for restraints that present obvious threats to competition given their nature and context, but which are not so nakedly harmful that they make it into the per se category.[177]

The standard determinants of by object/per se and by effect/RoR. The criteria used to determine anticompetitiveness are not fixed, which leaves margin to take into account the special features of the decentralized economy.[178] The courts recognize that agreements arise in different economic contexts and so to be able to determine appropriate treatment, different considerations may need to come into the picture.

The CoJ has ruled that in the assessment of by object anticompetitiveness 'regard must be had inter alia to the *content* of [the agreement's] provisions, its *objectives* and the *economic and legal context* of which it forms a part' (emphasis added),[179] and when determining that context, it is 'appropriate to take into

[174] *Chicago Board of Trade v. United States*, 246 U.S. 231 (1918).

[175] See Opinion of Advocate General Kokott in Case C-8/08 T-Mobile Netherlands BV et al v Raad van bestuur van de Nederlandse Mededingingsautoriteit EU:C:2009:110, para 43.

[176] See Saskia King, 'The Object Box: Law, Policy or Myth?' 7 European Competition Journal 269; Alison Jones, 'Left Behind by Modernisation? Restrictions by Object under Article 101(1)' European Competition Journal 649, 658 et seq. See also Commission Decision of 8 May 2011 IV/36.957/F3 Glaxo Wellcome and others, where even if though the offence was deemed by object anticompetitive, its effects were still examined. For the United States, see *California Dental Association v. FTC*, 526 U.S. 756, 779 ('The truth is that our categories of analysis of anticompetitive effect are less fixed than terms like "*per se*," "quick look," and "rule of reason" tend to make them appear') (italics in the original).

[177] *FTC v. Indiana Federation of Dentists*, 476 U.S. 447, 459 (1986).

[178] See eg *California Dental Association* (n 176) at 781 ('What is required . . . is an enquiry meet for the case, looking to the circumstances, details, and logic of a restraint').

[179] Case C-67/13 P Groupement des cartes bancaires (CB) v Commission EU:C:2014:2204, para 53.

consideration the *nature of the goods or services* affected, as well as the real conditions of *the functioning and structure of the market* or markets in question'.[180] The content, objectives, and economic and legal context, are factors that always weigh in, but the acknowledgment that these factors are considered inter alia leaves room for additional considerations.[181] For instance, in *Allianz Hungária*, where the agreements in question fixed the hourly charge to be paid by the insurance company to repair shops and linked the rate to the number of insurance contracts sold by each shop, the CoJ took into account the incentive mechanism embedded into the rate, the number of markets that were affected, the vertical relationship of insurance companies and repair shops, the potential for elimination of competition in the relevant markets, and the fact that the rates had decided on the basis of 'recommended prices' of a trade association.[182] In *Cartes Bancaires*, where the issue in question was the legality of the fee structure of an inter-bank interoperability system, the CoJ highlighted the particular role of the two-sided market that the interoperability system was operating in.[183]

If an agreement is deemed not to be by object anticompetitive, then a full investigation into its effects is warranted. For an agreement to have the effect of restricting competition, the CoJ has ruled that it must be 'liable to have an appreciable adverse impact on the parameters of competition, such as the price, the quantity and quality of the goods or services'.[184] In *Brasserie de Haecht* the CoJ mirrored the language of the by object assessment in stipulating how the by effects assessment works by ruling that 'an agreement cannot be examined in isolation from the earlier context, that is, from the factual or legal circumstances causing it to prevent, restrict or distort competition'.[185] In this analysis, various case-specific factors can become relevant; for instance, in *Société Technique Minière*, which concerned the legality of clauses granting an exclusive right of sale, relevant factors included the 'nature and quantity, limited or otherwise, of the products covered by the agreement, the position and importance of the grantor and the concessionnaire on the market for the products concerned, the isolated nature of the disputed agreement or, alternatively, its position in a series of agreements, the severity of the clauses intended to protect the exclusive dealership or, alternatively, the opportunities allowed for other commercial competitors in the same products by way of parallel re-exportation and importation'.[186]

[180] ibid.
[181] See eg Case T-472/13 H. Lundbeck A/S and Lundbeck Ltd v Commission ECLI:EU:T:2016:449, paras 339 et seq.
[182] Case C-32/11 Allianz Hungária Biztosító Zrt. And Others v Gazdasági Versenyhivatal ECLI:EU:C:2013:160, paras 39–49.
[183] Groupement des cartes bancaires (n 179) para 79.
[184] MasterCard (CoJ) (n 130) para 93.
[185] Case C-23/67 Brasserie De Haecht v Wilkin Janssen ECLI:EU:C:1967:54, at 414.
[186] Case 56–65 Société Technique Minière (STM) v Maschinenbau Ulm GmbH (MBU) ECLI:EU:C:1966:38, at 250.

In the United States, the criteria to distinguish between per se and RoR are less clearly defined. In *Business Electronics*, the Supreme Court defined per se restraints as those 'that would always or almost always tend to restrict competition and decrease output'.[187] In *Leegin*, the Supreme Court ruled that the per se treatment is appropriate for restraints that have '"manifestly anticompetitive" effects . . . and "lack . . . any redeeming virtue"'.[188] In an attempt to draw a spectrum of appropriate treatment the Supreme Court in *California Dental Association* commented on the degree of scrutiny required so as to choose between per se, RoR, and quick look; it ruled that:

> [w]hat is required, rather, is an enquiry meet for the case, looking to the circumstances, details, and logic of a restraint. The object is to see whether the experience of the market has been so clear, or necessarily will be, that a confident conclusion about the principal tendency of a restriction will follow from a quick (or at least quicker) look, in place of a more sedulous one. And of course what we see may vary over time, if rule-of-reason analyses in case after case reach identical conclusions.[189]

Once the court is convinced that a summary per se treatment is not appropriate, it will examine a number of factors to ascertain the reasonableness of the restraint based on the RoR. In that assessment, the landmark case of *Chicago Board of Trade* ruled that 'the court must ordinarily consider the facts peculiar to the business, its condition before and after the restraint was imposed, the nature of the restraint, and its effect, actual or probable. The history of the restraint, the evil believed to exist, the reason for adopting the particular remedy, the purpose or end sought to be attained, are all relevant facts'.[190] The joint Federal Trade Commission and Department of Justice Antitrust Guidelines for Collaborations Among Competitors adopts and expands on these criteria.[191]

In addition, in both EU competition law and US antitrust law, although the parties' intention is not a necessary factor in determining whether a type of coordination between undertakings is restrictive, it can be taken into account where it can shed light into its nature, aim, and structure.[192] However, the mere fact that an agreement also pursues legitimate objectives is not sufficient to preclude a finding of restriction of competition by object.[193]

[187] *Business Electronics Corp. v. Sharp Electronics Corp.*, 485 U.S. 717, 723 (1988).
[188] *Leegin Creative Leather Products, Inc. v. PSKS, Inc.*, 551 U.S. 877 (2007) (quoting *Continental T.V., Inc. v. GTE Sylvania Inc.*, 433 U.S. 36, 50 (1977) and *Northwest Wholesale Stationers, Inc. v. Pacific Stationery & Printing Co.*, 472 U.S. 284, 289 (1985)).
[189] *California Dental Association* (n 176) 781.
[190] *Chicago Board of Trade* (n 174) 231.
[191] Federal Trade Commission & Department of Justice, 'Antitrust Guidelines for Collaborations Among Competitors' (April 2000), sec 3.3.
[192] Dole Food Company (n 47) para 118; *Chicago Board of Trade* (n 174) 238.
[193] Case C-209/07 Beef Industry Development Society and Barry Brothers EU:C:2008:643, para 21.

In summary, while some basic factors such as the purpose, logic, content, legal and economic context and circumstances, as well as prior experience of courts with a certain practice,[194] are always relevant in determining the appropriate treatment, additional factors pertinent to the case are not only welcome but expected. This flexibility allows room for considering the idiosyncratic nature of DLT markets.

The by object/effect and per se/RoR considerations in the decentralized economy. While all of the above remains fully applicable in the decentralized economy, one cannot disregard that the decentralized economy has unique salient features that may inform the purpose, logic, content, and legal and economic context and circumstances, along with other effects-oriented considerations of agreements and restraints concluded within. As documented in Chapter 1, the decentralized economy is characterized by social production and pervasive governance dynamics,[195] and the conduct of economic actors within it can further encompass considerations that may depart from those of traditional firms and traditional understandings of merit-based competition.[196] Social production reflects commons-based principles as it comprises diverse stakeholders without a central firm-based coordinator, which is the usual organizational form competition law is familiar with. Social production instead is regulated by governance structures both embedded in the production systems and external to them. These governance structures encompass collective decision-making processes, which can be formal or informal, written or customary, enforced or ignored, or stable or fast evolving. Crucially, social production and governance in the decentralized economy may express considerations that are foreign to traditional competition law, such as the ethos and purpose of a decentralized economy,[197] the promotion of social good (however defined) and wealth redistribution,[198] the role of technology in society,[199] inclusion and representation,[200] and social power dynamics.[201]

To the extent that such considerations infiltrate business conduct and motivate collaborative behaviour, it is only natural that they inform an agreement's or restraint's purpose, logic, content, legal and economic context, and circumstances as well as effects. This is not to say that invoking the decentralized economy's

[194] Opinion of Advocate General Mazák in Case C-439/09 Pierre Fabre Dermo-Cosmétique SAS v Président de l'Autorité de la concurrence and Ministre de l'Économie, de l'Industrie et de l'Emploi ECLI:EU:C:2011:113, para 27; *Broadcast Music* (n 131) 9.

[195] Chapter 1 sections D.ii and D.iii.

[196] See Chapter 7 section B.ii.

[197] Nigel Dodd, 'The Social Life of Bitcoin' (2018) 35 Theory, Culture & Society 35.

[198] David Golumbia, *The Politics of Bitcoin Software as Right-Wing Extremism* (University of Minnesota Press 2016) chs 2 and 4.

[199] Toni Caradonna, 'Blockchain and Society' (2020) 43 Informatik Spektrum 40.

[200] Qiqi Gao and Jiteng Zhang, *Artificial Intelligence Governance and the Blockchain Revolution* (Springer 2024) ch 4.

[201] Malcolm Campbell-Verduyn, 'The Distributions of Distributed Governance: Power, Instability and Complexity in Polycentric Data Ordering' in Carolina Aguerre, Malcolm Campbell-Verduyn and Jan Aart Scholte, *Global Digital Data Governance* (Routledge 2024). See also Chapter 5 section B.ii.

special features can justify any conduct, but simply that they should be accounted for. Sources that can be consulted to help determine the purpose, logic, content, legal and economic context and circumstances of agreements and restraints include:

- **Whitepapers.** Many DLT products and services are accompanied by whitepapers that explain their motivation, goal, and basic functions.[202] Whitepapers have not been deemed legally binding (unless their content is part of documentation that is required by financial regulation, eg securities prospectus), and therefore compliance with them is not mandatory for those undertakings that participate in the development of the relevant products and services. To some degree, however, they set out goals and boundaries that undertakings agree to comply with to ensure the success of the product or service, and in that sense they can be informative sources on how participating undertakings are expected to conduct themselves and why.
- **Governance bylaws and processes enacted or customary.** Governance expresses the rules and norms that regulate decision-making in the development and management of DLT products and services and their consensus.[203] As such, governance rules and norms are determinative for how participating undertakings work together and can explain their cooperative conduct.[204] The difficulty with governance as a determinant of the modus operandi of DLT products and services is that governance sources can be both written and formal and customary and informal.[205] Customary and informal rules—while adhered to—may be difficult to detect and verify, which undermines their authoritativeness, even if they may in fact be influential. Further complications may arise when written rules and customary norms conflict with each other, or when they are silent on a matter and the decision-making develops as an incident unfolds.[206] This was more of an issue in the early days of

[202] Sergey Kasatkin, 'The Legal Content of a White Paper for an ICO (Initial Coins Offering)' (2022) 31 Information & Communications Technology Law 81.

[203] Ying-Ying Hsieh, Jean-Philippe Vergne, and Sha Wang, 'The Internal and External Governance of Blockchain-Based Organizations' in Malcolm Campbell-Verduyn, *Bitcoin and Beyond: Cryptocurrencies, Blockchains, and Global Governance* (2018) 48–50; Yue Liu and others, 'Defining Blockchain Governance Principles: A Comprehensive Framework' (2022) 109 Information Systems 102090; Roman Beck, Christoph Müller-Bloch, and John Leslie King, 'Governance in the Blockchain Economy: A Framework and Research Agenda' (2018) 19 Journal of the Association for Information Systems 1020.

[204] Project Liberty and BlockchainGov, 'Interim Report on Blockchain Governance Practices: Insights' (2023) at 9.

[205] Primavera De Filippi, Morshed Mannan, and Wessel Reijers, 'Blockchain Technology and the Rule of Code: Regulation via Governance' (2022) hal-03883249. On sources of governance see Liu and others (n 203); Jersain Zadamig Llamas Covarrubias and Irving Norehem Llamas Covarrubias, 'Different Types of Government and Governance in the Blockchain' (2021) 10 Journal of Governance and Regulation 8.

[206] See Nadine Kathrin Ostern and Guido Perscheid, 'Solve for Blockchain: Toward A Framework for Navigating Blockchain Tensions' (2021) 11 ICIS 2021 Proceedings 1.

the industry's development, but it can still happen with young projects. The various Bitcoin hard forks are examples of such governance crises characterized by blurry decision-making.[207]

- **Articles of association.** Some products and services are developed by organizations set up specifically for that goal.[208] These organizations assume a legal form and adopt articles of association, which are not only themselves agreements/restraints caught under Article 101 TFEU and Section 1 of the Sherman Act, but their decisions can also fall under those provisions. Articles of association may document governance aspects or considerations that would otherwise appear in governance rules and whitepapers, but they can have broader stipulations, such as formalizing relationships between participating undertakings, or between the association and third parties. In any case, articles of association regulate members' behaviour and can provide useful indicia on the purpose and context of the association and colour on members' conduct.

As emphasized previously, the unique features of DLT markets, as reflected in the above sources, do not in themselves invalidate the usual requirements and criteria competition law has established for the assessment of collusive activity; they only inform them. Some of the above sources will be interpreted to reflect general principles, while others may point to specific rules. Much can be said about the general principles, ethos, zeitgeist, origins, and character of the decentralized economy, but one should be careful to limit their influence on competition law's criteria. Instead, more specific rules and those that more directly and closely influence the challenged conduct should be given more weight in determining an agreement's or restraint's purpose, logic, content, legal and economic context and circumstances as well as effects.

[207] See Stephen DiRose and Mo Mansouri, 'Comparison and Analysis of Governance Mechanisms Employed by Blockchain-Based Distributed Autonomous Organizations', *2018 13th Annual Conference on System of Systems Engineering (SoSE)* (IEEE 2018) 198–200.

[208] See eg the Hedera Council, which brings together organizations tasked with governing the Hedera project. See <https://hedera.com/council>.

ADDENDUM

On 25 February 2025, the Grand Chamber of the Court of Justice delivered its preliminary ruling decision in the *Android Auto* case.[1] The decision created a new refusal to deal standard to be applied in cases where the input/infrastructure to which access is sought was not developed solely for the needs of the dominant undertaking's own business but with a view to enabling third-party undertakings to use it. The case arose in the context of access to the Android Auto platform, and so platforms are definitely covered under the new standard, but the decision can be read to apply to any input/infrastructure that was not developed exclusively for the dominant undertaking's internal use.

Because many products/services in the decentralized economy function as platforms, such as exchanges and smart contracts, the decision becomes of particular importance, as it replaces the criteria established in *Bronner*.[2]

According to the new standard:

1. Access to the input/infrastructure does not need to be indispensable but merely make the competing product/service more attractive. The refusal 'is capable of constituting an abuse of a dominant position even though that platform is not indispensable for the commercial operation of that app on a downstream market, but is such as to make that app more attractive to consumers, where that platform has not been developed by the undertaking in a dominant position solely for the needs of its own business' (para 52).
2. Competition does not need to be eliminated but merely hindered. It is necessary to assess 'whether that conduct on the part of the undertaking in a dominant position was such as to hinder competition on the market concerned being maintained or to hinder its growth, taking into account all the relevant factual circumstances' (para 61).
3. The fact that the input/infrastructure cannot readily accommodate requests for access is not an objective justification for the refusal. The dominant undertaking is required to develop the necessary interoperability technology 'within a period which is reasonable and necessary for that purpose and in

[1] Case C-233/23 Alphabet and Others v Autorità Garante della Concorrenza e del Mercato ECLI:EU:C:2025:110.

[2] Case C-7/97 Oscar Bronner GmbH & Co. KG v Mediaprint Zeitungs- und Zeitschriftenverlag GmbH et al ECLI:EU:C:1998:569

> return for, depending on the circumstances, appropriate financial consideration, taking into account the needs of the third-party undertaking which requested that development, the actual cost of the development and the right of the undertaking in a dominant position to derive an appropriate benefit from it.' This does not apply if developing it would 'compromise the integrity or security of the platform concerned, or where it would be impossible for other technical reasons to ensure that interoperability ...' (para 81).

For a more detailed analysis see Konstantinos Stylianou, 'Platform Competition after the Android Auto Case' (2025) available at https://papers.ssrn.com/abstract=5171789.

Index

For the benefit of digital users, indexed terms that span two pages (e.g., 52–53) may, on occasion, appear on only one of those pages.

Tables and figures are indicated by an italic *t* and *f* following the page number.

AAVE 96–97, 97*f*
ADA *see* Cardano
altcoin 58, 151
ancillary restraint *see* ancillary restriction
ancillary restriction 220–21, 239, 242–45, 252–53
architectural power 16–17, 116, 126–30
as-efficient-competitor (test) 177, 184
ASIC 55–56, 133, 138–39, 159–60, 187–88
asset pool 52–64
Automated Market Maker *see* market maker

BCH *see* Bitcoin Cash
Binance 108*t*, 164n.93, 195, 195n.89, 210–11, 237
  Binance hack incident (2019) 237
Bitcoin 16, 21–22, 24, 58, 58*f*, 62–63, 81n.12, 81*f*, 84, 84*f*, 88, 88*f*, 90*f*, 91–92, 91n.35, 91*f*, 92*f*, 93–94, 94*f*, 102–3, 107, 108, 112–13, 120–21, 125, 134–35, 135n.102, 138–39, 144–45, 148, 151, 163*f*, 166, 167*f*, 168–69, 169n.115, 178–80, 187n.67, 191, 196–97, 199–200, 206n.147, 207, 257
Bitcoin Cash 91–92, 91nn.35–36, 91*f*, 125, 134–35, 187n.67, 220n.6
BSV 91–92, 91n.36, 125, 195n.89, 220n.6
BTC *see* Bitcoin

Cardano 55, 75, 75*f*
CBDC *see* Central Bank Digital Currency
Central Bank Digital Currency 3, 7, 16, 27, 29, 32–34, 148–52, 153*t*, 203, 234–35
centralization *see* decentralization
Coinbase 30–31, 53–54, 60, 108*t*, 110*f*, 112, 168–69, 196–97, 199–200
commons-based (system) 13–15, 256
concentration 8–9, 11, 64, 105–6, 106*t*, 111, 119, 120–21, 126–27, 134, 138–39, 155*f*, 158*t*, 168–69, 173–74
congestion 54–56
consensus 5–6, 11, 12, 17, 19, 28–30, 31, 32–33, 42–43, 50–52, 54–55, 75, 93, 96–97, 98–99, 101, 101n.66, 136n.112, 138–39, 160n.80, 162, 164, 166, 167, 169, 178–80, 186, 187–88, 191, 198–99, 202, 203–4, 222, 225, 227, 236–37, 239, 241–42, 244–45, 246, 257
consortium *see* joint venture
cryptoasset 6–7, 7n.28, 10, 17, 26–27, 30–31, 32–33, 53, 58, 67–71, 68nn.94–95, 70*f*, 84, 85–105, 85n.25, 91*f*, 94*f*, 98n.50, 102n.68, 106–7, 109–11, 117–23, 124–26, 128, 134–35, 139, 144–45, 148–54, 150*f*, 153*t*, 169, 178–80, 187n.67, 194–95, 195n.89, 196–98, 206–7, 209–11, 215–16, 221, 228, 237, 248–49, 250–51
cryptocommodity 86, 122n.37, 192
cryptocurrency *see* cryptoasset
crypto-exchange 6–7, 14–15, 25, 33–34, 52–54, 56–57, 59–64, 64n.72, 68, 80, 106–13, 108*t*, 110*f*, 124–25, 126, 143, 144–45, 152, 163–64, 164n.93, 166–67, 168–69, 195, 196–98, 207, 208, 210–11, 215–16, 237, 244–45
  decentralized exchange 30–31, 60, 96–97, 164, 208–9, 244–45

DAO *see* Decentralized Autonomous Organization
dApp *see* decentralized application
decentralization 11–13, 81–82, 119–20, 138–39, 155, 157, 187–88
decentralized application 96–97, 152–54, 154n.56
Decentralized Autonomous Organization 59n.52, 65, 136, 178–80, 187–88, 190n.75, 250–51
  MakerDAO 22
decentralized exchange *see* crypto-exchange
Decentralized Finance 6–7, 30–31, 59–64, 75–76, 85–98, 97*f*, 164, 187–88, 187n.67, 244–45, 248–49
DeFi *see* Decentralized Finance
delisting 123–26, 195n.89, 196–97, 199–200, 206–13, 215–16, 220n.6
developer *see* protocol developer

DEX *see* decentralized exchange
Diem 128

economies 11, 47–48, 67–68, 123–24, 145–46, 151, 157–69, 158*t*, 246
ecosystem 13n.54, 14, 16–17, 33–34, 98, 116, 126–29, 130, 134, 135, 136–37, 138–39, 152–54, 195n.88, 203, 215–16, 223–24
engagement power 16–17, 116, 131–34
EOS 84, 84*f*, 93–94, 223–24
  EOS irregular voting incident (2018) 223–24
Ethereum 17, 31–32, 44, 55, 60, 62–63, 64*t*, 76, 87, 93–94, 99–100, 108, 130, 138–39, 141, 178–80, 190n.75, 203, 206n.147, 211–12, 247
  Ethereum DAO incident (2016) 178–80
  Ethereum Parity incident (2017) 87
ETH *see* Ethereum
exchange *see* crypto-exchange or Information exchange

fiat currency *see* fiat money
fiat money 7n.28, 106–7, 109–11, 124–25, 126, 127, 148–49, 151–52, 153*t*, 166
Financial Conduct Authority 161n.84
fork 90–92, 92*f*, 116, 125, 127, 134–35, 135n.102, 139n.129, 140, 161, 178–80, 190n.75, 191, 212–13, 236–37, 257
foundation *see* protocol developer

governance 5–6, 8, 11, 12, 17–21, 19*t*, 20n.84, 22, 31–32, 50, 51, 75, 84, 116, 126–30, 131, 132, 137–39, 152–54, 156–57, 174, 178–81, 183, 186–94, 186n.65, 187n.67, 189n.72, 190n.75, 202, 203–4, 212–13, 223–24, 227–28, 237, 239, 241–42, 250–51, 256, 257–58
  governance abuse 20, 171–258

hash *see* hashrate
hashrate 55–56, 81*f*, 99–102, 100n.60, 101n.64, 104, 105, 106*t*, 118–19, 155*f*, 167*f*

ICO *see* Initial Coin Offering
imputability 16, 16n.73, 35–44, 42*f*, 196–97, 208
information (exchange of) 8–9, 135–36, 219–21, 220n.6, 228–39, 237n.96, 244, 251–52
Initial Coin Offering 141, 152–54
intent 26, 27, 120n.27, 129, 178–80, 205n.144, 210, 214–15, 219–20, 224–27, 230–31, 232–33, 233–34n.81, 234, 236–37, 237n.96, 240–41, 251, 254, 255
interoperability 19, 32–33, 73, 116, 135–37, 137n.114, 200–1, 234–35, 245–46, 248–49, 253–54

joint venture 42, 180, 202–3, 220–21, 239, 245–53, 246n.141, 250n.161, 252n.171

Libra *see* Diem

manipulation 20, 85, 86, 95–96, 107, 108–9, 110*f*, 117–23, 120n.27, 121n.32, 122n.37, 149, 156n.65, 160, 161, 183, 186–87, 187n.67, 192, 240–41, 248
market capitalization 84, 84*f*, 85–93, 89–90*f*, 97–101, 97*f*, 107, 169n.115, 178–80
  realized capitalization 89, 90*f*
market maker 62–63, 64n.72, 64*t*, 210, 244–45, 248
Markets in Cryptoassets Regulation (MiCA) 5n.12, 10, 10n.45
maximal extractable value (MEV) 161, 206–13
merit (competition) *see* normal competition
metaverse 59n.52, 64–75, 130, 132–33, 200, 215–16
MiCA *see* Markets in Cryptoassets Regulation
miner *see* mining
mining 6–7, 11–12, 14–15, 16, 17–18, 20, 21–22, 25, 26, 28–30, 35–44, 36*f*, 42*f*, 45–169, 55n.36, 99n.56, 100n.60, 103*f*, 106*t*, 119n.20, 155n.61, 155*f*, 156n.65, 163*f*, 167*f*, 187, 187n.67, 191, 197–98, 211, 212–13, 220n.6, 221, 221n.10, 236–37, 244
  mining pool 17, 25, 29–30, 42–44, 45–169, 81*f*, 106*t*, 119n.20, 155*f*, 191, 200, 212–13, 237
mixer 95, 250–51
multihoming 105, 147–48, 150–51, 152, 157

NFT *see* Non-fungible token
no economic sense (test) 61–62, 118–19, 177, 188
Non-fungible token 52–53, 62
normal competition 15–16, 175–83, 188–89, 190, 212–13, 230, 248–49, 256

objective justification 201–2, 220–21, 239, 242–45
objective necessity *see* objective justification
off-chain 18–19, 19*t*, 20, 128–29, 164, 194
oligopoly 150, 154n.60, 157, 165–66, 217, 221n.8, 223–24, 223n.16, 237n.96
on-chain 18–19, 19*t*, 20, 128–29, 164, 195
open source software 14–15, 30–31
oracle 132, 154, 154n.58
output 48n.7, 52–53, 54–56, 57, 61n.59, 86, 94n.42, 99–102, 103–4, 116n.2, 117, 157–58, 159–60, 165, 166, 180, 191, 219–20, 233, 255

permissioned (network) 12, 19–20, 50–51, 195–96, 201–4, 231–35
permissionless (network) 12, 50–51, 85, 112, 156–57, 202, 221, 236, 236n.92
plus factor 229–31
pool *See* mining pool; staking pool, or asset pool
PoS *see* proof of stake
PoW *see* proof of work
proof of stake 17, 28–29, 54–56, 98–100, 101, 102–3, 104–5, 138, 162
proof of work 17, 28–29, 54–56, 93, 98–100, 101, 102–3, 104–5, 138, 139, 159–60, 162
protocol developer 4–6, 14–15, 16, 17–18, 25, 31–32, 35–44, 36*f*, 42*f*, 44n.90, 75, 87–88, 90–91, 93, 128, 130, 138–39, 191, 196–98, 220n.6, 237, 249–50

ripple 31–32, 63, 93, 145, 156–57, 156–57n.67

SEC *see* Securities and Exchange Commission
Securities and Exchange Commission 9–10, 112, 144–45
smart contract 42–43, 60, 84, 87–88, 132, 136, 187, 187n.67, 207–9, 210, 222, 232–33, 250–51
social production P1 8, 13–17, 16n.73, 19–20, 24, 26, 116, 130, 131, 137–38, 174, 178–80, 181–82, 186–87, 189, 250–51, 256
SSNIP 52–54, 52n.21
SSNRQ 56
stablecoin 7, 7n.28, 16, 22, 86, 120n.27, 121–22, 122n.37, 126, 134, 151, 153*t*, 192, 195, 211–12
staker *see* staking
staking 6–7, 17, 26, 28–30, 36*f*, 42–43, 42*f*, 50–51, 54–56, 75, 96–97, 98–99, 100, 102, 104–6, 117–23, 120n.24, 130, 138, 155, 156–57, 158*t*, 212–13
  staking pool 29–30, 42–44, 75, 98–106, 119–20, 155–57
standard-setting 180–81, 203, 239, 241, 245–53
switching 52–53, 54, 55–56, 132–33, 145, 147–48, 150–52, 153*t*, 167–68, 187–88

Tether 7n.28, 63, 64*t*, 86, 121–22, 122n.37, 122n.42, 126, 134, 192, 211–12
token 20–21, 22, 29, 51–52, 64–65, 73–76, 86, 87–93, 91*f*, 95, 98–99, 116, 126, 130, 132–33, 136, 140–41, 148–50, 150*f*, 152–54, 163–64, 164n.93, 166, 203, 206, 207, 215–16
tokenomics 8, 20–22
total value locked 64*t*, 85–86, 96–98, 97*f*
trading volume 107–9, 111
transaction count 84, 84*f*, 85–86, 93–96, 149
transaction fee 21–22, 29, 54–56, 102–3, 103*f*, 118–19, 130, 163, 215–16, 244–45
transaction value 83
transaction volume 59, 63, 64, 64*t*, 83, 84, 85–86, 95–96, 96*f*, 108*t*, 111, 199–200
TVL *see* total value locked

Uniswap 30–31, 60, 64*t*, 97, 244n.136
USDT *see* Tether

wash trading 95, 109
whitepaper 19*t*, 29n.35, 102n.68, 128–29, 138–39, 181, 189–90, 228, 257, 258

XRP *see* ripple